ACTING
The Creative Process
Third Edition

ACTING
The Creative Process
Third Edition

Hardie Albright
Arnita Albright

Wadsworth Publishing Company
Belmont, California
A Division of Wadsworth, Inc.

Senior Editor: Rebecca Hayden
Production Editor: Mary Arbogast
Copy Editor: John Hamburger
Art Director: Cynthia Bassett
Designer: Don Fujimoto
Illustrators: Hardie Albright, Michael Hobson, Ginny Mickelson
Cover Photo: Bill Ganslen

The cover photo is from the American Conservatory Theatre's production of *Hotel Paradiso* by Georges Feydeau.

The frontispiece shows Richard Chamberlain as Cyrano in CTG/Ahmanson Theatre of the Music Center's production of *Cyrano de Bergerac* by Edmund Rostand.

Printed in the United States of America

1 2 3 4 5 6 7 8 9 10—84 83 82 81 80

Library of Congress Cataloging in Publication Data

Albright, Hardie, 1903–
  Acting, the creative process.

  Includes bibliographies and index.
  1. Acting. I. Albright, Arnita, joint author.
II. Title.
PN2061.A65 1980   792'.028   79-23949
ISBN 0-534-00744-9

FOREWORD

Sir John Gielgud, recently asked by an interviewer to give the basic requirements for an actor, unhesitatingly named three: "Imagination, self-discipline, industry," and, as an afterthought, added quickly, "voice, of course, is wildly important." How do young, talented people satisfy these requirements? Mainly by hard work in steadily controlled training.

The conscientious student of acting, whether in high school, college, workshop, or even working alone, will profit considerably from mature, professional advice. A course of study offered with such hard-earned authority may sometimes equal the knowledge acquired by working for a long period with a professional company of actors.

When I first perused the manuscript for the first edition—actually lecture notes for Hardie Albright's university extension course—it was this practical, truly professional approach toward the education of prospective actors that impressed me most. Only actors with a solid occupational background—and teachers of wide experience—could arrange a textbook that so sensibly combines theory with ample practical exercise. The Albrights succeed in personalizing essential points of the acting process in order to free them from cold didactics. They always relate theories to the thoughts of practicing successful actors. So when they quote Alec Guinness on voice training, or Laurence Olivier on the physical aspects of acting—to cite only two of the numerous examples—they inspire the student to relate elements of the acting process to something a fine actor has said, as if the student had really talked to the actor about it.

The authors wisely avoid editorial bias. In this book, readers are encouraged to reach their own conclusions after hearing all sides. All acting theories and methods, from Stanislavski and Bertolt Brecht to the latest avant-garde, are discussed and skillfully applied to exercise scenes selected from the master dramas in world literature. The authors are particularly lucid in defining the various acting styles that have developed out of historical and practical needs.

Only actors who have done it themselves can convincingly explain how to act Greek tragedy and comedy, Commedia dell'Arte, Shakespeare, Restoration, Ibsen, or the Theatre of the Absurd. It is this special quality that distinguishes this book from many others.

In a time when repertory theatres are being built all over the United States, there is one pressing need: to provide well-trained actors who will be able to perform the great plays of the past and the present. Every effort must be made to meet this challenge. Hardie and Arnita Albright's book shows the way.

William W. Melnitz
Dean Emeritus, College of Fine Arts
University of California, Los Angeles

PREFACE

This third edition of *Acting: The Creative Process,* has been prepared in memory of the late Hardie Albright by his wife, Arnita, who has taken special care to preserve the content and format of the previous edition. The blending of techniques, philosophy, and history of acting remain, and the approach and style are intact, since both students and instructors have indicated their approval. There are over one hundred thirty exercises illustrating points made in the text, many of which are new to this edition. The subjects of mask, mime, voice, and characterization have been extended; and numerous changes and substitutions of scenes have been made in the styles section.

Throughout this text it is assumed that a modicum of talent combined with a great deal of fortitude will assist acting students to maintain the devotion necessary to achieve their goals. The book begins with exercises that will help develop the body and the voice as instruments of communication. Next, the students are exposed to techniques of creating pantomime and improvisation. Following a study of the theatre environment and its disciplines, students are encouraged to build their own acting methods for creating characterization and sensory experience. Much stress is placed on present-day acting methods, on physical–spatial–spiritual training, and on creating fresh and original metaphors. There is also emphasis on the more traditional approaches to realistic theatre.

Knowledge of more modern acting approaches is mandatory for an actor contemplating work in today's splintered theatre world, where innovative and even revolutionary plays are offered alongside traditional and classical dramas. Various approaches are presented, as acting students must be prepared to establish their own methods for successful, continuous creativity and progress. They must be able to make intelligent choices among the various ways of solving problems and achieving goals in today's theatre.

The "Styles in Acting" section, which has been extensively used and highly praised, explains the great historical acting styles. The chapter devoted to Greek drama, for example, includes excerpts from *Oedipus the King, The Birds,* and *Lysistrata.* Discussions of Roman and Medieval drama are included, along with play excerpts from these two historical periods of the theatre. Following those are chapters devoted to the Commedia dell'Arte, Shakespeare, Moliere, the Restoration, and the eighteenth century. The acting process is then considered in the light of the nineteenth-century dramaturgy of Wilde, Ibsen, Strindberg, and Chekhov. The twentieth century is represented by Shaw, O'Neill, and Brecht. Among the twenty-five excerpts are such works as *The Ghost Sonata, Pygmalion, Long Day's Journey into Night,* and *The Good Woman of Setzuan.* Finally, there is discussion of contemporary and innovative theatre, including excerpts from Ionesco, Pinter, van Itallie, Zindel, and Beckett, whose *Waiting for Godot* is highlighted in this new edition.

This book has been written for both the novice and the initiated acting student; for the beginner who must start at the beginning, working toward complexity, and for the more accomplished who must periodically return to the basics to keep the craft well honed and in balance. If artists lose the ability to return to basics, they risk becoming lost in the myriad details, nuances, and habits involved in the advanced stages of study or of a career. When students have been immersed in varied approaches and processes of the craft, a return to the beginning stimulates a renewed sense of purpose. Simplicity of statement results. Basic elements suggest deeper meanings when reviewed in the light of advanced study. One of the main keys to creativity is found in the review of early concepts.

This book is dedicated to the idea that today's actors must have a broader kind of training than those of the recent past. Their bodies must be malleable and their minds alert. Both must be kept in that workable state as long as the actor practices his or her craft. Actors must be thoroughly acquainted with all acting styles, historical as well as contemporary. And, above all, they must nurture their creative abilities to reach toward the future. This book encourages the development of an intellectual capacity that allows a deep understanding of the theatre of past and present. Only this approach will assure a capacity to accept new concepts.

The contributions and suggestions of numerous instructors who have used the previous editions have been incorporated into the text, with special thanks to Forest Feighner, Edinboro State College; Pamela Fields, Scottsdale Community College; Helen W. Kellum, University of Mississippi; Gilbert L. Rathbun, Seton Hall University; and Peter Rodney, Elmira College. The author particularly acknowledges the valuable criticism and assistance of George C. Fosgate of the University of Minnesota at Morris.

CONTENTS

13. The Commedia dell'Arte 210

Plots and actors   Acting technique—farce, clown vs. comedian
Preparation for *The Twins*   Rehearsal: *The Twins*
Further reading

14. Shakespeare (1564–1616) 218

The actors of the Globe   Importance of Shakespeare   An actor
named Shakespeare   Shakespeare the dramatist   The
Elizabethan audience   The music of Shakespeare   Atmosphere
Color   Rhythm and rests   Prose and poetry   Shakespeare
and you   Acting style for Shakespeare   Preparation for
Hamlet—character portrayals, background   Rehearsal: *Hamlet,*
Act III, scene iv   Further reading

15. Moliere (1622–1673) 242

Moliere as an actor   Apprenticeship   Moliere's style
The stamp of the Commedia   Zest in playing farce-comedy
Moliere as director   Preparation for *George Dandin*   Rehearsal:
George Dandin, an adaptation from act III, scene viii   Preparation
for *Tartuffe*   Rehearsal: *Tartuffe,* an adaptation from act II, scene ii
Further reading

16. The Restoration and the Eighteenth Century 256

Characteristics of Restoration comedy   First English books on
acting   Actors without plays   David Garrick   Sarah Siddons
Edmund Kean   High comedy   Rehearsal: *The Way of the World,*
an adaptation from act IV, scene i   RICHARD BRINSLEY SHERIDAN
(1751–1816)   Preparation for *The School for Scandal*—the character
of Lady Teazle, other characters   Rehearsal: *The School for
Scandal,* act IV, scene iii   Further reading

17. Nineteenth-Century Drama 280

Nineteenth-century melodrama   Preparation for *The Octoroon*
Rehearsal: *The Octoroon,* an excerpt from act II   Further reading
OSCAR WILDE (1854–1900)   Preparation for *The Importance of Being
Earnest*   Rehearsal: *The Importance of Being Earnest,* an excerpt
from act II   Further reading   Naturalism, realism, and the fourth
wall   HENRICK IBSEN (1828–1906)   Preparation for *The Master
Builder*   Characterization   Rehearsal: *The Master Builder,* an
excerpt from act I   Further reading   ANTON CHEKHOV (1860–1904)
Preparation for *The Three Sisters*   Rehearsal: *The Three Sisters,*
an excerpt from act III   Further reading   AUGUST STRINDBERG
(1849–1912)   Revolution in the making   Preparation for *The
Ghost Sonata*   Rehearsal: *The Ghost Sonata,* an excerpt from
scene ii   Further reading

LIST OF PLAYS

LIST OF EXERCISES

USING PARTS I AND II TOGETHER

You may find these excerpts useful during your early studies even though your playing style is not fully perfected.

It is important that these excerpts be used specifically for the purpose suggested. Any additional stress on other dramatic concepts can dilute the purpose of the exercises. Full attention to each excerpt and its style should await the time when you can apply all of the elements covered in Part I.

It is not always necessary to use the complete excerpt to work on the specific skills mentioned. But it is necessary to read and understand the full play before using an excerpt for any purpose.

The experience gained through using any of these suggested excerpts will not only help you to solidify the skills you are studying in Part I, but will assist you in preparing for the studies in Part II.

Excerpts other than those suggested may certainly be used when applicable.

PART I

Chapter 1 Discovering Yourself
Balance

PART II

Noah, A Morality Play, page 205
This excerpt can be used to extend balance from an individual skill to a group skill. The nine players involved must find ways of distributing and redistributing themselves through movement to give variation to the scene while at the same time maintaining a balanced audience view of the characters. This effort will lead to the beginning of *ensemble* playing because it requires interdependence among players.

Interdependence (Ensemble)

George Dandin, Moliere, page 247
Tartuffe, Moliere, page 251
Total cast enthusiasm and coopera-

Using Parts I and II Together

tion are required for successful ensemble playing of these excerpts. (See the quote from Sir Tyrone Guthrie on p. 89.)

Animal Characterizations

The Birds, Aristophanes, page 187
Since these characters are actually birds, the excerpt is ready-made for our purpose. It is a physical and comical farce.

Noah, A Morality Play, page 205
Both entertainment and instruction result as these characters pantomime various animals entering the ark.

Read the quote from Irene Worth on page 146. For Madame Ranevskaya in Chekhov's *Cherry Orchard* Miss Worth chose to use a swan characterization during pre-rehearsal exercises.

Chapter 2 Mime and Masks
Mime

The School for Scandal, Sheridan, page 273
All or sections of this excerpt are delightful to use as final exercises in mime. Two seated players can impart a great deal of the sense of the lines through use of their upper bodies, heads, hands, and arms. A third person may read the dialogue.

Masks

Waiting for Godot, Beckett, page 340
Estragon and Vladimir may both be played by one person who changes masks to assist in accomplishing change of character. This will use the player's background in mime as well as forcing complete clarification between the two characters. It can be reminiscent of the low-comedy clown whose act consists of changing hats.

Chapter 3 The Actor's Voice and Speech
Words

Richard III, V, iii, Shakespeare, page 227
A notable example of words chosen for their impact on the dramatic incident.

Sound

Life of Marcus Antonius, Plutarch, page 229

Antony and Cleopatra, II, ii, Shakespeare, page 230

The student who learns and presents both of these excerpts, which deal with the same description (borrowed by Shakespeare from Plautus), will experience the differences between prose and poetry. Shakespeare's words, rhythms, and composition call for the best that good voice can achieve.

Verse
Sustaining
Reaction
Listening
Ensemble

Hamlet, III, iv, Shakespeare, 234

a. Speaking verse.
b. Establishing backgrounds of characters through interpretation and physical behavior.
c. Sustaining audience interest through variation, in Hamlet's longer speeches.
d. Reacting and listening, especially obvious in part of the Queen.
e. Ensemble: A fine experience in interdependence between two characters.

Group Voices

Oedipus the King, Sophocles, page 183

The chorus at the end of this excerpt (page 186) offers good opportunity for developing *breath, strength,* and *tonal quality* of individual voices. *Clarity, articulation,* and *phrasing* should be so perfect in group performance that every word is understandable even at the rear of an auditorium *(projection).*

Pitch

The Bald Soprano, Ionesco, page 343

An experiment in creating monotony through voice without losing audience interest.

Phrasing
Pausing
Timing

American Buffalo, Mamet, page 359

Enlightening especially when used with a Shakespearian excerpt to point up differences between the two in rhythms, tempos, language, and attitudes in contemporary and regional speech, social mores, and dramatic verse.

Chapter 4 Improvisation

All types of dramaturgy can be enhanced in performance with

The Master Builder, Ibsen, page 296

the use of pertinent improvisational exercises. The ability of the student to devise for a purpose is extremely desirable. The following excerpts should be considered an extension of the chapter on improvisation.

The character Hilda Wangle, often called a "child-woman," is particularly useful for developing improvisations out of childhood memories. It can be challenging at the same time to devise childhood improvs that clarify the character of Halvard Solness, whose traits are less obviously those of youth.

The Importance of Being Earnest, Wilde, page 286
The frivolous artificiality of this super-farce lends itself nicely to creative development of characters using animal, bird, insect, or vegetation improvs.

Long Day's Journey into Night, O'Neill, page 318
The deeply tragic character of the mother offers opportunities to search for helpful methods of improvisation. An assortment of improvs might be used and finally blended into the total character.

The Good Woman of Setzuan, Brecht, page 329
In Expressionistic drama, improvs may be devised for assisting in the creation of a single character composed of two personalities. The problem of the actor or actress who plays both Shen Te and Shui Ta is to arrive at a single personality that encompasses both sets of traits. The danger is that this character can be a bore unless the audience identifies with both personalities.

Chapter 5 The Actor's Environment
Proscenium vs. Center Staging

American Buffalo, Mamet, page 359
The Effect of Gamma Rays on Man-in-the-Moon Marigolds, Zindel, page 357
When two separate casts are assigned to either of these plays, one performs as if from a proscenium stage while the other plans its performance for a center stage. The members of the audience become critics of the results.

Audience Communication

Hamlet, III, iv, Shakespeare, page 234
Begin with the Queen's speech on

page 235, "What have I done—" and continue through Hamlet's long speech, which ends on page 236. Two students playing the Queen and Hamlet try communicating with the audience in each of the following ways.

a. Through gesture and body movement only, while the speeches are read by a third person.

b. Through emotional voice tones and sounds (no words), while speeches are read by a third person.

c. Through speaking the lines only, without gesture or movement.

Rapport

The Octoroon, Boucicault, page 282
A direct way to initiate actors to the sensation of rapport with an audience is to use the nineteenth-century melodramatic "aside." Several appear in this excerpt.

The School for Scandal, Sheridan, page 273

The Importance of Being Earnest, Wilde, page 286
Among others, these excerpts are really fun when played directly for rapport with the audience.

Chapter 6 Building Your Own Acting Method

Concentration

"Interview" from *America Hurrah!*, van Itallie, page 353
This repetitious excerpt requires total concentration to keep its tempo flowing.

Observation

Pygmalion, Shaw, page 312
Lysistrata, Aristophanes, page 191
Although any of the excerpts in Part II can be used for developing observation, it is perhaps easier for the beginner to relate to the characters in the excerpts suggested: *Pygmalion* because its theme is so well known, and *Lysistrata* because its theme examines the liberated woman.

Imagination

The Twins, a Commedia scenario, page 215
Imagination is a basic requirement for playing part or all of this scenario.

Gesture

Oedipus the King, Sophocles, page 183
A good culminating exercise for ges-

ture; large and simplified gestures are required here.

The Octoroon, Boucicault, page 282
Broad, overdone gesturing is required for the tableaus in this melodrama.

The Three Sisters, Chekhov, page 300
Subtle, suggestive gesture is necessary in this scene.

Waiting for Godot, Beckett, page 340
This tragi-comic scene requires the poignant yet obvious gestures of burlesque.

Rhythm

The Homecoming, Pinter, page 346
American Buffalo, Mamet, page 359
Hamlet, Shakespeare, page 234
Contrasting kinds of rhythms in speech and movement can be discovered in the delivery of the excerpts from these three plays.

Atmosphere

The School for Scandal, Sheridan, page 273
Successful portrayal of this scene depends much on the atmosphere created by the frivolous, high-comedy characters.

Long Day's Journey into Night, O'Neill, page 321
Atmosphere suggests the underlying tragedy in O'Neill's realistic characters.

Chapter 7 Characterization
Play Analysis

Beginning Students:
The Master Builder, Ibsen, page 296
Pygmalion, Shaw, page 312
Long Day's Journey into Night, O'Neill, pages 318 and 321
The Effect of Gamma Rays on Man-in-the-Moon Marigolds, Zindel, page 357
Although no analysis can be thorough unless you study the complete play, these excerpts can be used as "practice runs" after you've read the complete play.

Advanced Students:
Hamlet, Shakespeare, page 234
Tartuffe, Moliere, page 251
The Good Woman of Setzuan, Brecht, page 329
Waiting for Godot, Beckett, page 340

Character Analysis	The excerpts used for play analysis can also be conveniently used for character analysis since this will save a great deal of study time.
Character from Dialogue	*Oedipus the King*, Sophocles, page 183 *The Twin Menaechmi*, Plautus, page 196 *The Way of the World*, Congreve, page 269
Character from Other Characters	*Hamlet*, Shakespeare, page 234 *Waiting for Godot*, Beckett, page 340 *American Buffalo*, Mamet, page 360
Progression	*The Master Builder*, Ibsen, page 296 *Oedipus the King*, Sophocles, page 183 These excerpts make particular use of character and plot progression within the scene.
Tragic Characters	*Hamlet*, Shakespeare, page 234 (Hamlet) *Long Day's Journey into Night*, O'Neill, page 318 (Mary) *Oedipus the King*, Sophocles, page 183 (Oedipus)
Comic Characters	*The Birds*, Aristophanes, page 187 *The Twin Menaechmi*, Plautus, page 196 *Tartuffe*, Moliere, page 251 *The Way of the World*, Congreve, page 269 *The Importance of Being Earnest*, Wilde, page 286
Tragi-comic Characters	*Waiting for Godot*, Beckett, page 340 *American Buffalo*, Mamet page 359
Surrealistic Characters	*The Ghost Sonata*, Strindberg, page 305 *The Homecoming*, Pinter, page 346 *The Bald Soprano*, Ionesco, page 343
Improvised Characters	*Noah, A Morality Play*, page 205 *The Twins*, a Commedia scenario, page 215
Subtext and Inner Monologue	*The Three Sisters*, Chekhov, page 300 *The Homecoming*, Pinter, page 346 *Waiting for Godot*, Beckett, page 340 "Interview" from *America Hurrah!*, van Itallie, page 353
Non-textual Scenes	*Hamlet*, Shakespeare, page 234 *The Twin Menaechmi*, Plautus, page 196 *The Good Woman of Setzuan*, Brecht, page 329

Devise pre-entrance scenes for the main characters in the preceding excerpts.

Chapter 8 Sensibility and Emotion

Oedipus the King, Sophocles, page 183
Hamlet, Shakespeare, page 234
The Effect of Gamma Rays on Man-in-the-Moon Marigolds, Zindel, page 357
The Good Woman of Setzuan, Brecht, page 329
Long Day's Journey into Night, O'Neill, pages 318 and 321
Waiting for Godot, Beckett, page 340

Eva Le Gallienne as Fanny Cavendish in the 1976 production of The Royal Family *in New York and on national tour.*

This book is lovingly dedicated to Eva Le Gallienne. It was Miss Le Gallienne who plucked Hardie Albright from the Carnegie-Mellon Drama School where he had played a memorable *Hamlet* and graduated cum laude. His first professional work was with her famous Civic Repertory Theatre. It is undoubtedly due in great part to Eva Le Gallienne's accomplished dream of the New York Civic Repertory Theatre that we owe today's resurgence of theatre as a fine art available to all the public. Miss Le Gallienne has said, "There should be in every large community a true theatre, and people's repertory theatre, presenting at normal prices the finest examples of international dramatic art—a place where one can find recreation and mental and spiritual stimulation."

Part I
THE CREATIVE PROCESS

1
DISCOVERING YOURSELF

The actor's art consists of making a disciplined instrument from an undisciplined human being. It is a very complex and absurd art which is only possible thanks to the duality of each individual: his profound being and his identity. It is an art which tears the actor apart since, on one hand, he must develop his power of sensibility to the extreme of hysteria, and, on the other hand, he must develop through will power a constant self-control.*

Jean-Louis Barrault
French producer-actor

*By permission of the Clarendon Press, Oxford, England. (Photo from *The Theatre of Jean-Louis Barrault,* used by permission of Barrie and Rockliffe, London.)

So great is the desire of some beginning students to act that, far too often, they begin by acting scenes from plays. This encourages them to use clichés or to mimic professionals they have admired. How much wiser they would be if they developed their own individualities and resources, and if they studied how their imaginations and physical beings affect their reflexes and emotions.

Other students might spend hours in psychological discussions about a play and a character. But the time always comes when they must get up on their feet—*and act*. So, why not begin that way? Unless study can be communicated physically, it has no value in theatre. While actors must study their characters, it must be done first through their bodies and their spontaneous reactions to given situations.

How many of us have seen something beautiful in nature and said, "Oh, if I could only paint!" The difference between us and the artist, who also appreciates beauty, is that the artist has learned to record his reactions by using colors and brushes to create certain effects. Actor-artists are in the same kind of situation. They must learn to use the actor's instruments skillfully in order to express their creativity.

First things must come first, and that is where we begin this book—by developing impulses, reflexes, and images. Then we learn to make these visible through body action, ultimately achieving an automatism of our physical equipment. This will promote integration of conceptual judgments and emotional responses.

A complete technique of acting cannot be mastered at one time. It must be studied in sections, sequentially. Then, when all parts become organically assimilated, they can be combined into a creative acting process. And the study continues for a lifetime.

A study in action-movement by the Bauhaus, Germany. (Courtesy of Frau Tut Schlemmer.)

Movement is at the foundation of acting. All inner impulses must be expressed through the body. Acting can be compared to a Jackson Pollock painting because the *meaning is in the action*. It took many devoted years for Pollock to arrive at his wedding of motion and its message. In the beginning he laid great boards or canvases on the ground, loaded a large brush with paint, and, by swinging his arm or flicking his wrist, he splattered as one would splatter a flat for a stage set. If you have the opportunity to practice splattering a flat (cover yourself with overalls) you will discover the delicate control involved in placing the droplets to make a certain effect. Through the movement of lines interacting with color and value (similar to body movement interacting with sound and pitch), Pollock achieved physical control over his tools and media. This is exactly the same procedure that you, as actors and actresses, will follow: control over your available tools and the ability to manipulate them. Jackson Pollock, through his varied spots and splatters on canvas, elicits mood reactions and the imaginative participation of his viewers. In theatre, a fundamental requirement is your ability to move in a manner that elicits a particular desired response. Your work with mime in chapter 2 will help to solidify this process.

If you watch children at play, you will see that they do not imitate reality, they create it. A cardboard box becomes a space vehicle, a broom handle a sword. It was for very good reasons that Shakespeare referred to actors as players.

Reactivating a joyful, childlike approach in adults may be the key to unlocking the acting mystique. A spontaneous human response to ideas or a set of circumstances, free use of the imagination, and acceptance of an abstract fantasy world are elements of acting that are usually most lacking in the mature mind. Those incapable of accepting the exercises we use to develop images, impulses, and imagination through physical training may never accept such other elements as dedication, self-discipline, and devotion to ideas, which are absolute demands in acting.

The exercises throughout this book are valuable in their immediacy, and in their use of instinct and imagination. They will also help train both body and voice as receptive instruments. That bright American star, Ina Claire, once said, "If [an actor] has complete control of his body, his mind, his emotion and his will, he can make an audience react as he wishes it to react."[1]

Exercises should not be rehearsed over and over, as if preparing for an audience. That would interfere with their spontaneity. They are for use in private classes *as a learning experience.*

RELAXATION

If you allow tension to enter yourself at any time during your work as an actor, you will set up an invisible wall between you (the *communicating force*) and your audience (the *receiving force*). Your intended message will not penetrate this wall, and your audience will receive a strange combination of your own anxiety mixed with the words of the character you are playing. Thus the playwright's intentions will be lost and you, the actor, will have failed in your work.

[1]Morton Eustis, *Players at Work* (New York: Theatre Arts Books, 1937), p. 81.

Training is a vital part of the American Conservatory Theatre's program. Classes in physical development, mime, voice, and theatre games are included in the daily schedule of the acting company of the Conservatory. (Photo by Clyde Hare, courtesy of the American Conservatory Theatre.)

The following exercises are not only designed to relax you before doing other exercises, but to serve you before rehearsals, before reading the play, before "going on," and so on. Each exercise must begin in total relaxation. The more you can relax your body, the greater will be the synchronization between your physical and mental efforts.

When performing these exercises, wear anything that does not bind but allows free movement; body suits, leotards, or even bathing suits are suitable. No shoes should be worn, as you will want to feel the security of the ground under you.

Total relaxation is a combined state of mind and body. It is a state of openness, in which you are ready to receive mentally and to put forth physically. When fully relaxed, you should be free of any intellectual blocks and your body loose and ready. For an actor, this is a state of preparedness.

There are various methods of achieving such a situation. For some, yoga or Transcendental Meditation are helpful. For others, physical exercise is often the answer. For the actor, it is a matter of reducing tension in every part of the body, while consciously eliminating all mental images and thought processes. Thought processes are more difficult to eliminate than mental images, as you will see if you close your eyes and try to remove everything from your mind except nothingness. Yet even a moment or two in this state can put you in touch with your inner self. The result will be a wonderful sensation of uninhibited strength. Your body becomes ready and your mind becomes open and alert.

Exercise 1 **RELAXATION: PASSIVE**

Lie flat on the floor, arms loosely at your sides. Take a deep breath. Readjust for total comfort. Now, starting either with your toes or your head, alternately tense and relax each part of your body, one part at a time. Breathing easily, speak quietly to yourself as you proceed. "Spread my toes . . . relax . . . point my foot . . . relax," and so on. Tense and then relax every part of your body; each finger, your scalp, your jaw, your face muscles, everything. When your entire body has become, *and remains,* relaxed, then allow your mind to divest itself of the responsibility it has had. As a gift to your mind and body, take a full breath and allow an audible sigh of contentment. Maintain this state as long as you can. From this state of restfulness, your body is ready to respond and your mind is in control and alert.

Exercise 2 **RELAXATION: ACTIVE**

Repeat exercise 1. At the end, while you are still lying flat on the floor, think of your breathing as your energy source. Issue a command such as "Lift my right arm," "Open my mouth," or "Growl." Both motion and sound should be involved. Slowly allow your energy to permeate your body until, consciously, area by area, you have come to a standing position or beyond that into any real physical activity. Finally, return to a standing position, free, relaxed, and expectant.

If you are properly relaxed, you will be in balance. Conversely, if you are in balance you will be properly relaxed.

Balance is natural. Nature and humanity are successful when in balance. It is natural for us to treasure balance and to strive for it. We are tense and distraught when denied it. The actor uses this knowledge to enhance his ability to communicate.

Exercise 3 RELAXATION: BALANCE

Standing. When you stand erect and in perfect balance, you are both relaxed and ready. This means that you stand in such a way that the gravitational pull on your body is accomplished without tensing any muscle, either of body or voice. Your breathing will be full and easy.

Think of your body as a skeletal puppet, each section balanced on the one below it. Imagine a wire running from the base of the spine, up through, and out the top of the head. Do not throw out the chest, suck in the stomach, or lift the chin. These sections of the body will fall into place naturally. Thus, with the wire taut, arms hanging loosely, and legs set slightly apart, you are in *symmetrical balance*.

Sitting. Imagine that the taut wire is lowered enough so that you are sitting on a stool. Your legs will be bent at hip and knee. Your arms may hang down or rest in the lap. But your torso is still erect and at ease. Thus, it becomes obvious that restful balance need not always be exactly symmetrical. In fact, you are usually in some asymmetrical position. Asymmetry can also involve perfect balance. When you change the position of one part of your body, you can compensate by a change elsewhere.

symmetrical
balance

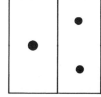
asymmetrical
balance

The illustrations, each showing two rectangles, demonstrate how in either square, the weight of one rectangle balances the weight of the other. Substituting your body for either of the squares, you can imagine that you can attain various positions of alert ease, provided you maintain balance, along with the uninhibited relaxation you achieved in exercise 1.

The balance theory affects all phases of an actor's craft: the relation of the body to the parts within it, the mind to the body, the voice to the body, body to character, voice to character, character to other characters, character to the play, one scene to other scenes, concept to presentation, and other aspects that will occur to you as art. The playwright, the director, the actor, the costumer, and the scenic and lighting designers must all be aware of fine balance. For if, within the parts or within the whole, one thing falls out of balance, the total seems off-key, rhythm is disturbed, communication is interrupted, and audience attention wavers.

Exercise 4 PHYSICAL RELAXATION

These movements are a continuation of the tensing and relaxing in exercise 1. The physical motion is more intense, and is geared toward the limbering warm-ups to come. All exercises work best when you are quiet in body, so that you may think beyond yourself.

Stand next to a chair, so that it will be handy should you need support. Now, slowly raise your arms as high as possible. Reach! Stretch! Now slowly balance on the balls of your feet. Shout if you feel like it. Then relax slowly; bend over, allowing all the force and energy to pour out with your breath. Now raise your head slowly and imagine you are breathing country air. Smell the grass you lay down on when you were ten. Fill your lungs with it. Now relax again, exhaling slowly. Let your heavy head drop. Feel the muscles stretching at the back of your neck. Hold this position, turning the head slowly from side to side. Follow this routine as many times as necessary to release tension.

Now sit in the chair. Adjust your body until you feel comfortable. Let your arms fall to the side, with feet set forward comfortably so that your heels are touching the floor. Now lean back and think about lying on a sunny beach or sitting on the bridge of a ship, moving gently with the swell. Next, bend over until your head is near your knees. Blood is draining from those centers of tension in your neck.

Slowly get up and take a long, deep breath. Bend your arms at the elbows, allowing the hands to hang limp. Now shake them. Stop. Stretch the fingers. Now, supporting yourself with your hand on the chair, raise your knee slowly; first the right, then the left. Do this several times, and stretch those knees up as far as they will go.

At the American Shakespeare Festival and Theatre Academy, Stratford, Connecticut, the actor's training program includes strenuous physical work. (Courtesy of American Shakespeare Festival Theatre and Academy.)

Exercise 5 RELAXATION: THE EGG, THE EGG ROLL, THE TRIPOD

The Egg. Lie flat on the floor. Sit up. Then raise your knees and bend over until you can clasp your hands about your legs. Slowly lower your head, stretching the back of your neck. Stay in this position until you feel tensions lifting from your spine.

The Egg Roll. Without changing your position, begin a rocking motion, back and forth, until you roll back on your spine. Then roll back down on your feet.

The egg.

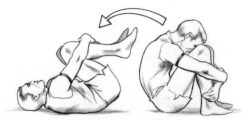

The egg roll.

The Tripod. Now lie prone again. Begin by bending your knees up with back still flat on the floor. Allow the force of this movement to arch your spine, permitting you to place your hands under the hips and your elbows on floor to support the weight of your body. Now raise your legs straight above your head. Stay in this position for at least one minute, or until the blood can flow into the upper part of your body from the feet.

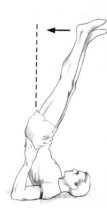

The tripod.

When performing exercises, don't be concerned with how you look—only with what you feel. Concentrate on some reason why you are standing in front of these people. As an example, pretend you are looking for some familiar face in the audience, or imagine that you are at an airport waiting for some close friend to arrive at the passenger gate. Use your imagination to invent other circumstances. Actors need to approach all physical tasks, not only with the body and voice, but also through objectives and motivations that come from within. These inner ideas may originate from remembrance of personal experience or they may be completely imaginative.

In the early stages, you may find it difficult to be imaginative. But this will disappear as you move through the exercises, designed to increase awareness. Freedom and the facility to use the imagination will become a natural part of your acting equipment. The most important point is that you should concentrate on these circumstances or images in detail before performing any physical act.

WARM-UPS

All sessions should begin with some limbering-up activity such as stretching, yawning, grimacing, stooping, squatting, etc. These warm-ups should be performed for five or ten minutes, not only before each exercise session, but also before rehearsals and performances. Warm-ups are no longer considered experimental, but are now standard procedure—even in the professional theatre.

Exercise 6   **WARM-UP: BREATHING**

The group stands erect and relaxed, facing one member who leads in deep breathing exercises.

1. Take in deep breath through the nose only, hold, and exhale, making the "Ohm-m-m-m" sound.[2]
2. Take in deep breath through the nose and mouth, hold longer than before, and exhale with a nasal sound.

---

[2]The use of humming as a way of massaging the voice is recommended by Kristin Linklatter, who also believes that the training of the body, the voice, and the person should be a synthesized process. Kristin Linklatter, *Freeing the Natural Voice* (New York: Drama Book Specialists, 1976), p. 202.

3. Continue, each time holding breath longer than before and making different vowel sounds while exhaling.
4. End by shaking arms and body in short palsied movements, and twisting the muscles of the face into grotesque, masklike formations.

The exercises described are only movements. *You* must supply the inner impulse for doing them. They should not be thought of as calisthenics, but as a means of stimulating ideas through physical actions.

Here is one of the main exercises used by the cast of *Oh! Calcutta!* before every performance.

Exercise 7 **WARM-UP: THE CALCUTTA**

Perform to rhythm. Stand relaxed. Raise arms to shoulder height so that there is room between each performer. Now step forward twisting lower body while keeping head, neck, and shoulders as a unit. Center of balance should shift with each step from right to left as hips twist.

The calcutta.

The above exercise might be transformed into an exercise in coordination by lowering the arms on every third count and raising them on the fourth, always staying with the beat.

Perform warm-up exercises based on the needs of the particular group, and not necessarily in the sequence published here.

The circle.

Exercise 8 **WARM-UP: THE CIRCLE**

1. Walk in time around a circle to some music. At a count or signal, rotate arms and hands, still keeping to the beat while walking.
2. Walk with knees bent, hands on hips.
3. Walk with stiff legs, pointing the toes on each step.
4. Walk two steps, then leap for two counts. Repeat.
5. Rotate trunk from the waist up, with hands on hips, as you trot.

Walking, leaping.

As in all exercises, the students should imagine some *reason* (real or imaginary) for their actions. For instance, in the first part of this exercise, you may be giving signals, like an official at a football game or an officer on an aircraft carrier. Use your imagination and think of images for all exercises.

Exercise 9 **WARM-UP: THE PEANUT PUSH**

Perform in place. Begin on hands and knees. Bend over, arms in front with palms flat on floor. At the signal, lower head to permit chin to push an imaginary peanut. Raise head and shift weight back to knees, then forward again to push the peanut. Do only a few times at first. Later, it can be performed up to fifteen times.

The peanut push.

Do not practice these exercises in front of mirrors because, if you do, you will imitate what you see instead of what you feel. When looking at yourself in a mirror, the normal tendency is either to adjust yourself physically to conform to your preconceived self-image or to adjust yourself mentally to enhance what you see. The actor and actress must overcome this habit in order to arrive at the selflessness required for creative behavior.

Most people are constantly playing a part. This part may be the person they would like to be, the one others want them to be, or a sublimation for some failure. Before any creative acting can be done, all such pretensions must be removed along with the tensions causing them. An actor expresses things he would normally hide behind his defenses.

Training is hard work. It is mental as well as physical discipline. If you approach the exercises and problems in this book with sincere dedication, they will work for you as they have for others. They require no technique, no props or costumes, only a synthesis of imagination, instinct, and natural movement.

Some of the exercises are original, while others are adaptations inspired by such authorities as Jerzy Grotowski, Viola Spolin, Constantin Stanislavski, F. Matthias Alexander, and others. All the exercises have been tested under workshop conditions. Begin each problem by creative rest and concentration. Start only when the action is sincerely felt; then, begin all movements in your body center.

As you do these exercises, do not work for *results* and don't worry about how you look. Exercises must develop spontaneously and organically if they are to become living experiences. Above all, do not think of these exercises as childish. They can be the beginning of your work on the creation of a character because they give you a direct line on how to express physical being and presence.

Exercise 10 **VISUAL IMAGES, IMPORTANT AS WORDS**

We begin by having everyone in the group take a place within a circle. The circle is the form used by tribal man for getting people together. It is the "all hands around" part of folk dancing. The circle has a magic, which shifts emphasis from the individual to more communal interests. The group revolves as a recording is played. Physical

Spontaneous group reactions. (Photo by Fletcher Drake, courtesy of the Living Stage, a project of the Arena Stage in Washington, D.C.)

contact, action, and sounds are combined. People chant, cry, laugh, speak in monosyllables, grunt, groan, and clap hands in rhythm. By externalizing in this way, inner images and ideas that cannot be verbalized seem to occur magically.

An imaginary object (a beach ball?) is tossed from one player to another as they continue walking or trotting around the circle. The imaginary object changes shape, weight, and texture. Sometimes it is hot or cold, or it may have various scents. Spontaneous reactions are encouraged, ranging from joy to terror, fear, disgust, etc., all timed in reaction to the recording.

Beginning with total freedom, players are using their bodies and senses as instruments of communication. Complete relaxation and a joyful spirit of child's play are essentials. Never forget that we are trying to reach inner feelings by first relating them to the physical act.

Some of the exercises that follow are training for the individual; others are oriented toward a group. Eventually, acting involves vibrations with others: players, director, and audience. By adjusting to a social situation, individuals experience self-confidence and assurance through the sharing of a common goal, and come to consider themselves part of a select group, within which members have been chosen for the special qualities they can contribute. This assures each student of the value of contacting others mentally, physically, and emotionally. In turn, such vibrations encourage individual spontaneity and fresh responses to problems.

In a group problem, a member is asked to look directly into the eyes of another, and describe in words what he sees as he touches the other's face. After such tactile human contact, with its resultant lowering of barriers, it would be difficult for any individual to think only of himself and not to think of the oneness of the group.

In ensemble exercises, gestures without words, movement without character, or other isolated problems may be indicated. But all are meant to lead the students into self-discovery and to locate areas of deficiency so that they may correct them and improve as actors. During physical exercises the atmosphere should be free and loose, one that fosters participation in game playing—unlike rehearsals, which are held in a climate of dedication toward the opening of a play.

EXPRESSIVE MOVEMENTS

Walking is but one facet of acting, and many other aspects must be perfected, such as gesture, speech, improvisation, characterizations, and emotions. That is why we must begin simply and develop our work in sequence.

Exercise 11 **WALKING WITH IMAGES**

The following describes only the mechanical actions. You should decide the impulse for each action, the ignition that starts the motor.

1. Walk, expressing calm and dignity. (Suggestion: visualize a coronation.)
2. Walk, expressing haste or impatience. (Do not think about hurrying, but about what is making you hurry.)
3. Walk, expressing opposition or uncertainty.
4. Walk, expressing fatigue. (What are the circumstances?)
5. Walk, expressing dread or fright. (What is frightening you? How does it look? Picture its size, color, shape, etc.)
6. Walk, expressing stealth. (What is the stimulus for such action?)

As in all exercises, you should begin with the impulse and allow it to flow organically into your body.
Imagine you are:

7. Walking on a skyscraper girder.
8. Thirty years older than you are. Now, perform #7 again.
9. Walking in joy, anger, despair.
10. Walking against a strong wind, holding a large flag.
11. Walking blindfolded into a tunnel, with hands tied behind your back.
12. Walking in a cloud or nightmare.
13. Walking in rubber boots in mud.
14. Walking in bare feet in the desert.

Before each exercise, close your eyes and concentrate. Feel the movement inside and act only when you are motivated, sincerely and definitely.

Exercise 12 **SPACE EXPLORATION**

With other members of the class, walk around the stage at will:

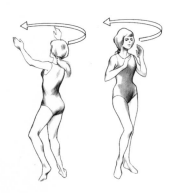

1. Pretend you are all in pitch dark by closing your eyes. When one player avoids colliding with another, he moves in a circle and claps his hands, once, to indicate success. Begin slowly, then increase tempo.
2. One player moves through a tightly packed crowd of noisy New Year's celebrants.
3. A player brings news of a presidential assassination to various groups at a cocktail party. (Use gibberish sounds.)
4. Several players are told they are in a small room and are sightless. Problem: by listening, touching, and receiving impulses from outside, they are to measure the confines of the space.
5. Two players are told they have long extended poles attached to their arms. They are to probe and discover the space of the acting area.

INTERDEPENDENCE

Ensemble playing is as valuable to the individual player as to a group. Each actor must be confident that he can depend on others and that there is complete cooperation. This interdependence among a company of actors could be compared to the buddy system among skin divers.

Exercise 13 **INTERDEPENDENCE**

Five or six players form a circle and join hands. Another player stands within that circle. At a signal, she stiffens her body and falls back.[3] The others catch her and she continues falling to the right, left, and front, until she has complete confidence in her fellow players.

ANIMAL CHARACTERIZATIONS

Playwrights often use similes as a kind of shorthand to indicate the mood or feeling of a character; quite often these are based on animals. For example, "she claws like a tigress"; "she moves like a snake"; a character is "mousy" or "he wolfs his food." The actor should learn to translate these similes into action and feeling.

Visit your local zoo and study the different animals. Note how their entire bodies contribute to movement. They are superb at expressing emotions such as fear, love, hate, hunger, pain, fatigue, and boredom. The reactions of animals are not complicated by built-in repression and censorship, as ours are, and are excellent examples of how one conveys primary emotions through organic action.

The use of exercises in creating animal images has often been the butt of jokes made by those who do not understand the process of building a characterization. In the kangaroo, monkey, cobra, and cat exercises, we are trying to *feel* like the particular animal by assuming

---

[3]In exercises, the signal to begin is often a click sound, such as a rider uses when on a horse.

its physical attributes. Some day you may find that you can abstract something from such exercises in order to visualize and absorb simian or catlike qualities in a part.[4]

Exercise 14 **ANIMALS**

1. Jump, imitating a kangaroo.
2. Walk on all fours like a cat; then strain chest, arms, and shoulder muscles by raising head, allowing pelvis to drop as back arches. Then drop head and tighten abdominals. Hold for count of three. Arch back again, while making catlike fricative sounds.

Cat.

3. Walk on all fours like a rhesus monkey with bent rear legs, and stiff arms supported on knuckles. Visualize a long tail at rear. Find the animal's basic tempo of movement: the short quick actions, sitting back on hind legs, then leaping again to action.

Cobra.

4. Simulate a cobra. From a horizontal position, face down, forehead resting on floor, bend elbows out so that flat palms are under the thorax. Slowly lift back the head only, straining neck muscles. Turn head slowly right and left. Gradually push up with the arms until they are straight, bending the spine back, stretching as far as possible. Hold. Return slowly to first position by bending arms at elbow, placing forehead on floor, and palms under thorax. Repeat. (Lower body does not move in this exercise.)

[4]See discussion on metamorphosis by Irene Worth in chapter 7.

FURTHER READING: DISCOVERING YOURSELF

These books are recommended for additional study at this point. For a more complete list see the "Additional Reading" list at the end of the book.

Alexander, F. Matthias. *The Resurrection of the Body.* Edited by Edward Maisel. New York: University Books, 1969.

Benedetti, Robert L. *The Actor at Work.* rev. ed. Englewood Cliffs, N.J.: Prentice-Hall, 1976.

King, Nancy. *Giving Form to Feeling.* New York: Drama Book Specialists, 1975.

King, Nancy. *Theatre Movement: The Actor and His Space* (100 Training Exercises). New York: Drama Book Specialists, 1971.

Oxenford, Lynn. *Design for Movement.* New York: Theatre Arts Books, 1951.

Penrod, James. *Movement for the Performing Artist.* Palo Alto, Calif.: Mayfield, 1974.

Pisk, Litz. *The Actor and His Body.* New York: Theatre Arts Books, 1976.

Rubin, Lucille S., ed. *Movement for the Actor.* New York: Drama Book Specialists, n.d.

2
MIME AND MASKS

The pantomimist mimes the water and becomes fish, he mimes the wind and becomes tempest, he mimes the fire and becomes flame, he mimes the feelings and becomes passion, he mimes the thing and becomes object, he transforms himself into a tree and becomes a bird, he becomes animated nature.*

Marcel Marceau

*From foreword to *Le Mime Marcel Marceau,* Harald Von Pawlikowski-Cholewa, Paris: Overseas Publications Vaduz, 1963. (Brown Brothers photo.)

All of us are mimes—the man in the White House, and the man in the street. We shrug our shoulders, nod, shake our heads, point our fingers, place our thumbs up or down, and replace speech with an ancient art known as pantomime. Pantomime is a concise and beautiful language.

When we see Marcel Marceau walking without moving, climbing invisible stairs, catching imaginary butterflies, leaning on nonexistent mantelpieces, or performing any of his extraordinary mimes, few of us realize the antiquity of this art. For pantomime is the oldest form of dramatic expression, and the most universal. It has been a part of all primitive cultures.

In ancient Egypt and India, pantomime had already developed artistic forms. In Greece, performers enacted fables of heroes and gods. Later, in fifth-century Rome, topical subjects were used, and there was a special school for the development of pantomime. The Commedia dell'Arte amplified the form by adding improvisational dialogue. In England today, popular entertainments during the holidays are called pantomimes, but these involve music, dancing, songs, dramatic speech, and slapstick clowning.

Mime, as we know the term, is language using no words. It is acting in which all physical images are stylized. Gestures are used sparingly, but are intensified; each movement is completed before another is begun. The only sounds made by a mime are those of objects—the swish of bullets, the squeaking of doors, the pop of opening champagne bottles, etc. These are accepted conventions, but the sounds typical of people are not.

When performers laugh, sneeze, or cry out, it is done silently and communicated only by movement. When mimes need a mantelpiece to lean on or a chair to sit on, these are created out of air. When handling imaginary objects, such as bottles, teacups, flowers, or telephones, mimes create for the audience a complete memory of the actual object: its size, shape, weight, color, smell, and touch. Movements in mime are carefully designed so that they honestly

Sprightly street mime Robert Shields practices pure theatre on the streets of San Francisco to the delight of his loyal lunch hour fans. (Courtesy of Robert Shields and Lorene Yarnell.)

interpret the sizes and shapes of objects. The viewer is purposely allowed to see a mime's hand open and then close around an object so that the object's size and shape are clearly projected. Mimes must be careful not to violate the confines of imaginary objects that they have already established. That is, they must never "walk through" a table or a chair, or forget that they are holding a glass. The glass should be put down before beginning another action. All gestures are enlarged, bigger than life. This is a necessity in the large, open theatres of today.

Although movements are enlarged, they are, as in all acting, stimulated from inside the actor. And like the verbal actor, the silent actor must have complete control over every part of the physical self. Indeed, physical training is a fundamental part of the present-day conditioning of all actors. Gilmore Brown, who trained many well-known actors at the Pasadena Playhouse, once told the author, "The director's great problem is to get the actor to use his body as a metaphorical vehicle for the expression of a dramatic idea."

Since the mime is denied the use of verbal language, physical and spiritual studies are extremely intense. For the mime, the body is the instrument through which the spirit speaks. Mime relies especially on pacing, timing, simplicity of presentation, and the ability to distill meaning until the essence alone remains. An understanding of these elements will increase the range of any actor's abilities. The actor whose body is trained as thoroughly as that of the mime will be better prepared for success in the acting profession. Actors and actresses who train their minds and spirits to use their bodies as instruments with the clarity of the mime will achieve a sturdy base on which to build further acting fundamentals.

Total training in the art of mime cannot be included here, for lack of space. But the following are a few pertinent examples of some accepted methods.

THE BODY OF THE MIME

The mime must undergo rigorous physical exercises so that he can express himself with each part of the body. Then, a range of communicative body expression will be available, whether it involves a twist of the hips or a crook of a finger. The mime's ability to move every part of the body with agility and grace is certainly an advantage to the total actor.

It should be understood that such movements are exercises, but not yet mime. Claude Kipnis remarks in *The Mime Book* that the moment of true mime happens when the inner spirit and the outer physical expression occur together.[1] When you begin studying mime, you must first intellectually recognize the inner urge; then the phys-

Claude Kipnis, mime, in Eve and the Serpent. *(Photo by Edith Chustka.)*

[1]Claude Kipnis, *The Mime Book* (New York: Harper & Row, 1975).

ical expression can appear. As you progress, the intellectual and physical interrelate, and the moment of true mime occurs.

As an actor, you will need to emulate the mime's procedure. You will need to examine the play and the character minutely, so that the inner spirit of the character can pervade the physical movements you will finally put to use. The mime works similarly except that speech is eliminated. Material must therefore be consolidated. It becomes obvious, then, that before you can dwell on the inner motivations, your body must be prepared to react to them.

In my discussions with some of the best-known contemporary mimes, one fact is especially clear. The famous Czechoslovakian mime, Antonin Hodek, says, "In-depth work in every phase of the art of the dance—ballet, free form, ethnic—is an ongoing requirement. Also physical control is developed by such studies as acrobatics, tumbling, and juggling. Study in the martial arts of judo, kung fu, fencing, sword play, etc., are invaluable in creating balance, stance, mental agility—any of which may be needed at any time." To prepare yourself for the varied requirements of contemporary acting, you too will need the physical enrichment of such training.[2]

Antonin Hodek, mime. (Courtesy of Antonin Hodek.)

Traditionally the mime works with each part of the physical being separately, garnering every possible facet of its expressive capabilities. The exercises that follow are for the head alone. You will be expected to devise your own exercises for the torso, arms, legs, feet, hands, wrists, fingers, and so on. By making the effort to design your own exercises, you will be starting the actor's lifelong habit of self-searching. This will help sharpen the awareness of the inner and outer aspects of yourself and your fellow man. The format suggested for the head exercises will form a basis for designing your own mime exercises. This will help prepare you physically, while at the same time planting the seeds for the ensuing parts of your work. It is an intellectual and spiritual study of yourself and the world surrounding you.

Exercise 15 **MIME: THE HEAD**

Assume a relaxed standing or seated position, with your head facing forward and a neutral expression on your face. Do not move any part of the body other than the one alluded to in the instructions. Work slowly or your intentions will be muddled.

1. Move head slowly front to back.
2. Turn head slowly front to right.
3. Tilt head slowly front to right.
4. Combine the above variously. For example, nod front while tilting left, etc.

[2]Actor Henry Brandon points out that those who are working consistently today are those proficient in every possible phase of the performing arts.

5. Vary the speeds with which you accomplish any of the above.
6. Give a descriptive interpretation to each of the above. Examples:
   Turn head *slowly* front to left.
   a. "Could I possibly have heard you correctly?" *or*
   b. "Do I have to listen to all that again?" *or*
   c. "That's impossible!"
   Turn head *swiftly* from front to left.
   a. "What was *that*?" *or*
   b. "I dare you!" *or*
   c. "That's a lie!"

You may recognize in the above exercises the well-known "take" used by most comedians and famous clowns. Charlie Chaplin, Red Skelton, Jack Benny, Jackie Gleason, Art Carney, Danny Kaye, Dick Van Dyke, Carol Burnett all mastered this delicate art. The "take" is a wordless pause, controlled by the performer, which is filled by the audience's imagination.

You may make a game of these exercises if you wish. If you are alone, try to label your movement with a word or phrase that describes the attitude or feeling you have portrayed. If you are with a group, let the others guess what you intended that single movement to express. Remember that, as clearly as you may have performed, each viewer will have a personal interpretation. Your ability to control audience reaction fully will come only after long study and experience. Part of the game should involve devising as many variations of the exercises as you can.

Some mimes use the neutral white mask, either painted on or worn, often with markings that help to project a particular character. Others use the expressive tools of the face: eyes, nose, mouth, forehead, cheeks, teeth, etc.

Exercise 16 **MIME: THE FACE**

Try the previous head exercises, adding as follows:

1. eyes very wide open
2. eyes opening slowly
3. nostrils extended
4. mouth in wide smile
5. lips pursed
6. forehead, frowning
7. eyebrows up
8. cheeks puffed out
9. cheeks sucked in
10. teeth prominently displayed

Give a descriptive interpretation to each of the above variations that explains the exact reason for each expression. You will note that the combinations seem endless, even using these few suggestions.

Mimes Robert Shields and Lorene Yarnell spend three to four hours rehearsing each morning, including eye, brow, and nostril exercises, to maintain what they call the "relaxed intensity necessary for mime." Shields has said that the intensity of the eyes triggers everything else; that he and Miss Yarnell work from the premise that the eyes are the key to mime. Their ability to avoid blinking is phenomenal.

Young American husband and wife mimes Robert Shields and Lorene Yarnell have appeared at fairs, in concert, and on many popular TV shows to great acclaim. (Courtesy of Robert Shields and Lorene Yarnell.)

Exercise 17 **MIME: THE EYES**

Pretend to be gagged and bound to a chair. By use of your eyes only, inform someone where to look for an object.

Exercise 18 **MIME: OTHER PARTS OF THE BODY**

In mime, you should study the same procedures for each movable part within the body as you have for the head. Imagine the countless possibilities of gesture and body language that can result from controlled combinations of the:

1. neck, which can thrust forward or back . . .
2. shoulders, which can shrug, droop . . .
3. chest, which can swell, slouch . . .
4. center torso, sucked in, puffed out . . .
5. hips, which can swivel, bend . . .

Try to enumerate some of the possibilities of movement in the:

1. legs—upper, lower, knee
2. feet—ankles, toes
3. arms—upper, lower, elbow
4. hands—wrist, fingers

Using the pattern of study suggested for the head, devise exercises for every other part of the body. Try to discover how each part can help you communicate an idea, an emotion, an attitude.

THE MIND OF THE MIME

There are certain required abilities for the mime, which provide the actor with mental enrichment as well as heightened body control. The "clic" is one of these. It is the ability to remember, for instance, the height of a table so that when the hand is about to strike it, that hand will stop its motion at the correct level. The ability to remember the exact size, contour, and texture of objects, as well as their weight and resistance to motion, is of primary concern. As Marcel Marceau moves inside a transparent box, we know its substance is hard like glass rather than soft like drapes because of the way he controls his hands against the surface of the box. The surface has no give, its resistance is complete.

THE SPIRIT OF THE MIME

Both actor and mime dwell deeply on the inner spirit, working constantly to free it through physical means. Both are free to use any theatrical means of communication, including costumes, props, and sound. But the sounds used by the mime may not be verbal. Therefore, the mime must use the most effective and simplified method of transmitting a message. This is sometimes through the elimination of extraneous material, and sometimes through tasteful exaggeration. It is here that the mime differs essentially from the actor.

The mime portrays the essence of things, creating reality in a silent but specific way. The actor, on the other hand, must superimpose on that essence a deep involvement with both the delicacies of characterization and the psychological reasons for behavior suggested by the playwright. The mime is necessarily a philosopher—like the clown, the jester, and the performers of Commedia dell'Arte—and finds material in the mysteries and ironies of life itself. The mime both stimulates and manipulates the rich imaginations of the audience. The actor must understand this technique, and move beyond it to grasp and re-create the realities of the play and the beauty of the spoken word. The actor's art *encompasses* mime, rather than being a separate art from mime.

Exercise 19 **HANDLING OBJECTS**

Practice handling imaginary objects of various sizes, weights, and textures.

1. Blow up a balloon. Tie it off. Puncture it. React.
2. Enter carrying a full suitcase. Set it down. Empty it. Carry it off.
3. Play a dart game with an imaginary partner. Toss your own darts. Take them out of the board. Watch your partner's efforts. Devise a finish.
4. Comb your long, straight hair. Braid it.
5. Break an egg into a frying pan. Scramble it as it cooks. Lift the pan from the fire. The handle is hot.
6. Furnish a room from your imagination. Show the location, size, and shape of tables and chairs by using them.

Exercise 20 **BEING AN OBJECT #1**

Housecleaning. You are to become the cleaner, as well as the objects used in cleaning—a dust cloth, a carpet sweeper, a spray can, a squeegee for windows, etc.

Car or motorcycle. You are to be the motor, the tires, the steering wheel or the handlebars, and the highway.

If your character is an object—perhaps a bird, a clock, or a gun—it will be necessary to think into yourself everything that *is* the object. This may be achieved by translating the essence of the object into sensory impressions that can be recognized by the audience. For instance, the clock ticks, its hands move round and round, its pendulum swings back and forth, its repetition is constant, consistent, and rhythmical.

Exercise 21 **BEING AN OBJECT #2**

Suppose you were to proceed with the clock object. How, as a mime, could you impart the ticking of a clock? It is possible, of course, to use nonverbal sounds. So, you could click and cluck with your tongue. You could snap your fingers in an evenly spaced rhythm, or tap your toe or heel. But suppose you deny yourself these more obvious possibilities? Try limiting yourself to pure body movement. As earlier mime exercises have revealed, you have a great many choices of possible body movement. There are so many, in fact (large or small, short or long, quick or languorous, strong or weak, delicate or coarse) that you had better decide exactly what kind of timepiece you wish to emulate. Is it a watch, an alarm clock, or perhaps a ponderous old grandfather's clock? Will you decide to mime the ticking by rhythmically extending the muscles of your nostrils; or by slowly swaying your buttocks back and forth?

What additional movement can you add to clarify your object? Will you sit, stand, or roam about? Why? Will you feel adorable, clumsy, blatant, grand? Why? Does time seem to fly or lag? Why? Is the clock running down? Does an alarm ring? Are there chimes? Is there a second hand? Is it a digital timepiece? What other information does it give beyond the time?

Whatever object you choose must be *thought into* with thoroughness. It will be helpful to make a list of every possible communicable characteristic inherent in the object you choose. For those traits that seem impossible to translate into movement, you will have to imagine what you can do to *suggest* the look or feeling to your audience, so that they can imagine it on their own. Once you have made a list, rearrange and reassemble it into a motion presentation. Now proceed on your own:

1. Choose an object.
2. List its title and its elements.
3. Perform the mime.
4. Read your list to the viewers.
5. Listen to their critique of your successes and failures.

Exercise 22 **MIMETIC GESTURE**

By means of only body gestures, express the following phrases:

1. Please go away.
2. About this long.
3. I have a stomachache.

4. Get up and get out of here.
5. Come over here, I want to say something to you.
6. I won, I won!
7. He zigzagged all over the road, then fell down.
8. Pull over to the side and stop the car.

When communicating several thoughts, do each one *and finish it* before introducing another thought. Do not blur your gestures together.

Exercise 23 **CHARACTER PANTOMIMES**

Spend one minute on each of the following character pantomimes:

1. A retired scientist selecting fruit in a supermarket.
2. A golfer getting ready to make a stroke, while having trouble with a bee.
3. A doctor examining a ticklish patient. You are the patient.
4. A waiter carrying a tray and serving, hoping not to sneeze.
5. A cowboy in a lingerie shop.
6. A mechanic handling tools.
7. A musician fingering an instrument.
8. A father watching a little league game.
9. A PTA speaker wearing tight shoes.
10. A typist having trouble with the machine.
11. A nurse examining a shy patient. You are the patient.
12. A waitress clearing a table and picking up an inadequate tip from a former customer.
13. A housewife knitting socks and listening to a TV soap opera.
14. A parent holding someone else's child.
15. An old lady threading a needle.
16. A B-girl at a bar.
17. A mother at a little league game.

It is interesting to superimpose animal or plant characteristics on character pantomimes. Try the slinkiness of a panther, the deviousness of a cat, the gaudiness of a flower, or the submissiveness of a willow.

Exercise 24 **ANIMAL AND PLANT PANTOMIMES**

This exercise must be done in two parts. For your first mime, you must, as in exercise 21, extract all the salient points characteristic of a chosen animal or plant, and give a short presentation communicating the results. For your second mime, you should apply these traits to a person, adapting them and allowing them to influence the character you portray. Don't choose a character first and then attempt to apply usable animal or plant traits to it. The good of this exercise results from following the routine as it is presented here. The purpose of the second mime is to help you learn to transfer animal or plant traits into human forms. It may improve your second mime if you read the section on mimetic improvisation later in this chapter. And for inspiration, read the story on page 146 by actress Irene Worth. This shows that the finest professionals constantly return to basic concepts.

Suggestions For First Mime: After you have chosen an animal or plant, consult the following partial checklist, which may help to start you off. Add as many additional observations as you can. Try to translate every detail that occurs to you into movement that either suggests the animal or plant to your audience or gives them the impetus to imagine it. Examine your chosen plant or animal for:

1. *First impact:* First impression. See page 117 for the description of the Gestalt theory of perception. Your first impression may well become the overall theme of your mime.

2. *Secondary impacts:* Additional impressions, which can become extremely minute as you proceed.

3. *External elements*
   size: largeness, smallness
   shape: formal, informal
   color: dull, bright, dark, light
   form: thick, thin, graceful, sharp
   texture: rough, smooth

4. *Internal elements:* Actions resulting from and reactions to the following:
   fear, joy, hunger, need
   earth, sun, fire, smoke
   wind, breeze, rain, noise
   light, dark, cold, heat

5. *Progression*
   insemination
   growth
   stages of development
   completed growth
   requirements for growth (rain, shelter, food, etc.)
   hindrances to growth

6. *Relate* all discoveries back to first impact, and finally back to your original choice of animal or plant.

7. *Rehearse* possible movements before a mirror.

8. *Correlate* and arrange, choose and discard, search for the essences, and write it all down. Then rehearse your mime for presentation, using the best movements you have found.

Suggestions for Second Mime: The transference of animal, plant, or object characteristics to those displayed by humans is a fascinating problem. Many words in spoken language seem to apply particularly to people. *Frailty, innocence,* and *bravado,* for instance, are not normally used in connections other than human. You must, therefore, be thoughtful both when identifying and when transferring traits. The dictionary is a never-ending source, full of surprising ideas for this kind of searching. We would not ordinarily think of bravado in connection with a plant. Yet the form, or attitude, or aura of a plant can *suggest* bravado. There is a kind of cactus called epiphyllum (orchid cactus), whose greenery is clumsy, spiny, and spindly, but which suddenly bursts forth with a short-lived, most exquisite, large, and brilliant bloom. This plant certainly communicates a loud, distinct "Hah!" That's bravado.

In preparing your second mime you will have to devise translations. For example, in what ways could the demeanor of an ostrich be applied to human character? The long, erect neck, the seemingly bold and brazen stare, the stilted manner of picking up and placing the legs and feet, the relatively slow raising and lowering of wings, the ability to move suddenly from a static pose to incredible speed, and the overall impact of disdain and haughty control. These are wonderful traits to try to place on a human character. Even though you can't lengthen your neck or flap your wings, you can still seem to. Your posture, your walk, the tilt of your head, the speed of your movements (or lack of it), the pride in your appearance, and the pace of your decision-making process can all *suggest* character.

Reread the previous paragraph. Don't read only the words. Go slowly enough to allow pictures to form in your imagination as you read. And enjoy yourself. This is a creative process.

Exercise 25 **PANTOMIMES**

1. You are an army nurse or a male medic in a field hospital. You have accidentally discovered a bomb. You try to get some native attendants to get the bomb squad, but they understand no English.
2. A deaf mute is about to touch a hot stove. You try to prevent this.
3. You are in a foundry where the noise is deafening. Warn a co-worker of immediate danger.
4. You are in a TV studio, about to go on camera, when you notice that your partner's clothing is unzipped. You cannot speak or whisper, so you use gestures instead.
5. You are in a boat with your young child, fishing on a clear lake. You see a large bass and try to indicate that the line should be where you have seen the fish.
6. You tell a story to both an old and a young person, who sit at your feet and whistle their reactions. It is a story about a princess, a castle, and a handsome prince—but there are no words to it, only gestures because it is a memory.[3]

The story is less important in miming than the execution of physical images. They should be presented in their essence—precise, clean-cut, and, as we have said, larger than life.

MIMETIC IMPROVISATION

Improvisation is the natural ally of the mime. Like the performers of Commedia dell'Arte, the mime creates directly from a simple plan or scenario.[4] Strengthened by the ability to observe, improvisation

[3]From Jean-Claude van Itallie's one-act play, *War* (New York: Dramatist Play Service, 1967), p. 13.

[4]*Scenario* as defined by *Webster's* is "an outline or synopsis of a play; especially a plot outline used by actors of the Commedia dell'Arte." A screenplay or shooting script is also called a scenario. Further and more involved discussions and exercises with scenarios appear with the study on improvisation on page 65. See also page 215 for a Commedia dell'Arte scenario.

serves the mime by allowing the inner self to surface and to influence intellectual and physical behavior. The following exercise will serve as an introduction to the more in-depth study of improvisation in chapter 4.

In order to extend your imagination, the next exercise will assist you in learning to devise scenarios (plans) of your own. Later you will discover additional categories. But for simplification here, each mimetic improvisation requires a character, a situation, and some action.

Character   For the actor, character is usually defined within the play. But for the mime there is no such convenient background. A mimed character must be thoroughly clarified by other means— drawn from within or plucked out of a rich storehouse of observed behavior. The actor who is practiced in mime is enriched because of this knowledge; conversely, the mime who has studied acting is more accomplished, as well.

Situation   This is the place, time, and position in which the character is located.

Action   This is the impetus to move the character forward or backward from the present into the future or the past.

Exercise 26   **MIMETIC IMPROVISATIONS**

In exercise 23 the character, situation, and action were selected for you. Now *you* will choose from each of the lists below and arrange a short, written scenario of your own. After you have performed it, the scenario will be read to the class. A critique can then take place.

The ability to do this well will have great value for you when play, scene, and character analysis are studied in chapter 7. From the examples supplied, you will have to mix and match from among the various possibilities.

Possible characters:

A teenage girl or boy much in love

A lazy country bumpkin, much too fat

A suspicious mother or father

A person filled with nervous anxiety

A naive adult

Possible situations:

Sitting on a park bench on a hot summer day

In a department store at closing time at Christmas

Standing in a long line at the bank

Waiting in a doctor's office

Driving someone else's car

Possible actions:

Asking for a day off

Remembering a similar situation years ago

Trying to hurry

Arguing to no avail

Writing a letter

Example scenarios for pantomime (selected from above):

1. (*character*) A teenage girl or boy much in love (*situation*) sitting on a park bench on a hot summer day (*action*) writing a letter.
2. (*character*) A person filled with nervous anxiety (*situation*) driving someone else's car (*action*) trying to hurry.

Before proceeding further, you should make notes suggesting physical actions that may help to communicate your scenario. The act of improvising will add to your inventiveness. For each of the three categories, you must ask yourself questions, and answer each with imagination and clarity. *For scenario 1 above:*

QUESTIONS	POSSIBLE ANSWERS	POSSIBLE BUSINESS
Character: How will you tell an audience that you are a teenage girl?	Dig continuously into your purse and pull a brush through your hair.	Lay the brush on the bench by mistake and search frantically when it isn't in the purse.
How can you show that you are in love?	Gaze adoringly and often at your token engagement ring.	Ring is much too heavy and too large. You fuss with it. It falls off. You finally hold it on by keeping your finger bent.
Situation: How will people know it is a hot day?	Pat your damp forehead with kleenex. Try tying your hair up.	The kleenex is used up so you use your blouse. Your boyfriend is coming so you must let the hair down in spite of the heat.
What makes it clear that it is a park bench?	People walk by. Someone sits next to you. You feed the birds from your lunch.	A child gives you her balloon. You buy an ice cream cone from a vendor. The child bothers you, you give it the ice cream. Birds interrupt you, you throw them the whole sandwich.

Action: What makes it obvious you are writing a letter?	You tear paper from your notebook. You shake your pen to start it flowing.	The pen runs dry. You find a pencil. The point breaks so you bite it to find more lead.

When two or more people are involved, there should be a conference with written results. The presentation should be as carefully rehearsed as an intricate dance routine or a musical composition. A mime does not always work alone. Ensemble playing in pantomime can be very beautiful and entertaining.

Exercise 27 **MIME: ROMEO AND JULIET**

A fine exercise involves miming *Romeo and Juliet*, beginning with act IV, scene iii and continuing to the end of the play. Cut, trim, and consolidate as necessary.

Samuel Beckett has written a fascinating scenario, *Act without Words, A Mime for One Player.*[5] It is well worth the effort to study and perform. It requires highly integrated behind-the-scenes assistance, involving two or three persons.

[5]Samuel Beckett, *Act without Words, A Mime for One Player* (New York: Grove Press, 1958). Published with the play *Endgame.*

Ensemble playing in pantomime. (Courtesy of Claude Kipnis. Photo by Edith Chustka.)

MASKS AS TOOLS

We have been using mime as a way of searching into methods for identifying and communicating aspects of thought processes and character. With this preparation, you can proceed into further character involvement by experimenting with masks. In working with masks, it is important to realize that the exercises are an outgrowth from mime, not connected directly with it.

Working with masks does not permit the convenience of facial expression. Too often we depend on facial expression for the greater part of our nonverbal communication. But such a dependence can be dangerous, especially for those in films. Film magnifies and intensifies to such an extent that players must remember that the audience is as close to them as the camera.

Although masks have always been a part of theatre, their use as tools for the acting student is relatively recent. This use was developed by Michel St. Denis, among others, at the Old Vic Theatre in London.[6] In unpublished notes regarding his work with masks, Michel St. Denis points out that working with masks forces the observation of character. The mask encourages the body to blend with it. Self-examination then becomes easier, and the actor's apprehension is minimized. St. Denis observes that the use of masks causes internal feelings to surface, resulting in clean, powerful body reactions. He values the fact that the mask depersonalizes, while it both reveals and rejects. Personality and character traits that are normally communicated through facial expression are hidden when a mask is worn. The mask does not allow the player to depend on this convenient method of transmitting messages. In so doing, the mask also rejects the overlying innuendos, complications, and confusions that facial expression usually superimposes on direct body language. Wearing a mask, therefore, forces the players to use all parts of their bodies fully to communicate information or sensation. Masked players initially find that their inadequacies are revealed, and later that their bodies can become competent communicators. Communication when using a mask requires simple, strong, controlled movement—sustained and sure.

The following format for working with masks parallels that used by Michel St. Denis and John Houseman. There are, in addition, many other exciting approaches that will encourage your development.[7]

The Neutral Mask

Initially, you should use only the neutral mask. It is important to continue to work neutrally for two to three months, since the elementary techniques will develop during this time.

---

[6]Michel St. Denis introduced masks as tools at the Drama Division of the Juilliard School in New York. John Houseman, formerly at Juilliard, brought the method to the University of Southern California Performing Arts Department. Mr. Houseman has graciously edited the material presented here.

[7]Rolfe Bari, *Behind the Mask* (Oakland, Calif.: Persona Products, 1977).

The neutral mask used in a group improvization. (Courtesy of the Claude Kipnis Group. Photo by Edith Chustka.)

The neutral masks are full, rigid, blank faces—all white. Both male and female masks should be provided. Halloween masks can be sprayed with white paint. Or masks can be made by laying several thicknesses of one-inch strips of newsprint or paper toweling, impregnated with diluted white glue, over a thoroughly greased (Vaseline) Styrofoam head form—the kind available for wigs. Four types should be available: childhood, adolescence, maturity, and age. Once the masks have been placed over their faces, the students should study themselves in a mirror as long as necessary for them to transcend their own personalities—thus opening themselves to the point where they can accept suggestion freely. An abstraction takes place; foreign images become possible.

Use of the neutral mask requires a pure "body-brain technique." The actors will not be allowed to speak. The easier effects of voice tone and facial expressions are denied to them. They lack the means ordinarily used to convey emotions. To project a particular character, the actor must use the whole body—together with an intellectual drive, resulting in expression on a higher, broader, more complete level.

Exercise 28 **NEUTRAL MASK**

Time: one to two minutes
As the actor stands masked and neutralized, both spiritually and physically, suggestions should be presented to him through words,

snatches of music, and rhythmic sounds. His reactions to these stimuli should take the form of facets of the character type that has entered his mind—whether it be human, animal, or some other.

It is important to remember that this is not mime. This is abstract movement that uses the body as its tool and the mind as its directing force.

The Character Mask

The most successful work with character masks is done with half-masks of the type used in Commedia dell'Arte. These masks leave the lower portion of the face free so that sound from the actor can be heard. The various character types should be extreme in design. A capable artist-craftsman should prepare these papier-mâché masks.

Exercise 29 **CHARACTER MASK**

1. Choose a mask. Look at it; study it; identify yourself with it.
2. Put on the mask and take some time, perhaps using a mirror, to make a marriage between the character of the mask and your own character, as you have adapted it to the mask.
3. Once this new character has solidified, you may devise your own characterizations. Do not use set pieces. Simply allow the new character to perform normal, ordinary tasks. The manner in which you perform will be dictated by the mask-influenced character. So you will not need word or sound suggestions, as you did with the neutral mask. Self-imposed stimuli will occur to you such as:

listen	watch	argue	work
search	sit	walk	leave
amble	discuss	escape	arrive

4. Do not speak. Only noises or sounds are permitted. Wordless sounds can be intensely indicative of character. There are *whines* of petulance, fear, anxiety, and criticism. There are *moans* of loneliness, pain, boredom, and grief. And there are *grunts* of satisfaction, inattention, and concentration. A constant, repetitious staccato tone can suggest, for instance, an annoying or insistent personality. A low-pitched humming, with variation in its intensity, could indicate quiet, argumentative discussion.
5. Try attaching various sounds (suggested below) to the character types they suggest. And attempt to attach the various character types below to the sounds.

Sounds:

clucking	growling	barking	whispering
whistling	chirping	cheering	sighing
mumbling			

Types:

indecisive	thoughtful	blustering	coy
pushy	successful	timid	lackadaisical
rowdy	crotchety		

Again, remember that while mime may be considered a preparation for this kind of character exercise, this is not mime. Mime has to do with imitation, simulation, and copying, and has an overcast of buffoonery. These mask exercises, on the other hand, require the creation of an original character—a mental-physical development triggered by the appearance of the mask and its amalgamation with the individual actor. Each person's results will differ from every other's, due to the variety of individual perceptions.

Exercise 30 **MASKS (GROUP)**

Time: two to five minutes

The preceding two exercises have helped mold actors capable of assimilating new characters and transforming themselves. At this stage, the following short scenarios may be done.

1. Often, two or three actors can work together on a scenario. After deciding on their mask characters, the actors agree on a simple scenario.
2. A scenario typically includes a locale, a reason for being there, and a problem. For instance:
   a. a department store; a shoe sale; a difficult customer
   b. home at Christmas; opening presents; a gift to be assembled is missing a part.
   c. a park with a bench; feeding the birds; the bench is only large enough for two people
3. First, present the scenarios with only movement and unidentifiable sounds. Try the same ones again, incorporating actual speech. These last are for more advanced students.

FURTHER READING: MIME AND MASKS

(See also the "Additional Reading" list at the end of the book.)

Alberts, David. *Pantomime: Elements and Exercises.* Lawrence: Regents Press of the University of Kansas, 1971.

Barlanghy, Istvan. *Mime Training and Exercises.* New Rochelle, New York: Sportshelf & Soccer Associates, 1967.

Decroux, Etienne. *Words on Mime.* New York: Drama Book Specialists, 1979.

Hunt, Douglas, and Hunt, Kari, *Pantomime: The Silent Theatre.* New York: Atheneum, 1968. Recommended.

Kipnis, Claude. *The Mime Book.* New York: Harper & Row, 1975.

Pawlikowski-Cholewa, Harald von. *Marcel Marceau.* New York: Taplinger, 1964. Excellent pictures of the "master" at work.

Rolfe, Bari. *Behind the Mask.* Oakland, Calif. Persona Products, 1977.

Shepard, Richmond. *Mime: The Technique of Silence.* New York: Drama Book Specialists, 1971. An easy-to-follow book for the beginner. Good clear explanations and drawings.

3
THE ACTOR'S VOICE AND SPEECH

I think a classical background of acting gives a performer many things; he can stand well, walk well, speak well, be heard above all. I think all the great actors had good voices. There have been many glamorous-looking men and women in the theatre who have been matinee idols without being able to touch the higher reaches of their profession, because they have let down vocally.*

Sir Alec Guinness

*Reprinted by permission of Calendar magazine, *Los Angeles Times*. (Photo by permission of Columbia Pictures)

The way people speak reveals their background, education, and social standing, as well as their state of health and emotion at the moment. To those we meet we may sound friendly or persuasive, monotonous or affected. One who possesses a pleasant and convincing way of speaking has a lifetime asset. Conversely, poor speech can be a permanent handicap.

For the actor, good speech is a necessity. Standards of speaking in acting are higher than in any other profession. An actor depends on voice to convey thought, emotion, and characterization. Voice has usually been the first-mentioned characteristic in descriptions of the celebrated actors of the past. It is gratifying to hear an actor with a resonant and flexible voice, using it to transmit meaning and emotion to an audience.

Obviously, the first duty of the actor is to be *heard;* and yet he must sound conversational. The written speeches must seem to be spoken for the first time, but the hesitations and corrections of everyday speech onstage seriously interfere with the flow of the play.

In this country, soon after the arrival of Stanislavski's System, there was an extended period when many interpreters of that System (Method) minimized the training of body and voice while concentrating almost entirely on the development of the inner self. Their fear was that the actors might seem artificial. They expected that the inner self alone could bring forth an uninhibited performance. This resulted in pitifully inadequate actors whose speech was slovenly and inaudible and whose movements were ugly and clumsy. These actors overlooked the fact that nothing on the stage is real. It is the actor's magic that should make it appear real. Fortunately the passage of time has clarified the Stanislavski Method, which now takes its correct place within the total process of training the actor.

The distinction between voice and speech should be clarified at once. While speech is an acquired skill, voice is instinctive. No baby needs learn to cry or croon, whereas speech is a difficult and complicated acquisition. Though we might use a hundred muscles to speak one word, most of us take this skill for granted. Once it is learned, we must continue to practice our speech, or else it atrophies. Speech is affected by many factors: regional and family environments, physical and psychological conditions, and others too technical for our present consideration. Certainly body conditions can affect speech. Anxiety and tenseness can result in speaking too quickly. A phlegmatic attitude results in an indifferent or boring delivery. The actor can only be convincing in emotional moments when both voice and body are coordinated.

Human speech is produced by:

1. A *motor*, largely composed of respirator muscles in the general region of the diaphragm. Its function in speech is to provide power for the expulsion, regulation, and control of air.
2. A *vibrator*, which is chiefly concerned with the vocal folds (or bands). Its function is to produce tone by sound waves and vibration of air.
3. A *resonator*, chiefly in the cavities of the throat, mouth, and nose. Its function is to reinforce or amplify sound waves, giving them resonance.

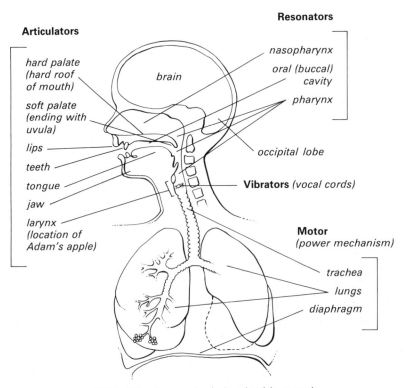

Parts of the human body involved in speech.

4. The *articulators,* composed mainly of the lips, teeth, tongue, upper gums, hard and soft palate, the uvula, and lower jaw. These give shape and character to each speech sound, as the phonated or nonphonated breath stream is expelled through the nose and throat.

BREATHING

Projection, sustained tone, and the timing of vocalization are dependent in most part on control of the breath stream. The mechanism of breathing consists of the rib cage, diaphragm, lungs, and trachea, leading up to the larynx and vibrating folds.[1] As you inhale, the powerful diaphragmatic muscle that forms the dome-shaped floor of the thoracic cavity contracts and descends; air fills the lungs. When you breathe quietly without speaking, the relaxation of the diaphragm and the rib cage slowly force out the air. In normal breathing, inhalation is active and exhalation passive; the time cycle for each is equal. But in breathing for speech, both inhalation and exhalation are *controlled,* as is the time cycle. This control allows the actor to sustain a tone, to exhale with economy while speaking, and to alter timing of phrases and pauses. Skill in other phases of the speech process depends on this breathing control, for it influences tone, resonance, articulation, and rhythm patterns.

Exercise 31 **BREATHING**

1. *Clavicular breathing:* Stand and relax. Then inhale, while at the same time raising your shoulders and collarbone. Exhale. Breathe this way several times, then try speaking a sentence. (Clavicular breathing should be avoided, since it inhibits diaphragmatic control and usually results in fatigue.)

2. *Upper thoracic breathing:* Stand and relax. Place your open palm against your breastbone and raise the chest as you inhale. Repeat. Now read the same sentence.

3. *Medial breathing:* Relax again, and as you inhale this time, press your palms against the lower ribs, moving the ribs outward and slightly upward. Repeat, then try your control of breathing as you speak the sentence.

4. *Diaphragmatic-abdominal breathing:* Stand at ease and inhale as you place your right palm over the soft part of the abdomen just under the ribs and your left palm against the ribs and abdominal wall. Repeat, then try the sentence.

5. *Deep breathing.* Take a deep breath, inhale to the bottom of your lungs. Now exhale slowly by blowing through pursed lips. Repeat.

6. *Controlled breathing.* Take a full deep breath and count silently: IN, 1, 2, 3, 4, 5; HOLD, 6, 7, 8, 9, 10, and OUT. Now increase by two counts each time you repeat the exercise.

---

[1]Elise Hahn et al., *Basic Voice Training for Speech* (New York: McGraw-Hill, 1957), pp. 24–55. Used by permission.

SOUND

Much of your voice quality depends on the amount of breath inhaled and the rate (force) of exhaling. Place your hand on your rib cage. Breathe with short panting breaths. You can feel the rising and falling motion. Now breathe in long and deeply. Note the expansion of your chest as your lungs fill with air. Experiment in the same way again, but this time place your hand on your abdomen, above your waist at the center and front of your body. This is the location of your diaphragm. Feel the movement as you inhale and exhale. The diaphragm is the power source, and controls in large part the kind of sound you emit. A gentle sigh will give forth no substantially audible sound. A heavy sigh will carry with it the beginning of vocalized sound. The level and kind of sound depend only partly on the amount of breath expelled. Voiced sound is also affected by the way the breath is expelled.

Push out a sudden blast of air from your diaphragm. This is the same kind of power you use when you cough or when you yell. Try coughing or yelling as you hold your hand on your diaphragm. You will feel the similarity.

ARTICULATION

When you impede or modify your breath power, you are articulating. The illustration on page 38 shows the various general areas concerned with manipulation (impeding) of the breath power. Intensity refers to the rate at which energy is given off from the power source. When you prepare to shout, you automatically increase inhalation and exert pronounced pressure on the lungs. The release of this pressure through the trachea to the vocal folds causes a vibration that increases the loudness of the sound. If you maintain pressure to sustain this tone, release is controlled in the diaphragmatic-abdominal region, not in the throat.

Articulation is not confined to speech alone. Both verbal and nonverbal sounds are articulated, since both are manipulated by the articulating mechanism. To prepare for investigating the technical aspects of articulation, we will do a simple exercise to demonstrate several ways a single sound can be impeded. The method in which you impede this sound will be influenced by the inner need to express. The phrases in the exercise will suggest this inner need.

Exercise 32 **ARTICULATION: AN EXAMPLE**

Sound without words and sound as an accompaniment to the formality of words are important parts of physical expression.

Without opening the mouth, emit the humming sound, m-m-m-m-m-m, before speaking each of the following phrases. The kind of hum should vary and be expressive of each phrase.

M-m-m-m-m-m. . . . I'll have to think about it.

M-m-m-m-m-m. . . . That hurts!

M-m-m-m-m-m. . . . You're absolutely right.

M-m-m-m-m-m. . . . It feels good to relax.

Repeat each while holding one hand against your throat and the other on your diaphragm. Note the variations in both breath power and amount of constriction of the throat muscles.

Repeat each phrase, first with the mouth closed as you make the m-m-m-m-m-m sound and next with the mouth open. Note the vast differences in the resulting sounds.

This exercise has introduced you to the idea of articulation. We have said that we must move from one facet of an actor's preparation to another. Wherever possible, we will pair each step to an inner feeling, thus establishing the interdependence between interior and exterior expression. Kristin Linklatter suggests that the creative impulse is actually the synthesis of voice-sound and body-movement, which simultaneously emanate from an inner energy. Good additional exercises may be found in her writings.[2]

With regard to the combination of sound and the impulse causing it, think back over the last exercise. Note that the resulting sound was controlled by (1) the inner impulse, which comes from (2) the idea within the phrase, which stimulates (3) the breathing mechanism, which causes (4) emission by way of the articulation muscles. The different results you achieved, all from the same sound, were caused by the various ways you controlled your diaphragm and your vocal mechanisms.

Insofar as the Linklatter theory applies, you may discover that a habitual body movement or gesture involuntarily accompanied each sound. If not, it will help at this time to choose a single, simple movement that you associate with each thought; perhaps a shrug, a recoil, or a nod. The interrelations between sounds and movements can vary greatly. Different combinations can result in different kinds of communication. Try combining a single movement with a single sound. Identify verbally what you have tried to communicate. Proceed by combining more than one movement with a single sound. Try more than one sound with a single movement. How much more can you communicate by judiciously choosing combinations of sound and motion?

Exercise 33 **CONTROL THROUGH ARTICULATION**

In this exercise you will experiment with control by manipulating the various articulating mechanisms noted in the illustration on page 38.

---

[2]Kristin Linklatter, *Freeing the Natural Voice* (New York: Drama Book Specialists, 1976).

Using the same m-m-m-m-m-m sound, with your mouth closed, listen to the assortment of sounds emitted when:

1. the tongue is relaxed in the mouth
2. the tongue is tight to the roof of the mouth
3. throat muscles are tensed or relaxed
4. the soft palate (rear of tongue) is closed, relaxed

Try the same articulation positions, but this time push a sudden blast of air from your diaphragm. If you consider the innumerable possible articulatory positions, either singly or in combination with each other, you will realize the vast number of sounds at your disposal. Add to these the various positions of the lower jaw—with mouth open and with mouth closed. With these, you can achieve guttural grunts and growls, nasal twangs, bell-like open tones, and many others.

Vowels and Diphthongs

As with all facets of the actor's work, the study of articulation can be very involved. We introduce it to you here, hoping that you will investigate it further, along with the other phases of voice and speech.[3] The articulation of vowels and diphthongs is accomplished by specific positions of the lips, tongue, and lower jaw. (Diphthongs are a blend of two vowel sounds.)

Exercise 34 **ARTICULATION: VOWELS AND DIPHTHONGS**

Note the various positions of your lips, tongue, and jaw as you slowly say the following, changing from one to the next:

moo	mist	*may*
maw	mud	*my*
ma	murder	*moist*
man	noose	*mew*
men	nook	*now*
me	no	

(The italicized sounds are diphthongs.)
Repeat these sounds, recording them on tape if possible, until you are sure that each sound is completely distinct from the others.

A speech teacher has made the excellent suggestion that vowels be renamed *tones*, a word denoting *sounds* rather than *letters*. Vowels are the main vehicles of speech. All vowel sounds are voiced.[4] Their characteristic is that the outward stream of breath is not stopped or interrupted. The pure vowels are classified as front, middle, and

[3]See "Further Reading: The Actor's Voice and Speech" at the end of this chapter.
[4]Some experts disagree. Touch your throat and *whisper* a, e, i, o, and u. Can you do it and not use voice?

	FRONT		MIDDLE		BACK	
High ↑						
	beat	[i]	[ɚ] mother		[u]	room
	bit	[I]	[ɜ] [ɝ] bird		[U]	book
tongue position	bet	[ɛ]	[ə] sofa		[o]	open
	bait	[e]	[ʌ] up		[ɔ]	saw
	bat	[æ]	[a]	[ɑ]		father
Low ↓			ask			(The Boston "broad A")

back, depending on the position of the tongue when making the sounds. The tongue is a much larger and more influential instrument in speech than most people imagine. Pure vowels are made by a single position of the mouth, whereas a diphthong is a combination of two vowels with the tongue gliding smoothly from one position to another (which it may not necessarily reach). Old actors referred to a diphthong as a "vowel and a vanish."

The bracketed symbols you see in the figure are taken from the International Phonetics Alphabet (IPA) chart that appears at the end of this chapter, along with an explanation and discussion of its uses.

With the vowel chart before you, follow the line from left to right as you read aloud, first the word, then the isolated vowel sound as underlined. Now practice saying the words below, and note in the mirror the adjustments made by your lips, jaw, and tongue, and where the sounds are made.

late, hat, yes, calm, ask (general American), ask (English or Bostonian), seem, hit, reap

In the following list, practice the complete word, and then isolate the vowel sounds:

feet, women, fatal, ever, plaid, true, put, protrude, aunt

Exercise 35 **ARTICULATION: SUSTAINING TONES**

Only vowels may be sustained. Consonants cannot.

Stand and relax. Next place both palms on the abdomen, just under the rib cage. Inhale. Imagine that a fist is being aimed at your middle. Tighten the muscles. Exhale as you shout *"HAH!"* Relax. Again inhale. As you exhale, shout *"HAY!"* Again, assume the same position and conditions, but shout *"HEE!"* Again, *"HOH!"* Relax. Assume the same position and the same conditions, but this time conserve breath in order to sustain the vowels:

1. HAH h-h-h-h-h!
2. HAY a-a-a-a-a!
3. HEE e-e-e-e-e!
4. HOH o-o-o-o-o!
5. HI i-i-i-i-i!

Note that in preparation for each sustained tone, you first fill your lungs with an adequate supply of air to "motorize" the long tone. The normal breathing cycle is altered. We actually take more breath than the body requires. This is a necessity in sustaining tones.

Consonants

Unlike vowels, which are produced by breath traveling through *un-interrupted* passages to become tones, consonants are hewn and shaped into crisp, clean sounds by tongue, lips, and teeth.[5] A less fanciful and more accurate definition is given by Hahn:

> *To produce consonants, the breath stream is stopped momentarily at a particular place in the mouth, or made to flow through a narrow passageway, or diverted through the nose. The positions for the articulation of consonants are therefore much more definite than for vowels.*[6]

Some consonants are voiceless, as in *p, t, k, s, f, h*; others are voiced, as in *b, d, g, v, w, n,* and *l*. Voiced sounds are the result of actions or movements of the vocal folds and the vibrations of air in the resonating cavities. Voiceless sounds are the opposite of voiced. You may always check the difference by placing your fingers on your throat as you speak a word.

Consonants require rapid, efficient adjustments of lips, tongue, and cheeks. They carry the main burden of speech, giving it clarity, vigor, and beauty. Common faults in the phonation of consonants are either a tendency to be overprecise, or to slur the sounds so that they are unintelligible. Consonants should be spoken so that there is no doubt as to the sound. Never expose an audience to such sounds as "Bra'way" for Broadway, "belong'inks" for belongings, or "may-an" for man unless these pronunciations contribute to your characterization.

Exercise 36   **ARTICULATION: CONSONANTS**

There are several technical categories within the consonants. For our purposes, at this stage of your work, you mainly need to become aware of the various kinds of movements that must take place. Using the vowel and diphthong sounds given above, go through the whole

---

[5]For detailed descriptions of consonants, see Margaret McLean, *Good American Speech* (New York: E. P. Dutton, 1952), chap. 3.

[6]Hahn et al., *Basic Voice Training for Speech.*

list, placing a different consonant before each. Do it slowly, noting the changes that take place with the lips, all parts of the tongue, and the positions of the jaw. For example:

moo, boo, coo, doo, etc.

maw, baw, caw, daw, etc.

ma, ba, ca, da, etc.

Do not omit combined consonant sounds as below.

th, as in *think*	*s,* as in *pleasure*
th, as in *the*	*ch*, as in *Charlie*
sh, as in *she*	*ng* as in *bring*

Note that the *m, n,* and *ng* sounds are called nasal or guttural because it is necessary to use the soft palate (back of the tongue) to form them.

PROJECTION

Projection is the ability to be heard and understood at distances both near and far. Although related to loudness, it does not involve loudness alone. An actor may speak very quietly and, with proper projection, be heard and understood by everyone "out front." On stage, actors may seem to be speaking to each other, but they should always be aware that their words must reach all over the house.

The ability to project results from the combined control of your breathing apparatus and your articulation, working in conjunction with one another. A full breath exhaled with a powerful thrust does not insure projection. Projection can fail when articulation is incorrect, limited, or sloppy; when the mental image (intent) is not clearly thought out; or when the necessity to be heard and understood has not been fully comprehended. The various combinations of your breathing power and articulation are limited only by your ability to control the power and thrust, and your inner compulsion to express. The first can be developed technically. The second will develop only in proportion to your awareness of your control, coupled with your growing insight into the emotional possibilities and needs of the character. Exercise 32 is an early effort to express a thought or feeling by combining it with a simplified articulated sound. In exercises for projection we will always try to combine expressive need with the power mechanism, breath.

Exercise 37 **PROJECTION: RELAXATION**

Approach projection exercises in a relaxed frame of mind. We have called relaxation a state of preparedness. Preparedness embraces confidence. Confidence erases anxiety. Therefore, if you are confident of success as you build your ability to project, you will eliminate any chance of *hyperventilation* (taking in too many breaths without adequate exhalation). Try these two ways of calling, "Hey" across campus or to the rear of the auditorium. You will immediately understand the necessity of relaxation for projection.

1. Your inner need (intent) is to attract attention. Take a complete breath. Let the breath power come from a thrust of the diaphragm as you call, "Hey." The successful result is like the swift power of the string of a bow as it releases an arrow. It is the same power you used as a child to blow a bean through a tube.
2. Using the same inner need, take a complete breath allowing the rib cage to expand fully. Hold the rib cage expanded as you call, "Hey." You will note that while tensing to hold the rib cage expanded, you have actually cut off breath power. Relax. Try number 1 again.

Exercise 38 **PROJECTION: CLARITY (INTENT)**

Both articulation and inner need are here imposed on your energy source, breath. This game will help show how much clarity assists projection, and how much clarity depends on intent. Speak the line, "Peter Piper picked a peck of pickled peppers." Now clarify an intent. To do this ask:

Question:

1. *To whom* am I speaking?
2. *Why* am I speaking to them?
3. *Where* am I and *where* are they?

Answer:

1. I am speaking to a group of farm workers.
2. They complain that a peck is too much to pick. I must change their minds.
3. They are scattered about a small field. I am standing on a truck bed in the field.

Speak the line again. You will note that your intent causes you to accent certain words, perhaps even to pause within the speech: "Peter *Piper* picked a *peck* of pickled peppers!"

The intent, along with the correct amount of breath power and fully articulated sounds, results in successful projection. In other words, you will then be understood by your listeners. This is fundamentally because you have involved them in your intent. Therefore, they have opened themselves to your effort. If you have an eager listener, half the battle is won.

In order to check the influence of different articulation of the same line, change your intent as follows:

1. Speak to a group of six-year-old children playing a game.

2. They are the first team receiving instructions to pick only *pickled* peppers. The second team must not hear, so you will have to seem to whisper.

3. The first team is hiding behind bushes around the garden. The second team is farther away.

Speak the line again.

Note that in this example the word *pickled* is articulated entirely differently than in the previous example, because of your change of intent. Remember that your audience must be a party to what you have said. It often helps to imagine that the field workers or the children are actually scattered among the audience itself.

Exercise 39　**PROJECTION: BREATH SUPPLY AND CONTROL**

Review the various points we have discussed regarding breath power, articulation, and projection. Study the following excerpts, and prepare to read them in class—first to the front row of an auditorium, second to the center, and third to the rear. Underline the words you wish to stress, and mark the pauses that best bring out the meaning. But also remember that you must renew your breath supply. You will find that renewing the breath does not always mean taking in a full supply. A catch breath often suffices, is less obvious, and is quite natural. Your method of breathing can often be suggested by an author's use of punctuation. A comma or dash can be a convenient breathing time, and can also enhance the meaning of the lines.

First is a quote by Bertolt Brecht from *Mother Courage:*

I feel sorry for a commander like that—when maybe he had something big in mind, something they'd talk about in times to come, something they'd raise a statue to him for, the conquest of the whole world for example—Lord, the worms have got into these biscuits!—he works his hands to the bone and then the common riffraf don't support him because all they care about is a jug of beer or a bit of company.

The second quote is from Shakespeare's *Sonnet 65:*

Since brasse, nor stress, nor earth, nor boundless sea,
But sad mortallity ore-swaies their power,
How with this rage shall beautie hold a plea,
Whose action is no stronger than a flower?

PHRASING, PAUSING, AND TIMING

A phrase is a thought unit. Pauses serve as oral punctuation marks. Both depend on the meaning of the lines, and each contributes, not only to the intelligibility, but to the emotional impact of the character and the play. If we hurry in speaking a phrase, we can subordinate it. By pausing judiciously, we can accent it. By varying tones, we can alter moods and build interest.

Many different effects are enhanced by good timing. Timing is a delicate art, which only experience and instinct can guide. It is the interaction of two components: the rate of speed with which you speak and the use of pauses between the words. Most people comprehend best when a continuous flow of words is spoken at the rate of no more than 160 words per minute. Excellent articulation is needed at faster speeds.

Timed pauses can be effective theatrical techniques. Comedian Jack Benny became famous for his use of the pause. Much of his humor was based on this technique.

When a ball is thrown toward you, there is an instant when you must gauge the distance and coordinate your muscles to catch it. You learn how to catch the ball by practice and instinct. It is the same with timing onstage, for timing represents a personal interpretation of deviations from a measured beat. It involves the actor's instinct for understanding the propitious moment to be silent or to speak. This instinctive reaction can be different at each performance because no two audiences are alike. The ability to anticipate audience response is an instinct, especially for an inexperienced player. Some actors are born with a fine sense of timing; others must learn it by long exposure to different audiences. Comedians know that timing is instinctive; but some have first learned it mechanically, by counting beats. As an example, here are a few lines from Oscar Wilde's *The Importance of Being Earnest*:

Lady Bracknell: —are your parents still living?
Jack: I have lost both my parents.
Lady Bracknell: Both? [*count one-two-three*] That seems like carelessness.

Exercise 40   **TIMING**

Use the excerpts from exercise 35. This time experiment with (1) variations in speaking speed, and (2) variations in pauses. Use these to clarify or change your interpretations and to hold the attention of your audience. Your breathing patterns will vary accordingly.

Pauses

Pauses are a valuable tool for any actor. Perhaps *stillness* would be a more descriptive term, for it indicates that such moments are creative, rather than just silent intervals. There are many such moments in that fine thriller *Dial M for Murder*, but these stillnesses advance the plot with action, even though silently.

In Stanislavski's prompt book for his production of *The Lower Depths*, pauses are indicated by plus signs.[7] He used these not only

---

[7]A *prompt book* is a complete copy of the play that includes notations from the director and other production personnel regarding both interpretive and technical aspects of the play. It is used by the prompter, who develops and uses it during all rehearsals and performances.

to indicate beats between speeches, but even between words of dialogue spoken by different characters. Such pauses are like rests in music. An actor may suggest where he feels pauses should be made, but the final decision rests with the director who is out front and has an overall view of the entire production.

Silences are not necessarily dead pauses in which all dramatic action stops. They often indicate that characters are trying to remember something or trying to reach a decision. Such pauses really sustain the drama, add to the characterizations, and are often more effective than dialogue. This is especially true in plays by Harold Pinter, who has become known for them.

Even in films, the pause is important. Film star Glenn Ford has said, "I don't think a good director should get nervous when there's a bit of silence. Some directors think that there's nothing going on if you're not talking all the time. But many times the silences are more eloquent than talk. They are moments when the audience can do the acting. I'm not trying to get out of work, but in a good silent scene, all the talking can take place in the audience's heads."[8]

Glenn Ford. (Photo courtesy of JMK Public Relations.)

Exercise 41 **PAUSES**

Choose a speech from a favorite play, and mark a plus sign where you intend to pause, either for meaning or dramatic intent. Read it aloud, or better yet memorize the speech and the pauses, and then read the speech to your class.

TONE AND RESONATION

Some musical instruments produce sound through the vibration of strings stretched over a sounding box, or *resonator*. Other instruments produce sound when air is propelled through tubes. Human speech sounds are produced as the breath stream passes over the vocal bands and sets them in vibration, much as the lips of a trumpet player are set into vibration. Although the exact nature of these vibrations is not known, it is evident that they initiate disturbances or vibrations in the air column of the tracheobronchial tree, the larynx (Adam's apple), the pharynx (throat), the buccal cavity (mouth), the nose, and the nasopharynx. These disturbances produce sound waves in the outer air, which are transmitted to the listener. The shape, size, texture, and firmness of the walls of these cavities—together with factors such as movements of the epiglottis, soft palate, tongue, jaw, and lips—modify and amplify these tones, building up certain overtones and damping others, until we produce the complex tone we identify as voice.[9]

---

[8]Digby Diehl, "The Western Today," *TV Guide*, April 1, 1972, p. 23. Reprinted with permission from *TV Guide* ® magazine. Copyright © 1972 by Triangle Publications, Inc., Radnor, Pennsylvania.

[9]See G. W. Gray and C. M. Wise, *The Basis of Speech* (New York: Harper, 1946).

All these working parts of speech should be free of muscular tensions and obstructions. We are usually able to recognize a friend just by voice. If our friend is not feeling well or has a cold, we are apt to say, "You don't sound like yourself." The cold or illness has altered the tone emitted by the resonators.

Exercise 42 **STIMULATION OF TONE AND RESONATORS**

The resonators are most important to an actor. To enrich your vocal faculties, imitate different natural and mechanical sounds such as a foghorn, a coyote barking, an old man coughing, a motorcycle starting up, etc. Place each of these in the resonator most suitable to carry the sound. (Check the diagram on page 38.)

1. head
2. mouth
3. nasal
4. occipital
5. laryngeal
6. abdominal

PITCH

A good voice is pitched at the level best-suited for the particular individual. While seated at a piano, read aloud some written material. Try to identify a level of pitch you most often use, and locate a note on the piano that approximates your level. This project is more effective when another person listens for your pitch and locates the tinue using the piano to estimate your *optimum pitch*. Sing down to the lowest note you can produce with ease. From this note, sing up the lowest note you can produce with ease. From this note, sing up the musical scale. Experiment until you locate the pitch that allows the greatest ease and richest tone. If your habitual pitch and your optimum pitch levels are the same, you should be congratulated. If not, then you should attempt to bring the pitch you customarily use closer to the pitch that allows for the most effective use of your vocal instrument. Through consistent daily attention you can easily change your habitual pitch level. This alone is proof that you can also increase your range.

RANGE

An effective range adds variety and interest to speech. Your *range* is the difference between your lowest and highest notes. Actors use variations in pitch to illustrate the temperament or personality of characters they portray. Such variations may also be used to transmit moods for certain words, phrases, or ideas. These variations from optimum pitch are called *melody*, a word actors frequently associate with Shakespearean playing. A simple change within a *single* phonation, either an upward or a downward glide, is called *inflection*. Try saying, "Where have you been?" with a rising inflection at the end, and then with a falling inflection, noting the change of meaning between the two. Changes in pitch within a *group* of phonations are known as *intonation*. When speakers repeat these changes so that they form a pattern and become monotonous, we say they are "intoning." *Always work for variety in your voice tones!*

ARTICULATION AND PRONUNCIATION

Most of us in America grow up learning "lazy" language. As long as we are understood, we are content. We are satisfied with utility when we might have beauty of speech. The sad fact is that most people do not hear themselves accurately. We believe we are making one sound when in fact it is quite another. Also many do not realize that a word is not a single blur of a sound but is made up of a sequence of sounds. For instance, there are many different sounds in a word like "extinct." In pronouncing a word, a speaker may move so quickly from one sound to another that individual sounds are not easily detected.

If you wish to improve your speech, you must first isolate each faulty sound and correct it. This is going to sound overprecise in the beginning, but it is the only way to improve. Later on you will find yourself speaking naturally and you will lose the tendency toward slovenly, lazy speech.

Articulation has been defined as the process of forming meaningful oral symbols by manipulation of the tongue, lips, lower jaw, and palate. The breath stream is interrupted or constricted, and with the aid of resonance forms into understandable sounds.[10] While articulation deals with proper manipulation of the articulators, *pronunciation* is the skill of producing acceptable sounds and correct accents. This includes the ability to form vowels and consonants properly and to divide words into syllables and accent them correctly.

What is correct pronunciation? Is it the speech of the well bred in England and the educated in America? Such standards are unreliable. Nor can we depend on the spelling of a word to know how it should be pronounced. In real life, correct pronunciation depends on the occasion. But on the stage pronunciation must be appropriate to the character portrayed and the play that is acted. It would certainly not be appropriate to use localized accents of American speech when acting in one of the great classical dramas. Such a mistake could destroy an otherwise perfect illusion of another time, another place. On the other hand, correct English will not do for certain

An exercise for articulation and breath control. (Photo by Clayde Hare, courtesy of American Conservatory Theatre.)

[10]*See* Lyman Judson and Andrew Weaver, *Voice Science* (New York: Appleton-Century-Crofts, 1942).

other plays. In the United States there is no such thing as "standard English." Pronunciation differs in each locality, and even among individuals of each locality. The so-called general American dialect is divided into many subgroups, and since no norm can be found, the term is meaningless. No matter how an American tries to alter his pronunciation, it will be localized.

But for the actor, the problem is simpler. After a study of the play and the character, he decides on an artistically correct pronunciation for the particular part and play. "Stage English" is used only by the unoriginal and uncreative. An actor should not only look, think, and feel like the character, he must also *sound* like him. Don't feel that you are being affected when using unfamiliar speech on a stage. Like your costume and makeup, it is part of your characterization. Your objective should be to blend all the parts into a total concept so that no one part is isolated. Only then will the audience "believe."

HEARING

In the next few days, make it a point to study the manner in which your friends articulate. Do they:

Omit some sounds, saying "pro'bly" for probably, "c'pany" for company, "lay'ees an' gen'l'mm" for ladies and gentlemen?

Make additions, such as "athey'letic" for athletic, "naw" for no?

Substitute, saying, "tinth" for tenth, "git" for get, "Toosday" for Tuesday, "as't" for asked, "becuz" for because, "arn't" for aren't?

Run syllables together, making an uninterrupted string of gibberish such as "Wotchagotdare?" "Howybin?" "Wazzamatta?"

Exercise 43   **SELF-ANALYSIS**

Record your own speech using a tape recorder. In this way you will be able to make an impersonal self-analysis. As you play it back, be honestly critical. The only way you can improve is by isolating faults. Here are some words to practice; articulate all sounds and accent correct syllables:

monkey	February	door	potato	Wednesday
decision	deep	man	yell	egg
fat	yes	nose	sick	Pete
judged	cold	quiet	house	take
bait	can	Broadway	homage	task
bit	can't	sudden	Puck	water
bet	grandma	shrunken	daddy	loose
bat	and	God	punch	lose
Have you eaten?	that	guard	pseudo	anything
asked	clams	peace	photo	land
Didn't you?	calm	strength	piano	laugh
unanimity	clapped	pieced	folio	orange

psychology	tongue	the	fixed	Zsa Zsa
extinct	on	shoe	wing	ardvark
throw	light	shrink	shrub	vegetable

Americans pronounce the following words differently, depending on the locality. Compare your pronunciation with the dictionary preference:

appreciate	often	ammonia	status
conflict	ration	extraordinary	almond
interesting	hanger	hangar	protein
genuine	again	coupon	tedious

Now try recording from plays some of your favorite long speeches, as well as ordinary conversation. As you play it back check your speech for these faults:

Lack of breath control: Is your speech too fast, too slow? Do you take a breath and speak until that breath is exhausted? Are you frequently asked to repeat what you have said?

Obstructions in mouth, throat, and nasal passages: If the sound of your voice indicates obstruction, see a doctor and have the cause corrected.

Muscular tension: Do you sound tense, your voice strained or wavering?

Harshness, resulting from prominence of overtones.

Throatiness (or guttural sound), caused when tongue narrows the pharyngeal passage.

Nasality, excess resonance in nasal passages.

Adenoidal or "cold in the nose" speech.

Strident, hard, piercing, annoying speech (the "hard sell" voice).

Monotonous, lack of variety.

Weak, thin voice, faulty pitch, does not carry; very undesirable.

Lack of volume, too loud, too soft, caused by lack of proper control.

Whatever the thought, the actor is only able to express it through the physical means of speech, gesture, and bodily movement. An actor brings images and impressions to the audience through voice. When a voice is trained as an instrument responsive to thoughts, it can express colorations, silences, and vibrations of force or gentleness, which words alone cannot express.

Speech is an integrated skill. Although each facet may be explored separately, the entire vocal process must be developed as a unit. If your breathing and phonation are poor, no amount of drilling will perfect your articulation. Your skill in using vowels and consonants depends on phrasing and the quality of your voice, as much as on the ability to hear and create sounds. To those who are convinced that an actor's voice is one of the chief means of communicating with an audience, this chapter will be all too brief and

cursory. It has been necessary to limit the material here in order to cover subjects not found in other acting books.

GROUP VOICES

Group sound has always been a part of the theatre. The choruses of Greek drama are used in many ways to enhance those plays. Group sound is also used as an integral part of Peter Schaeffer's *Equus*. In *Equus*, the characters who are not actually playing in a scene are seated in darkness or semidarkness awaiting their entrances. Mr. Schaeffer uses these players as a chorus, which emits nonverbal background sounds to heighten moments within the drama. The "*Equus* sound" is carefully described in the printed play; both horse and human sounds are used. The effect is exceedingly poignant, exciting, and more personalized than an offstage effect would be.

It is often surprising what the individual can accomplish with the voice when it has been subjected to group exercises. Working within a group can free a timid or self-conscious person. Students will normally extend themselves in group work far beyond what they will initially do alone.

Dai Bradley in a scene with one of the horses from Peter Schaeffer's Equus. *(Courtesy of Huntington Hartford Theatre, Los Angeles. Photo by Van Williams.)*

Exercise 44   **GROUP VOICES**

A group should consist of five or more persons. One of the members should act as director. The director will indicate the sounds and changes to be made by the group. Everyone should have an opportunity to direct, since evaluation and creative attitudes are a large part of this exercise.

Use open vowel sounds:

[e] ay	eh [ɛ]
[ə] aw	oh [o]
[ɑ] ah	uh [ʌ]
[i] ee	oo [u]

1. Elongate each sound, as in singing. Hold the sound as long as possible.
2. Combine two or more sounds such as *ah-ee, ay-oo*, or *oh-ah-ee.* As a group of voices emits the combined sounds, members should use their own natural pitches. The director should control the start, finish, and variations of loudness, softness, etc.
3. Experiment with open sounds:
   a. Emit a sound and hold it as long as possible. Take a catch breath and continue the sound. The sound will appear continuous if each member of the group takes a breath at a different time.
   b. Start the sound very softly. Let it slowly swell to loud. Return to soft again.

   c. Start the sound very loud, diminish suddenly to soft, and end abruptly.

   d. Start the sound on a soft, low pitch; swell to a loud, high pitch; and end by fading slowly into silence.

   e. Start by fading in from silence slowly to a middle pitch. Stop abruptly.

   f. Try part of the group with one sound, while others emit another.

   g. Try part of the group working with continuous sound, while others interrupt with short sounds.

   h. Continue by doing variations of combined sounds, changing their pitch, loudness, length, and kind of attack and finish.[11]

You can develop short presentations (one to three minutes) that will communicate any choice of statement. Just as the mime is limited to body language, you will be limited to pure sound. No movement or verbalizing is permitted. Developing statements is similar to orchestration for music, or choreography for dance. Discuss the sensations your sounds evoke. Your chosen director should help guide the assembled sounds into statements, since often your own idea of what you are imparting may be quite different from what actually comes forth. If possible, use a tape recorder to check your progress.

4. Possible statements:

   a. A train in the distance is rumbling toward the station. It comes nearer and nearer until it finally screeches to a swift halt.

   b. The quiet of an ocean beach is broken by the momentum of water gathering into a wave. The wave crashes onto the beach and quietly subsides as the water returns to the sea to begin the cycle again and again.

   c. Freeway traffic, roaring in the distance, is punctuated by ambulance sirens.

   d. A fearful crowd watches helplessly as rescue operations near a mine accident continue interminably.

   e. The earth of the meadow is warm and peaceful. The spring flowers are appearing. Birds are building nests. Rain falls gently.

For the actor, group voice rehearsal can sharpen the awareness of range in the voice, and of tonal effectiveness in interpretation. It lends strength and flexibility to the individual voice. Articulation gains accuracy when exercises move from those of pure sound into group readings of pertinent selections of poetry or prose. The following suggested selections are useful for group readings:

Foreboding by Don Blanding

The King of the Yellow Butterflies by Vachel Lindsay

The Tale of Custard, the Dragon by Ogden Nash

---

[11]The *attack* is the initial approach to the emission of a sound.

You Will Die from the Shi King Book of Odes, 500 B.C., translated by H. A. Giles.

The Tempest act IV, scene 1 by William Shakespeare *from* "These our actors . . ." *to* ". . . and our little life is rounded with a sleep."

A SYSTEM FOR CORRECT PRONUNCIATION

The many divergencies in our spelling are well known. For example, the first *k* in knock has no sound, and yet in *king* it sounds like a *k*. *A* is pronounced in many ways, but always spelled *a*. Indeed, our spelling has little relation to pronunciation. For instance, check the spelling against the sound of the following: *go, do, dove, women, woman, not*.

Hardly any one of the sounds in our language is represented by a single symbol. This is but one reason why we recommend the International Phonetic Alphabet (IPA). This system employs symbols, each symbol representing a single sound, and each sound representing a single symbol. The IPA can be of great help in eliminating substandard speech and dialectical variations and in detecting mispronunciations and improving articulation. It encourages accurate hearing. The IPA system is authoritative. When you use it, you may be assured you are right. It will give you the confidence an actor must have.

Modern dictionaries represent sounds by respelling words and using alphabetical symbols, with dots and marks to indicate pronunciation. These *diacritical marks* may be adequate for the layman, but for those who specialize in speech, the IPA system is more effective. The publishers of dictionaries have devised different systems, no two exactly alike.

The IPA has the additional advantage of being international. Its symbols represent the same sounds in any language, an asset when actors are working with foreign phrases and dialects. By use of the IPA system actors can write speech phonetically, just as they hear it when listening to a speech model or studying voice tapes when following a course in speech self-improvement.

Look now at the IPA chart. You already know from your own alphabet many of the symbols and the sounds they indicate. You are already well on your way to memorizing the IPA system.

Speech is an exciting and rewarding study. For those who wish more technical and detailed studies, a vast library has accumulated in the past twenty years.

Phonetic Symbol	Key Word		Webster's	Funk & Wagnall's	American College
[i]	*ea*t	[it]	ē	ī	ē
[ɪ]	*i*t	[ɪt]	ĭ	i	ĭ
[e]	*cha*os	[keɒs]	ā	—	ā
[ɛ]	*e*ver	[ɛvɚ]	ĕ	e	ĕ
[æ]	*a*t	[æt]	ă	a	ă
[a]	*a*sk	[ask]	a	ɛɪ	—
[u]	m*oo*n	[mun]	ōō	ū	ōō
[ʊ]	b*oo*k	[bʊk]	oo	u	oo
[o]	*o*bey	[obeɪ]	ō	o	ō
[ɔ]	*a*ll	[ɔl]	o	ē̵	o
[ɒ]	*o*ften	[ɒfn]	ŏ	ɵ	ŏ
[ɑ]	*fa*ther	[faðɚ]	ä	ā	ä
[ʌ]	*u*p	[ʌp]	ŭ	U	ŭ
[ə]	*a*bout	[əbaʊt]	ā̵	ə	ə
[ɝ]	b*ir*d	[bɝd]	ur	Ūr	ur
[ɜ]	b*ir*d	[bɜd]	u	Ū	u
[ɚ]	weath*er*	[wɛðɚ]	ē̵	—	ər
[ɑɪ]	t*i*me	[tɑɪm]	ī	ɑi	ī
[ɔɪ]	b*oy*	[bɔɪ]	ɵi	ɵi	oi
[ɑʊ]	s*ou*nd	[sɑʊnd]	oi	ɑu	ou
[eɪ]	d*ay*	[deɪ]	ā	ē	ā
[oʊ]	g*o*	[goʊ]	ō	ō	ō
[ɛɚ]	*air*	[ɛɚ]	ar	ār	ar
[m]	*m*ay	[meɪ]	m	m	m
[n]	*n*o	[noʊ]	n	n	n
[ŋ]	ri*ng*	[rɪŋ]	ng, ŋ	ŋ	ng
[p]	*p*ay	[peɪ]	p	p	p
[b]	*b*ay	[beɪ]	b	b	b
[t]	*t*ime	[tɑɪm]	t	t	t
[d]	*d*ime	[dɑɪm]	d	d	d
[k]	*c*ome	[kʌm]	k	k	k
[g]	*g*o	[go]	g	g	g
[f]	*f*eel	[fil]	f	f	f
[v]	*v*eal	[vil]	v	v	v
[θ]	*th*ink	[θɪŋk]	th	th	th
[ð]	*th*em	[ðɛm]	th	th	th
[s]	*s*oon	[sun]	s	s	s
[z]	*z*oo	[zu]	z	z	z
[ʃ]	*sh*ip	[ʃɪp]	sh	sh	sh
[ʒ]	mea*s*ure	[mɛʒɚ]	zh	ʒ	zh
[h]	*h*ow	[hɑʊ]	h	h	h
[w]	*w*ater	[wɑtɚ]	w	w	w
[j]	*y*es	[jɛs]	y	y	y
[r]	*r*ed	[rɛd]	r	r	r
[l]	*l*eap	[lip]	l	l	l
[tʃ]	*ch*ur*ch*	[tʃɚtʃ]	ch	ch	ch
[dʒ]	*j*ud*g*e	[dʒʌdʒ]	j	j	j

From Elise Hahn et al., *Basic Voice Training for Speech* (New York: McGraw-Hill, 1957), pp. 24–55.

FURTHER READING: THE ACTOR'S VOICE AND SPEECH

For a more complete list see the "Additional Reading" list at the end of the book. Materials for dialect study and training will be found there also.

Berry, Cecily. *Voice and the Actor.* New York: Macmillan, 1974.

Brigance, William N., and Henderson, Florence. *A Drill Manual for Improving Speech.* New York: Lippincott, 1939. This book is a treasure of effective drills for improving speech.

Hahn, Elise, et al. *Basic Voice Training for Speech.* New York: McGraw-Hill, 1957. Recommended.

Lessac, Arthur. *The Use and Training of the Human Voice.* 2d ed. New York: Drama Book Specialists, 1967.

Linklatter, Kristin. *Freeing the Natural Voice.* New York: Drama Book Specialists, 1976.

Machlin, Evangeline. *Speech for the Stage.* New York: Theatre Arts Books, 1970.

Turner, J. Clifford. *Voice and Speech for the Theatre.* 3d ed. Revised by Malcolm Morrison. New York: Drama Book Specialists, 1977.

4
IMPROVISATION

Before I start work on a part, I read the script; but when shooting starts, I like improvisation right on the set. Even when I'm not consciously thinking about a part, I'm really thinking about it all the time.*

Sophia Loren
Academy Award Best Actress, 1961 (for *Two Women*)

*© 1962 Lillian Ross. From *The Player, A Profile of an Art,* by Lillian Ross and Helen Ross, Simon and Schuster. Originally published in *The New Yorker.* (Photo by permission of Carlo Ponti.)

In the theatre, improvisation is a means by which players can develop and make use of stimulated imaginations. Dr. George Fosgate of the University of Minnesota suggests that there are two general classifications within improvisational work. The first is geared toward the exploration and sharpening of a player's acting tools. Some call this category "theatre games." Though the games are fun, it is well to remember that the main reason for playing the games is to alert the players to ways of applying these sharpened tools for perfecting the acting craft. In other words, once you learn how to improvise, you can use the method to enlarge upon and enhance character and meaning. The second classification is allied to the "nontextual scene." This is a scene, which is not written by the author, but occurs aside from the action of the play. It is devised as a means by which players can locate the authentic impulses of a scene or a play. This kind of improvisation will be discussed in chapter 7 on characterization. Both types of improvisation are used to enhance understanding of the play, and have nothing to do with play writing. They should never be used as ends in themselves.

We are concerned here with learning how to improvise. During that process, the demands of improvisation will demonstrate its value. The actor begins the process by discovering the established realities, as given by the playwright, or by supplying the given circumstances through the use of the "who-what-why formula" discussed later. Through improvisation, the players supply words and actions while performing, *without previous rehearsals*. Although pantomime may be improvised, the process is not the same.

In the theatre, actors are taught to respect the authority of the play, the playwright, and the director. But improvisations provide release from such authority, allowing actors to come in direct contact with the essence of a dramatic, or comic, situation and characterization. They are no longer concerned with memorizing and speaking lines written by an author. The actors' main concerns here are to discover ideas and responses deep in their subconscious by realizing the character in a situation.

Most of the "improvisations" we see on television are previously rehearsed and performed again and again. It is rare to see improvisation capable of the sharply intuitive ability of penetrating the heart of a situation, a quality, or a relationship swiftly enough to bring it out with exactly the right gesture or comment. While you can expect shapelessness and confusion during improvisation, this should occur in the privacy of the workshop. It takes time for the actor to explore and realize new situations. In a strict sense, improvisation is a tool used for training and study—not for the commercialism of public performances.

As a prelude to true improvisation, it can be useful to apply *intent* to a previously memorized piece of no-content dialogue. You have already become aware of the effects of intent on voice in exercises 32 and 38. The following is a study of the effect of intent on verbalization. While it temporarily denies you the practice of solidifying creative thoughts by means of words, it can be a convenience for learning certain aspects of the acting craft.

Exercise 45 **PRELIMINARY IMPROVISATION**

Memorize the following no-content dialogue. Each person (A and B) should prepare by assuming a definite frame of mind, resulting from some previous hypothetical occurrence. The partners should not be aware of each other's attitudes before beginning the dialogue. In this way, the actions and reactions will necessarily be improvised.

A: Hi.

B: Hi.

A: How goes it?

B: Okay.

A: Good.

B: And you?

A: Okay.

B: Are you coming or going?

A: Neither.

B: Oh.

A: Yeah.

B: Yeah.

A: Well . . .

B: How come?

A: How come what?

B: Are you sticking around?

A: Guess so.

B: Oh, okay.

A: Okay.

B: See you.

A: See you.

One of the purposes of improvisation is to familiarize actors with the significant moving parts of a play through an active reference or an experience they can grasp. If the experience is to be meaningful, the player will need to know the structural qualities of a play and scene. He will need to learn how a scene relates to the entire play— the theme, plot, and characters. Your study of the play on page 115 will help to clarify this requirement. By the time you reach that chapter, improvisation will have become easy for you.

There are other advantages to be gained by performing improvisations. They teach actors how to plan their work, how to respond imaginatively to the given circumstances, and how to develop a dramatic or comic incident. In improvisation, the players relate closely with one another and gain confidence in their acting potential. It often happens that one of the actors will accidently hit upon something truthful to which the other players can react in kind.

During rehearsals, improvisation is invaluable in clarifying a scene, some business,[1] or the motivation. It also discourages imitation and stereotypical reactions, which too often plague inexperienced players.

As a learning experience, improvisation:

encourages creation of fresh images.

provides experience in stepping into the world of illusion.

encourages careful preparation through the understanding of dramatic presentation.

provides a student with the means to extend himself from a limited natural environment into wider experiences.

teaches the value of flexibility, collaboration, and point of focus.

trains in concentration, observation, and communication.

gives training in crediting "the illusion of the first time,"[2] and in following impulses.

provides experience in working from a plan, or overall artistic design.

THE GIVEN CIRCUMSTANCES

When you act in a play, the time, the place, the situation, and the character are provided for you by the playwright. When you improvise, *you* must provide some or all of these factors. Although this

---

[1]*Business* is silent action important to plot and illustrative of character.

[2]"Illusion of the first time" means giving the audience the impression that the lines and situation are impromptu.

form is impromptu, it is best done when there is first an overall plan or artistic design. Improvisation begins with some established realities, a problem stated, or a given circumstance. In order to develop this given premise, certain correlatives are usually needed, and should be supplied, before the improvisation can be considered ready for performing. These include:

Who are the characters?

What happens (situation)?

Why did it happen (motivation, theme)?

Where does it happen?

When does it happen—today, yesterday, tomorrow?

Rarely are all of these components stated in a given circumstance. Any missing points must be supplied by the actors based upon what has been given or implied. When this is not possible, then the actors must create the missing elements imaginatively. When more than one student is involved in an improvisation, all members should discuss and agree on the who-what-why and, from the information they have, invent a plan that dramatizes their answers. Most plans will be improved by the addition of conflict (what happens and why), sequential development, and a conclusion.

As an illustration, let us take a given circumstance.

A and B have a heated argument in the home of C, who tries to make peace, but finds himself attacked by both.

Now let us apply the formula to it:

Who? A and B.

What? Are having a heated argument.

Where? In the home of C.

Here are characters, a situation, a conflict, and sequential development. The missing elements of *when* and *why* will need to be supplied by us. The theme might be: "Don't stick your nose into other people's business."

To perform this scene as an improvisation, we must create a rough scenario by supplying characterizations. And we must break up the action into "beats," or small developing scenes, beginning with the premise:

A and B are having an argument . . .

Are they friends, relatives, strangers, business partners? How old are they? Suggest backgrounds through body postures, habits, etc. Are they in disagreement about money, wives, gossip, cars, business, ethics, politics, children, religion, or what? (Decide which will contribute most to your improvisation.) Will you build this scene from a quite innocuous remark to loud insults and threats? Or will you begin with high emotions? Which will be best dramatically? How will you vary tempo and audibility when C enters the scene?

In the home of C . . .

What brings them together? What sort of home has C? Is this meeting social or business? Does C enter from another part of the house or is he present when the argument begins? What is C's relationship to A and/or B? Is he a friend to both? A stranger? What answers will contribute most to the improvisation? Trace all the possibilities.

Who tries to make peace . . .

Obviously this action constitutes a fresh development, a new scene, needed for dramatic interest because of what has happened in the first scene. It entails a physical change in positions—an encounter—as C takes central position. If C comes physically between A and B, this would be understood by the audience as a visual symbol of intervention between opposing forces. The movement alone activates the theme, or point of focus, of this little scene. We must decide the reasons for C's intervention. Will animosity between the men jeopardize some future plan of C's? Or perhaps it is simply that he does not want the neighbors to hear, or the baby wakened. What points of argument does he make as he tries to stop the conflict? His statements could lead us into the next scene, in which A and B turn on him.

But finds himself attacked by both.

Why do they object to his peace-making efforts? Do they attack him physically, or only verbally? How is it concluded? Do they knock him out, call the police, call others in, or walk away friends, leaving C their common enemy?

SCENARIO—PLAN OF PROCEDURE

Decisive answers to questions such as the above will constitute a plan sufficient to begin an improvisation, provided all performers understand it. You will note that no dialogue has been planned, merely sequential development and content for each "beat."

Before improvising, the three actors assigned the problem will have to agree on what is to happen, the order it will occur, and the characterizations they will assume. Narrative, definitive characterization, and emotional reactions are left to be extemporized. The plan of procedure (or *scenario*) will be better remembered by all three if written down and not left to oral agreement.

Before performing, the players should free themselves of all preconceptions and contact their specific material directly, allowing their sensory equipment and the characterizations to create fresh impulses. This direct contact is one of the main reasons for improvis-

Center Theatre Group/Mark Taper Forum's Improvisational Theatre Project work is directed by John Dennis at the Mark Taper Forum of the Music Center in Los Angeles. (Photo by Steven Keull, courtesy of the Center Theatre Group.)

ing. Long speeches or soliloquies should be discouraged. Whatever narrative is necessary should be presented physically, in action, rather than by rhetoric. *Don't tell us, show us!*

After performing several improvisations, the importance of imaginative planning, spontaneous responses, and concentration on the given circumstance will become clear. Short improvisations are best; otherwise students may run low on inspiration.

Since they are self-initiated and self-directed, improvisations provide the highest level of independent study for individuals. They permit students to make their own minds work as they want them to, independent of a director's wishes. This allows an actor individual incentive.

EVALUATIONS

After each exercise in improvising, there should be an evaluation, not only of what has actually been presented but also of the planning. Other students should decide how effective players have been in solving their problems. Unless one is watchful, improvisations can slip away from the problem as stated, ending up as a comfortable presentation of what students feel they do best.

As in the physical exercises, the spirit of play should not be lost in doing "improvs." However, giggling and clowning should not be encouraged. Of course, there are times when something happens accidentally that is genuinely amusing; and a laugh at this time will relieve tension. However, when the work of the players is being ridiculed, actors should not play the fool.

When beginning improvisational work, it is best for students to choose roles near their own age and interests. Previous physical exercises should have loosened up any reticence, so that at this point there should be no problem in forcing anyone to participate against his will.

Everyday conversations and casual movements do not make the points so necessary to improvisations. *Action and words must be distilled.* Tempo, suspense, and complication should be built into the scenario. In each exercise, try for the physical as well as the spiritual sensations in the situation.

The who-what-why formula used to develop an improvisation is, in reality, a kind of prototype for dramatic composition. Another method, used sometimes, is similar to the who-what-why, except that different words are used:

Situation: What happened?

Characters: To whom did it happen?

Locale: Where did it happen?

Motivation: Why did it happen?

Atmosphere: When did it happen?

Whichever method you choose, always move simply from one objective and action to another.

ENRICHING AN IMPROVISATION BY ADDING ELEMENTS

Exercise 46   **IMPROVISATION #1**

Let us begin with an everyday nondramatic occurrence and add only one element at a time.

Two people meet	Improvise "who."
Two friends meet	Improvise. Now add the "when."
Two old friends meet	Improvise. Now add the "what."
Two old friends meet and fail to recognize each other . . .	Improvise (situation). Now add the "where."
. . . as both are boarding a plane for Europe.	Improvise. Now add the "why."
One is a CIA agent who does not wish to be recognized and his old friend is a gregarious insurance salesman.	Improvise.

By inventing motivations (the "why") we have also helped in the characterizations and given a conflict relationship between our two old friends. One is hiding, the other probing.

Exercise 47 **IMPROVISATION #2: THE "WHY" ELEMENT**

Begin by using only the "why" (motivation) element.

Each student selects a mood such as anger, suspicion, fear, expectancy, happiness, etc.

Each is to improvise a scene consisting of one simple line, "I'll get it," in answer to a telephone or door bell ringing.

All else must be supplied by the player.

Exercise 48 **IMPROVISATION #3: THE "WHERE" ELEMENT**

Use only "where" (locale).

Statement of the problem: *A man is standing in line.*

Questions to be answered by the players: What line? Where is this line? Who is the man? Why is he standing in this line?

This is the starting point of a play that was presented off-off Broadway, *Line* by Israel Horowitz.

Exercise 49 **IMPROVISATION #4: THE "WHAT" ELEMENT**

In this series of improvisations, the problems state one or two elements. Others are to be supplied by the students when planning what they will do. Mostly, these situations give the "what" element; the others must be added. Try to choose elements that relate to each other.

1. A robbery in a busy bank.
2. A suburban home catches fire.
3. A teacher returns to her classroom to find the students in an uproar.
4. A job interviewer discovers that one of his idols is applying to him (or her) for a job.
5. A girl is temporarily blinded by seeing what she believes to be a UFO. A friend is with her.

Exercise 50 **IMPROVISATION #5: THE "WHEN" ELEMENT**

Supply the "when" element, and any other needed, to the "who" and "what" that follow:

1. Newlyweds are expecting their first guests.
2. A houseguest is preparing a meal.
3. An elderly person is having peanut butter for dinner.
4. A child hears the telephone ringing.
5. A bride or groom is reading a recipe from a can label while setting the table.

Exercise 51 **IMPROVISATION #6: THE "WHEN" ELEMENT**

Set up several improvisations in which people prepare to take a trip on a plane. Suggestions:

1. A girl learns her mother is seriously ill in another state. She makes arrangements to travel to her, which includes getting permission from her boss.
2. A Cuban exile has reasons to return to Cuba and plans to hijack the plane.
3. A TV comic, who is a "white knuckle flyer," must fly to fulfill an engagement.
4. A student is late for registration.
5. A bankrupt businessman looking for "greener fields."
6. A dignified matron impatient with delays.
7. A strike organizer.
8. An elderly foreign woman on her first flight.
9. A reporter for a national magazine on an assignment.
10. A couple on their honeymoon.
11. A rich, former cowboy star.

Once actors become facile at improvisation, they may wish to experiment further with the technique. Selected improvisational scenes may be combined into a collage, giving a total result that is somewhat different from the effect created by the individual parts. Perform each of the above improvisations singly and then do another in which all these people are waiting to board a jet at 4 A.M. Retain the characters and moods established in previous improvisations. The boarding gate will not be open for some time, but the passengers cluster around the entrance hoping to have first choice of seats. As they wait they strike up conversations.

Exercise 52 **IMPROVISATION #7: MISCELLANEOUS**

1. Play an emotional scene without overt emotional display.
2. Create a printing plant in which the actors improvise the noises and actions of machines. This may require a visit to an actual plant.
3. Choose a basically narrative description of some character from a famous novel. Reconstruct the narrative into an active or dramatic improvisation. Student should look, sound, and feel like the character. At a signal from the director, another actor takes over the characterization, then another, etc. (*Note:* Several actors should work on this problem so that all are prepared. They need not collaborate as in other improvisations.)
4. *Character:* A tough, wounded Marine is being loaded into a helicopter.
5. Use banal dialogue, such as "Nice day," "What's doing?" "How'ya been?" etc., in:
   a. A dramatic situation.

Bugs/Guns, a presentation for young people, directed by John Dennis and performed by the Improvisational Theatre Project from Los Angeles' Center Theatre Group/Mark Taper Forum in spring 1977. (Photo by Jay Thompson, courtesy of the Center Theatre Group.)

    b. A comedy situation.

    c. A situation using characters that are recognizable, functional, predictable, or one dimensional, such as: Smokey the Bear, the Devil, St. Peter, Santa Claus, Pride, Sloth, etc.

    d. Use the same one-dimensional characters as in #5c. Give them some human (two-dimensional) attributes that will reveal such things as home life, disappointment, or success.

    e. Use the same characters as in #5c and #5d. This time give them three dimensions, bringing out individual qualities, such as inner conflicts, background, psychological drives, all rooted in lifelike situations. Note how the posterlike simplicity of the one-dimensional characters disappears as they are complicated by individual human attributes. Note that when the basic traits of a one-dimensional character, like Santa Claus, are diffused by adding further dimensions, the original character no longer seems like itself. The simplified caricature traits have been lost.

6. A women shoplifter being interrogated by a nearsighted desk sergeant.

7. An improvisation between Adam and the Creator, Noah and his sons, a girl and her alter ego, etc.

8. *Situation:* a freeway accident. Students create characters and improvise action and dialogue. *Suggestions:* argument, exchanging names and addresses and finding they know each other.

9. *Premise:* A series of mishaps caused by attempts to answer phone. May be used for different students portraying different characters. Begins in a bathtub. Phone rings, tries to reach towel—it falls in water. Phone continues ringing—decides to let it ring; finally reaches for robe—slips on floor. Phone continues—wipes feet on bath mat blocking door; struggles to force open door; while trying to dry self with robe, knocks over vase still trying to force door. Gets out, answers phone—and says "wrong number"—hangs up. Gets back into tub and sighs with relief. Phone rings again.

10. Memorize the lines of a short scene from a play. Use the same inflections and tempo you would in speaking the author's lines but speak gibberish instead in the following characters:

    a. As two ghostly spirits. (An amusing improvisation when done using two bed sheets.)

    b. As two angels. (Use makeshift halos or wings.)

    c. As two robots.

11. Adapt colloquial speech to a short scene from Shakespeare, using the characters' names and situations. *Suggestions:*

    a. Nurse and Juliet from *Romeo and Juliet,* act III, scene 2.

    b. Launce and dog from *Two Gentlemen of Verona,* act II, scene 3. (Use people as props and animals.)

    c. Hamlet and Polonius from *Hamlet,* act II, scene 2.

    d. *Taming of the Shrew,* introduction, scene 2.

    The most satisfactory way to create your own improvisations for special requirements is to begin with characters in a situation. In this context we may define a *situation* as an incident or event in which characters are involved with each other or with outside forces. The types of characters that seem to work best in improvisation are those that relate to each other. They can also relate to some object or to an idea. Such relationships help to motivate characters toward some goal or desire.

POINT OF FOCUS

Any object, event, or thought on which all players agree is the *focal point* of the improvisation. This point might be compared to the ball in a ball game on which all the players concentrate. People who improvise can never remind themselves too often, "Keep your eye on the point of focus." The established realities are stated in the problem, scene, or play—in other words, by what is supplied to the actor by the author or idea. The things that are *not* stated must be supplied by the actor.

An improvisation should consist of a conflict and have *development*. It should never be planned so that it ends as it began. Some students have a proclivity for devising improvisations dealing with human suffering, frustration, and despair. Such experiences seem easier to remember than happier moments, which we are more reluctant to share with others. But do so whenever possible, as they lift the spirit and encourage security in a player.

John Dennis's Improvisational Theatre Project for the Center Theatre Group of Los Angeles performs for a Saturday matinee crowd. (Photo by Steven Keull, courtesy of the Center Theatre Group.)

Exercise 53   **IMPROVISATION #8**

Suggestions for Characters

A person with a gambling problem

A person influenced by East Indian philosophy

An ambitious young music student

A brilliant but arrogant young student

A plain but wealthy young woman

A young married

A young mother

A bill collector

A person of ideals

A ranch hand

A perfume salesperson

A detective

A man hater

A teacher

A real estate agent

A sign painter

Suggestions for Situations

Select two of the above characters and involve them in one of the following situations:

Undergo an experience that results in a change of viewpoint.

Forsake cherished goals to carry out a moral duty.

Seek a crafty way to avoid misfortune.

Because annoyed by unwelcome attention from the opposite sex, pretend to have a spouse.

Become involved, through curiosity, in an unusual enterprise.

Become implicated in an accident that has its bright side.

Find an obligation at variance with pleasure or ambition.

A threatening complication results from misjudgment.

Seek revenge for a fancied wrong that proves baseless.

Secretly hide another from danger.

Happen upon an important secret that might endanger personal ambitions; a decision must be made.

Become involved in a situation in which there seems no solution, but one is found accidentally.

Involved in a risky situation, a shy young person proves heroic.

Assume the personality of a criminal in a legitimate enterprise.

Exercise 54   **IMPROVISATION #9: MORE SUGGESTIONS**

Locations

A veterinary office

A mental hospital

A welfare office

A drive-in movie

A Venetian ballroom in the 14th century

A weight-reducing gym

The Little Big Horn

A boutique

An elevator

A jewelry store

A gangster funeral

A pie bakery

A free clinic

A fire

A monkey house in a zoo

Characters

A bill collector	A cook
A photographer	A traveler
A dress designer	A police officer
A real estate agent	A travel agent
A teacher	A pilot

Situations

Shopping for a mattress

Making a date

Pretending to be another

Getting a license

Being rescued or rescuing someone

Becoming involved in a petty theft

A jury attempting to reach a verdict

Being late for an important appointment

Informing a dying girl that no more can be done for her

Talking to a hard-to-please lady at an employment agency

Handling an irate customer

Apologizing for another you know to be wrong

Becoming involved in a harmless act that could appear otherwise

Two people trying to hide a fateful secret from the world

Attempting to unravel mistaken identity without each other knowing

Being impelled by unusual motives to engage in a crafty enterprise

Undergoing an experience that results in character changes

Applying for a job

Conflicting personalities

Experiencing love at first sight

Exercise 55 **IMPROVISATION #10: CHARACTERS**

Several personalities are being interviewed on a talk show. After the moderator introduces each, he questions them about their work, their views on various topics, and asks about their future plans. Students playing the interviewed persons develop complete characters unlike themselves. *Suggestions:*

A housewife who has invented something now on the market

A European movie star

A black mayor

A student lawyer

A hillbilly who operates a still

A college professor who has just written a book on the feminist movement

A lady lobbyist from Washington

A housewife with a talking dog

An actress who has just opened in a play

An editor of a woman's magazine

Exercise 56 **IMPROVISATION #11**

Depth of concentration can be developed through work on interrupted improvisations. The objective here is to move with facility from one character to another. When new characters or situations are verbally presented, the speaking player should begin to communicate the changes without ceasing the learned speech.

1. The player chooses a well-known character, perhaps a political or sports figure or a TV news reporter. As that character, he performs a learned speech or poem, such as the Gettysburg address, "The Lord's Prayer," or the words of the "Star-Spangled Banner."
2. Give the player new characters while he continues with the learned speech: a cheerleader, a coach at half-time, a child reciting from memory, a grocery checker.
3. Suggest new situations in which to perform the learned speech: a funeral, a graduation, a political rally.

Exercise 57 **IMPROVISATION #12**

During this interrupted improvisation, the objective is to follow up dramatic leads as quickly as they present themselves.

A Chorus Line, the Broadway musical hit created by Michael Bennett and winner of nine Tony awards and a Pulitzer prize. (Courtesy of the New York Shakespeare Festival.)

1. One actor chooses and performs a simple physical action: painting a fence, sweeping the floor, jogging.
2. Other actors choose related actions and develop a scene using words.
3. Another actor arrives with a new, unrelated action.
4. Others adapt to the new action as quickly as possible.

Try working several groups at the same time. Actors should move from one group to another, adapting as they move.

IMPROVISATION AND PLAY WRITING

Improvisations are sometimes used in the creation of new plays for off-off-Broadway production. In workshops, directors give "notions" to actors as a starting point. Later, these notions are solidified; the "author" uses paste pot and scissors to jigsaw them into plays. The results are not so much play texts as assemblages. Nevertheless, when time allows this kind of method can produce results.

Despite claims of originality, this technique for creating drama is not exactly fresh. Down through theatrical history, a great deal of drama has been created by actors using no scripts. Offhand, who can name the playwrights of the Commedia dell'Arte or, for that matter, the authors of the morality plays?

Several years before off-off Broadway, *A Hatful of Rain* was developed through improvisations. Joan Littlefield has been using improvisations for some time to produce such plays as *A Taste of Honey* and *Oh! What a Lovely War.* According to the "playwright," *Comings and*

Goings was created by the actors as, "an enjoyment of technique, pure virtuosity on the part of the actors." *The Open Theatre*, led by Joseph Chaikin, conducted improvisations on the Book of Genesis and later performed these professionally under the title, *The Serpent*. Peter Brook's productions of *US* and *Marat/Sade* owe much to improvisations.

The successful musical *A Chorus Line* is an interesting example of a concept developed slowly through improvisation. It began with actual tape recordings of various hopefuls auditioning for a show. The result is a new kind of musical that blends speech and song with dance. Director-choreographer Michael Bennett led its growth in New York's Public Theatre workshop. This provided a situation in which the material had a chance to flow by itself and to jell without the pressure of an opening date. Increasing numbers of theatrical productions have gained full professional acceptance by beginning modestly and slowly evolving while the polishing is being accomplished.

There can be no doubt that today improvisations are the "in" thing. However, when improvisations are presented commercially as plays, there is the ever-present danger that actors will become too enraptured with their own involvement, exposing a slipshod amateurism and self-indulgence. To hire a hall, to pay for the printing of tickets, to furnish lights and scenery, all require playing to more than a single audience and, therefore, repeating something that has been rehearsed, set, and completed. This is the exact opposite of improvisation.

FURTHER READING: IMPROVISATION

Barker, Clive. *Theatre Games.* New York: Drama Book Specialists, 1977.

Dezseran, Louis John. *The Student Actor's Handbook: Theatre Games and Exercises.* Palo Alto, Calif.: Mayfield, 1975.

Elkind, Samuel. *Improvisation Handbook.* Glenview, Ill.: Scott, Foresman, 1978.

Held, Jack P. *Improvisational Acting.* Belmont, Calif.: Wadsworth, 1970.

Hodgson, John, and Richards, Ernest. *Improvisation, Discovery and Creativity in Drama.* 2d ed. London: Methuen. New York: Barnes & Noble, 1974.

Slade, Peter. *Experience of Spontaneity.* New York: Fernhill House Ltd., 1969.

Spolin, Viola. *Improvisation for the Theatre.* Evanston, Ill.: Northwestern University Press, 1963.

5
THE ACTOR'S ENVIRONMENT

The actor is the only man who goes onto a stage and knows he's lying. You go onstage to say something written by somebody else—and you may not believe him—but you transform these words into some strange kind of extraordinary truth. The actor never stops working. The painter doesn't, the writer doesn't, the artists don't. We're always watchful, always learning.*

Richard Burton

*From American Broadcasting Company television interview by ABC's Bob Young and Walter Wager, editor of *Playbill*. By permission.

DIFFERENT STAGES

A great majority of productions in high schools and colleges are mounted on proscenium stages. For nearly two hundred years plays have been written for the proscenium stage and are most effectively staged on it. These are the plays of realism. The audience is seated on one side of a raised platform and the actors and action are set within a frame. It is the theatre of curtains, borders, and wings.

This was not always so. Festivals and ceremonies in earlier cultures used a form much the same as the one diversely known as theatre-in-the-round, open, arena, circus, environmental, space, circle, or center theatre. Another form now used extensively is Shakespeare's thrust stage, in which the audience is seated on three sides of the stage.

Proscenium Staging

In proscenium staging the actor is concerned with acting positions as indicated in the accompanying sketch. Study these positions until the terms are familiar to you: up left (UL), down center (DC), right center (RC), and a walk or cross (X). Upstage (U) and downstage (D)

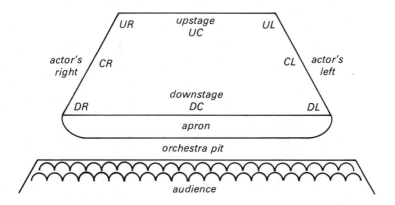

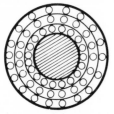

primitive

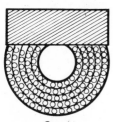

Greek

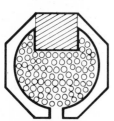

Elizabethan (thrust)

proscenium

circle or arena

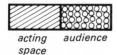

*acting   audience
space*

are so indicated because early stages were built on an incline to allow the audience an unblocked view of all actors, even those farthest away from them. From that we get the term *upstaging*, which means taking unfair advantage of a fellow-player positioned downstage. Some such raked stages still exist, notably Piper's Opera House in Virginia City, Nevada. Directions such as *stage right* or *left* always indicate the actor's right or left as he faces the audience. *Onstage* means toward center, while *offstage* indicates the periphery of the acting area.

Exercise 58   STAGE POSITIONS: PROSCENIUM

Acting is *doing*. You will remember the various positions better if you get up on stage and take the following positions, keeping in mind the placement of furniture in the illustration. Better yet, ask someone to read the directions as you walk them.

Enter up right center (URC) from right (R).

Cross (X) down left (DL), open door, and look out ¾ left (L).

Cross (X) upstage center (USC) to piano and look in bench.

Cross (X) to desk up right (UR) to desk and search in it, full back.

Cross down right (CDR) to fireplace, stir fire.

Cross (X) below sofa to table at left (L).

Cross up right (XUR) to desk, pick up paper.

Turn up center (UC) to French windows.

Turn right (R) and left (L) to see offstage.

Cross down left (XDL) to small table down left (DL).

Sit upstage of table (T) looking at paper.

Cross downstage (XDS) of sofa to fireplace right (R).

Throw paper in fireplace.

Published plays catering to nonprofessionals frequently indicate stage directions in this code. More creative directors prefer to plan stage movements according to their interpretation of a play.

Sight lines are imaginary lines indicating the audience's line of vi-

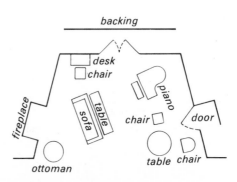

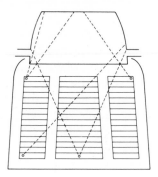

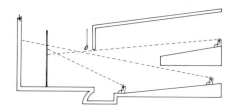

Lines of sight.

sion from different parts of the house. Scenery, props, and furniture are all arranged with these sight lines in mind. The actors must also be conscious of them during preparatory rehearsals. Otherwise one actor can "cover" or "block" the audience's view of other actors or an important piece of business (usually some silent action important to the plot). Examples of stage business could be the opening of a letter, the lighting of a cigarette, or even a look. *Stage business* is frequently confused with *stage movement*. The latter is geographical, whereas business is usually illustrative of a character. The following is an illustration of stage movement. When an actor's position is CL and he is playing a scene with someone at C, then his upstage (or right) foot should be a little before his left. This allows his body to be angled DS and gives the audience a good three-quarters view of his face and expression. Such positioning may not be important for modern plays, but for the classics it makes a considerable aesthetic difference.

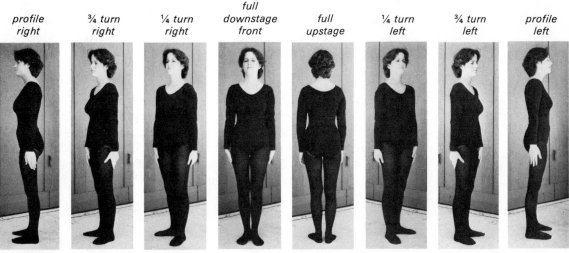

| *profile right* | *¾ turn right* | *¼ turn right* | *full downstage front* | *full upstage* | *¼ turn left* | *¾ turn left* | *profile left* |

←——— *stage right* *stage left* ———→

Thrust Staging

Many of the acting positions for thrust staging are the same as in proscenium, except that visual dynamics are altered. In thrust staging, the line parallel to the footlights is eliminated, and players literally step out of the picture frame. On a thrust stage the actor faces spectators on three sides, not just one. When playing on a thrust stage, entrances and exits are made in several ways. Actors can enter or exit just as they do on a proscenium stage, but they also enter or exit by way of passages under the raised stage or seating areas.[1] While curtains or other scenic devices can be used at rear as scene dividers, a main curtain is seldom used on thrust stages. In lieu of curtains, elaborate lighting devices from the front highlight scenes on various sections of the stage, leaving others in darkness.

Arena or Center Staging

In arena theatres, actors are usually on a level with the audience or, as in the Arena Stage in Washington, D.C., the audience is seated on steeply banked rows. In either case, the height of the acting area can be altered by the use of platforms. Actors can be "discovered at rise" less easily on the center than on the proscenium stage; but spotlights are often used for this purpose on center stages.[2] The circular or four-sided arrangement includes aisles that assume duty as actor's entrances, exits, and sometimes even playing space. Lighting and support stands are not masked or concealed; they are accepted as part of the nonillusionary aspects of arena staging. Because of the difficulty in making changes, scenery (usually only set pieces) and furniture must be kept at a minimum.

Actors find that more normal face-to-face positions are possible on this stage. Makeup and costumes must pass minute scrutiny, and characterizations must be constantly maintained because of the proximity of the spectators. The stage positions and sight lines of the proscenium or thrust are useless on an arena stage. Positions for actors are usually designated as North, East, South, or West of center, or are located by aisle numbers or numerals on a clock face. Though it might seem that more voice volume is required on center stages, actors often find this is not so. Inactive characters are normally placed against set pieces or aisles where they will not block the view of the spectators. Actors working on an arena stage should consider their positions as part of a constantly changing series of movements, in which a dominant character moves to a central position, and supporting players to the periphery, of the circle. However, all moves should be the result of motivation—attitudes, moods, or reactions of the characters to what is happening in the play.

Formerly, arena and thrust stages were believed suitable only to

---

[1]These passageways have the unattractive name, "vomitoria."

[2]"Discovered at rise" refers to the player or players on stage when the curtain rises.

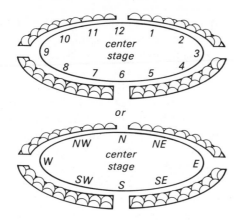

the classics—the plays of Shakespeare, Molière, or the Greek poets—none of which were written to be played on a proscenium stage. But today all sorts of plays are produced on thrust or arena stages. These theatres are especially receptive to the new nonillusionary, more spectacular plays. But plays by Eugene O'Neill and Harold Pinter have also been given interesting arena productions. The actor's work on creating characters need not be affected by the technical adjustments he will need to make between performing on thrust, proscenium, or arena stages.

Exercise 59　**EXPLORING ACTING SPACE**

For groups contemplating the use of a center or thrust stage for the first time, it might be well to move now into the room that will be used for performances. If possible, avoid rehearsing an outdoor or space-oriented production on a proscenium stage.

1. Fill the acting area in geometrical patterns, such as star, checkerboard, circle, etc. Move everyone into a tight circle at dead center, then spiral out in N. E. S. W. Columns. Move out to periphery and back.
2. Try groups of three people just off center.
3. Walk everyone around the periphery clockwise; turn and reverse.
4. Play a scene that has previously been done on proscenium stage using exact movements. Does it play as well in the new acting area? What adjustments must be made for central or thrust staging?

STAGE ACTION

When actors are onstage they become part of an ever-changing, ever-moving stage picture. The objective is to convey the dramatic progression of a play *in movement*. Stage groupings are not still pictures, but kinetic elements that flow from one to another. This action, however, must never seem mechanical, done just for the sake of motion, but must be properly motivated. *Invent for yourself some reason why your character moves to a particular position at a particular time, and be able to justify it should your director ask.*

Both director and actors must consider various reasons for stage movement, and then select one that seems most expressive of the character and the play. The actor, then, is not moving out of a chair because he has been told to do so, or because the director thinks a scene has been static for too long. He is moving because he is so motivated. By justifying each move, the actor adds to his characterization and to the interrelationships between characters. Moving, speaking, and reacting are the results of a living response to continuous thought process and the use of improvisation.

In rehearsing isolated scenes, actors are not afforded an opportunity to experience the natural flow of an entire play. Nor are they able to test their ability to sustain the effort necessary when playing a long part. Instead, they become accustomed to concentrating and expending physical energies for only a short period.

Nevertheless, it is hardly possible for every rehearsal to be a complete run-through. Certain scenes will need more time and special attention than others. A rehearsal may include working on various scenes throughout the play, but you must always keep in mind the location of these scenes and how they fit into the development of the entire play. That is the way an audience will experience them—not as isolated scenes. An opening scene of narrative and character exploration will not require the speed or the intensity of a scene near the climax. The playwright has made an effort to keep interest rising by disclosing situations in careful steps, one scene growing progressively out of the preceding one and relating to it.

Audience Focus

The most important consideration for arrangements of characters onstage is to identify the proper focus for an audience. Principal characters in a play have a great deal more to say than the others because they are the chief means of communicating the story to an audience. Obviously, such characters, with important scenes, should be placed in dominant positions because the audience has more interest in them. Such positioning should never be made into old-fashioned groupings or "stage pictures." Actors should never be considered as solid mass but as unfettered action forces—*stasis* must become *kinesis*.[3]

Also, for an actor, it is much better to be in the right position onstage when delivering an important line, speech, or piece of business. If he isn't, he will need to use all his ingenuity to produce the same effect.

---

[3]*Stasis* implies absence of movement. *Kinesis* is the Greek word meaning motion.

Entrances and Exits

The mechanics of getting into or out of a room should not be the primary concern of an actor playing a part. It is one of the few things we do onstage much as we do offstage. Different characters enter and exit in different ways depending on "the moment" or the dramatic atmosphere of the scene. The mood of the character entering or leaving the stage is important. The previous and subsequent action affect the kinds of entrances and exits made.

Avoid long walks when leaving the stage. They are seldom dramatic. Something else should be happening to cover your exit. To break up a long walk, divide up your last speeches and take a few steps between, so that you are near the door for your final lines. There are times, however, when a long silent walk is effective, especially at the end of a scene or act.

Stage Balance

It is considered one of the actor's responsibilities to balance the stage. That is, he must be sure that he is neither covering others nor being blocked from the view of the audience by other actors. Also, clustering too many characters on one side of the stage is disturbing to the audience. The term "dressing" is used when this happens. A director has every right to expect an advanced student to be aware of stage balance and be able to "dress" when other actors move. If you visualize the lines of sight as shown in the previous illustration, you are not apt to hear the director shouting from the house, "Dress the stage!" In this instance, the director means that the actor is to move out, break up the huddle—but always by inventing some proper motivation for so doing.

Exercise 60 **STAGE BALANCE**

1. Four people group in a half-circle, facing front. Student at center reads an interesting speech while others concentrate on the reader, except that one of the four has previously been instructed to hedge back on a certain word in the speech. This demonstrates how an audience's attention can be lost by an apparently innocuous move.
2. Now place the reader downstage right (DSR) with the other four players upstage right (USR). Note how the attention is lost by the imbalance.
3. Now place the reader upstage left (USL), with the others downstage right (DSR).

THEATRE RELATIONSHIPS

The Actor and His Audience

Leslie Howard once said that acting was part audience and part actor, and that the combination was a "sublime communion." A play is not a play until it is played before an audience. And an actor is not acting until he is in contact with his audience; otherwise he is merely rehearsing. An audience is much more than a group of spectators. It is part of the team that makes theatre.

In order to better understand what makes up an audience, let us imagine a group of pedestrians walking along a street. They have no common interest at the moment, no focus of attention. Now suppose that a car stops at the curb; and it is a new and long-awaited model. All eyes focus on the car and everyone begins discussing it. From individual pedestrians, the group has now changed into an audience. Psychologists consider an audience an entity because of common interests.

A phenomenon of the actor-audience relationship, and a most important consideration for the actor, is the *feedback*, or response. The actor communicates with the audience and, in turn, the audience responds by visible or audible means. This response, in turn, stimulates the actor to greater endeavors. It is a kind of circular game, and the ball is communication. Actors communicate with the audience in three ways: first, by gesture and body movement; second, audibly by the voice; and third, by emotion.

By convincing the audience of their sincerity, actors create rapport. It is not so important *that the actors believe* what they are acting, but that *the audience believes* everything the actors do on a stage.

Actors can learn a great deal about acting from an audience. It can show them where they have misjudged certain lines or scenes. It can even show them errors in characterization and interpretation of the character. It can reveal entire vistas of development they never realized in the character and the play.

The highest-rated television shows are now filmed when the cast is performing before a live audience, evidence of the vital importance of this actor-audience relationship.

The Actor and the Director

"There is something incomparably intimate and productive in the work with the actor entrusted to me," writes the great Polish director, Jerzy Grotowski. "He [the actor] must be attentive and confident and free, for our labor is to explore his possibilities to the utmost. His growth is attended by observation, astonishment, and desire to help; my growth is projected into him, or rather, is found in him—and our common growth becomes a revelation—what is achieved is a total acceptance of one human being for another."[4]

Grotowski's point is well taken that the attitude between actors and director should be that of fellow-inquirers. Both director and actors need an introductory period of discovery. This helps to create a provocative, searching climate in which the actors can understand their characters by developing concepts and relationships within themselves. This intuitive search into characterization often begins with only the smallest clue. Ideally, the director will stir the actors' imaginations into an understanding of the characters before any attempt is made to act the roles. Justification for a character's behavior is the responsibility of both director and actor. The director's further responsibility is to relate all characterizations to his visualization of the production as a whole. Imagination is creative only when controlled and directed toward some goal.

Both actors and the director should try to avoid stereotypes and stock responses. If there is a feeling for the play and its milieu, the actions and motivations of the characters will be reflected in a plausible and meaningful way. The search should concentrate on subtle and explicit reasons as given in the play for the behavior of characters. The problem of the actor-director relationship then becomes one of utilizing this knowledge in the actor's creation of a characterization. Different directors may use various methods of procedure:

1. Physical Approach
   Instinctive
   Positive
   Arrive at emotion and characterization by first reproducing physical acts.

---

[4]Jerzy Grotowski, *Towards a Poor Theatre* (New York: Simon and Schuster, 1968), p. 25. Copyright © 1968 Jerzy Grotowski and Odin Teatrets Forlag.

2. Emotional Approach
   Memory recall
   Comparison of similar experiences
3. Demonstration
   This method is seldom used today. Great directors of the past used it—Molière, Max Reinhardt, George M. Cohan—but they were also fine actors. Few directors are competent enough actors to demonstrate to an actor how to play a scene.

Peter Falk. (Photo courtesy of Universal TV, Publicity Department, and Robinson Associates.)

An actor who is fortunate enough to work with a director of sensitivity and experience is bound to improve, as many ideas generate from such a collaboration. A good director will not only serve the actor, but will become a sounding board for ideas. He will be the actor's audience when there is no other. Stage and screen actor Peter Falk has a somewhat different idea of the director-actor relationship. "Actors make their own performances," he says. "The director can make a contribution. Certainly he's got to provide the right atmosphere—that's number one. You gotta get rid of tension. You gotta get rid of insecurity."[5]

The Actor and Other Actors

In the preparation of a play, there is usually a kind of camaraderie among those involved, especially among cast members. Although petty jealousies sometimes cause friction, do not allow them to continue or the morale of the entire company will suffer.

Each member of the cast should be instilled with pride in the company as a whole. There should be a spirit of cooperation and an eagerness to help each other. A "good trouper" has pride in the work of all his fellow-players.

Ensemble playing means playing together. Listen to other actors when they have learned most of the lines. Acting involves reacting as much as acting. There are defensible theories that it is reacting that most interests an audience. Watch TV dramas; an actor speaks a line to another, and then quickly you see a close-up of the other actor, showing his reaction to what has been said.

In Louis Calvert's book *Problems of an Actor* he tells of a leading man who said to the villain of the play, "That was a good hand I got tonight, wasn't it?" The villain replied, "That was a good hand *we* got, yes." The hero bristled, "You had nothing to do with it, it's *my* scene!" At the next performance, the villain refused to react when the hero denounced him, and there was no response from the audience. The actor-hero was forced to admit that a denunciation scene is no good unless the one being denounced reacts.

No matter how childlike, egocentric, and mad actors may seem, there is always within them a consciousness of belonging to an an-

[5]Dick Hobson, "America Discovers Columbo," *TV Guide,* March 25, 1972, p. 30.

cient order. In order to join, a ritual of self-sacrifice has been followed, unspoken vows have been solemnized, even another language has been learned. True, the actor is often ambitious for himself and envious of another's success. But beyond this there is always a pride and an awareness that all actors are kin.

Over the years they worked together, Alfred Lunt and his actress-wife, Lynn Fontanne, developed an effect that sounded amazingly like extemporaneous conversation. "Cues," in the ordinary sense, were disregarded. They frequently spoke simultaneously but, always, important words or phrases were heard.

One of the values of ensemble was nicely put by the late Sir Tyrone Guthrie:

An interplay between two actors, by the exchange of looks and subtleties of vocal color and of rhythm can only occur when two imaginative actors react to suggestions of the other's performance, when they create and feel their scenes together. [6]

Exercise 61   **ENSEMBLE #1**

A coiled rope is thrown into the air, high above the group. The shape it takes when landing on the floor is then used by the group as a pattern for freely inventing attitudes, or ideas. Each time the rope is thrown the group creates a new arrangement.

What might these groupings convey to an audience?

Exercise 62   **ENSEMBLE #2**

Your entire group is in a subway car, jostling each other and swaying with the movement of the car. At intervals, the train stops, passengers get off, and others get on. Some sit and stare, others listen or join in conversations—or resent them.

The object of this exercise is *physical human contact.* See what comes of it.

Next is an exercise Peter Brook uses to show the possibilities of ensemble playing and the results of sensitivity training.

Exercise 63   **ENSEMBLE #3**

Select a phrase of ten or fifteen words from a well-known speech. One word is given to each actor. Standing in a circle with hands joined, they speak the words one after another until the entire speech flows and sounds like living speech.

[6]Tyrone Guthrie, *In Various Directions* (New York: Macmillan, 1965), p. 106.

Exercise 64 **ENSEMBLE #4**

In life, we are all affected by contacts with others. Often such contact modifies our behavior, even our personalities. Characters in plays also often change through contact with other characters. Improvise:

1. A boy in his father's office trying to get an increase in his allowance.
2. Outside, the boy meets a teacher or a boyfriend and is negative about the increase.
3. Then, at a malt shop with his girl, he is positive and cheery about the increase.

How does each affect the boy? He acts—they react—and he reacts from that. How?

SOME RESPONSIBILITIES OF THE ACTOR

Certain duties and behavior patterns are the sole responsibility of the actor. Directors and production personnel depend on actors to perform these correctly.

Learning Lines

The task of memorizing lines seems of some concern to inexperienced actors. Under ideal conditions, lines should not be memorized before completely understanding the role. Many essential decisions can alter the learning process. Lines may be changed or cut; if they have been learned, it is difficult to unlearn them and then to relearn the alterations.

Individuals seem to be affected variously by their different senses, and therefore approach learning lines in different ways. Some of the broad categories listed below may be more useful to you than others. Some may help initially, but will be discarded for others as rehearsals proceed. If you are most successful *visualizing* the printed lines, by all means begin that way. But if *hearing* the words is easier, speak them aloud and have a friend read the lines that are not your own. A "photographic memory" that allows one to visualize the printed page would be convenient during an examination, but a player would experience great difficulty depending on this alone for learning lines.

Think about what the following methods mean to you personally:

visual: seeing the lines on the page

aural: hearing the lines repeatedly

kinetic: relating the lines to stage action

interpretive: connecting the lines to their meaning within the scene, and relating them to the way your character would feel

The usual procedure is to begin with the visual, move into the aural, adapt during rehearsals to the kinetic, and stamp in indelibly using the interpretive.

In chapter 7 on characterization you will learn how to study the play before beginning rehearsals. This study will do more than anything else toward helping you to implant lines. Whatever means the actor uses to learn lines, once the memory is functioning, the method of doing so can then be eliminated, leaving the mind and emotions free to cope with more immediate problems.

Each actor must find his own most comfortable way of learning lines. Jack Lemmon has said that, for him, knowing lines too well presents a problem because it can prevent him from sounding natural—from seeming to be saying them for the first time. This could be so for some film actors. José Ferrer, on the other hand, looks forward to having learned his lines completely. After that, he says, things begin to bloom and grow. Rehearsal, for Ferrer, is the most thrilling period of all.

A few misguided actors delay learning their lines, using the excuse that they must understand the play, the character, or the director's plans before doing so. Frequently this is just an excuse for lack of interest or just plain laziness. *Once the director orders that all lines are to be memorized by a certain time, there must be no procrastination on the part of actors.*

In film and television production, actors are required to memorize lines before appearing on the sound stage, perhaps without ever meeting the director or the other actors with whom they will be working. This kind of memorization is extremely difficult, so the actors must develop some kind of system that enables them to remember the whole sequence. Sometimes they can find key words that form a pattern they can remember. At other times, the actors assign a letter or a number to each thought and then remember the thoughts in proper sequence by referring to this code. This technique, known as the associative method, is not at all ideal and is used only when necessary. When lines are memorized in this way, it takes a great deal of ingenuity during shooting to make them seem natural.

In television and in some films it is best to learn the lines while keeping the overall sense of the scene always in mind. In the daily soaps and weekly serials, shooting is so swift and script changes are so numerous that word-for-word memorization is almost impossible. For this type of acting an ad lib that is in keeping with the sense of the script is actually most effective. But such informality is not acceptable in legitimate theatre.

Exercise 65   **MEMORY**

Choose one of the phrases below and explain to your group all of the details as you remember them:

a scent of perfume or cologne

a funny school photograph

an old familiar tune

reminiscing with an old friend

New Year's Eve

your first date

your first dance

your earliest remembrance as a child

Conquering Anxiety

Anxiety together with anticipation can cause the physical trauma known as *stage fright*. Actors must find ways of counteracting this sensation so that, if it appears, it will not influence their performances. Stage fright is the occupational disease of all speakers and actors. The better the actor, the more sensitive he is and the more susceptible to emotion. Callous actors are seldom very good actors; they lack the means to transmit emotion to an audience.

"Opening night jitters" are usually evidenced by poor eye contact, rapid heartbeat, constriction of muscles, a tremor in the voice and hands, a hollow feeling in the stomach, dry mouth, lack of coordination, and a marked loss of skill. We had best accept the malady as being common to all and try to work out some treatment.

First of all, remember that it is healthy to be concerned, to care. But if an actor cares too deeply, he develops fear and becomes insecure, tense, and anxious, a condition in which he cannot function and be creative.

Some actors think of an opening night audience as a monster with a thousand heads. To help alleviate their fears, they might better think of the audience as human beings exactly like themselves who are willing, even eager, to communicate with the actors.

One of the most common causes of stage fright is lack of preparation. Self-confidence is dependent upon a sense of personal adequacy to meet the situation. Be positive that you are properly prepared, that you know your lines and your character. Focus on that character, never on yourself.

Stage fright can be diminished by narrowing your point of focus, blocking out all but your first words or the immediate scene to be played. Fear is the lack of knowledge. Walk into a strange, dark room and you are apprehensive. But if the room is your own dark room, you have no fear. You know the room even though you cannot see.

Sincere students will seize every opportunity to appear before an audience no matter whether at an audition or at a lecture where they just ask questions from the floor. Actors must learn to be at ease before the public, and this can only be accomplished by practice.

Theatrical Customs

There should never be any noise or horseplay backstage or in the dressing rooms. The theatre is an ancient and respected place. Show the same decorum here as you would in a library or church. Discipline is very important in the theatre; self-discipline is equally important to the individual actor.

One of the rules of theatre is that an actor does not go into the audience section during performances. An actor in costume and makeup greeting friends in the lobby, during or after a performance, is the sure mark of the glory-seeking amateur. Get out of makeup and costume as quickly as possible and then wait backstage for your friends. Tell them beforehand, "Please come backstage to the dressing room after the performance."

Make it a habit to check the bulletin board (or as it is called in the profession, the *call-board*) before and after each performance or rehearsal. It is the company's newspaper and law-giver.

The stage manager or his assistant call out terms that let the actors know how much time remains before the curtain goes up. When any one of the following are called out individually—"half-hour," "fifteen minutes," "five minutes," "places," or "beginners, first act"—you can gauge the time you have to spend with makeup and costume preparations. When the callboy knocks on your dressing-room door, calls your name, and gives you the time, answer him with a "thank you." Your response is the only way he can check whether or not you are present and getting ready. Some playhouses require that actors sign in before the half-hour. If actors have not signed in or phoned by that time, then their understudies are prepared.

Costumes and Makeup

Costumes should be thought of as clothes. If you throw your clothes on the floor or crumple them on chairs, it is time you learned better. Always hang up your costumes. Remember, it is to your advantage that you look as well as possible while onstage. If your boots are dusty, polish them; if your costume blouse is soiled, ask that it be cleaned or get permission to clean it yourself. It is this kind of attention to detail that makes the difference between the ordinary and extraordinary actor.

Many nonprofessionals do not realize that the purpose of makeup is to compensate for the washing-out effect of stage lighting on natural skin colors. Makeup should never *look* like makeup, except in nonrealistic, stylized productions (where it serves a planned purpose). In most amateur and professional productions, the actors must design and apply their own makeup. In films and television, this job is done by professional makeup artists. When makeup is left up to the actors, they should study the subject carefully.

Some actors feel strongly that makeup has great influence on their

Richard Burton in costume.

Henry Brandon (left) and as Squire Cribbs (right) in the original production of The Drunkard, or the Fallen Saved, *Hollywood. (Photos courtesy of Henry Brandon.)*

development of the character. This was certainly true with Paul Muni, who always spent many hours before rehearsals perfecting the look of the character he would soon play. At age twenty-three, Henry Brandon played the original Squire Cribbs in the early American melodrama, *The Drunkard, or the Fallen Saved.* The look he developed, coupled with studied manipulation of his costume, set this character for him and for many who played that part during the following thirty years.

For both Muni and Brandon, the preoccupation with makeup was one of the ways of *becoming* the character. According to Brandon, the re-creation of his face, and the exaggeration and sublimation of its various planes and contours, was in great part the catalyst that nightly moved him out of himself and into his part. Choices of posture, movement, voice tones, and rhythms evolved from the need to correlate the body and spirit character with the newly designed face. The process is similar to the use of masks in character development.

FURTHER READING: THE ACTOR'S ENVIRONMENT

(See the "Additional Reading" list at the end of the book.)

6
BUILDING YOUR OWN ACTING METHOD

You are playing Othello, you give it all you've got. The author says to you, "You've given it all you've got? Good! You've done that? Fine. Now, more! More! M-O-R-E!" And your heart and your guts and your brain are pulp, and the part feeds on them. Acting great parts devours you. Great parts are cannibals.*

Laurence Olivier

*Interview with Laurence Olivier by Kenneth Harris, *Los Angeles Times,* Calendar section, March 2, 1969. Reprinted by permission of the Observer Foreign News Service. (Photo shows Laurence Olivier in the film version of the National Theatre of Great Britain Production of *Othello.* Courtesy of British Home Entertainment, Ltd.)

As we have already said, too often students begin the study of acting by performing small scenes from plays when, in fact, they are ill-prepared to cope with the many problems that arise in creating a characterization. There is little growth in this. You have to get down to the basics. Acting requires a planned and structured approach, a sequential study beginning with flexing acting muscles on exercises and getting to know the tools with which you will work. This involves respecting yourself, the work done in class, and your fellow-students' attempts to improve. An actor lives on dedication to his work.

Assuming that you have benefitted from the exercises thus far, we can now approach other, more complicated matters. In this chapter, we start using some tools with which you can eventually build your own acting method—concentration, observation, imagination, the creation of atmosphere, and the use of gestures, mimicry, rhythm, and self-discipline. And these will require beginning with a relaxed body and a free mind.

CONCENTRATION

Do you remember how, as a child, you used a magnifying glass to concentrate the sun's rays until they burned a hole in paper? An actor needs that sort of concentration. In today's world we live in an atmosphere of distractions: traffic noises, telephones, sirens, the news, and our own private jitters over the future. As a result, many of us are simply losing our powers of concentration.

However, you cannot *will* yourself to concentrate any more than you can will yourself to relax. Concentration is like listening on a telephone. You must give it your undivided attention; any small distraction certainly destroys your point of focus. Think of boredom as the opposite of concentration. Even such a simple everyday act as picking up a fork at dinner is a highly concentrated process, involving observation (sight and sound), stimuli (desire), and many muscles of the body. With proper concentration, an actor will always listen intently to what a fellow-player is saying and react to what has been said. With proper concentration, an actor develops what has been called "public meditation." It has been said that British star Paul Scofield concentrates so completely that he even asks for a prompt while still in character. The depth of absorption an actor needs is almost impossible to describe in words, but the following exercise may impress you with the sort of concentration you should give your work at rehearsals and performances.

Exercise 66   **CONCENTRATION #1 (GROUP)**

We need a chair placed in the center of the room, and six volunteers to help in the demonstration. One person sits in the chair facing front, the other five stand in a semicircle around the chair. The seated player reads aloud some material, and it must be read intelligently.

Other players try to distract him in any way possible, except by physical contact. After one minute, the player standing at the reader's left takes the seat, and the former reader takes his place standing at right. This exercise continues until all players have had their minute in the "hot seat." The class will decide which player was best able to concentrate and read most intelligently.

Exercise 67   **CONCENTRATION #2**

1. Fix your eyes on some focal point such as the reflection of your own eyes when looking into a full-length mirror. Hold this concentration without blinking for as long as possible.
2. The game of Indian wrestling is also effective in developing eye-to-eye contact and concentration. Watching an adversary's eyes for signs of weakness makes a good Indian wrestler.

Exercise 68   **CONCENTRATION #3**

Concentration is commonly facilitated by using a silent inner monologue. This is simply talking to yourself. It assists in gaining control over circumstances. Check and you will notice how you think to yourself in verbalized terms. Often, when putting things away, you will silently say, "This goes here and this goes there...." Or when you are hurrying to leave home you probably ask yourself, "Do I have my key, money, tickets?"

Transfer this technique to:

1. savoring the taste of ice cream as you eat a scoop of mashed potatoes
2. knocking at a door as you await the appearance of your blind date
3. retracing your activities as you try to locate a misplaced key

Concentration is not merely required during the development of your character in the play. Often, as in repertory, where several

plays are in process at the same time, it will be necessary for you to
rehearse a new show while you are still playing in another. For such
circumstances the inner monologue is very useful because it can
help direct your concentration to the work at hand whether it be
rehearsal or performance.

OBSERVATION

Human nature is one of the actor's most important studies. Experienced actors give it more attention than beginners. "If there's unhappiness around you, you're likely to be observing it rather than
feeling it directly," Sir John Gielgud says. "You constantly catch
yourself trying to study how people really feel emotion. . . . If I see
a bad accident, I watch the expressions on the faces of people. The
dramatic side of every emotional experience seems to be always first
with the actor. You jot it down. When you see somebody dead for
the first time, you can't resist making notes of the way you yourself
feel."[1]

Knowledge of human experience is as much a part of the actor's
equipment as the attention to the quality of his voice and body control. It is by constant investigation that the actor trains himself, adding to his fertility and increasing his range. As you study and observe character, use your imagination of course, but always build on
what you have actually seen and felt.

*John Gielgud. (Photo courtesy
of International Famous Artists.)*

Exercise 69   **OBSERVATION #1**

Describe orally to the class someone you know, without giving names.

Exercise 70   **OBSERVATION #2**

Go to a park, an airport, or a hotel lobby, anyplace where you can sit
quietly and concentrate as you observe people. You may find that one
particular person intrigues you more than the others. Ask yourself
questions about this individual and then answer them from your imagination. Ask yourself why this particular person caught your eye. Try
to decide what makes this person tick. Why does he (or she) behave
this way? What are his goals in life? What is he like inside? When you
return to class, don't describe what you have observed, but act a
character you have created from your observation and imagination.

Academy award nominee Walter Matthau often wanders about
anonymously in large groups. He favors cafeterias. "I love the
chance it gives me to browse around in people's external behavior. I
can look around as much as I like. Not that you ever imitate people

---

[1]© 1962 Lillian Ross. From *The Player, A Profile of an Art*, by Lillian Ross and Helen Ross,
Simon and Schuster. Originally published in *The New Yorker*.

as such. But you get the feel and the smell and the taste of how they behave. I soak that up wherever I am. Then, when I'm onstage, I use it."[2]

Just how accurate is your ability to see—and remember? Most of us overestimate the efficiency of our imagery. In truth, our memory of what we have seen is sometimes vague, hazy, and often inaccurate. Actors must be scrupulously observant. They must be able to view a scene or see a fleeting gesture, and remember it in every detail.

Exercise 71 **"SEEING"**

```
S  J A O
H  I N T
W  T F P
G  S O A
```

Study the letters in the square. Take your time. Be sure you can visualize it in your mind's eye—that you have impressed each letter in your brain and left an impression there.

   Have you got it? All right, cover the figure, and don't uncover it. Now close your eyes and "read" the letters from that image in your mind. That's easy, isn't it? Close your eyes again and read the letters *diagonally*, first right to left, then left to right. That's another matter, isn't it? You have learned the letters by rote. You haven't really "seen" the entire square. If you had, the visual image would be complete and you would be able to read it from any direction with equal ease and speed.

IMAGINATION

Some students are blessed with vivid imaginations. In others this quality must be cultivated, *and it can be done.* Imagination is not something vague and mysterious; the dictionary tells us that it is "the picturing power or act of the mind; the constructive or creating faculty." Isn't everyone born with that? Even some animals demonstrate the faculty of imagination. Have you ever watched a cat playing with an imaginary mouse? That cat was creating something out of memory, instinct, and imagination.

Certainly all children possess imagination. They live in a world where the real is not separated from the imagined. A child doesn't lie; he is as innocent of deception as he is of truth. When she was four years old, actress Sandy Duncan had a friend she named Ann Puffenfuffer. The friend did not exist, except in Sandy's fantasy. She would walk and talk with Ann. When Sandy asked her mother for a glass of water, she wanted another for Ann. One day her mother asked Sandy, "Whatever happened to Ann? You don't talk about her anymore." "She's dead," Sandy said flatly. "A car hit her."[3]

The creative fertility of childhood imagination usually interferes with our mature goals of reality and materialism. By adulthood,

Sandy Duncan. (Photo by permission of Sandy Duncan and Walt Disney Productions. © MCMLXX Walt Disney Productions. World rights reserved.)

[2]Ibid., p. 422.

[3]Arnold Hano, "Funny Face," *TV Guide*, September 18, 1971. Reprinted with permission of *TV Guide*® magazine. Copyright © 1971 by Triangle Publications, Inc., Radnor, Pennsylvania.

many of us have literally trained ourselves out of imagination. An actor needs to revive that childlike approach to pretending. The purpose of cultivating an active imagination in the actor is to give him a solid experience of living in a particular situation. Then, when he is called on to create a character, he will feel the atmosphere of the play and become emotionally involved in it.

Creative talents need constant development. Daydreams are imaginative, but they are not creative. In order to transform wishes into creative activity, we need to concentrate, to remember clearly, to analyze, and then to visualize the new or to construct the new on the old.

Exercise 72 **IMAGINATION #1**

1. Perform some simple everyday function, first as you would do it as you are; then, pretend you are four inches smaller—taller—twenty pounds heavier—forty years older.
2. Tell a simple story. Now add some physical infirmity; for example, you are crippled or have just been shot.

Exercise 73 **IMAGINATION #2: PEOPLE PUPPETS**

Puppets are built to perform certain bodily tasks. Each is an individual. A clown puppet is made loose jointed so that he can assume ridiculous postures, while a ballerina is made to move slowly and gracefully.

Design a puppet character for yourself and perform a short action. Remember to be constantly aware of the strings from above controlling you. A puppet walks by having his knee strings pulled up, gestures are made by moving strings on the wrist, while strings from the right and left shoulders carry most of the puppet's weight. At the back is one string that enables it to bend over and sit.

(In the Motel scene of the award-winning *America Hurrah!* the cast of characters are all marionettes.)

Exercise 74 **POINT OF FOCUS**

There is a letter on a table. The table may be anywhere, anytime, anyplace, but such details must be communicated. The character may be any person the student wishes, but must be presented *visually* because there is no speech, only pantomime.

Each student performs solo, in character, while others serve as his or her audience. The only essential is that the student read the letter and show some reaction. It is a situation, a crisis, funny or sad. Concentrate on that letter; it is the point of focus. Then you must show a reaction. What is the size of the imaginary letter? Is it typed, handwritten, or what? Is it from a man or a woman? What does it say? Show us by your reaction.

It is an advantage to the student-actor if he learns quickly that there is a vast difference between *what he thinks he is showing an audience and what the audience actually sees and understands.* In the discussion afterward, the observers explain what they understood; then the performer tells what he intended to show. In this exercise it is impossible to judge the effectiveness of the actor's work unless we know what he thought he was doing.

Exercise 75   **IMAGINATION AND COMMUNICATION**

Collect an assortment of objects from an attic or rummage sale. These should be items of clothing or accessories, personal things once owned and used by people. Each player examines the pack and selects an object that stimulates his imagination. The player imagines the sort of person who once used it—his intellectual, emotional, and physical attributes. He decides how this person thought, felt, and moved. As each player feels prepared, he assumes the fancied character, using improvised words or only silent action. The others should guess occupation, age, mentality, and emotional attitudes of the created character.

If you find that others have either not understood the character or misinterpreted your presentation, figure out how you can improve your communication to clarify your meaning. Think of your communication as if it were the work of a graphic artist presenting a visual advertisement for a billboard or a magazine. The initial impact of the ad must gain the viewer's attention. The secondary impact serves to hold the attention, and all further impacts embroider those that precede them.

If you are not sending your messages clearly, it may be that the ideas you wish to transmit are garbled. Simplify your presentation, and choose the most telling attributes of your character: the voice, the kind of movement, its recent past, its present need. Let these aspects permeate your work so that the initial impact of your communication will prepare your audience correctly. Economy of physical movement is vitally important. Often, the secondary, more subtle, impacts will fall into place by themselves, thus filling out your interpretation. Once a strong, positive statement has been communicated, the audience imagination will do a great deal of the detail work on its own. A review of the requirements for mime can assist here.

Laurence Olivier and Maggie Smith in Othello. *(By permission of the National Theatre of Great Britain.)*

GESTURES

An actor has many ways to communicate with an audience. Body and voice have always been considered most valuable tools, but there are others. A shrug, the lifting of an eyebrow, even a grunt—all may convey special meanings. Think of gesture as a vibration from thought, put lyrically. Beginners often make the mistake of believing that each spoken word should be accompanied by some movement of the arms or hands. All words are not of equal importance. Use gestures sparingly. *They should be used only to express something that you have not been able to express otherwise.* Peter Brook defines a *gesture* as "a statement or wordless language" to be used only when emotion and words will not convey the meaning.

The type and the form gestures take will vary with different characters and play styles. Hands in pockets; flicks of the wrist; and short, jerky, or incompleted movements that we call gestures may be all right for a Pinter play, but would be unsuitable for Shakespeare. Classical drama requires that gestures be free, open, and completed—in keeping with the lyrical intentions.

Movement is correlated as much with gesture as it is with rhythm. Few gestures can be made without involving the entire body to some degree. When properly chosen and executed, a gesture can do a great deal to illustrate character, giving the audience an immediate image of a person. Some actors are inclined to use gestures on stage that are personal to themselves, rather than those of their characters.

Laurence Olivier has said:

John Dehner. (Photo courtesy of Arwin Productions, CBS, and the William Morris Agency.)

Sometimes on the top of a bus I see a man. I begin to wonder about him. I see him do something, make a gesture. Why does he do it like that? Because he must be like this. And if he is like this, he would do (gesture) in a certain situation (gesture). Sometimes months later, when I am thinking about a bit of business, I hit on a gesture, or a movement, or a look which I feel instinctively is right. Perhaps not till later; perhaps weeks after I have been making that gesture I realize that it came from the man on top of the bus. [4]

Popular television character actor John Dehner has said, "I've learned that the hardest thing for an actor to do is the simplest everyday gesture—opening a door, picking up a suitcase, sitting down on a chair." [5]

Exercise 76 **SMALL GESTURES**

Determine the differences between the hands of an auto mechanic and those of a pianist. Perform some ordinary tasks as each might, such as opening a can or packing a suitcase.

Exercise 77 **HAND GESTURES**

A boy and a girl are concealed behind a screen, leaving only their hands exposed at top. Work out a little action or story within a simple

---

[4]Interview with Laurence Olivier by Kenneth Harris, *Los Angeles Times*, Calendar section, March 2, 1969. Reprinted by permission of the Observer Foreign News Service.
[5]*TV Guide*, November 27, 1971.

framework. An elaborate plot is beyond the needs of this exercise. Props such as flowers, boxes, or money might be used with good effect. In fact, anything could be used that can be recognized by sight and is small enough to be handled. The exercise is enhanced when a recording is used. Students are usually astounded at how much can be conveyed by so little.

Exercise 78 **GESTURES**

Select a phrase from some dramatic work or a poem, which, in your opinion, might be accompanied by gestures. Face the members of your group and, using only gestures and emotions, convey the meaning of the phrase without the use of speech or mouthing. When finished, indicate by some gesture of finality; but remain in place for evaluation. The test of how well you have chosen the phrase and how well the gestures have conveyed the meaning will be indicated by how quickly others guess that meaning. Frequently, they will guess the actual phrase.

The old game of charades is an excellent exercise in the use of gestures to transmit meaning.

Although pantomime employs gesture, it also requires action of the entire body rather than a particular part. At this time, we are interested in the entire body.

Exercise 79 **GESTURE AND MOVEMENT #1 (GROUP)**

One player reads from a short scene involving no more than four characters. Previously, actors have been assigned parts. Players are to supply gestures as the scene is read.

This exercise is more challenging when actors are hearing the lines for the first time and are reacting spontaneously.

Exercise 80 **GESTURE AND MOVEMENT #2**

You are in a phone booth making a call. We cannot hear your conversation, but by your movement and gestures you are to convey to us which one of the following is on the other end of the line:

your mother	your boss
a boyfriend	your dentist
a girlfriend	a florist
your hair dresser	a bill collector
your doctor	an auto mechanic

An interesting approach to gesture is to consider it a spilling over of excess emotion. And from this point of view, a "gesture" may be either a body movement or a vocal sound that has not been verbalized. Sighs, groans, grunts, and squeals all fall into this nonverbal category.

Exercise 81 **GESTURE: VOCAL**

Try, without body motion, to emit a sound that indicates a reaction to
the following:

1. You find your old pet dog dead.
2. A total stranger is driving your car away.
3. You have just barked your shin.
4. That touchdown wins the game!
5. The ground you are digging in is hard.
6. The gift you open is a real surprise.
7. The letter you open advises that you will not graduate.

How many kinds of sighs can you emit? Groans? Grunts? Note that
you will have to think them out in order to communicate your exact
meaning.

RHYTHM

Architecture can be judged by its relationship to the space surrounding it. In the same way rhythm can only be appreciated when it is
related to surrounding atmosphere and space, that is, to its silences
and immobility. A rest in music is an interruption of sound, and yet
is part of that music. No one would enjoy a symphony played at
exactly the same tempo and volume. So it is with the performance of
a play. It must also have stops, retards, syncopations, and structural
emphasis.

Each actor in a play contributes a rhythm for his character, which
is developed during rehearsals. The constant repetition of lines,
movement, and silences serve to blend his rhythm with the rhythms
of the other characters. There is a time during final rehearsals when
the play takes on a music of its own. This imprinted behavior is a
form of security, which actors always depend on during performances.

Rhythm is the impulse behind words and movement. It is time,
pace, and meter all rolled into one. A regular walking step is a
natural model of measure for dividing time into equal parts. Muscles
are made for movement; and movement is rhythm involving time in
space. It is impossible to conceive and convey a rhythm without
thinking of a physical movement. It is not enough that an actor possesses natural rhythm. He must evolve it into a precise tool by developing and controlling the muscles of his body. Rhythm control
informs the actor of the exact time to pause, to move, or to be still
and silent. If an actor comes onstage using a walk that is timed to an
uneven rhythm, the audience will be immediately alerted to some
disturbance in the natural flow of the play.

Tempo is often confused with meter. Tempo most often involves
the timing of a scene or entire play, the rate at which the unit of time

is either increased or decreased. It is more properly used as a director's term. But rhythm is more personal, and generally describes the instrumentality of the actor.

Exercise 82 **METER**

Read lines from one of the Greek tragedies to the accompaniment of a percussion instrument. Vary the rhythmic patterns and silences.

Exercise 83 **MECHANICAL RHYTHM**

Here is an exercise Peter Brook uses. All members of the group are to memorize a soliloquy or verse of their choosing. Divide the piece into three sections; then, using no special expressive delivery, three individuals are to read the piece, in turn, but as a unit.

1. As quickly as possible.
2. Retard pace slowly.
3. Accent certain previously selected words using beats or silences for other words.

Exercise 84 **RHYTHMIC MOVEMENT AND COORDINATION**

The objective of this exercise is to develop a feeling for time and rhythm. Use for all members of the workshop group. Use a metronome or drum. Students should be trained to distinguish between various divisions of time and various accents within the divisions of time. For example, this exercise moves constantly in four-beat divisions (speaking as they walk will help).

1. Group begins by walking around the action circle in response to a regular beat.
Step—step—step—step.
Step—step—step—step.
2. At a given signal and without breaking rhythm, change the first STEP to a STOMP.
STOMP—step—step—step.
STOMP—step—step—step.
3. When all are accustomed to this rhythm, change the second STEP to a REST.
STOMP—REST—step—step.
STOMP—REST—step—step.
4. Assorted variations of your own invention can continue the complication and concentration. Try clapping with each step on every other group of four beats.
STOMP—REST—step—step.
Clap—clap—clap—clap.
STOMP—REST—step—step.
Clap—clap—clap—clap.

After constant repetition, muscular actions pass outside the control of the brain into automatism. You may want to combine or substitute speech or song with the already imprinted behavior.

We have all noted the magic of combined and dissociated rhythms in nature, machinery, traffic, and in all life around us. Listen for rhythmic sounds and groups of sounds that surround you. Try isolating one from the others. Then devise a set of rhythms of your own.

When asked if he had any "particular hobby horse" he rode in his work as actor-director, Laurence Olivier said: "I rely greatly on rhythm. I think that is the one thing I understand . . . the exploitation of rhythm, change of expression, change of pace in crossing the stage. Keep the audience surprised, shout when they're not expecting it, keep them on their toes . . . change from minute to minute."[6]

CREATION OF ATMOSPHERE

It is an important ingredient of theatre. Creation of atmosphere, or mood, is the responsibility of both director and actor. An individual actor can create his own mood, which can later be incorporated into the general atmosphere of the play, as the director desires. Let's try creating some without words.

Exercise 85　**CREATING MOODS (GROUP)**

1. This is a class exercise. Improvise mood and action only. A crowd of mourners is returning from a funeral on a bright, sunny day. Now do the same, but on a dark rainy day.

2. Improvise mood and action only: A discouraged and weary woman tries to do her housework in her dreary walk-up flat located on the lower east side, New York City. Her son enters with news that he has a job.

3. Improvise mood and action only for a situation set on an isolated island in the South Seas. You are in a tin-roofed, general store and it has been raining for days. The heat is unbearable. Convey this to the class.[7]

4. Improvise mood and action only: You are in the performer's tent of a small European circus. This is where the performers take a last minute check before "going on." Clowns are testing props, athletes are limbering up, and the owner and his wife are bustling about among equestrians, strong men, etc. Offstage, we hear the announcer and the circus band (use a recording). A stranger enters and stands silently at one side. Slowly, one by one, they turn to him. After a moment of wonder, the owner walks up to the stranger.

[6]Interview with Laurence Olivier by Kenneth Harris, *Los Angeles Times*, Calendar section, March 2, 1969. Reprinted by permission of the Observer Foreign News Service.

[7]Part 3 of exercise is from Somerset Maugham's *Rain*, 4 is from Leonid Andreyev's *He Who Gets Slapped*, 5 is from Lillian Hellman's *The Little Foxes*, 6 is from Anton Chekhov's *The Cherry Orchard*, and 7 is from Eugene Ionesco's *The Chairs*.

5. Improvise dialogue and action: A wife is being angrily harangued by her husband for something she has done, but behind this anger is the lifetime of unhappiness she has caused him. She sits quietly watching him, bristling with hate. The husband is in a wheelchair, a very sick man. His fury brings on one of his frequent heart attacks. He attempts to take medicine, but spills it and cries out for her to bring him another bottle from upstairs. She does not move; she actually wills him to die. He manages to crawl to the stairs crying out for help from the servants. Still she does not move. Create the atmosphere of the old South, the heat, the characters, and the inner conflicts.

6. Improvise dialogue and action: A family is leaving the home where they have spent most of their lives. The younger members and their friends look to the future. They gather luggage and clothing. Their concern is to catch the train into the new life in the city. The mother moves about the room where she leaves so many memories. The objects each remind her of the years she has lived among them. Finally, when everyone leaves, the old servant appears, having decided he will stay here with the past.

7. Improvise dialogue and action: An old janitor and his wife are no longer capable of facing the reality of their depressing lives, so they invent a reality based on their dreams. The couple act out a grand party where they are hosts to distinguished guests. The most important person in the world will address the gathering. They prepare the room for his speech, gathering chairs before greeting imaginary guests. When all is settled, the speaker arrives—but he is a mute.

Create your own dialogue first, then read what each playwright has written for the same dramatic situation.

Discoveries from observation tend to be associated most often with the building of characters. But this is a limited point of view. The performance of characters is also affected by the kind of observation that stimulates mood. For instance, when Hamlet sees the ghost of his father, the atmosphere of the play is quite different from the scene during which the players reenact his father's murder. The actor playing Hamlet must be aware that while Hamlet's character remains the same, his performance of the character differs according to the moods of the various scenes in the play. Actors and actresses must be ever alert to atmosphere and mood, since these add variation to characterization. A sensitivity to the aura of objects can be helpful for development of pure atmosphere or mood.

Exercise 86 **ANIMATED INANIMATES**

In exercise 85 you were given situations and locations that could produce atmosphere. But inanimate objects also have the power to elicit sense reactions of which we are not always aware. Whether the reactions are stimulated by recall or by the inherent qualities of the object itself, your ability to recognize and apply them will broaden the scope for atmosphere or mood creation.

Choose some particular object or specimen from home or from nature—just some small insignificant object, such as a discard, a flower, a rock, or a twig. Select something that you have seen so often that you take it for granted.

1. Now take the object in your hand and *look at it as if for the first time.* Examine it for color. Is it a solid color? Multicolored? Is there some design or pattern to it? Look deeply. Is it flat or contoured? How many dimensions or planes has it? Now feel it; smell it; bring all your senses into the observation.

   a. Describe in writing any moods you can recall because of the qualities of that object.

   b. Make a written list of the actual moods suggested to you by the object itself.

   Example: The object is a smooth, flat pebble. You may say to yourself:

   a. I can remember flicking this kind of pebble over the water so that it skipped three or four times. I had to practice a long time, but I finally was better at it than the kid next door. This pebble puts me into a mood of pride, even elation, over the accomplishment.

   b. This pebble is bluish gray, a somber color.
   This pebble is smooth, after many years under rushing water. It is old.
   This pebble is from the creek bed—lost, buried there.
   This pebble has been battered about by many forces.
   This pebble was once a craggy piece of rock; its impudence is gone forever.
   This pebble fills me with sadness and fatigue, even though I love the comfort of its gentle surface.

2. Using the above procedure, contemplate your chosen inanimate object until you have arrived at an atmosphere or mood.

3. Translate your emotional reactions into action. Give a short pantomime of the thoughts or feelings evoked. After you have performed, produce the article and trace your thought or emotional construction from the inanimate to the animate.

4. With a partner, use the no-content dialogue on page 62, performing it in the atmosphere your object has suggested.

MIMICRY

Few drama instructors would doubt that a mimetic sense is of value to a player. In learning any art, one goes through a period of imitation. However, we should not deceive ourselves. Imitation is not a creative process. It is reproducing an art already accomplished. It bears the same resemblance to acting as a photograph of a famous painting does to the original.

Beginning actors must take care that their admiration for a favorite star does not (consciously or unconsciously) lead them to imitate that celebrity's personal aura. They would be wasting valuable time in a study of the package without examining the product inside.

Rather than working to achieve a cold reproduction of the outer evidences or technique of another actor, they would do better to study the inner motivating force—the cause as well as the results.

Some of your own individuality should be expressed in every part you play. A character, as written, is only some symbols on paper. You must bring these marks to life. The playwright has gone as far as he can. He realizes—or should realize—that his play is no play until it is acted by actors. Authors are often amazed when they see what actors have been able to accomplish through their artistry. Don't mimic another actor; be yourself and the character. Determine that you are going to do more than lend your body and voice to the part.

There is a difference between copying and being influenced. Many great artists have been influenced by those who preceded them. It is said that Beethoven was influenced by Mozart and Haydn. Modern artists Modigliani and Picasso freely admitted that their rediscovery of the beauty of African primitive art influenced much of their own creative thinking. The point is that before you allow yourself to be influenced, you must be capable of good judgment and the ability to evaluate. You must be able to recognize the basic elements of the creative art and to understand how those elements have been used. Your critical judgment, which is a product of your own individuality, will increase as you use it. Eventually, you will be able to allow the beauty of a great actor's work to sift through yourself, emerging at last as your own creation.

There is a type of actor using mimicry who *is* creative—*the impressionist*. He does more than mimic celebrities. He selects their most individual traits, both inner and outer manifestations, distills these to an essence, and then holds them up for ridicule by the use of caricature. This requires not only careful selection of characteristic traits, but also a vivid imagination. The result is a creative act in itself.

SELF-DISCIPLINE IN THE ACTOR

Art without discipline approaches exhibitionism. In references to acting, this means that psychologically, actors who are unable to establish disciplined behavior controls appear as petulant, childish show-offs. A baby assumes that the world exists just to meet its needs. The little ego is completely self-loving. At the age of three or four years (or sooner), the ego's demands are disturbed by the development of the superego, as the child becomes aware of a world existing outside itself. When a child begins to wonder what is right and what is wrong, he is beginning to develop a conscience. The conscience must come to terms with the ego; they must exist in an inner balance. If the ego refuses to be superseded by the superego, then we have such reactions as "I hate myself," "I don't feel like it," "Don't bother me." Ego is making a last-ditch stand, fighting for unrestrained expression of instinct against conscience. The adolescent girl sometimes despises her femininity; the adolescent boy may reject responsibility. Normally, the superego wins and establishes certain standards for the self. The outside world looms larger as we grow up. The ego still exists, but it learns to satisfy itself by special skills and interests. But the battle is usually hard fought. Procrastination, postponement, hostility, and indolence are the weapons used by the ego in the struggle. While the struggle is never over, a certain balance is eventually reached within the individual.

Let us assume that a working arrangement has been reached between instinct and conscience. Let us also assume that a person is set on acting as a career. In training, this individual has been told to use and rely on emotion, to excite and release the very emotions the student has only recently learned to control. This may be just the straw that will upset that delicate inner balance. The infantile ego may become free again to scream and storm for the world to serve its needs. No question about it, this does happen! We see it often when actors are apprehensive, anxious, and mentally and physically exhausted from long, exacting rehearsals. At this time, when the usual controls are weakened, the leading lady may suddenly "blow her top" and storm off the stage in a rage. G. K. Chesterton said, "The tragedy of the artistic temperament is that it cannot produce any art."

In becoming an actor, a most important and difficult task is to learn the use of the power of the will to its full capacity. Freedom may be sweet wine, but if you drink too much, its very sweetness can make you ill. An actor is popularly and mistakenly believed to be a free soul, living morally and physically as he pleases—a child of nature and a creature of instinct. This has never been true of actors worthy of the name. When an ambitious young actress travels to New York or Hollywood "to become a star," she suddenly finds herself free—of hometown, parents, and parental expectations—only to find that what she expects of *herself* is much more demanding. She must assume responsibility for, and mastery of, herself. She must become her own disciplinarian, for no one is going to guard her interests but herself. She must fight her own indulgences, adopt a tough policy, and eventually acquire a pride in exerting her willpower.

Freedom? The ambitious person is never free. He must compete. Ambition drives him on. He must be constantly learning. And learning means changing, giving up something he has for something he wants more.

We all resent limits and boundaries. We confuse rational control of self with denial of the sweet things in life, and we have difficulty setting limits for ourselves. But the ability to live richly and rewardingly depends on the integration of the ego and the superego.

In another sense, discipline can promote freedom. The graphic artist Corita Kent has pointed out that we must set limitations in order to be free. At first this may sound impossible. Yet, each creative effort actually involves narrowing down the myriad possible choices to a few with which we can most easily contend. For example, the graphic artist may choose to limit her color to black, white, and one hue; her tools to only a palette knife, and her design to balanced symmetry. She thus frees herself of all the other possibilities, allowing herself to solve limited problems more thoroughly. Similarly, the actor must build an acting method one step at a time, concentrating on a limited choice of acting elements for each theatrical problem to be solved. However long and successful his career, he will return again and again to specific exercises and thinking processes in order to create the most perfect result.

FURTHER READING: BUILDING YOUR OWN ACTING METHOD

(See also "Additional Reading" list at the end of the book under *Acting.*)

Boleslavsky, Richard. *Acting: The First Six Lessons.* New York: Theatre Arts Books, 1933.

Chaikin, Joseph. *The Presence of the Actor.* New York: Atheneum, 1972.

Clurman, Harold. Interview in *Behind the Scenes.* Edited by Joseph F. McCrindle. New York: Holt, Rinehart & Winston, 1964.

Cohen, Robert. *Acting Power.* Palo Alto, Calif.: Mayfield, 1978.

Hagen, Uta, with Frankel, Haskel. *Respect for Acting.* New York: Macmillan, 1973.

McGaw, Charles. *Acting Is Believing.* 3d ed. New York: Holt, Rinehart & Winston, 1975.

Strasberg, Lee. *Strasberg at the Actor's Studio.* Edited by Robert H. Hethmon. New York: Viking, 1965.

Stanislavski, Constantin. *An Actor Prepares.* Translated by Elizabeth Reynolds Hapgood. New York: Theatre Arts Books, 1933.

Weissman, Phillip. *Creativity in the Theatre.* New York: Dell, 1966.

7
CHARACTERIZATION

Half the actor's battle is won
once a clear picture of the character is firmly engraved in his
senses.*

Helen Hayes
**Academy Award Best Actress
1931/32 (for *The Sin of Madelin
Claudet*) and Best Supporting
Actress 1971 (for *Airport*)**

*From Morton Eustis, *Players at Work, Act-
ing According to the Actors,* Theatre Arts
Books, 1937, p. 18. (Photo by Marcus
Blechman, courtesy Lucy Kroll Agency.)

The fundamentals of acting remain forever constant: They are the same for Shakespeare as for Chekhov. The actors first study the play, including their characters and their relationships to the play and the other characters. They must then determine what the characters are inside, and develop the means to communicate these characters to an audience. These are the fundamentals of an acting design.

Somewhere along the line you must be concerned with the needs of the play, the author, and the times for which the author wrote. All playwrights write out of the urgencies of their time. Each play reflects a certain civilization and a set of mores. Some actors find it difficult to assume fully the characteristics of historical periods, and out of frustration attempt to project themselves, with their alien values and standards, into another time. For Chekhov, you need a realistic approach, for Shakespeare an enlargement of reality. These needs are forever changing with the fashion in plays, but the artistic design in acting is perpetual.

When creating a part, the actor begins by studying the play. Thorough early study builds a strong support for the work to come. Next comes experimenting, selecting, refining, and finally the addition of detail. Aside from the idea, the technique, or the actor who created it, the audience must accept the characterization as an identity. The character must seem a living, breathing human being, whether horrible or wonderful. Acting, like any other art, must communicate something. Originality, skill, design, emotional and psychological interests are the means, not the ends.

STUDY OF THE PLAY

Actors must be prepared to loan themselves as completely to the symbolic language of Ionesco as to the poetry of Shakespeare. A receptive frame of mind is important. On first reading, Virginia Woolf suggests that one must banish all preconceptions and try to become the author, to be the author's accomplice.[1] She cautions that if you have any reservations, you are preventing yourself from getting the utmost value. If you open your mind as wide as possible, you will enter the presence of a human being unlike any other. This is good advice for the actor who is preparing to cope with the broad range of theatrical material today.

Analytical Procedure

As you study, it is important that you understand your intent and that you hold strictly to it. There are several reasons for analyzing the play and each has a distinct purpose. When analyzing for character traits within specific scenes, it may be tempting to revert to contemplating the total drama. The actor must develop strong powers of concentration.

Often during the study of the play it will be possible to read material written elsewhere about the play. In such cases the serious student must be alert to different words or phrases that have similar meanings. This is evident in the words *events*, *beats*,[2] *incidents*, and *units of action*, all of which are explained in the next few paragraphs.

Before an actor can act, he must have a play or story. In our exercises, we have worked with many. A story can be very simple indeed. It can last two hours or one minute. The essentials are characters in a situation and some sequential development. It must also have something basically human at its center.

It is not necessary that a story be a written play. The actors of the Commedia dell'Arte used only a scenario. Marcel Marceau and Red Skelton are able to dispense with words entirely. On the other hand, Charles Laughton could read a passage from the Bible, doing so without movement, settings, or costumes, and thrill an audience with his imaginative powers. Indeed, acting can be deprived of much that we think of as theatre, and still be theatre. The indispensable elements seem to be—an audience, an actor with imagination, and a story. John Gassner has defined a play as a sequence of events in which characters express themselves through what happens to them, what they do, or fail to do.

Actors preparing to play parts in a play must study the structure of the play, its genre, its language, and its characters. From this analysis, they will begin to understand the overall objective, the facts, and the sequence of events. Then they will see how the attitudes of the characters motivate the play's objective, create its given circumstances, and provide the main drive.

Next, they must consider the incidents activating the objective, those sequential and accumulative organizations of physical actions that provide involvement and conflict in the lives of the characters.

---

[1]From Sheridan Baker, *The Essayist*, 2nd ed. (New York: Thomas Y. Crowell, 1972.)
[2]*Beats* are usually considered the smallest *units of action*.

In general, a character is created by some or all of the following components:

1. a playwright's lines and descriptions of characters
2. the emphasis the director places on the character
3. the actor's contribution, mentally and physically
4. what other characters say about that character
5. what that character *does* in the play
6. the character's ideas, ideals, goals, beliefs, and emotions
7. the character's past, heredity, present environment, and appearance
8. the general quality of imagination contributed by all those involved

The creation of a character entails an analysis of its social, psychological, and physical aspects. These are based on the play and the director's concept of the production. Read the play as a play. That is, imagine it as it will be produced, up on a stage, with the characters and the settings. Don't just read the words. Try to experience the *feeling* of the words, what the author is trying to communicate.

First Reading   When you first analyze the play, you read it as if you were the audience—for its total theatrical impact. Your purpose is to discover the overall objective, often called the *super-objective*, of the play. You want to understand the message the playwright wishes to impart through the telling of the story. So you will allow the general feeling of the play to permeate your consciousness.

While you search for the overall objective during this early analysis, you should be aware of two closely associated qualities. These are the *genre* of the play, which designates its type or style of drama, and the *kind of language*, which will vary according to the genre.

This and the ensuing procedures are an extension of the Gestalt theory of perception—a most valuable concept for the actor. While there are many ramifications of the theory, the essential thought for us here is that initially we perceive a thing as a whole, in its totality; only after this original perception can we begin to perceive the parts that make up the whole, thus giving depth to our understanding.

You can visualize this theory in the accompanying illustration. When you first look at it, you perceive a square. It is not until later that you will note that this square is made up of four right angles. This same applies to a tree, with its branches and leaves; to a building, with its bricks and windows; or to a play, with its acts, scenes, and beats (units of action).

Second Reading   During this reading your purpose is to analyze the play for its *contributing objectives*. These are the minor driving forces that have been used to produce the super-objective. As the contributing objectives become apparent, the facts will give you the *story line.* The arrangement of these facts will reveal the *structure* of the play. After this analysis, you will be able to allocate both main and contributing objectives to the characters. This will give you a general idea of the personalities of both the primary and secondary characters.

Third Reading   During your third and further readings, you will consciously separate the play: first, act by act; next, scene by scene; and finally, beat by beat. In each of these you will discover both primary and contributing objectives for each character. For each objective, you must be able to answer the question, "Why?"

This analysis should be written down and thoroughly discussed by all the actors and the director before rehearsals begin. Group discussion will illuminate, and very possibly change, your own points of view. Once mutual understanding and agreement have been reached, rehearsals can begin.

Everyone connected with the production of a play should study it in this analytical way—the director, the costumer, the set and lighting designers, and so on—each for his own needs. For the actor, this systematic breakdown and rebuilding will promote understanding of the play and help to create a character. This also increases the actor's ability to play in harmony with fellow actors for the purpose of communicating the super-objective.

We continue now with a more detailed analysis of what occurs during the various readings of the play.

Detailed Study

First Reading: Super-Objective; Genre and Language   A good way to pinpoint the overall objective of a play is to identify the play's line of action (often called the *spine* of the play). Ask yourself, "How does this play begin?" and "How does it end?" What happens between the beginning and the end is the line of action. If you can state this in one or two short sentences, you have probably isolated the super-objective.

Using *Romeo and Juliet* as an example, the statement could be, "The play begins with two young people in love who encounter problems. The difficulties mount because of a family feud and the intervention of unkind fate, until a solution is found in their deaths." The super-objective could be stated: "True love finds a tragic solution to the obstacles of both man and fate."

As you read different plays you will begin to notice that the historical time of their writing, the social mores of their settings, the distinctive rhythms of their language, and often the treatment of subject matter will denote the play's genre, or type. It may be, among others, Greek drama, a comedy of errors, or Theatre of the Absurd. Each of these represents a specific style. The acting in a Greek drama is very broad, larger than life—in voice, gesture, and essence. A comedy of manners, on the other hand, requires a sly, flippant, rather racy delivery. Samuel Beckett's *Waiting for Godot* is performed in the style of the Commedia dell'Arte, with overtones of burlesque.

Your concept of your character will be much influenced by the genre of the play. It would certainly be inappropriate to conceive and play the characters of Romeo or Juliet using a Greek style or the staccato language of Pinter or Ionesco. This means that you must look into the historical backgrounds and social tendencies in your play. You should read, inspect the art and fashion of the times, and look into possible geographical influences.

Second Reading: Contributing Objectives, Individual Goals, and Character Traits   This time as you analyze, list the facts that create the story line. Each of these facts includes a contributing objective and its respective goal, which affects each character. Be sure, when you try an analysis of your own, that you list *all the facts* before you proceed to pinpoint each objective, each goal, and finally the visible traits of each character.

In dramas where the character traits are less obvious, you must put your creative imagination to work. In all drama the character traits become more well defined as the play progresses. This means you will have to return to the beginning and perhaps correct or add to a character's traits as you come to understand them more fully as the tale unfolds.

We will use the first scene of Shakespeare's *Romeo and Juliet* to demonstrate this kind of analytical procedure. The speeches here have been heavily cut for reasons of brevity. It is suggested that you read the scene in its full form, including the Prologue, which actually explains the whole play.

This example involves only the first few lines of the play. You will note that the master craftsman wastes no time in revealing the immediate point of the plot. As you proceed with your analysis, you will note that some characters are less important to the total drama than others. It would be incorrect to study these lesser personalities to the depth and extent required for those that more properly "carry" the play.

Romeo and Juliet

William Shakespeare
An Excerpt from Act I, Scene i

CAST: **Sampson   Citizens**

Gregory   Capulet

Abram   Montague

Benvolio   Prince

Tybalt

SCENE: *Verona. A public place.*

SYNOPSIS: *Capulet servants, Sampson and Gregory, enter, bantering jokingly about their masters' longstanding feud with the Montague family. A quarrel and sword play develop as Abram, a Montague servant, enters with friends. The mock fight becomes serious when young Tybalt, a Capulet, and Benvolio, a Montague, join them. It intensifies with the arrival of Capulet and Montague and their wives. It is in full, noisy sway when the Prince of Verona arrives and stops it.*

Sampson: Gregory, o' my word, we'll not carry coals.

Gregory: No, for then we should be colliers.

Sampson: I strike quickly, being moved.

Gregory: But thou art not quickly moved to strike.

Sampson: A dog of the house of Montague moves me.

Gregory: The quarrel is between our masters, and us their men.

Sampson: 'Tis all one, I will show myself a tyrant: when I have fought with the men, I will be cruel with the maids, and cut off their heads.

Gregory: Draw thy tool; here comes of the house of Montagues.

Sampson: Let us take the law of our sides; let them begin.

Gregory: I will frown as I pass by; and let them take it as they list.

Sampson: Nay, as they dare. I will bite my thumb at them; which is a disgrace at them, if they bear it.

(Enter Abram)

Abram: Do you bite your thumb at us, sir?

Sampson: I do bite my thumb, sir.

Abram: Do you bite your thumb at us, sir?

Gregory: Do you quarrel, sir?

Abram: Quarrel, sir? No, sir.

Sampson: If you do, sir, I am for you; I serve as good a man as you.

Abram: No better.

(Enter Benvolio, at a distance)

Gregory: [*aside to Sampson*] Say—better; here comes one of my master's kinsmen.

Sampson: Draw, if you be men.—Gregory, remember thy swashing blow.

(They fight)

Benvolio: Part, fools; put up your swords; you know not what you do.

(Beats down their swords)
(Enter Tybalt)

Tybalt: What, art thou drawn among these heartless hinds?
Turn thee, Benvolio look upon thy death.

Simon Ward, who played the title role in the film Young Winston, *appears here as Romeo with Sinead Cusack as Juliet in Shakespeare's* Romeo and Juliet. *(Courtesy of Her Britannic Majesty's Consulate-General.)*

Benvolio: I do but keep the peace; put up thy sword,
    Or manage it to part these men with me.
Tybalt: What, draw, and talk of peace! I hate the word,
    As I hate hell, all Montagues, and thee:
    Have at thee, coward.

                 (They fight)
    (Enter various citizens who join the fight)
Citizens: Down with the Capulets! Down with the Montagues!
               (Enter Capulet)
Capulet: What noise is this?— Give me my long sword, ho!
    My sword, I say!—Old Montague is come,
    And flourishes his blade in spite of me.
               (Enter Montague)
Montague: Thou villain Capulet,—hold me not, let me go.
          (Enter Prince with Attendants)
Prince: Rebellious subjects, enemies to peace,
    Profaners of this neighbour-stained steel,—
    Will they not hear?—what ho! you men, you beasts,—
    Throw your mistemper'd weapons to the ground,
    And hear the sentence of your movèd prince.
    If ever you disturb our streets again,
    Your lives shall pay the forfeit of the peace.
    For this time, all the rest depart away:
    You, Capulet, shall go along with me;
    And, Montague, come you this afternoon.
    Once more, on pain of death, all men depart.

Analysis: Example

STORY LINE: FACTS	CONTRIBUTING OBJECTIVE	INDIVIDUAL GOAL	CHARACTER TRAITS
1. *Servants* of Capulet and Montague families brawl and start fighting.	1. To introduce the feuding situation	1. To goad other family's servants	1. Playful, relaxed, and carefree; inconsequential except as employer's lives affect their own
2. *Young relatives* of the two families join the brawl.	2. To intensify the importance of the feud	2. To hurt or kill each other	2. Quick tempers; close family attachments
3. *Capulet and Montague,* the family heads, arrive and burst into the brawl—now a full-fledged fight.	3. To establish stubborn, unrelenting parental attitudes	3. To emerge victorious	3. Display of strength and family leadership
4. *Prince of Verona* stops the fight and admonishes all.	4. To suggest the imminent dangers of the feuding situation	4. To keep the peace	4. Detached grandeur

It is impossible to determine the correct objective and traits of a character until you have subjected the whole play to the more general analysis above. Contributing objectives and their goals will obviously throw additional light on your character's self as the play progresses. So, your procedure should involve first, listing the story line facts; second, filling in the contributing objectives; and third, determining each individual goal. It is the individual goal that will most reveal your character's traits.

Exercise 87   **ANALYZING A PLAY**

This exercise may be the most valuable and useful effort you can make as an actor. With a play of your own choice, do a complete analysis following the previous procedure. You will simplify your work and arrive at better conclusions if you follow the Gestalt theory of perception described earlier. Note the large events first; then break the analysis down into its smaller units. You will be using this same analysis for the work on character progression, which follows later in this chapter.

Structure of the Play   Once the facts have been listed, with their objectives and goals, the structure of the play will be revealed. The structure is chosen by the playwright either because of the historical time in which he writes or because of the requirements of the play's objectives. The kind of structure can dictate the style of the play. Conversely a choice of style can dictate the kind of structure.

Most of our dramatic literature gives us a structure with a comfortable beginning, middle, and end. Play structure can be plotted on a graph. The graph is often used by directors and choreographers to indicate the movement of the play. When lines plotted on a graph are seen as a picture, the physical, emotional, and intellectual climaxes, as well as subtle aspects of the plot, can be readily identified. Much of contemporary theatre, including Theatre of the Absurd, has purposely manipulated structure in order to communicate a super-objective indicative of modern times. Seemingly odd or uncomfortable structure has been used for many purposes—often simply to jolt the audience out of its complacence. One of the most artful manipulators in this area is Samuel Beckett. In *Waiting for Godot*, he has managed, by means of repetitive and circular structure, to affect audiences deeply. Many people, unable to accept the bitter message, have found it difficult to sit through the play. This is a beautiful example of an artisan's ability to use communicative technique purposefully.

Third and Further Readings   By rereading and reviewing your detailed analysis of the play, you will find that the playwright has arranged several series of objectives into a structure that forms (1) *acts*, which consist of (2) *scenes*, which consist of (3) character encounters, or *beats*. In each of these categories, the smaller objectives assist in explaining and furthering the next larger category. Eventually, the largest category—the total play with its super-objective—has been accomplished.

The encounters—the smallest of the categories—are usually called beats. And in each of these encounters you can find a specific conflict, affirmation, thought, or emotion that is there only because it is necessary to the revelation of action or behavior within the story line of the scene, the act, and finally the play. It is through the beats that you will discover many of the mysteries and delicacies of your character in the play.

By now you have ferreted out everything in the play that sheds light on all its characters, their behavior, and the reasons for their behavior. No character can be developed without this foreknowledge. And no characterization can be complete without a full understanding of all the other characters in the play. Only now, having analyzed the full play, can you receive meaningful answers to further questions regarding the characters. Because you know and understand the text, you will be able to enlarge and refine character by also seeing and using the *subtext*—the unwritten words, the sensed suggestions and intimations. (Subtext will be dealt with in greater detail later in this chapter.)

No definition of a play's objective will apply equally to all plays. But a majority of plays are structured; that is, they have a sequential and accumulative organization of actions or situations, which provide involvement and conflict in the lives of the characters. Without characters and situation, there can be no drama.

Usually the dramatic pressure centers on a protagonist. He is the one who wants something so sincerely that he is willing to fight, or even sacrifice his life, for it. That something may be love, power, duty, money, politics, freedom, country, morality, honesty, ethics, revenge, or life itself. Hopefully, the audience will see something in this character's struggle that relates to them. So in a general way, *the particular becomes the universal.*

Along with the central character (or activist) there are, in most plays, secondary characters almost as important to the plot as the protagonist. They may be allied with or against the protagonist. We would be unable to tell the story of Romeo and Juliet without mentioning their parents. Macbeth has Macduff and Lady Macbeth. The only reason these are secondary characters is that it is not their story. Taking another view, secondary characters could become leading characters; but the play as written makes them contributors to the protagonist's struggles, either by aiding or opposing.

Having thoroughly analyzed the play, you now must study the various facets involved in achieving the ability to communicate your concepts of character. Each facet will, in its own way, assist you in developing the character more completely. Although we must consider these facets one at a time, you are responsible for retaining the information from each as you proceed. As you build your character, do not neglect any facet of the process. The subjects of subtext, inner monologue, nontextual scenes, and metamorphosis (which appear at the end of this chapter) must all be interrelated in your analysis of the play.

THE CHARACTER IN THE PLAY

An actor should not begin working on his characterization until he has a thorough knowledge of the complete play. Do not skim over the parts that do not concern your character, or you may deprive yourself of information that could help you. Study the period for which the play was written. A girl of fourteen in a Shakespearean play is quite different from one in a farce by Oscar Wilde, or one in a modern play, such as *The Effect of Gamma Rays on Man-in-the-Moon Marigolds.*

A playwright uses his characters as symbols through which he conveys his meanings. All artists deal in symbols; the playwright's symbols are endowed with human traits and drives that allow an audience to identify with them. Without characters, a play would simply be a series of events. We empathize with Romeo, or even with a villain like Richard III; good or bad, we recognize their humanity and associate with them.

Only events and actions relating to people are theatrically effective. A devastating flood or hurricane sweeps the Atlantic coast. This is an event, an action, but our interest is always in the effect of the event on people, their lives and homes. We all remember Falstaff, Sherlock Holmes, Oliver Twist, Scarlett O'Hara, or Holden Caulfield. Most of us can close our eyes and see them. But how readily do we remember their stories?

The words of a playwright serve as an actor's blueprint for the creative job that lies ahead. Simply speaking lines that are committed to memory may be lecture or oratory, but certainly not acting. The actor's art involves adding flesh and blood, strength and weakness, desire, mind and soul.

ENTERING THE CHARACTER

While studying the play, you have become familiar with the playwright's words. Obviously, through these words you can learn a great deal about your character. The relevant words may be those of your own character or they may be those of another character, which shed light on your own. But beyond the written words there are implications you must discover for yourself. Usually the written words communicate plot or scene development. The character's buried intents—those parts of his personality that deeply influence his behavior—are revealed in more subtle ways. If the dialogue in

Two contemporary masters of character, Sir Ralph Richardson and Sir John Giel-
gud, as they appear in the Broadway production of Harold Pinter's No Man's Land.
(Courtesy of Ralph Richardson and John Gielgud.)

the play does not suggest these buried intents to you, it will be
necessary for you to imagine them.

We all have such underlying drives; often they are hidden because they are unattractive or socially unacceptable. We inhibit their
appearance. The actor must learn to overcome such inhibitions because of the need to use buried intents in characterization, no
matter how unattractive.

We are socially conditioned to hide certain aspects of our characters. We use tactics to disguise our intents: a laugh to cover em-
barassment, silence to elude reply on a controversial subject, excessive talk to hide indecision or lack of knowledge, or a flippant
attitude to dismiss a guilty thought. Even within ourselves we find
ways to ignore our own lust or envy or to rationalize dishonesty or
greed. From childhood onward we have encountered varying degrees of success with such tactics. Some are conscious and some are
not. We adopt and use those that serve us best. Each character in
every play shares such attitudes, mannerisms, and tactics; these
must be discovered.

"Getting inside a character" means that the actor is lending his
body, mind, and voice to be motivated, even possessed, by the
character. This almost religious attitude toward character creation
has many precedents. Mythological tradition holds that images give
power. The aboriginals, from ancient to modern times, have wor-
shipped their hero-ancestors. And folklore gives the creator of images the role of sorcerer or magician—witness the festivals of
Dionysus and later the miracle plays. Such convictions are founded
on two premises—the nonartist's awe of inspiration and the artist's
skill at transposing vision into object. This synthesis of spiritual and

visual sensibilities allows the created character to dominate. This image is transmitted to an audience by means of symbols and impulses. Only training and discipline can perfect the actor in this art. Judith Groch has written:

> The ability to regroup the fragments of experience mentally in new and significant combinations, to move backward and forward in thought, to go where we have not been, to be where we cannot go, and to re-create, even if imperfectly, another person's feelings, is the supreme gift of our responsive, uniquely personal human brain.[3]

We can understand a character's physical actions from what he says or does, or how he looks. Richard III boasts of his ambitions and his villainy. He speaks directly to the audience—which is narrative—and then proceeds to do everything he has talked about. Lady Anne's loathing of him shows us that others consider him a villain. Later, although he is physically repulsive to her, she becomes his queen; this shows us another side of Richard—his evil, but irresistible, magnetism. Here then are a few ways in which the actor might study his character:

1. by what the character says and does
2. by what others say of the character
3. by how the character affects and manipulates others
4. by the physical appearance of the character

Using this list as a guide, the examples that follow will indicate two different ways to analyze through the words of the play: directly and by implication. Refer back to each of the four statements for studying character.

Example of Analysis through Words by Direct Indication

Statement 1. In *Hamlet* he describes part of his own character as he bemoans his weakness in the famous monologue at the end of Act II: "O, what a rogue and peasant slave am I! . . ."[4]

Statement 2. In the previous *Romeo and Juliet* excerpt from Act I, Scene i, the Prince's words give an early description of the Capulet and Montague families. The words used are: "rebellious subjects, enemies to peace, profaners, beasts, mistemper'd."

Statement 3. In *Romeo and Juliet*, Romeo's misunderstood refusal to fight Tybalt results in Mercutio taking the initiative; this causes Mer-

---

[3]Judith Groch, *The Right to Create* (Boston: Little, Brown, 1969), p. 41.

[4]Should you find the classics somewhat difficult at your present level of ability, a general picture may be formed by referring to Frank N. Magill, ed., *Masterplots*, 12 vols. (Englewood Cliffs, N.J.: Salem Press). *Romeo and Juliet* can be found in vol. 10 of the revised 1976 edition. The critique, story, and critical evaluation is by Kenneth John Atchity. *Hamlet* is in vol. 5. Other variorums are available.

cutio's death and finally also the death of Tybalt. In Romeo we discover loyalty (to his new kinsman by marriage). In Mercutio we find how much he values the honor of the Montague family.

Statement 4. In *Death of a Salesman*, Willie Loman's desperation shows in his fatigued and beaten posture. His once broad shoulders slump. His clothes drape in sad defeat. The spring is gone from his step. Not even memory can restore the bravado of his early dreams.

Exercise 88 **ANALYZING DIRECTLY THROUGH WORDS**

Choose characters in familiar plays. Isolate dialogue or monologue to accompany each of the four statements previously listed for studying character through *direct indication* from the words of the play.

Example of Analysis through Words by Implication

Statement 1. In *Hamlet*, when Hamlet talks with Ophelia so strangely during Act III, Scene i, the implication is that he is quite mad. And Ophelia seems quite convinced when she replies, "O, what a noble mind is here o'erthrown!" Is this, in your opinion, true?

Statement 2. When Hamlet arranges for the Players to do a scene duplicating the act of his uncle murdering his father, he is implying his uncle's actual guilt. This occurs in Act III, Scene ii. Or in act 3 of Lillian Hellman's *The Little Foxes*, when the husband, Horace, outlines to his wife, Regina, how he proposes to change his will, he is implying Regina's spiritual complicity in the plot to use his money.[5]

Statement 3. In act 2 of David Mamet's *American Buffalo*, Teach describes a poker game that implies Don is naive and too trusting of his fellow man. This results in Don's agreeing to check out Fletch's information.

Statement 4. In Bertolt Brecht's *The Good Woman of Setzuan*, Shen Te's disguise as Shui Ta implies that she is a different person.

Exercise 89 **ANALYZING BY IMPLICATION THROUGH WORDS**

With a partner, choose known or imagined characters, each with clearly different personality traits. Discuss these traits thoroughly with each other. Devise a short argument to communicate and illuminate the characters:

1. by what they imply about the subject of the argument
2. by what they imply about each other or about people they both know
3. by the ways they achieve a goal regarding each other—through implication, not directly
4. by some indirect reference to physical appearance

[5]Lillian Hellman, *Collected Plays of Lillian Hellman* (Boston: Little, Brown, 1971), pp. 185–88.

Suggestion:

The characters might be two girls or two boys—one more handsome than intellectual and one more intellectual than handsome.

The argument might involve whether a third person of the opposite sex will accept an invitation to a weekend alone with one of them in a private vacation cabin.

Whenever we have a scene between two characters, we learn a great deal about each of them. In some plays there is often a contradiction between what the character says, and what he does. This adds another dimension, which is clearly demonstrated in Shakespeare's *Taming of the Shrew.* In this play, the character Petruchio delights audiences with the inconsistencies between his physical actions and the words he speaks. Petruchio's behavior belies his intent. While he says he wants to marry the shrew, Katherine, his behavior is more irritable and hot tempered than hers. It is in this contradictory manner that Petruchio cures Katherine, and the play ends happily.

When you are preparing to perform in a play, read it again and again. After thoughtful analysis, read it giving all your attention to your part. Have you found the objective of your particular character in the overall play? In each scene? Do you know what your character thinks and wants from life? French actor-producer Jean-Louis Barrault refers to this as the "What-am-I-doing-here?" step.[6] Find your character's objectives: Ask yourself all sorts of questions, and answer them using your imagination and what is presented by the playwright. You will recognize good answers by the way they validate, corroborate, and assimilate the character and the play. In this way you will be able to justify a logical and consecutive group of organic physical actions for the character, in the entire play and for each scene.

There is, of course, no way to say, "I now completely understand the character." Once implanted, the spiritual part of that personality will continue to grow, even in small ways, shedding its influence on physical actions and reactions. The main thing is to open the door to your awareness and to keep it open so that a wedding of the spiritual interior and the physical exterior will evolve. But do not try to *will* yourself into the feelings of your character. Instead, perform his physical actions. Your instincts and emotions will bring you to the creative moment when there is complete integration of the physical and spiritual aspects of a role.

UNDERSTANDING THE CHARACTER

We have been considering physical actions of characters and how they relate to objectives. But every character has both a physical and

[6]Jean-Louis Barrault, *The Theatre of Jean-Louis Barrault* (New York: Hill & Wang, 1961), p. 34.

a spiritual life. From the exercises given earlier, you have learned how organic physical actions and definite objectives can lead to deep inner responses. "The body is biddable," Stanislavski has said. "Feelings are capricious; therefore, if you cannot create a human spirit in your part of its own accord, create the physical being in your role."[7]

To gain a full understanding of a character as it relates to the play, you must achieve a deep, sympathetic understanding of the other characters involved in the drama. This is a twofold job. It means not only that you as a person must be appreciative of your fellow players' work, but also that you as your character must be thoroughly acquainted with them as their characters. Insight into your own character will deepen when you understand the other characters' points of view. While you are posing questions about your own character's behavior, you must also ask about the behavior of your fellow players. But the answers to the latter must come from your character's self, not your own.

It is for this important reason that, even though it may at first seem strange, women must make thoughtful studies of men's parts and vice versa. Certainly no woman should be deprived of working on *Hamlet*. And no man can be a total actor without having immersed himself at some time in *Medea*. Historically, the theatre has been enriched by women who have played the great classic male parts. And in much of the theatre's history all parts, male and female, were played by men. Fortunately for people of the theatre our contemporary social standards no longer make stark differentiations regarding the male and female roles in society. Today it is more a matter of appreciating full individual capabilities, regardless of sex, but without eliminating that lovely maxim, *"Vive la différence!"*

Exercise 90 **UNDERSTANDING OTHER CHARACTERS #1**

An exercise outlined by Charles Marowitz suggests that male and female actors should choose situations typical of their opposite genders and, as their own characters, improvise within those situations.[8] Situations for a male character might include applying nail polish, discovering pregnancy, dressing from lingerie on up. For a female, this might include shaving, first visit to see the new baby, or coaching a Little League game. Students are cautioned not to adopt the voice quality or to parody the opposite sex in any way. The objective is the faithful assimilation of a situation belonging to the opposite sex, performed as the character—not the actor—would perform it.

In real life we constantly think about why those around us speak and act as they do. In a play you are never alone. You are part of an

[7]Konstantin Stanislavski, *Creating a Role* (New York: Theatre Arts Books, 1961), p. 154.
[8]Charles Marowitz, *The Act of Being* (New York: Taplinger, 1978), Appendix 1.

interacting team. Even during a monologue you are in league with the audience. The way you act depends a great deal on the way you feel about your friend, your lover, your parent, your fellow player, and your audience, and how they feel about you. Reactions to a fellow character will depend on both your own character's self and your character's understanding of the other character's self.

Exercise 91 **UNDERSTANDING OTHER CHARACTERS #2**

If you want to go to a party but have no way to get there, in what different ways would you approach your father, an instructor, a popular rival, or your kid sister for a solution to your problem?

Improvise telephone conversations with two of these. How do the conversations differ because of your understanding of their characters?

The unfolding of the action-reaction chain, which depends so heavily on understanding, has been called *Relacom,* or "relationship communication."[9] As in exercise 91, it points up the intricacies inherent in communicating content as it is affected by relationships.

Once a play is "on its feet," you will find yourself tuning in to variations in the characters of audiences. Each audience has an identity of its own. To a seasoned actor the question, "How's the house tonight?" means much more than "How many people came?" He hopes for a tip-off on the personality of that entity out there, which changes at every performance. The audience reaction will affect the players and the play—the manner in which the communications are delivered.

Often an inexperienced actor or a professional lacking imagination will lean heavily on the playwright, expecting him to carry them. In such circumstances, the play presents the actors instead of the actors presenting the play.

The director's task is to stimulate his actors into individual creativity, to suggest possibilities, to find relationships between the actors and their characters, to encourage a sense of perception, and to serve as the actors' audience when they have none.

However, it is the actor who makes the final contact with the audience. He is the relay team's anchorman. It is the actor who will finally win or lose the event. This alone should be sufficient reason for the actor to know a character better than the playwright who created the character, or the director who collaborated with the actor. Understanding is the key to successful characterization. Some actors write biographies of their characters in order to get a more penetrating insight into their roles. Anthony Quinn is reported to have written 11,000 words on his part in the film *Flap*. His notes

Anthony Quinn. (Courtesy of Anthony Quinn and Warner Bros.)

[9]Robert Cohen, *Acting Power* (Palo Alto, Calif.: Mayfield, 1978), p. 53.

begin with "The character's character (very male), and his weight (139 pounds)"—and they continue for forty-five pages.[10]

When Rod Steiger was working on his characterization of Al Capone, he read the gangster's autobiography and all the newspapers of the time. Steiger asked himself, "What did this man *want?* I decided he wanted to be respected—he wanted recognition. I read the script and reread it, and somewhere inside me it clicks, and there's an 'Oh, Yes' in a secret place—I walk through a five-and-ten-cent store and associate objects with the part. Say I see a toothbrush. I'll think, How does he brush his teeth?—One thing I did for Al Capone was to take out all small gestures. I played it pretty big—I wore my coat draped over my shoulders, and my hat brim angled—because one thing I felt he wanted was to be big."[11]

Rod Steiger. (Courtesy of Rod Steiger and United Artists.)

CHARACTER PROGRESSION

Progression, sometimes called *the through-line,* involves linking one event together with the next. Each event is motivated by a previous event, and is therefore a reaction. Each reaction becomes an action, and then it motivates the next event.

In the traditionally structured play there is a progression in the story; that is, the play does not end the way it began. There is also a progression in characters. They are introduced, we learn something of their past and what they want, and then they are confronted with a situation or crisis. In the resulting conflict, they are either victorious or destroyed. Thus, progression keeps an audience interested in what is happening on stage.

The function of mounting dramatic scenes is to reveal the constantly shifting psychic lives of the characters. In the great dramatic classics, such as *Romeo and Juliet,* transitions in the leading characters can be traced scene by scene. Physical actions are motivated by different drives, but all eventually combine toward the total goal of the character.

During the discussion on study of the play, you were given a procedure for analysis, which revealed the story line in such a way that you could read its events as a synopsis of the entire play. You can also use this story line to analyze character progression. As you trace the progress of the plot by means of the changing objectives and goals, you can relate the progress of each character to the plot. Because of the conflicts faced and the kinds of solutions made, each character grows or changes—sometimes a great deal, sometimes only a little, sometimes progressing only to arrive back at its beginning state, but always changing.

---

[10]Interview by Joyce Haber, "Anthony Quinn Takes Film Work Seriously," *Los Angeles Times,* Calendar section, October 26, 1969, p. 19.

[11]© 1962 Lillian Ross. From Lillian Ross and Helen Ross, *The Player, A Profile of an Art* (New York: Simon and Schuster, 1962). Originally published in *The New Yorker.*

In a production, this character progression happens before the eyes of the spectators; yet the basic inner dynamism of the character is never lost. In any aspect of vital experience there is progression— some sequential development. Each living thing reacts to the outside world by constantly changing its total condition. When it ceases to do so, it is dead.

Unless you are fully aware of each stage of your character's progress, your interpretation will resemble a cardboard replica passing through the play. To clarify this progress you need only to refer to your written play analysis from exercise 87. Note the individual goals for your character, and the line of character progression will begin to emerge.

You can extend the information you already have by adding four more categories:

1. the character's basic inner dynamism
2. the character's main objective
3. the stimulus for each action
4. the reason for the character's reaction to the stimulus

The *inner dynamism* is the character's inner psychic drive. There will be further discussion of this as we proceed. The character's main objective is usually not the same as the super-objective of the play itself. A brief sample of analysis for character progression follows. We use only one action from Arthur Miller's *Death of a Salesman*. The character is Willie Loman. It is early in act 1.

1. *Inner dynamism:* His weak set of values.
2. *Main objective:* To be a success according to his values.
3. *The action:* Willie lapses into a memory of when his boys were young.
   The stimulus: His discomfort with the present.
4. *The reason for the reaction to the stimulus:* The need to maintain stature before his boys.

Once you correctly understand items 1 and 2, items 3 and 4 will fall into proper place. Without the character's inner dynamism and main objective, the stimuli and the reasons for reactions to those stimuli could be badly incorrect. For instance, if you decided that Willie Loman's inner dynamism is not his weak set of values, but rather his misunderstanding of the American free-enterprise system, every moment in the progress of both character and play would have to be different.

You are analyzing, not what happens in the play, but only what happens to your character—what it was initially, and, step by step, how it became what it was at the end. It is often difficult to put these things into mere words because a great deal of it must be sensed by you. Yet forcing verbalization will help to clarify those fuzzy areas that it is natural to try to bypass. Some feelings seem to defy verbalization. A character's inner dynamism is seldom a thing so obvious that it can be stated exactly. It is usually unclear to the character itself. It constitutes, in great part, the *dimension* of the character. The search for inner dynamism brings one into the realm of fantasy. How did Willie Loman become saddled with such a weak set of values? Why did he cling to those values? You will ask such questions of your character all the time you are working on it.

One thing is certain, the inner dynamism is peculiar to the character and has nothing to do with your own self. While you will make decisions about it, you will also sense that its peculiarities and the inherent form partially responsible for it are a great mystery that the magic and genius of the actor will find a way to suggest to the audience. If this seems an open-ended statement, it is just that. All the things you have discovered about the character still leave unidentifiable possibilities. But don't lose courage. The fact that you have set down a statement covering the inner dynamism carries with it the assurance that the character can progress.

You—the actor or actress—will know all the facets of your character even before the curtain rises. But the character traits belonging to that character will only be shown to the audience as the drama unfolds. What an error it would be to allow the audience to sense the final heights of Willie Loman's despair during the scenes that occur earlier in his marriage! As you read the play *Death of a Salesman* you will not find a straight, continuous line of progress for Willie's character. It is rather a complicated zigzag during which Willie must revert from his late despair back to his early joyous ambition, then again into despair, and so on through the play. This wrenching, erratic progress accentuates the pull and tug within the character's progress, at the same time as it weaves a web of distraction into the play's structure.

As you work on progression, it is important that you study an entire play. Otherwise you will be deprived of the experience of developing the complete character. It is only through the whole play that you will be able to grasp the many dimensions of character.

PHYSICAL COMMUNICATION

Once you have analyzed a character, your intellectual and emotional feelings must be transferred into physical communication. These feelings are communicated to the audience through sight and sound. The physical and verbal gestures that belong to the character must be developed along with your study of the words of the play, the implications the words suggest, and the inner intents of the character. If you, as the character, can imply and suggest with nonverbal physical and vocal gestures, the audience will begin to think for itself and become part of the performance. Your research into the style of the play and into the environmental and social backgrounds will assist in the choices you make. These choices will influence the manner in which you perform the gesture and emit the sound.

The purpose of exercises 92 and 93 is to clarify the meaning of *environmental influences*. These exercises will also demonstrate the facility required of actors, who must be able to correlate the intellectual results of study with a fruitful imagination. Attempt to discover how such study affects a character's actions and reactions.

Exercise 92 **SOCIAL ENVIRONMENT**

Study one of the plays below or substitute one of your own. Be prepared to justify your choices of gesture or voice due to the changed social and physical relationships of your character with others in the play. Isolate a scene and with a partner demonstrate how the chosen characters would be played if in:

The Little Foxes by Lillian Hellman, Regina's husband was a bully.

Hamlet by William Shakespeare, Hamlet's mother was a frivolous female.

Death of a Salesman by Arthur Miller, Willie Loman's wife Linda was a nag.

Waiting for Godot by Samuel Beckett, Vladimir was sensually fond of Estragon.

Exercise 93 **PHYSICAL ENVIRONMENT**

Using the same plays as in exercise 92, transfer the characters into a different locality and time. Which body and voice gestures would change? Which would not? Why? Some possible suggestions are to change:

The Little Foxes from a southern family to one in an Oregon mining camp.

Hamlet from seventeenth-century Denmark to a modern western cattle ranch.

Death of a Salesman from the eastern United States to Hollywood, California.

Waiting for Godot from an open space with a tree to a closed barn.

It is conceivable that a character might be so universal in concept that historical or temporal variations would have little effect.

THE ACTOR BECOMES THE CHARACTER

An actor-character relationship has been accomplished when an actor understands the behavior of a character. Then the actor can begin to sense anything false in the character's speech, movement, and intellectual processes, and can ensure that all lines and business are in harmony with the author's concept. An actor will only be able to create in direct proportion to sympathetic understanding of the character he is trying to portray.

Most psychologists accept the fact that, beyond the social influences of people such as parents, teachers, and peers, the way each of us behaves is predicated on our own personal views—that we are self-oriented. We do not behave in a certain way because of the way someone else feels or thinks. All experience is sifted through each individual; therefore all expression stems from self. The development of character involves a transition from your personal self into the self of the character. You, as the character, then become the person around which the other characters move. You, as the character, react to the rest of the players.

Exercise 94 **THE CHARACTER'S SELF**

This exercise should be done by both men and women. The following excerpt from *Hamlet* is the latter part of one of Shakespeare's most famous monologues. Preparation for presentation should include:

1. studying how you would react if you returned from school to learn that your mother had married the man who had killed your father
2. searching yourself in order to break down your personal inhibitions
3. examining the physical, psychological, and social aspects of Hamlet so that you can enter his character
4. reconstructing Hamlet's life previous to the time of the play
5. analyzing Hamlet's hopes and objectives for the future
6. learning or reading the following from *Hamlet,* Act I, Scene ii

Finding himself alone, Hamlet allows his deep grief to pour out. He is speaking of his mother. He is desolate and can scarcely believe the horrible situation is true.

> *Let me not think on't—Frailty, thy name is woman!—*
> *A little month; or ere those shoes were old,*
> *With which she follow'd my poor father's body,*
> *Like Niobe, all tears; — why she, even she, —*
> *O heaven! a beast, that wants discourse of reason,*
> *Would have mourn'd longer,—married with mine uncle,*
> *My father's brother; but no more like my father,*
> *Than I to Hercules: within a month;*
> *Ere yet the salt of most unrighteous tears*
> *Had left the flushing of her galled eyes,*
> *She married: O most wicked speed, to post*
> *With such dexterity to incestuous sheets;*
> *It is not, nor it cannot come to good;*
> *But break, my heart; for I must hold my tongue!*

If you do not know the play, it is time that you read it. If you find it difficult to understand, listen to cassettes and recordings or discourses on Hamlet. Or analyze it in class to the best of your present ability. There is no reason to fear or avoid the classics. The sooner you become acquainted with them, the better.

CHARACTER DELINEATION

Contrary to general opinion, acting is not a lazy man's pastime. A creative actor is never content to read lines written by an author and to be moved about the stage by a director like a pawn on a chessboard. Any actor worthy of the name does more than read a play once or twice. It is not enough for an actor to be able to follow the story and to decide what he will do with the part he has been assigned. Indeed, he does not view the work ahead from an actor's point of view at all, but from the character's. He begins by *absorbing* the play and allowing it to seep through his pores until it becomes a living part of himself. He knows that his character cannot be jammed into the confines of an actor's ego. A character only begins to live after the actor knows, understands, and is on intimate terms with him. Even then, the character will come in his own time when he feels no longer a stranger and when the actor is at repose. This moment of revelation will be clear to the actor. He may note a different pitch in his voice, or may become conscious of an unfamiliar gesture or a strange way of thinking, as actor and character fuse into one. When this metamorphosis is complete, the actor will begin to think, act, and even look like the character. Blind confidence will not accomplish this change; the actor must take logical steps to achieve it. Development comes systematically, piece by piece, requiring intensive concentration, investigation, and self-discipline from the actor, as well as systematic guidance by the director.

Character development is a question-and-answer game. You must research. Ask yourself questions and answer from either your own or some observed experience.

An artist creates—using the available materials to compose, by selection, observation, research, experience, inspiration, and discipline—something that had no existence before he set his hand and heart to it. "The artist need not have experienced in actual life every emotion he can express," states philosopher Susanne Langer in her provocative *Feeling and Form*. "It may be through manipulation of his created elements that he discovers new possibilities of feeling strange moods, perhaps greater concentrations of passions than his own temperament could ever produce."[12]

The following are four steps that an actor might follow in working

---

[12]Susanne Langer, *Feeling and Form* (New York: Charles Scribner's, 1953), p. 374.

on characterization. Extremely intricate and expanded procedures may be found in recent contemporary literature.[13]

1. *Orientation.* Study the play, the milieu in which the character lives, and the character's relationships to others in the play. Discover the individuality in the character. What makes him different from others in the play? Decide his mental and moral traits, his behavior, his dress. What is his importance to the play? To the plot? Who is he? What is he? When? Where? Why?

2. *Motivational Period.* What are his biological drives? What makes him do the things he does? What are his dominant characteristics? What does he say—or not say? What does he want? Locate a sentence or speech in the part that illuminates the essence of the character.

3. *Physical Aspects.* All movements are motivated by thought. (We decide to get up out of a chair before we do.) Select innerdynamics of the character that can be shown physically and audibly. Select the rate and tension of his movements, and physical aspects that can be adapted to the character. How does he fill space? Is he a small man, a fat one? What is the rhythm of his walk? The texture of his voice? Synthesize the character *in action.*

4. *Spiritual Aspects.* The character's ethics or morals are usually revealed during the play—to the audience and, sometimes, to himself.

During the period of selection, logical thinking may become blocked. If this occurs, the actor may find some value in relaxing his conscious effort, allowing time for his unconscious to contribute. Metaphysical abstractions or inspiration may appear suddenly when the actor's thoughts are totally detached from the problem, seeming to arise from no apparent logic. On closer examination, these are usually found to be the result of conscious thinking. By releasing pressure, you have allowed your unconscious to contribute. This does not imply that you should sit around waiting for inspiration to flutter over your head. It merely suggests that you relax if you reach an impasse. Should this fail, then return to your studies. We have already concluded that the creative process is part conscious or logical, and part unconscious or intuitive, and that these should be combined with hard work. There is no substitute for sticking to the problem. It is the key to both logic and intuition.

Exercise 95 **CREATING CHARACTERIZATION #1**
Begin with some simple, everyday duty, such as washing the face, reading a newspaper, threading a needle, etc.

---

[13]Robert L. Benedetti, *Actor at Work,* rev. ed. (Englewood Cliffs, N.J.: Prentice-Hall, 1976); Robert Cohen, *Acting Power* (Palo Alto, Calif.: Mayfield, 1978); Charles Marowitz, *The Act of Being* (New York: Taplinger, 1978).

Pantomime the action as you might do it.

Now, do it as several different characters might.

This can become a very provocative and rewarding exercise when a character from some well-known play is selected. Improvise a scene that is not in the play, but using the character from it. For instance: How would Lady Macbeth wash her face? She had to, you know.

To be valid, this search must begin with the facts as stated in the play: the author's description of the character, what is said by the character, what others say about him, and how he contributes to the play. In other words, an actor must work backward—from what happens to the character during the action to the *reasons* for what happens. You can use various means to determine the reasons for a character's actions, all of which require thoughtful study and imagination.

We know that actions and reactions, both physical and verbal, result from some kind of stimuli. Try to train your mind to search for the stimulus that causes the action. For instance:

THE ACTION	THE POSSIBLE STIMULI
1. You eat.	1. You are hungry. It is lunch time. It would be impolite to refuse.
2. You sit.	2. You are tired. Everyone else is seated. It is an order.

You can see that there are many possible stimuli for an action.

Exercise 96 **CREATING CHARACTERIZATION #2: MOTIVATION**

To test yourself, choose a familiar scene with two characters. Play it with a partner. Invent, play, and be ready to justify your own character's stimulus for:

1. abruptly leaving the room during the scene
2. refusing to speak during the scene
3. laughing during the scene

Switch characters with your partner and repeat.
How did the stimuli differ? Why? Were they physical or emotional stimuli?

The particular stimulus behind each of a character's actions can be discovered only through study of the play, the words, and the implications. When you have found the stimuli that belong to your character in that play, in that scene, and at that time, it is because you know and understand the character fully. The stimulus to action is the character's motivation.

Exercise 97   **CREATING CHARACTERIZATION #3: FROM THE OUTSIDE**

By observation, select an obvious external behavior or look such as:

a way of walking

a way of listening

a way of arguing

a kind of posture

Concentrating on it, allow your imagination to fantasize a complete character. Assume this character and read to a partner from a newspaper, a recipe, or the directions on a label. Your partner may interrupt with questions or remarks at any time. Exchange roles and repeat.

In this exercise, either by speaking or listening, you will have communicated a character that was originally conceived on the basis of external behavior. You will have chosen a starting point that was strong enough to sustain your imagination throughout. Your classmates should be able to tell you about your character at the finish.

There are endless possibilities for triggering awareness into character creation. Try devising characters for the no-content dialogue in exercise 45 by contemplating musical themes, ethnic rhythms, distinctive portraits, animal behavior (see exercise 14), or anything that stimulates your imagination.

Exercise 98   **CREATING CHARACTERIZATION #4: FROM THE INSIDE**

Choose a character from a familiar play. Study as deeply as you can the probable childhood relationships, home, school friends and enemies, ambitions, successes, failures, and how the character behaved and felt in such instances. Write it down, explaining as you write. Proceed in this way through adolescence, young adulthood, etc., up to the character's present age and social position. Remember, as you build this character's interior self, that the behavior and experiences of childhood influence those that occur later. Decide whether the reactions to failure strengthened or caused lifelong resentments. Did the reactions to success result in humility, braggadocio, or ambition?

When you have saturated yourself with your character's personality, proceed with a partner, as in the previous exercise. Check yourself with a tape recorder or by your classmates' impressions. How much of your character was revealed? Correctly? Incorrectly? What additional characteristics came forth? What aspects of your own self were obvious? Why?

The two exercises above exemplify both internal and external influences on your work. Physical movement evolves of itself, partly through recall and partly as a result of the traits of the new character. Once your character has begun to form and build, it will usually continue to grow on its own.

Exercise 99 **CHARACTER CONCEPTS BY THOUGHT PROGRESSION**

The objective in this exercise is to describe a character that an audience would believe capable of a given action. By use of logical thought patterns, we trace back and create a character whose background; age; and mental, moral, emotional, and physical aspects determine the character's actions. Stated differently, we are to give full justification for the action, by understanding the character himself.

This is not a physical exercise, but one involving thought progression and imagination. Students are not to mime or improvise, but to describe the thoughts, feelings, and behavior of a character whose actions would be believable to an audience.

Students should describe the following situations in the first person, from the protagonist's viewpoint, filling in the cause and effect for each.

1. A man (or woman) has walked to a parking lot two blocks away and finds that the keys to the car are in the office.
2. A girl slaps her mother in the face.
3. A mother slaps her daughter in the face, but for entirely different reasons from #2 above.
4. A young wife hears a noise during the night. She cannot arouse her sleeping husband and decides to investigate herself. When she enters the living room, she confronts a burglar.
5. A sensitive sixteen-year-old boy, a music student, is given his first summer job on a garbage disposal truck. After two days he quits, and attempts to explain it to his father.
6. Two office girls from Texas decide to spend their vacations together in New York. One is offered her plane fare by her employer, and she accepts. She explains why to her friend.
7. A freshman is dared by an upperclassman to call the White House and ask to speak to the president. He does, and the president comes to the phone.
8. A girl of humble circumstances has saved to buy a fashionable wardrobe in order to be admitted to a garden party of the socially prominent. At the party she overhears several guests ridiculing her clothes and awkward manner.
9. An overprotective mother objects to her daughter's dating. A very eligible young man calls and the mother either changes her attitude or not.
10. A protester sees a wounded policeman lying in the street, and helps him to his feet and to an ambulance.

At a later session, each student is to provide an improvisation using the circumstances given. Students may use voice to express stream of consciousness or monologue. Each should relate some personal experiences to the characterization, whether actual or vicarious. This exercise will be judged on how well the student has shown:

the age of the character

the emotional aspects of the character

whether there was an obvious difference between the actor and the character

whether the thoughts, feelings, and actions were explored in such a way that an audience would accept the character in the given circumstances

SUBTEXT AND THE INNER MONOLOGUE

During a performance, much is often "said" by characters without speaking lines written by the author. In an earlier theatre these thoughts were audible to the audience and known as asides or soliloquies. Today, words alone are not as important as they were once. Other means are used. The expression on an actor's face, the movements and gestures, and the unspoken thoughts can speak louder to an audience than would soliloquies or asides. This also happens in everyday life. When we listen to someone who is talking, thoughts, impressions, and reactions are silently created in our minds. It has often been said—and it is certainly true—that a good actor knows how to listen well. When required, or thought useful, the use of an unspoken subtext, or silent *inner monologue* as Stanislavski called it, may help an audience to understand a character's private thoughts.

It should be pointed out here that the word *subtext* has a more inclusive meaning than the phrase *inner monologue*. Charles Marowitz links subtext with the "spiritual presence" of a performance.[14] One may conclude that with successful communication of the spiritual subtext, the audience comprehends even what the actors are not saying. There is a barrier between actor and audience if only the physical is imparted. The practice of using inner monologues can assist in establishing the growth of the often elusive, but so desirable, spiritual, subtextual presence.

Exercise 100   **SUBTEXT THROUGH INNER MONOLOGUE**

Choose a scene in which it is obvious that a character is not expressing his complete or honest thoughts through the lines as written. As you rehearse, try whispering these inner thoughts. Ask your fellow players to disregard these whispered thoughts during the few rehearsals it will take to establish the inner monologue in your mind. (Understand that these thoughts will be audible only during rehearsals.)

During performances, a solid imprint of thought processes will be operating. These processes will be revealed to the audience, not in words, but in facial expressions, voice tones, movements, and gestures. In short, the mind will be transmitting character revelations

[14]Marowitz, *The Act of Being*, p. 102.

even when you have nothing to say. Once mastered, this inner monologue will save you from standing on a stage looking lost in yourself as the actor, instead of being involved with your character and the others.

Exercise 101 **CREATING SUBTEXT #1**

This exercise is most pertinent when you choose a familiar character in a scene from a familiar play. In such cases, the situation has been provided by the playwright. Use a scene with two characters. Four actors will be required.

1. You are the first actor and will play one of the characters. At an agreed point, your partner, the second character, will diverge from the dialogue and begin to ask preplanned questions. The questions can be on any subject relating to the play or to the characters in the play. But the questions should be designed so that the answers can reveal feelings, actions, or attitudes that are not revealed in the play itself. Once the questions and answers begin, all the actors will be developing subtext. Their improvised words will bring forward ideas that can add meaning to the actual words of the play.
2. The third and fourth actors are to become facets of the first actor's character, such as anxiety, passivity, short temper, indecisiveness, patience, etc. Subtext will be developed from these facets of character.
3. The first actor will reply to the questioner in a preplanned way. Having taken their cues from this dialogue, third and fourth actors will also reply, but in the way that their chosen personality facets dictate. These two speak simultaneously with the first actor. Therefore concentration must be constant.

During this exercise all actors must exert great effort to keep the actual chosen character the same, even though the various facets of personality will speak different words in unique ways. The emerging subtext will help create depth of character.

The lines you speak (your dialogue) comprise the text. But the *meaning* of the words you speak is in the subtext. Playing from a full and meaningful subtext is much more than interpretation. The extent of subtext affects both the actor and the audience's interpretation of the play. Without communicated subtext, the audience will hear only the lines as written. The interpretation, then, will be shallow and only of surface quality.

Since you cannot add words to the written text, you must find ways of speaking the lines that reveal and suggest more than you have spoken aloud.

Exercise 102 **CREATING SUBTEXT #2**

1. Try to reveal as much subtext (underlying background, purpose, attitude, etc.) as possible as you speak the single words: "Hello," "Why?" "How?" "No," "Hah!"

2. Use the no-content dialogue in exercise 45 for the development of various subtextual meanings.

As you read various plays, you will notice scenes such as the kind suggested in exercise 100. Exercise 103 gives two obvious examples. It will, of course, be necessary to study the plays in their entirety before this exercise can be performed.

Exercise 103   **CREATING SUBTEXT #3**

The following scenes each have two characters; one character is the speaker and one is the listener. The participants in this exercise are to develop complete subtexts for both the listener and the speaker. Use the inner monologue technique explained in exercise 100.

1. *The Little Foxes,*[15] by Lillian Hellman; act 3, at Regina's entrance. *Characters:* Regina (the listener); Horace (the speaker). *Scene:* Regina discusses, then waits, as Horace tries in vain to get to his medicine. In the lines preceding this moment, the playwright gives strong clues from which to develop subtext for both characters.
2. *Old Times,*[16] by Harold Pinter; act 1, scene 1. *Characters:* Kate (the listener); Anna (the speaker). *Scene:* Anna's first long speech. How does Kate actually feel? It is typical of Harold Pinter to have left all subtext to the actor, director, and audience. In this play a good deal of decision making is required previous to rehearsal.

Exercise 104   **CREATING SUBTEXT #4**

The following portions of scenes from the "Styles in Acting" section (in part II of this book) are helpful for clarifying development of subtext. Try one and see how much meaning you can add to the playwright's lines by communicating subtext. While you cannot use your own words to say what you mean, you can intimate, suggest, and be influenced by your additional knowledge. Here is where your command of the acting tools and your study of the play become all important, for it is subtext that reveals intent. If possible, tape-record your first reading. Then record again after developing the subtext. *Suggested scenes:*

1. "Interview" from *America Hurrah!* by Jean-Claude van Itallie (page 353). Without subtext this could be as boring as listening to a typewriter.
2. *Waiting for Godot* by Samuel Beckett (page 340). Only subtext can help to keep an audience attentive throughout the whole of this play.
3. *The Homecoming* by Harold Pinter (page 346). Subtext involves reaction as much as it does action.

---

[15]Lillian Hellman, *The Little Foxes* (New York: Viking Compass, 1971), p. 125.
[16]Harold Pinter, *Old Times* (New York: Grove Press, 1971), p. 17.

ADDING TO CHARACTERIZATION THROUGH NONTEXTUAL SCENES

The words *nontextual* and *subtext* should not be confused with each other. While neither is written into the play, *nontextual* refers to scenes devised by the actor to assist in clarification of character and motivation *during the rehearsal period*. *Subtext* is implied and is a psychic connotation that is an actual part of the total character or play, and is communicated *during the performance*.

Improvisations of offstage scenes, not written by the playwright but employing subliminal, or unconscious, involvement of the characters, can be a great asset to the actor in preparing character. The audience is told what happens to Hamlet when he is sent to England. But if this action is dramatized by the actors in an improvisation, it will certainly deepen their understanding of the characters when Hamlet returns to Elsinore. The events on the voyage to England are going to make Hamlet a different person than when he left. By such offstage improvisations, an actor is afforded the opportunity of bringing something onstage rather than simply making an entrance. The creation of a character might be likened to fitting the pieces in a mosaic: Some pieces are best set in place tentatively and later adjusted to other pieces as the work on the complete design proceeds.

Exercise 105 **NONTEXTUAL SCENES**

Choose a character in any play and devise a short scene that could have taken place either before the character's entrance or after the exit. Limit yourself to one, two, or three characters.

1. Imagine a scene immediately before your entrance.
2. Imagine a scene occurring at some time in your character's past.
3. Imagine a scene in which you are a witness but are not personally involved.

THE METAMORPHOSIS

Most writers know that when they have studied their subject at length and collected stacks of notes, something more is still needed to give life to the material. The information is assimilated in the writer's brain. This knowledge, along with his own experiences, might stimulate the evolution of a fully realized characterization.

The intuitive search into characterization begins with discovery; some action of the mind produces a fresh insight or image. This might be accomplished by examining the character's needs or goals; his preplay history; his physical traits; his intellectual and emotional attributes; his present mode of living—in fact, everything the author has not explicitly stated. Or the impetus can be a line, an action, or some sympathetic recall that sets off the creative mechanism. The role must then be divided into physical actions for each act and scene in which the character is involved. The physical movements must all grow organically out of "the moments"—the events taking place in the play—and in sympathetic actions with other players.

Suppose that Hamlet is to be your character. After a complete study of the play, the period, and whatever else you have been able to find on the subject, you have decided that Hamlet's outstanding characteristic is his indecision in carrying out his objective—to avenge his father's murder. Consider this in relation to the play and the way you might transmit this to an audience. Ask yourself dozens of questions; then answer them. How does this relate to the play's line of action—the super-objective? Are there lines in the play that justify his indecision? Does Hamlet know he is indecisive? In Act II, Scene ii, he says:

> Yet I,
> A dull and muddy-mettled rascal, peak,
> Like John-a-dreams, unpregnant of my cause,
> And can say nothing: no not for a king,

Let us suppose that after testing indecision as a piece of our puzzle we have decided that it might do. As we rehearse, the subconscious may suddenly recapitulate, select, refine, and arrange related material. By consciously selecting an idea and experimenting with it, we will discover matters we knew only subconsciously. We put these ideas into action by improvisation and the use of our trained body and voice—our physical assets. Thus, the day-by-day work with technique during rehearsals eventually leads us to the emotional and spiritual Hamlet, and we are finally able to *enter into* the character, and to live with him.

This process is used to some degree by all good actors. Experienced actors may no longer be aware that they use it. When an experienced actor is assigned a part, all the cogs of the process mesh automatically. But a beginner must follow the creative process consciously at first, going from what is known to what is unknown, then allowing imagination to create metaphors. Imagination will seek its own mode of expression, and intuition will constantly relate this information to the personality, the consciousness, and the store of emotional memories, giving the concept the breath of life.

But in this process of metamorphosis, the concept will take on its own personality. The character is no longer the actor. Hamlet will reveal his own voice, body, and character. And with this step in the creative process, we reach a realm that escapes logic. What happens is beyond explanation or reality. From a disciple of nature, the actor becomes nature's creator. The actor and the character are hidden behind a veil; when we see them onstage they will be fused into one being. This is the magic of acting, the same magic practiced by

Irene Worth as Madame Ranevskaya in Anton Chekhov's The Cherry Orchard, directed by Andrei Serban, New York, 1977. (Photo by Friedman.)

aboriginal man. The vision born in the artist's mind has now become a physical image. The value of the image depends not on its proximity to reality, but on its association with the artist's psychic existence.

Irene Worth has given an interesting account of a metamorphic way to achieve assistance with characterization:

> When Andrei Serban was directing The Cherry Orchard for the 1977 production at Lincoln Center, he gave us an exercise in improvisation which was exciting and extraordinarily helpful. Three assistants, not actors, read the text of a scene as the actors mimed the action. This indirectly helped us to learn our lines with ease.
>
> He then asked us to select an animal which seemed closest to our character's nature and to express this essence through the animal's actions. It was liberating to lose one's human body and helped to free the actor from his natural shyness and self-consciousness. The following day we repeated the scene from the day before, the readers again speaking the words, dryly, without emotion, but this time we performed the scene as animals and for an extended period of time.
>
> These mute, anthropomorphic emotions were swift, powerful, poignant, very true, and the sequence of exercises made us concentrate on the character instead of ourselves. Both text and character were illuminated. Eventually, many of the new, unexpected actions were put to direct use in the play.

It is obvious that all this study, selection, improvisation, and construction must be done in an atmosphere of peace and relaxation. It must be done whenever the actor studies and rehearses, alone or in the company of sympathetic fellow artists. It cannot be done during performance when facing an audience. That may seem obvious, but there are actors who wait until a performance to "feel" their parts.

All artists have ethics. No painter in his right mind paints in front of a client. Rembrandt once got so angry with a visitor to his studio that he barked, "Don't poke your nose into my pictures, the smell of paint will kill you!" Stanislavski placed a certain emphasis on "feeling the part," but when he learned that some American disciples were placing undue emphasis on "affective memory," he clarified the matter in an article written shortly before his death for the 1947 edition of the Encyclopedia Britannica:

> —this does not mean that the actor must surrender himself on the stage to some hallucination as that when playing he should lose the sense of reality around him, to take scenery for real trees, etc. On the contrary, some part of his senses must remain free from the grip of the play to control everything he attempts and achieves as the performer in his part.

During a performance, the actor controls the prearranged image. This "phantasm," as Aristotle called it, is now under control; it is not controlling. This overall metaphor will have, within it, just enough room for spontaneity and inspirational moments to keep the performance fresh. In a letter dated 1769, the great actor David Garrick speaks of this moment of spontaneity coming upon the actor

Stanislavski shortly before his death. (Courtesy of the Ministry of Culture, USSR.)

during the warmth of the scene as if springing from a mine, and which, "—like an electric fire, shoots through the veins, marrow, bones and all, to every spectator."[17]

The ability to conceive, construct, and communicate an original portrayal to an audience is the measure of a good actor. The poor actor contents himself with copying another actor who had this faculty.

ACTORS' CHECKLIST

The following questions may help you during rehearsals to determine if you are on the right track in building your characterization, and may even show you where you can improve.

1. Does my performance help elucidate the main objective of the play?
2. Am I effectively expressing my character's objective?
3. Is the relationship of my character to the play and to other characters correct?
4. Am I expressing ideas by both physical and mental means?
5. Is my voice quality effective for the part? Do I speak distinctly? Do I project properly?
6. Is everything I do clear and do I communicate to the audience? (This is very different from projection.)
7. Are any of my scenes dull? Do they have a tempo and rhythm? Do my important scenes build to a climax?
8. Is anything I do repetitive? Have I followed the director's instructions?
9. Does my performance have color and does it reflect the mores of the period? Does it have humanity?
10. Am I doing everything possible to cooperate with my fellow players and our director?
11. Have I built my characterization from imagination and observation?
12. Am I completely relaxed at rehearsals?

"You study the character by living with him. When you rehearse, what the character is saying and how he is saying it begin to work in you. Even when you're sleeping, you're developing the character. It's solidifying in your unconscious. An actor shouldn't think on the stage. He must only do."—Walter Matthau (© 1962 Lillian Ross. From The Player, A Profile of an Art, *by Lillian Ross and Helen Ross, Simon and Schuster. Originally published in* The New Yorker. *Photo courtesy of William Morris Agency; by permission of Walter Matthau.)*

FURTHER READING: CHARACTERIZATION

(See also the "Additional Reading" list at the end of the book under *Acting*.)

Benedetti, Robert L. *The Actor at Work.* Rev. ed. Englewood Cliffs, N.J.: Prentice-Hall, 1976.

Cohen, Robert. *Acting Power.* Palo Alto, Calif.: Mayfield, 1978.

---

[17]David Garrick, *The Letters of David Garrick*, eds. David M. Little and George M. Kahrl (Cambridge, Mass.: The Belknap Press of Harvard University, 1963), vol. 2, p. 634, letter dated January 3, 1769.

Guthrie, Sir Tyrone. *Tyrone Guthrie on Acting*. New York: Viking, 1971.

Marowitz, Charles. *The Act of Being*. New York: Taplinger, 1978.

McGaw, Charles. *Acting Is Believing*. 3d ed. New York: Holt, Rinehart & Winston, 1975.

Osborn, Alex. *Achieving Characterization in Applied Imagination*. New York: Charles Scribner's, 1963.

Schechner, Richard. "Introduction: The Playwright as Wrighter." In Megan Terry, *Viet Rock and Other Plays*. New York: Simon and Schuster, 1966. This deals with "transformations."

Stanislavski, Constantin. *Building a Character*. Translated by Elizabeth Reynolds Hapgood. New York: Theatre Arts Books, 1949.

8
SENSIBILITY
AND EMOTION

An actor can never let himself be overcome by emotion. If he started to cry during a scene, there wouldn't be any play. Emotion can play a big part in acting. Sometimes a role can tear you to pieces. But it must always be controlled emotion.*

Alfred Lunt

*From Morton Eustis, *Players at Work, Acting According to the Actors,* Theatre Arts Books, 1937, p. 45. (Photo by permission of Alfred Lunt.)

The emphasis in the preceding chapters has been on exercises. We began with relaxation and the use of the body and voice as pliable, effective acting instruments. From this base, we moved into other exercises dealing with pantomime, improvisation, concentration, imagination, play analysis, and characterization.

The exercises are not intended as an end in themselves. They are a means of uniting exterior physical actions with the actor's sensibilities—interior impulses and feelings. Responses are never convincing if you attempt to *will* yourself to laugh or cry. Joy or sadness must come from within. Physical expressions for feelings are derived from analysis of the character and through the use of improvisation and emotional recall. These are immediate and direct means of "feeling the part."

Author Norman Mailer believes that

> *actors, particularly stage actors, are very literal people. It's very important to them whether the salt shaker is here, or here. After all, a stage actor is a man or woman who is, if you will, the president of an emotional factory which has to produce the same product at the same minute every night. And so, they attach all sorts of conditioned reflexes in the gearing of their emotions to the placement of objects. They may pretend that they want motivation, a reason to pick up a salt shaker. But the fact of the matter is that the only way you can produce a certain emotion at a certain hour every night and do it without killing yourself is to set up a whole series of conditioned reflexes. Therefore, just as a dog salivates when he hears a bell ring, so the actor begins to weep when he reaches for the salt shaker.*[1]

There are machines today that store facts and reach decisions based on those facts. We have some machines that "think" and others with a built-in "will," but to date we have no machine that "feels." Actors who cannot feel are machines. They cannot move an audience because they lack the human touch to interpret characters

[1]From Joseph Gelmis, *The Film Director as Superstar* (Garden City, N.Y.: Doubleday, 1970), pp. 45–46.

to an audience. This *Einfühlung*, or "feeling into," allows actors an instant bond with the audience. They certainly cannot transmit emotion to others unless they have experienced that emotion themselves. How is this done? How can an actor convey the feelings of a murderer when he has never murdered? Thornton Wilder answers in this way: "We have all murdered, in our thoughts, or been murdered. We have all seen the ridiculous in estimable persons, and ourselves. We have all known terror, as well as enchantment."[2]

CREATION AND RE-CREATION

Few laymen have any idea how professional actors condition themselves to play a role. While watching a play, the highest praise seems to be that actors are "feeling the part"; otherwise the critics say the actors are "insincere." The fact is that if actors feel the part at every performance, they will have no control over the elaborate and complicated machinery involved during the glandular and visceral changes brought on by emotion. Once this machinery is set into motion, it is difficult to stop. Even in everyday life, after a siege of anger, grief, or fear, we need a cooling-off interval, time again to gain control. On stage it is even more important that actors maintain control, because others are also involved. If an entire cast on stage were feeling the part and doing nothing else, the result would be more madhouse than theatre. The paradox is that actors cannot act unless they feel; but if they really feel, they cannot act.

Because this true paradox has been so controversial and remains confusing to many beginners and even to some professionals, I cannot stress often enough that *the time for actors to feel the part is when they study and rehearse.* They can show raw emotion and be critical because when there is no pressure, raw emotion can then be adapted, designed, and *selected*. Only this process makes acting an art.

Emotion makes no sharp boundary between the true and the untrue. We all remember Pavlov's experiments with dogs. He rang a bell each time the dogs were fed, and they learned to associate the sound of the bell with food. When they were sufficiently conditioned, he rang the bell, and the dogs reacted automatically: Saliva flowed, even though the food was not there. Were the dogs insincere?

In the creative acting process we must learn to use the three aspects of psychological life: thought, will, and emotion. We think out our problem, reach some decision, and, by force of will, reexcite emotion; then we select the response that is appropriate. Later, before the audience, the previously arranged synthesis or conditioning

[2]Thornton Wilder, *Three Plays by Thornton Wilder* (New York: Harper & Row, 1957), preface. By permission.

will re-create the emotion. The emotion can even be made to appear spontaneous (which in fact it will be), so the entire process will be sincere, controlled, and artistically true.

Clara Morris, one of America's first celebrated actresses, wrote:

> *There are, when I am on stage, three separate currents of thought in my mind: one in which I am keenly alive to Clara Morris, to all the details of the play, and to the other actors and how they act, and to the audience; another about the play and the character I represent; and finally, the thought that really gives me stimulus for acting.*[3]

To sum up our discussions thus far on emotion, we may conclude that the ability to summon emotion depends to a large extent on the development of our imaginations: to be able to imagine a world of appearances as a real world, to see what is not before our eyes, and to feel sensations from past experiences as if they were in the present. If we can develop such an imagination, we can create emotion in ourselves and transmit it to others.

Exercise 106 **BUILDING EMOTION**

This exercise demonstrates one method of making individuals aware of their own consciousness, and how they can be used as a motivating instrument in building emotion. The exercise has three parts. Do each part consecutively, as presented below.

1. Walk in from right. Remove jacket. Look front. Walk off left.
2. Now, choose a simple motivation—one with an emotional attitude. Use your own or one of the following suggestions. Before you walk on, fill your mind with it. (But do not say it aloud.) Exclude all other thoughts. Do not plan in any way, but simply allow yourself to be influenced by the chosen motivation. Now perform the same actions as above. Walk in from right, and so on. Your movements will be affected variously. Suggestions:
   a. Wow! What a day!
   b. I just can't do it. I won't!
   c. I hope I left it on the desk.
   d. What if the night watchman sees me?
3. Proceeding as in the first two parts of this exercise, use the same motivation and the same movements. But this time plan a procedure and an inner monologue that is suggested by your motivation. Begin saying it to yourself before you walk on, and continue through to its conclusion. It will be helpful if, during your inner monologue, you recall an emotion you have personally experienced. This is one of the most direct ways of transmitting a desired emotional effect.

---

[3]Lewis C. Strang, *Plays and Players of the Last Quarter Century*, vol. 2 (Boston: L. C. Page and Co., 1903), p. 240.

This is not a pantomime. It is simply inaudible speech directing external movement. The time involved will increase depending on your inner monologue. Caution: Thoughts, as in dreams, can race through the mind. In this exercise, consciously say to yourself each word of your inner monologue so that you will allow time for the physical actions to become obvious to your audience. For example, here is an expansion of motivation d, above:

If I don't get those books fixed tonight it will be too late. Then what? Where's that watchman? All right, if he sees me, I'll just act casual; you know, get a cup of water or something, ask about his kid—it'll be fine. That sandwich I bolted down is like a rock in my stomach. My mouth is dry. My hands are wet too.

As you review the directions in this exercise, you will realize that you are, step by step, elaborating on the original concept. In other words, you are developing the impetus that will free emotion.

The Moscow Art Players developed études, as they call such invented scenes, to a fine degree. As the actor becomes accustomed to this technique, he will be able to use it without the aid of an instructor. He will consciously invent words and react to them.

In preparing a part, analyze each situation in the play with which you will be concerned, put it in simple terms, switch this information to your storehouse of memory, and let it motivate the author's requirements of your character. In rehearsals, learn to select, refine, and control. Rely on gaining insight from inside. (Have you ever asked yourself, "Now, why did I do that?" Reasons can be found in that wonderful computer we call memory.) Learn to use messages from your memory. When you have no audience, ask your director what you have conveyed to him. Use him as your sounding board.

Each day we perform certain duties almost mechanically. Take one of your chores and add your imagination to it. Create a situation with your emotions. Relax. Transfer to automatic pilot and perform the duty.

Exercise 107　**SOUNDS CAN STIMULATE EMOTIONS #1**

1. Study the texture, pitch, volume, direction, and timing of human sounds, such as those associated with fear, anger, grief, happiness, suspicion, and *davening*.[4]
2. Make tapes of different mood sounds: a waltz, a siren, a merry-go-round, etc. The group should react physically to the moods presented in any way they feel moved.

---

[4]*Davening* is that rhythmic murmur or humming sound of repeated prayer or lament, such as old women make in church or at funerals.

Exercise 108 **SOUNDS CAN STIMULATE EMOTIONS #2**

Peter Brook uses this interesting approach to kindle a sharpened
awareness to the emotional effects of sound.[5]

1. Give each actor an object he can bang on—box, can, bottle, pot,
   spoon, or stick.
2. Explore the possibilities thoroughly by banging it on the floor, on
   the knee or forehead, with another object, tap with fingers, knuckles, teeth, etc. Change the loudness, bluntness, and swiftness of
   repetition.
3. Create dialogues between two or more sounds. Change rhythms.
   Add syncopation.
4. Re-create a well-known Shakespearean scene using only the objects to beat out the rhythm of the poetic words.
   a. Ignore the object and use the body instead.
   b. Now use your voice along with the body, but not with words. Let
      the voice produce pure sounds that emanate from within, send-
      ing forth messages without using word patterns.

Acting is one of the few art forms in which the creative moment
happens in the present, before the eyes and ears of the spectator.
The actor must therefore be able to produce an effective moment at
will, and spontaneously.

Exercise 109 **SENSE REACTIONS**

React to the following words by creating a sense stimulus for each:

Smell: a bakery, a fish market, low tide, a perfume shop

Sight: a miracle, maggots, a lake, an auto wreck, a tennis game

Hearing: tapping noises, birds, traffic, sirens

Touch: rain, velvet, thumbtacks, tree bark, marble, corrugated
cardboard

Taste: bitter medicine, ice cream, metal, honey

What counts in acting is the preparation for an action. You must
consciously think about the feeling of the action before that action is
taken. Muscular coordination must be built up with the correspond-
ing sensory and emotional data. The actor's feelings control bodily

[5]At the opening of his short play *The Serpent: A Ceremony* Jean-Claude van Itallie presents a
procession, in which the cast moves through the audience making just such nonverbal sounds
as these. The procession is a kind of prologue, which sets the mood for the audience through
sound and movement only. A full description by the playwright can be found in Otis L.
Guernsey, Jr., ed., *Best Plays for 1969–70; The Burns Mantle Yearbook* (New York: Dodd, Mead,
1970), p. 235.

reactions. Rising from a chair is a physical habit; the actor needs to know the feelings that control the decision to rise.

Exercise 110   **EMOTIONAL RECALL**

Use the following words to revive feelings. (These words describe the effects to be created. The circumstances that produce the emotions are to be supplied by the actor.)

hate	love	fire	water	rejection
joy	fear	flight	cave	heat
pain	cold	surf	blind	threat

EXPRESSING CHARACTER AND EMOTION BY PHYSICAL MEANS

Let us suppose that one of your group has been assigned a part in a play, has studied the play and the character, and has discussed both with the director. The actor has decided that the essence of the character is craftiness and a distrust of others. Has anyone in the group ever seen or known someone who gave them such an impression? If so, the actor should describe the person's appearance and then try to assume the character of the person *physically*. Perhaps someone has seen an animal that left such an impression of distrust and hostility.

In demonstrating physical aspects of characters, exercises are more effective if students are limited to the visual. You may have noted that all the simple exercises have certain limits that require you to isolate a particular aspect. In the following exercise, students should not speak or walk, but should concentrate on posture, stance, attitude, and facial expression. In other words, they must limit themselves to a display of the visual symbol—the outer image of the character that will represent and reflect the inner character.

Suppose the character is old. What happens physically in the aging process? Students should not begin their thinking with clichés for showing age: the bent back, the cane, or the piping voice. Instead, think of fading vision, faulty memory, unsteady balance, waning self-confidence, the stiffening joints of arthritis, how clothes hang, and the weariness and despair evidenced in body and facial expressions. Show the outer image of such a person. Perhaps our old man or old woman has lived a very active life. Perhaps he is a former wrestler or laborer and she a pioneer woman who has borne many children, driven teams of horses, and chopped firewood. How might each look?

Richard Mennen's production of Euripedes' The Bacchae *(406 B.C.)
for Sweet Briar College placed stress on the free use of the actors'
physical attributes, as demonstrated by these two scenes. (Courtesy of Richard Mennen.)*

Exercise 111   **CHARACTER ASSIGNMENTS**

In this exercise the students must only use physical attitudes and
movements. They must *show* their characters rather than rely on spoken words. It should not be difficult if each player has carefully studied
the play and the character.

The instructor assigns one character from a well-known play to
each student, who is to read and study the play out of class, with
particular attention to the assigned role. In a later session each student will present to the group a *visual* characterization. The student
may move about, perform short mimes, but may not speak. Afterward
the student must be able to justify any movements made by quoting
lines or actions from the play. (Notes are permissible when quoting
lines or the author's description of the character.)

As an example, Sir Tyrone Guthrie directed *The Taming of the
Shrew* with Petruchio as a shy, modest character. Are there lines in
the play that might justify this concept?

Some characters from dramatic literature, novels, and life are
suggested below. Additions might be supplied by the instructor.

Falstaff: Shakespeare tells us he is fat. What else is he? How will you show it?

Lady Macbeth: How does Shakespeare describe her? What do other characters in the play say about her? Do her actions in the play tell you what sort of woman she is? How will you show that? Translate Shakespeare's words into visual concepts.

A retired economics professor: What is his age? How will his profession be indicated? His subject?

Chris: In *Anna Christie,* by Eugene O'Neill.

Marchbanks: In *Candida,* by George Bernard Shaw.

Firs: In the *Cherry Orchard,* by Chekhov.

Mosca: In *Volpone,* by Ben Jonson.

Rosencrantz: In *Rosencrantz and Guildenstern Are Dead,* by Tom Stoppard.

Millamant: In *The Way of the World,* by Congreve. For further descriptions, refer to J. L. Styan's *The Dramatic Experience* (New York: Cambridge University Press, 1965), pp. 8–9.

An old librarian: Decide her age. Has she ever been married? Is she head librarian or an assistant? What are her hobbies? How does she dress and wear her hair? Is she a reader herself? What does she read?

Emotions are more vividly created by tangible motor sources than by intellectualizing and filtering the experience through words and abstractions. Your imagination responds much more readily to the shock of physical experience—to the sensations of body, weight, energy, and motion. The recurrence of physical sensations—such as smelling a flower or hearing a sound—can revive unconscious memories of long-forgotten emotional experiences.

Exercise 112   **EMOTIONAL CONTRASTS**

A group stands around a single player, shouting personal insults. While they are in every way disagreeable, the player answers them politely and with dignity. All players should allow their bodies to explore their personal expressions. Definite objectives such as this take the actors out of themselves and into another reality. Characterizations created by emotional means are dominated by a state of mind (or a mood) and by the alignment of the character's thoughts with the dramatic moment. Each player in this group should invent private circumstances for the wrath, just as the single player will need reasons for his reactions.

Exercise 113   **TRANSFERRING EMOTION BY THOUGHT**

You are walking to class. You have just been awarded the lead in the new school play. The midterm C you had expected turned out to be an

A. The world is a beautiful place. Be calm; relax into these warm thoughts. Allow your emotions to reflect your contentment and happiness. Now a stranger is coming from another direction and your eyes meet. Transfer your emotion *by thought*. Don't use any mechanical tricks but allow your feelings to direct whatever you do. If the stranger reflects your joy, you have communicated your feelings to another.

In the beginning, you will need to practice this, depending on your individual aptitude. Once mastered, emotion can be reexcited instinctively. Only *you* can develop this individual skill.

Exercise 114   **CREATING AND SUSTAINING EMOTIONS**

Improvise action and sound, but no dialogue. It is New Year's Eve, midnight. Place: a country-club dance. Everyone is on the dance floor, noisy and uninhibited; the band is playing as the crowd celebrates. A woman enters. Her little son has just been run over. Her husband is a waiter here, and she must reach him through the crowd.

Exercise 115   **CREATING CONTRASTING EMOTIONS**

Improvise action and sound, but no dialogue. Two weary old guards stand in the foyer of a big city museum. The atmosphere is austere in deference to the museum's treasures. From outside, a tide of childish giggles and screechings can be heard. Then an entire class of seventh-graders sweeps into the foyer, like surf hitting a beach. The guards move to restrain the youngsters, but the teacher anticipates them and controls the situation. Dignity regained, the class proceeds on its tour. The old men react to the near catastrophe, then in relief settle back into routine.

Exercise 116   **CREATING EMOTIONAL REACTIONS**

Improvise action, sound, and dialogue. Actual news item: A girl is murdered on a New York street in full view of a number of people. The two assailants escape unchallenged. A policeman finally arrives and questions every individual in the crowd. Each must explain why he or she did not interfere.

Exercise 117   **SENSE IMPRESSIONS**

Before the class meets, students are to prepare themselves by experiencing a sensory emotion, using the tongue, the nose, or the ear. Students might take a taste of hot pepper or lemon. They might go to the beach at low tide, visit a candy factory to sense different smells, or listen to disturbing or calming sounds. This exercise deals with the *senses only*. These suggestions are given to stimulate your own thinking. Undergo the *actual experience!* Do not rely on memory at this time. Later, in class, these experiences are to be translated into acting terms. *Memory* will then be used in class—*without the benefit of the stimuli.* The process is something like this:

1. Actual sensory experience *with* stimulus. (Taste the lemon.)
2. Observation of emotional and physical reactions. (How did you feel when you tasted the lemon? How did the experience affect you physically? Emotionally?)
3. Rehearse by re-creating your reaction from memory. Select, refine and clarify, then present the learned behavior to the class. At that time, the actual experience should be relived.

Caution: In attempting to reproduce an emotion, a common fault of beginners is in forcing themselves to feel. Sheer effort only defeats the purpose. The mind and body become tense and restricted. Begin with relaxation.

Exercise 118 **MEMORY RECALL**

Each student is to concentrate on a sensation, such as anxiety, pain, cold, heat, fatigue, pleasure, boredom, anticipation, hunger, or fear. Begin by recalling some time in your life when you actually experienced this emotion. Sit relaxed in a chair and begin telling the class about it. Describe the time and place, the clothes you wore and how they felt, your mental state, the color of the room. No detail should be left out, no matter how insignificant it may seem. As you begin seeing it all again in your mind's eye, allow your relaxed body to feel the emotions again just as it happened before. You have begun with narration. Now allow the emotion to take over, and gradually shift from past to present tense. It is happening now! Allow this to activate what you are now bringing out of your memory storehouse. Although body involvement may only be slight, the important thing is to go through the motions. As the memory and the body begin to work together, you should actually reexperience the emotion by a kind of subliminal guidance.

Exercise 119 **EMOTIONAL REACTIONS**

In this exercise, improvise physical actions only. Imagine you are spending the night in a haunted house. You do not believe in the supernatural but you are aroused by a knocking sound, faint at first but becoming louder. Next, you hear footsteps approaching and feel a chill in the air. Show your reactions, being careful not to use any clichés.

Tears

A difficulty often encountered is the inability to release ourselves from the self-restraint conditioned since childhood. Parents often shame youngsters when they cry, telling them it is not "grown up." When the children do grow up, they have a firm association in their minds between tears and shame.

Exercise 120 **TEARS**

A child's tears may be the result of actual pain, or a means of getting what he or she wants. Tears can also be the result of some disappointment, such as not getting what the child wants. Some stimuli that cause tears are: pain, desire, loss, sorrow, offense, injustice, anger, jealousy, hatred, and envy.

Search back in your memory, and remember when you once cried. Recall all the details of the circumstance. Follow the points carefully, as outlined in the exercise on memory recall, and try producing tears.

To produce the feeling for tears, remove that taint of shame from your mind and don't be concerned with how you look. Put yourself into the position of your character and the circumstances of the play. Call upon your emotional memory and your observation of people in similar situations. Think of what once made you cry. Then relax, concentrate, and give those emotions deep within you a chance to rise to the surface.

Maureen Stapleton quotes director Bobby Lewis as saying, "If crying were acting, my Aunt Rifke would be Duse." But Maureen feels that, "All you have to do to cry is set up the stimulus that will trigger the mechanism, and off you go. Laughing is much more difficult. On the whole, it's very hard to do a true laugh—a real laugh is so real you have no control over it."[6]

Laughter

Max Eastman holds that "the mechanism of comic laughter may never be explained." Others have said that we laugh because we don't want to cry. There is extensive literature on the subject, but there are no solutions as to how to produce laughter at will, because it cannot be self-willed and still ring true. We cannot dissect it, and there are no mechanical formulas for producing it. We must be content to know what it is, what causes it, and where it starts. Josh Billings said, "Laughing is feeling good all over but showing it in one spot." Although laughter is exclusive with man, Eastman tells us, "Dogs can laugh—but only with their tails."

Psychologists view laughter as a defensive weapon, as if giving proof that the great are not so great, or as a means of forestalling the other fellow's ridicule of us. Laughter is not an inborn instinct. We must learn to laugh, just as we learn to walk and talk. But it becomes a personal part of us. No police state can ever suppress laughter.

According to Aristotle, the ludicrous is "some defect or ugliness which is not painful or destructive." To understand this, we have only to remember that a baby's first laugh is apt to be stimulated by a momentary fear, then joy at the removal of that fear. A jack-in-the-box, the hunchback Punch of Punch and Judy, false faces, and lovable monsters, all follow Aristotle's theory.

Laughter cannot be accepted automatically as a sign of amusement. It may express wonder, embarrassment, or discomfiture. It

[6]© 1962 Lillian Ross. From *The Player, A Profile of an Art*, by Lillian Ross and Helen Ross, Simon and Schuster. Originally published in *The New Yorker*.

can be used as a weapon. We laugh at anything new. It can be used as an instrument for debunking. And when we laugh at a teacher's poor jokes, we do so for reasons other than amusement. It has been said that laughter can kill, and perhaps it can. One thing is certain; laughter likes society. Performers know that laughs are better when the house is full. We are not apt to laugh when we overhear a joke in a restaurant because we do not belong to the particular group enjoying it.

In summary, laughing expresses the emotions of joy or happiness, or it conceals other emotions, such as anger, shyness, derision, or contempt. We can conclude that laughter and tears both result from emotion coming from within. If you can re-create emotion, you can laugh.

CHARACTERIZATION IN THE NEWER PLAYS

In the so-called Absurd plays coming out of Europe and in today's nonstructured plays being written for Off and off-off Broadway, many innovations in play writing have been made.[7] There is typically a lack of a sequential build in a play; scenes are seldom cumulative. Whatever thread of story there is will often be shown in isolated, unrelated incidents and then left for the audience to develop as it will. The playwright disregards explanations of what has happened to the characters prior to the play. Changing elements of time and place are introduced, as well as scenes of ritual, camp, or vaudeville.

In the Absurd plays, characters are more or less abstract and expressionistic. They seem to undergo little or no personal development. Frequently, they exist in an Orwellian void, as in the plays by Samuel Beckett and Eugene Ionesco.

Characters in a typical off-off Broadway play are often one dimensional, as in *America Hurrah!* or *Gorilla Queen*. Referring to Jules Feiffer's plays, critic John Lahr says:

> *Characters have an immense intellectual resonance, but not necessarily a theatrical one. Performers find his plays difficult because they must perform in a strict and often ambiguous circumference of gestures and emotions. The characters do not offer the actors a chance for emotional self-revelation. Feiffer's people, like Jonson's Lovewits and Congreve's Witwoulds, become an articulate amalgam of general attitudes focused in a particular man.*[8]

The sensibility of a player confronted with such one-dimensional, intellectually conceived characters requires exquisite distillation of the larger concepts. The ability to call up an emotion is not enough. The emotional essence must be swiftly portrayed. Such deep, sure,

---

[7]A full explanation of the distinction between Off Broadway and off-off Broadway plays may be found on page 348 in the paragraph on experimental theatre in America.

[8]John Lahr, *Up Against the Fourth Wall* (New York: Grove Press, 1968), p. 81.

and complete emotional revelation tends to trigger intellectual recognition in the audience. This then carries forward, devising its own
reasons and explanations for the situations provided. A player must
be highly skilled in the ability to summon sensibility and emotion
quickly, and to use them with facility and purpose. While it would
seem that some of the characters in the newer plays have been purposefully drawn in a minimal way, players who can furnish added
sensibility will create living theatre from the printed page.

The characters in Samuel Beckett's *Waiting for Godot* offer many
opportunities to display complicated facets within a single interpretation. This is not to say that players should in any way interfere
with the playwright's overall objective. Rather, players must be
especially sensitive to the way that objective relates to the characters.

TRANSFORMATIONS

One of the techniques used in some of the newer plays has been
titled *transformations*. The term is used to describe shifting characterizations. Highly developed sensibility is required to play these
multifaceted parts. Each character has many different facets of
character within him, one being dominant and the most obvious. In
real life, we present this dominant image, or face, to the world. But
underneath are other faces that may burst through the skin of the
main identity at any time, revealing contradictions or complexities.
This process is unlike the dual roles in hundreds of plays from
Shakespeare to Bertolt Brecht to Jean Genet, in which one character
pretends to be another. In the experimental plays, split personalities
attempt to explore the many different personalities within one personality. The stated objective is that a continuity of progression will
occur because the same actor displays the various facets of a character.

It is a difficult acting job to make transformations convincing. Not
only is the actor required to assume several characters without previously preparing the audience, but he must be convincing in each.
Actors should not attempt any Stanislavskian psychological motivations, but should make these transformations only through physical
manifestations. The changes must be made abruptly; the number of
characters within the role each actor must create is hardly conducive
to penetration of any single role. If an actor switches from being a
condemned prisoner, to being his mother, and then to General Custer, the audience can be completely baffled.[9] This would be the case
unless that actor is sensitive and skilled in portraying various facets
of a single character, while still maintaining its basic traits.

[9]*Comings and Goings* by Megan Terry is a charming playlet written especially as a theatre
game or as a straight transformation play. It is included in the book *Viet Rock and Other Plays*
(New York: Simon and Schuster, 1967).

Exercise 121 **TRANSFORMATIONS #1**

Explore a many-faceted character by first performing a single character improvisation using established realities (given circumstances). Next devise another improvisation in which several different aspects of that same character are shown simultaneously. (See the excerpt from "Interview" by Jean-Claude van Itallie on page 353).

Exercise 122 **TRANSFORMATIONS #2 (GROUP)**

This exercise is for several actors. One student begins a narrative (such as where he was and what he was doing when the astronauts landed on the moon) using *first person narrative.* At a signal from the instructor another actor takes over, who must remember all the details established, but must elaborate on the story, keeping it in first person narrative.

FURTHER READING: SENSIBILITY AND EMOTION

(See also the "Additional Reading" list at the end of the book under *Acting*).

Chekhov, Michael. *To the Actor on the Technique of Acting.* New York: Harper & Row, 1953.

Cohen, Robert. *Acting Power.* Palo Alto, Calif.: Mayfield, 1978.

Hagen, Uta, with Frankel, Haskel. *Respect for Acting.* New York: Macmillan, 1973.

Ghiselin, Brewster, ed. *The Creative Process.* Berkeley: University of California Press, 1954; Mentor Books, 1955.

Marowitz, Charles. *Stanislavski and the Method.* New York: Citadel Press, 1964.

Schechner, Richard. "Introduction: The Playwright as Wrighter." In Megan Terry, *Viet Rock and Other Plays.* New York: Simon and Schuster, 1967. This deals with "transformations."

Stanislavski, Constantin. *An Actor Prepares.* Translated by Elizabeth Reynolds Hapgood. New York: Theatre Arts Books, 1933.

Wilson, Garff B. "Emotionalism in Acting." *Quarterly Journal of Speech,* February 1956, pp. 45–54.

Woodbury, Lael J. "The Externalization of Emotion." *Educational Theatre Journal,* October 1960, pp. 177–83.

Part II
STYLES IN ACTING

9
THE CHARACTER
AND ACTING STYLES

I think that classical plays require more imagination and more general training to be able to do. That's why I like playing Shakespeare better than anything else; because I think he wrote the greatest plays for people, and I think they require more to be brought to them. And I think one learns more through acting in classical plays than one does in anything else.*

Vivien Leigh
Academy Award Best Actress
1939 (for *Gone with the Wind)*

*From Lewis Funke and John E. Booth, *Actors Talk about Acting,* Random House, 1961, p. 239. Reprinted by permission of Random House.

Thornton Wilder has said, "Every masterpiece was created this morning." There are plays dealing with elements so externally human that they transcend their own time. Such a play is called a classic, and it deserves to be placed alongside a Beethoven symphony, a Rembrandt painting, a Gothic cathedral, or a Michelangelo sculpture. Such great art brings an entire age into sharp focus. Contrast the austere simplicity of Greek architecture with the elaborate and lacy detail of Gothic churches. We learn much about a civilization when we study its art.

When we experience the theatre of a people, we become involved in their emotional, spiritual, and physical concerns. An Elizabethan play, staged with its originial excitement, makes us almost taste Falstaff's "pint of sack," feel the cobblestones underfoot, smell the streets and the marketplaces, and hear the pipes and the *hautboys*.[1] When we see a play by Richard Sheridan, we get a sense of the eighteenth-century man. We almost share his love of brocade and silk on the skin; we hear the harpischord and keep time to the stately minuet. In short, a play reaches us through our senses as well as our intellect, and can express more of an age than a dozen history books. The ever-present question is not whether theatre is contemporary or traditional, but whether it will be absorbing to an audience.

IMPORTANCE OF GREAT PLAYS

It has been said that the purpose of drama is to show man struggling with the problems of being alive. Most great plays do indeed deal with conflict between man and himself, his god, or other men. Hidden beneath these conflicts are specifics that must be explored by the actor. To the actor it matters a great deal who this person is who

---

[1]*Hautboys* are oboes.

grapples with life. The person may be a king of Thebes, a drug addict, or a perfumed elegant. Into what sort of world has the king been placed? Is the drug addict in America or in an oriental civilization that tolerates rather than censures the addiction? The perfumed elegant could blend easily into the eighteenth century, but in Russia during the revolution he would be completely out of place. When we act in the plays of another time, we must understand how the people thought and felt.

Sir Michael Redgrave has said there is a style for Shakespeare and a style for Chekhov. A play is created out of a need of a people, and reflects the hopes, desires, and attitudes of that people. This need is ever-changing, ever in a state of flux, as people themselves change. A dramatic masterpiece isolated from its time is not easily understood by present-day audiences unless those responsible for its production have prepared themselves with a knowledge of the period and style in which it originated. Only in this way will the urgency and force of first life be restored to it. It is not enough to imitate physical components, such as an Elizabethan stage or Greek costumes. We must understand the people of that time, and their social and economic goals. We should also be aware of the conditions under which the actors worked and the standards of acting they set for themselves. Knowledge of this kind can but add richness and texture to a performance.

AN ACTING METHOD FOR EACH PLAY

If we transplant a play from its native earth, we must take some of that earth with it, or the play will never flower. And each play has a climate in which it lives, part of which is the style for acting it. If the play is to be properly presented, this climate or atmosphere must be transmitted to the audience.

If theatregoers fail to support a particular type of play, then it is replaced by plays they will support. Historically the avant-garde plays have been resisted by audiences. Time must often pass between the vision of the playwright and acceptance by audiences.

At left, Trojan Women, *and at right,* The Taming of the Shrew, *performed by the Indiana Theatre Company. (Courtesy of Richard Mennen.)*

During that passage of time, a culling out process occurs. Drama that is supported by audiences will contain both the socially accepted views of its time and the style of presentation of the era for which it has been written. Often some levels of society will accept or reject innovation before others. But the passage of time settles any disputes. Our own contemporary drama has yet to achieve a final historical place. Meanwhile, today's actors and actresses must find ways to communicate what is presently being produced.

When it became obvious that audiences wanted plays of realism, then actors found a method to suit. The heroic method of the Greek actor is wrong for Chekhov, just as the realist style of acting is wrong for *Medea*. Suppose an actress is called upon to play Shakespeare's *Cleopatra*; she would approach this part in an entirely different way than she would Shaw's *Cleopatra*. Why? Both are Cleopatra. Let us also suppose that our actress is interested in history and believes she knows the "real" Cleopatra. If she tries to get this into her portrayal, she only adds inconsequentials. It would make no sense artistically. But to create a Cleopatra within the context of the given play and to act it in the style of that play makes for harmony and a complete artistic design.

TODAY'S FASHIONS IN ACTING

Forty years ago, acting students were taught according to individual teachers' interpretations of the Stanislavski system. In time, such students become teachers, and taught their versions of "the Method." This resulted in actors who placed excessive stress on psychological realism and truth. But then came the revolution! Today's young and imaginative directors and playwrights no longer submit to the confinements of realism, with its box sets and kitchen sinks.

The new plays are no longer exclusively realistic. Some are not even tightly structured as plays, but are inspired by improvisations and theatre games. Language is less authentic than it is imaginative. In addition to plays of the existential-absurdist school, there is a definite interest in the production of classical and semiclassical dramas.

The dilemma of the actor trained exclusively in psychological realism is that his body and speech are not sufficiently developed to cope with the sheer physical challenges of today's theatre. And so, most of the old guard "methodists" now find themselves in films, where the confinement of the camera and the proximity of the mike diminish the necessity for certain voice skills and physical coordination.

One of England's most esteemed actresses, Dame Edith Evans, has observed:

There are too many actors today and they don't speak up. They won't take advice either. . . . There is no discipline today. Kids are snapped up for the telly and films as soon as they learn to stand up straight. They have no training and many of them go to psychiatrists. . . . It's over here [in America] that you do that sort of thing, where you have so many Method actors. There are a frightful lot of chi-chi classes in the Method, but it's such bunk. To me there is only good acting and bad acting. [2]

Acting instructors are now confronting the fundamental problems of working with the body and voice. There is a concerted effort to find means of training young actors who will be capable of playing the outsized roles found in the classics and in the imaginative dramas being presented for a new generation. This methodology must include the training of supple, receptive bodies and voices, with power and range. These are the actor's chief tools, and have been so considered by all great actors since Aeschylus.

IMPORTANCE OF DIFFERENT STYLES IN ACTING

Today an actor is required to know many different styles of acting. Theatre has become decentralized. All over the United States there are permanent and successful companies that have developed their own discriminating audiences. These audiences demand a more varied theatrical fare than when New York audiences alone called the tune. A beginner's first job may be in Florida playing Genet or in Minneapolis playing Shakespeare. And he cannot approach work on either of these as he would approach Ibsen. A recent survey of theatres, even in New York, revealed that current productions included plays by van Itallie, Ibsen, Molière, Shaw, Genet, Albee, Chekhov, Shakespeare, Euripides, and O'Neill—a sampling of twenty-five centuries of theatrical history.

You are going to become familiar with various acting styles: first by learning something of the times in which they flourished, why they are what they are; and then by working in actual classics from different periods, to acquire personal experience in a variety of styles. The great historical plays contain universal human experiences, illusions, myths, and truths that make them just as valid today as they were in previous generations. But there is always a disparity between truth and form; these we must leave for the actor to homogenize.

Six-time Oscar nominee Arthur Kennedy has said:

To me, when they speak of the range of an actor, it doesn't mean to play a Mexican peasant or an older or a younger man. It means to play different styles. The problem facing American actors today is the lack of experience to play these styles. This kind of training, with few exceptions, does not exist. [3]

Arthur Kennedy. (Photo courtesy of Phil Gersh Agency.)

[2]Rex Reed, *Do You Sleep in the Nude?* (New York: New American Library, 1968), p. 139. Interview with Dame Edith Evans. Appeared in Chicago-Tribune Syndicate. Reprinted by permission of the author.

[3]By permission of Arthur Kennedy.

But *style*, when applied to an individual actor, is an entirely different matter. When we speak of the styles of John Gielgud or Ralph Richardson, we are referring to a distinctive quality they possess, which enables them to project their particular personalities to an audience. There is also a difference between the exploitation of a personality and an individual style. Laurence Olivier has style, but it is always *in the part*. *Style* is form and finish in an actor, a kind of precision, ease, and confidence, along with the quality Walter Huston called "intention." It is manner without mannerisms. It is a quality always admired—in a thoroughbred horse, an Olympic champion, or in an actor.

But a *style of acting* entails an approach to a play through study of the particular period that gave it birth. It refers to any device or process that creatively reflects the mode of a play's genesis. It can supply depth, authority, and authenticity to portrayals and production—a sense of being in the right time and the right place. Martin Esslin has said,

> *Every age has a common aspect which makes the most divergent elements of the epoch instantly recognizable as stemming from it: A baroque Jesuit may have been at daggers drawn against a baroque Protestant or a baroque freethinker; yet their style, their mode of thinking, their whole attitude, will be instantly recognizable to us as having a common basis.* [4]

When he is performing, an actor's attitude and state of mind is always obvious to an audience. It is a part of the created empathy. In our context, style is a means for the actor to become imbued in the atmosphere and mood of a particular play so that he can provide a framework for his creative ideas and concepts. A spectator can "tune in" to a style remote from his own time, exactly as he can tune in to a painting that represents a life-style or period different from his own.

Ever since a Polish author named Jan Kott wrote *Shakespeare Our Contemporary*, we have been deluged with productions ostensibly dedicated to bringing Shakespeare "closer to the people" by making his plays "relevant." Poor Shakespeare, who has been bowdlerized, vulgarized, and bastardized for three centuries. Shades of Naham Tate! [5] I will describe only one of the adaptations inspired by Mr. Kott, who cannot read Shakespeare in English. The play was Shakespeare's *Henry V*, and this production erected considerable obstacles between the play and the audience. The stage was a jungle gym, cluttered with jump ropes, pipes, and swings. The players were literally players—clapping, shouting, and chasing each other through the pipes. Canterbury and Ely were rag-doll clowns. The avowed

[4]Martin Esslin, *Brief Chronicles, Essays on Modern Theatre* (London: Temple Smith, 1970), p. 238.

[5]Naham Tate (1652–1715) was an English poet laureate, whose name is connected with a long series of mangled versions of Shakespeare's plays.

intent was, of course, to open up the play to a contemporary audience. Instead, the lines were muffled between shenanigans and were completely lost. Such concepts seem to be a flat denial of the original intent, and appear to be an apology for attempting Shakespeare at all. I once described one of these gimmick-ridden productions of *Hamlet* to my old friend B. Iden Payne.[6] When I had finished, Iden sighed and quietly remarked, "What a pity. . . . It's such a *good* play."

Another serious fault is to force the classics, especially Shakespeare, into our modern speech idiom. Attempts to sound natural by breaking up the formal style only muddle the clarity of the language. A speech, such as "The ages of man . . . ," is not born on the spur of the moment.

To reorient themselves, to become saturated in the intellectual and psychological attitudes of a day far different from their own, is not easy for contemporary actors. They must, like Alice, step through the looking glass into an entirely different world. But it is a rewarding venture. Those who can act in the classics find that great dramatic literature feeds and nourishes them. The classics give actors fluidity, grace, and variety, and redouble their faith in their abilities.

In order to concentrate on one particular style of acting at a time, we apply ourselves to periods of history that have stamped their own characteristics on acting. But, just as they do now, different acting styles frequently coexisted in the same period. The popular and accepted style of the eighteenth century was romantic, flamboyant, and recitative. But pioneers such as David Garrick, Talma, and "the Siddons" were calling attention to themselves by a more naturalistic method.[7] Today, now that realism is old and tired, we find interest in the acting school of the avant-garde and in Brecht's alienation theories of acting. There is also a revived demand for the style of acting required for the classics. We shall consider all these acting methods in chronological order, beginning with civilization's first acting style—that of the Greeks.

USE OF SHORT SCENES

Our rich legacy of classical dramatic literature is sometimes neglected. In hopes of spotlighting the richness of classical theatre, excerpts have been chosen from many plays that have outlived the authors who wrote them, the public for which they were written, and will most probably survive all of us. These plays are the very foundation of living and perpetual theatre.

---

[6]Ben Iden Payne will be remembered as an eminent director of Shakespeare.

[7]Francois Joseph Talma (1763–1826) was a great French actor. Further discussion of Sarah Kemble Siddons and William Siddons can be found in chapter 16.

Classical drama cannot be appreciated by merely reading the printed page, any more than a symphony can be appreciated by reading its score. The missing, basic factor is the interpretative, creative magic of the actor, which turns words into humanity. *Oedipus*, *Macbeth*, and *Tartuffe* were not written to be read, but to be acted as living theatre.

Whenever possible, the "obligatory scene" (as it was once called) has been used; that is, the moment when the conflicting forces of the play clash—the climax or turning point of the entire drama. There can be no pretense that a short scene is a substitute for the complete play. However, by actual physical involvement with a scene, the student will, to some extent, experience the taste and feeling of the whole play. These excerpts are offered merely as samples to encourage the student into further exploration of dramatic literature. If only a minority of young people using this book are so stimulated, then the inclusion of these plays will have served a worthy purpose.

The criteria used in the selection of these scenes are that (1) they are suitable for young student-actors, (2) they illustrate points about acting and style, (3) they stimulate further exploration into the classics, and (4) they are effective and rewarding—that is, they give students a sense of accomplishment, so they will feel they have exerted time and effort on worthwhile material that will become part of their cultural education.

It is of the utmost importance that the play representing each style be read in its entirety before attempts are made to perform the chosen excerpt. The intent of each scene and the motivations of the characters depend on total and thorough analysis.

STAGING THE SCENES

All of these scenes can be performed in an ordinary room. It would be preferable to have a stage or platform, if possible, but even this is not necessary. There are only four vital elements—actors, a play, a director, and an audience (in this case, the class). You do not need lights, curtains, scenery, furniture, or props. You will need some chairs, a table, and a few wooden boxes to represent steps, rocks, and boundaries. The boundaries of the working space should be defined (either by chalk or tape) so that the actors learn how best to use their playing space. By use of these makeshift materials you will actually be duplicating the appurtenances of a professional rehearsal. When props are indicated, but are not available (for example, the tea service in *The Importance of Being Earnest*, or the double door in *Tartuffe*), this will stimulate an interesting problem in pantomime for the students. It will be their task to convey the identities of such objects to the spectators by use of their imaginations.

Characters should not be visible before entrances are indicated.

If this is impossible because of the confinements of the room, actors should stand with their backs to the audience until they are required in the scene.

Full costumes are unnecessary, but the instructor should be satisfied that carriage, movement, and manners coincide with the play and the period. Costume and fashion are so closely linked with the acting style of a period that it will often be necessary to imagine the clothing during rehearsal, or even to wear a makeshift rehearsal costume until dress parade or dress rehearsal.[8]

These rehearsals will give students practice in the interpretation, characterization, and creation of atmosphere necessary to portray people in dramatic situations. It is only when we understand the psychology of a character and the aesthetics of each type of play that we can, with intelligence and emotion, be prepared for acting problems. The preliminary study and notes for each exercise are planned to make the acting more satisfying and enjoyable. Your performance will reveal whatever thought, research, and study you put into a characterization.

The marginal notations suggest movements and motivations. They should be accepted merely as one way to stage the scene, and by no means the only way. You will have your own ideas, of course. Perhaps the notes will help stimulate your thinking into creative channels, even if only to disagree.

On the pages devoted to "preparation" we will explore some particulars of each play: the locale, the time; and the economic, social, and cultural status of the characters. The "atmosphere" is created in part by director, costume designer, set designer, and electrician, but, most importantly, it must be imbedded into each characterization. Before speaking a word, actors must know what constitutes the emotional tone, spirit, or individual aura of each play they perform.

Where does the province of the director end and the work of the actor begin? We must explore the relationship between the two along with the play. All directors should know the language and problems of the actor, and the actor must become familiar with the responsibilities of the director.

FURTHER READING: THE CHARACTER AND ACTING STYLES

For more specific references see the "Further Reading" lists following the chapters dealing with particular periods, styles, and playwrights. The list below should provide good basic reference sources for all of part II.

---

[8]*Dress parade* occurs once all costumes are ready to be worn by actors playing the parts. It is an actual parade across a stage so that director, costumer, and all others concerned can inspect for perfection, wearability, lighting effects, and so on.

Acting History

Duerr, Edwin. *The Length and Depth of Acting.* New York: Holt, Rinehart & Winston, 1962. An excellent and comprehensive history of the actor's art and craft from the beginnings to the mid-twentieth century. Also includes an extensive bibliography of primary and secondary source writings on acting in various periods.

Manners and Movement

Chisman, Isabel, and Raven-Hart, Hester E. *Manners and Movements in Costume Plays.* London: Kenyon-Deane Ltd.; Boston: Walter H. Baker, n.d. A short but informative book that includes manners, ceremonial amenities, weapons, dances, and more specific source references for particular problems.

Crawford, Jerry L., and Snyder, Joan. *Acting in Person and in Style.* Dubuque, Iowa: Wm. C. Brown, 1976. Contains a few errors in names and dates, but has some good approaches to various period styles.

Oxenford, Lynn. *Playing Period Plays.* Chicago: Coach House Press, 1974. The title speaks for itself. A good basic reference.

Playwrights

Gassner, John. *Masters of the Drama.* 3d ed. New York: Dover, 1954. Still the best basic reference work on playwrights from the Greeks to the mid-twentieth century.

Theatre History

Brockett, Oscar G. *History of the Theatre.* 3d ed. Boston: Allyn and Bacon, 1977. If you own only one theatre history book, it should be this one. It covers plays, playwrights, and physical theatre. It also contains an excellent and extensive bibliography.

10
GREEK DRAMA

We have less information on the Greek theatre than we have on any other. One indispensable document is Aristotle's *Poetics*, but this deals mostly with the theory of drama and literary criticism. Fortunately, we can learn from the paintings and sculpture of the time; some works of art even depict actors at work. We also have some Greek plays—thirty-three tragedies, eleven comedies—out of at least two thousand plays of superior quality that we know were written and produced in Athens between 480 and 380 B.C., when the population was no more than forty thousand citizens.

We also have the ruins of their theatres to convince us that only the broadest gestures and the fullest voices would have been practical. When working on the proscenium stage, gestures and movements may be intimate. However, anyone who has worked "in the round" knows that here broader actions are required. This gives us at least some idea of the great freedom and style practiced by the Greek actors.

The tradition of the actor-playwright-director began with the Greeks. Of the three immortals—Aeschylus, Sophocles, and Euripides—only Euripides did not act, but he did direct. It is interesting that all three were at one time associated with the priesthood, for that is where the profession of acting began.

ORIGINS

Even before the Greeks, primitive man depended on the actor-priest to create a sympathetic association between man and nature, by assuming the spirits of gods, animals, and natural forces. By acting out a visit of the rain god to a tribe, he caused them to believe that a visit from the real god would take place. The actor-priest, or medicine man, subsequently began enlarging his repertoire of characters. By assuming the spirit of a dead patriarch or an ancestor of the tribe, he created the first hero, and enacted the life struggles of that hero and the hero's dramatic encounter with death. *Oedipus* and *Medea* are

During the annual festival of Epidaurus, this ancient Greek amphitheatre is used to revive the great classics. (Courtesy of the Greek National Tourist Office.)

related to such reenactments. Animal and human sacrifices are part of the transference of life or the spirit from one individual to another. From its beginnings, acting has always been associated with spirit transference, magic, ritual, and mystery.

ACTORS OF ANCIENT GREECE

Greek actors began as amateurs, but gradually developed into highly trained professionals. At the height of their glory they had their own "Actor's Equity," with set rules controlling wages and conditions. They were exempt from military duty. One of the leading actors, Polus, received the equivalent of twelve hundred dollars for two days' performances—that's a professional! Even today, American theatre is not subsidized by the state, as was the Greeks'. Nor are our actors held in such respect—and accorded an almost religious deference. We must remember that in those times religion and theatre were very close. We can get a feeling for the Greek theatre by attending a Christmas or Easter ceremony of the high church, with its chants, choir, processions, costumes, symbolism, and stylized actions.

Greek audiences had high standards for acting. They considered the actor Aeschines so bad that they actually stoned him out of the business. Like Shakespeare's audience, the Greeks appreciated great plays as well as good acting. People from all walks of life were devoted to theatre. The great Greek plays were rich in drama, conflict, and profound characterizations.

Greek actors are known to have developed an unbelievable range in voice. They had special instructors in mime, dance, and gesture. During performances, the Greek actors were weighted down with

A modern revival of a Greek classic in an ancient amphitheatre. (Courtesy of the Greek National Tourist Office.)

heavy trappings; but because of their exhaustive training, they moved with grace and ease.

In our day of the confidential actor,[1] it is difficult for us to realize that all through the history of acting the voice was considered the actor's greatest asset. The Greek actor trained constantly with voice specialists. Supporting actors were also expected to sing as well as dance. In the course of a regular performance, an actor was required to be efficient in three types of voice production:

iambic trimeter: declamatory style with particular emphasis on enunciation

recitative: intoned with a musical accompaniment

lyrical: the song proper, written as a solo, duet, trio, or chorus

In addition, the actor was obliged to have at his command an entire catalogue of conventionalized movements—a complete repertoire of coordinations in body, voice, and gesture.

This was a theatre of the star system. The leading part was played by the chief actor, who was often the director and manager, as well. A play was said to be "done by" him. Oedipus, Electra, Medea, Antigone, male or female, he played all the roles. Another actor played the chief supporting roles. A utility actor (with a bass voice) would play passionate heralds, dignified kings, etc. All three might interchange parts, having a complete knowledge of the entire play, the verses, the dances, and the formalized gestures.

The sincerity of these actors is demonstrated by an incident involving the actor Polus. In his portrayal of Electra, he used the actual ashes of his own dead son, so that he might express the character's grief over Electra's dead brother's ashes. Here we have an actor in a period before Christ using the association method.

The acting style of the Greeks was vast in scope, larger than life, and formal in speech and gesture. Greek actors were never required to play a Willy Loman.[2] Such a suggestion would have been contemptible to them. They played hero-kings, even gods. Greek actors were esteemed, not only as artists, but as leaders of the community. With the decline of Greek civilization, the status of the actor sank to the level of a vagabond, and was not restored until much later. Even today it is questionable if actors have the venerated status of the ancient actors, in spite of the knighting of many English actors.

Judith Anderson and Henry Brandon as Medea and Jason in Euripedes' Medea, *produced by the U.S. National Touring Company, 1948–49.*

Exercise 123 **EMOTION IN SCULPTURE**

Study the art books in your library or, if possible, visit your museum and study the statues. Try to find the particular emotion the sculptor

---

[1]The *confidential actor* is a theatrical reference to today's actor, who depends on microphones and mechanical means for being heard. Now an actor can "whisper in confidence" into a mike in film, or on radio, television, and even the stage.

[2]Willy Loman is the chief character in Arthur Miller's *Death of a Salesman.*

sought to express. Was it dignity, fear, grief? Study how these artists gave grace to the human figure by the balance of weight, by the drape of a costume. You can learn much from these art masterpieces.

COSTUMES

Unlike the ordinary Athenian citizens, who did not cover their arms in the day-to-day business of life, the tragic actors wore ornamented costumes with long sleeves to give grace and flow to their gestures. These garments were usually striped or embroidered perpendicularly, and brilliantly colored. Think of this vivid coloring as you consider the statuesque image of the Greek actors. They were imposing, graceful, and beautiful, but not colorless like a marble statue. There was nothing cold about the Greek actor. Overgarments of saffron and purple often completed a wardrobe.

Members of the chorus were uniformly dressed, according to the characters they represented, whether old men, maidens, or women of the city. They wore sandals or were barefooted, as they had a great deal of dancing to do. Most scholars agree that leading actors wore thick-soled boots (*cothurni*). This footgear was very much like the boots worn by Chinese actors in ancient times and today. The high headdress (*onkus*) worn above the mask also added to the illusion of height. The long lines of the costumes, ornaments, mask, body padding, cothurnus, and onkus made the Greek heroic actors awesome and commanding figures.

MASKS

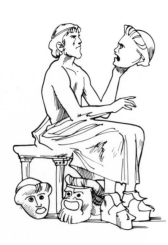

Often made of wood or cork, Greek masks were not designed to fit the face, but were placed over the head. Domed at the crown, they were intended in all details to further the impression of height. Some believe that the open mouth served to amplify the voice. To the Greeks, these masks were the symbol, the essence of a character. When manipulated by the actor, light played on the sculptured planes, giving the illusion of changing expressions. When using masks, actors cannot depend on facial expression to reveal their inner feelings. They must know the art of mime. Masks are not a hindrance, but an aid to expressing emotions if the body is used as a controlled instrument. No mincing or half-executed movements will do. The actors must be precise and calm in execution, using only the simplest movements. A mask transforms an actor from a creature of flesh and blood into a crystallized image of the character. Nuances of expression must be managed by manipulation of the mask and the entire body. By use of the mask, these actors were able to play many characters in quick succession ("doubling").

Several masks might be worn for the same character, for example, Oedipus. When he becomes convinced of his guilt, Oedipus leaves the stage, returning later with eyes gouged out and blood streaming from them. Gruesome? Not the way the Greeks performed it. The emotion was there, but by the use of the mask, violence and horror were eliminated. It was *artistically* true, but there was always an aesthetic distance.

The stylized lines of the mask transmitted emotion. In the great amphitheatres, human expression could not have been seen. The audience would not have accepted ordinary facial expression, which they considered vulgar on the stage. We must remember the Greek ideal of art. Ancient Greeks were interested in experiencing emotions, but only in terms of art. They expected an artistic arrangement of emotion, never the emotion itself.

PREPARATION FOR *OEDIPUS THE KING*

Before attempting the following scene from *Oedipus the King*, you should study the entire play. *Oedipus* has been called the world's greatest tragedy of fate, and one of the most solidly constructed dramas ever written.

Sophocles
(496–406 B.C.)

Exercise 124

You might test your knowledge of the play by answering the following questions:

1. What did the Delphic Oracle tell Oedipus' father?
2. Who was Jocasta?
3. Trace the events in the life of Oedipus from the time the Messenger brought him to Corinth until the opening of the play.
4. How much time passes between the beginning and end of this play?
5. What motivates Oedipus to search so relentlessly for his identity?
6. Describe the character of Oedipus. What sort of man is he? What is the tragic fault in his character?
7. Does Oedipus fit Aristotle's definition of a tragic hero as set down in *Poetics* XIII?
8. Are there any points of similarity between this story and a modern detective story? How is Oedipus different from a common murderer?
9. How does Oedipus change during the course of this play?
10. What reason does the author give that the murder of Laius was not investigated at the time of his death?
11. How can a modern actor identify himself with Oedipus?
12. Check the phrase that most nearly describes the theme of this play:
    a struggle for knowledge
    success does not bring happiness
    the struggle of a free man to avoid fate

a critique of rationalism
the uncertainty of human life
the irony of fate

13. In a few descriptive words, indicate the style of acting that should be used for this play.

14. Give several reasons why this play has lived 2,000 years and is still being produced.

If you find these questions difficult to answer, read *Oedipus* again—the entire play—before attempting to rehearse the scene. You must know where the pieces fit.

The scene given here has been chosen because it is the climax of a long series of investigations Oedipus makes to reveal the truth. During this scene, he learns the most damning truth of all. It is the turning point, the end of the hero's use of his free will against fate. Although he has felt the truth instinctively, he must go on searching, no matter what the cost. The revelation in this scene is the beginning of Oedipus' destruction.

The character of Oedipus is a prototype of the hero in quest of himself. This play demonstrates what Ibsen, centuries later, was to set down as rule for characters he created—that they must reveal past mistakes by retrospection. This play is so skillfully constructed that the audience always knows more than the hero. In his *Poetics*, Aristotle used the play *Oedipus* as a prime example of tragedy. What is the appeal of tragedy? It proves that man is a creature capable of heroic dignity and significance. By means of Sophocles' mastery of drama, we are able to witness a hero with a tragic flaw in a story that builds scene by scene to a towering climax. In this scene, just one old man, the Shepherd, can give the proof that will destroy Oedipus. The Shepherd not only fears for his life; he also has pity for the king. He cannot face his master, and it requires force to get the truth from the meek, old slave.

At first, the group should read the scene aloud, slowly and for sense, not emotion. As the class experiences the sense and meter, try to add not only the feeling of the characters but the larger-than-life style in which it was played. Feel the weight of the costumes. Remember that voices must fill an amphitheatre. And keep in mind the prestige and dignity enjoyed by the Greek actors.

A brief portion of the male Chorus that follows this scene is included here. The Chorus is composed of the elders of Thebes, who comment on the pitiful situation of man and of Oedipus. Sophocles used the Chorus throughout the play. The poetic beauty of these rhythmic lines, spoken in unison and with choreographed movement, lends powerful depth and meaning to the play. It is a good exercise for those students who have prepared themselves with the previous exercises on group voices.

REHEARSAL

Oedipus the King*

Sophocles
An Excerpt

CAST: Oedipus   **Shepherd**

Messenger   **Servants**

SCENE: *On the steps before the great palace of Thebes, Oedipus waits impatiently as the Messenger comes from L forcing the old Shepherd before him into the presence of the king. The Shepherd falls to his knees in fright and awe before Oedipus. There is a recognition of this between Oedipus and the Messenger. Oedipus takes a step toward them, and touches the Shepherd on the head. Throughout the scene, the Shepherd avoids any direct eye contact with the king. Positions are as follows: Oedipus at C, Shepherd to his L, and the Messenger DL of him. Up back to R there is a group of three servants to balance the group DL.*

Messenger: This is the man.

Oedipus: Well then old man! Look at me!

Tell me—you served Laius?

Shepherd: I was his slave.

Not bought by him, but reared in his house.

Oedipus: Doing what work? What was your way of life?[1]

Shepherd: For the best part of my life I tended flocks.

Oedipus: Where did they graze?

Shepherd: Sometimes *on*—[2] Citheron, sometimes *near* the mountain.

Oedipus: (*Pointing out the Messenger*) This man—do you
recall having ever met him there?

Shepherd: Not to say off-hand, from memory.[3]

Messenger: And no wonder, master![4]

But he will, when I remind him. We kept pasture
there three half-years,
he with his two flocks, I with one.
They grazed together from springtime to the rise
of Arcturus[5] in the fall.
Then I drove my sheep to our fold at home
And he brought his back to Laius.
(To the Shepherd)
Was this so as I tell it or not? [6]

1. A pause as he looks to the Messenger, who strikes him on the shoulder, then pulls him to his feet. Then he speaks.

2. Well aware that the name of the mountain is a dangerous word to utter.

3. Speaks quickly, trying to end the matter.

4. Messenger is angry at not being remembered, but decides to try kindness with the old man. He smiles, walks in front of the Shepherd, facing the king. He speaks in a friendly tone.

5. Arcturus: a star behind the dipper.

6. Puts his hand on the Shepherd's right shoulder.

*From Sophocles, *Oedipus the King*, trans. John Gassner, in *A Treasury of the Theatre* (Simon and Schuster, 1951). By permission of John Gassner.

7. Shepherd shrugs off the Messenger's hand with irritation.

8. Messenger is now between the two men.

9. Shepherd turns away, pretending not to have heard. Messenger seizes him, turning him back to face them.

10. In rage, Shepherd swings the Messenger to his left, but is arrested by the voice of the king.

11. Innocently.

12. Turns left to Messenger, snarling at him.

13. Falls to his knees, pleading as he sees the Servants UR moving back of king to threaten him.

14. Servants act to Oedipus' orders.

15. A loud cry.

16. Oedipus bombards him with questions like a district attorney pressing for a point. The following four lines of dialogue are spoken in fast tempo.

Shepherd: It was[7]—but it was a long time ago.

Messenger: And tell me now, do you remember giving me a boy,[8] an infant then, to rear as my own?

Shepherd: (*Frightened*) What do you mean?[9] Why do you ask me that?

Messenger: (*Pointing to Oedipus*) Here is the man, my friend, who was then the child.

Shepherd: (*Violently*) The plague take you! Hold your tongue![10]

Oedipus: How now? You have no right to blame him. The words that offend are yours.

Shepherd: Offend? How have I offended, master?[11]

Oedipus: In not telling us about the child.

Shepherd: He busies himself with no business of[12] his own. He speaks without knowing.

Oedipus: Herdsman! If you will not speak to please me, you shall be forced.

Shepherd: For God's love, master,[13] do not harm an old man!

Oedipus: (*To his servants*) Hold him fast; twist his arms behind him![14]

Shepherd: Wretch that I am![15] What do you want to know?

Oedipus: You gave him a child?[16] The child he asks about?

King Oedipus and the messenger force the truth from the old shepherd. As performed at the Burgtheatre, Vienna. (Photo copyright Hausmann.)

Shepherd: I gave it. Would I had died before!

Oedipus: You will now, if you do not speak the truth!

Shepherd: And it will be worse with me if I speak it.

Oedipus: The fellow trifles with us still[17]—evades the question.

Shepherd: (*As the servants twist his arms*) No,
no![18] I have told you that I gave him the child.

Oedipus: From whom did you have it?[19]
Did someone give it to you, or was it your own?

Shepherd: It was not mine.
Another gave it to me.

Oedipus: Which of these citizens?[20] From whose home?

Shepherd: Master, I beg of you—I beg you, do not ask it.

Oedipus: You are a dead man if I ask again.

Shepherd: It was a child, then—of the house of Laius.

Oedipus: A slave's child? Or born of the King's own family?

Shepherd: I stand on the knife-edge of dreadful
words;[21] I fear to speak.

Oedipus: And I, to hear.[22] Yet I must!

Shepherd: The child was called his son;[23]
but she within, your lady, could best say how it was.

Oedipus: Did she then give it to you?[24]

Shepherd: So it was,[25] my King.

Oedipus: For what purpose? Speak!

Shepherd: That I should do away with it.

Oedipus: Wretched woman! Her own child?

Shepherd: Yes, from fear of the evil prophecies.

Oedipus: What prophecies?

Shepherd: That he should kill his parents, it was said.

Oedipus: Why, then,[26] did you give him to this old man?

Shepherd: Through pity,[27] master.
I gave him the child,
thinking he would take it to another land, his own.
He did so but, alas, he saved it for the worst of sorrows.
For, if you are the man he says you are,[28]
then surely you were born to great misery!

Oedipus: (*Uttering the cry of a wounded animal*)[29]
Oh—Oh—Oh!
Everything is proved true—everything has come to pass!
light of the sun,
Never shall I look on you again,
I who am revealed
damned by the light I saw at birth,
damned by my marriage,
damned by the blood I shed.
         (*Oedipus rushes into the palace*)

17. A change in tone and tempo. Oedipus speaks almost to himself and obviously is somewhat discouraged. Shepherd has turned away, avoiding the king's eyes. One Servant turns his head to face Oedipus, who indicates that the others apply pressure to the arm.

18. Another and louder cry.

19. Louder still as he threatens the old man.

20. Staccato (same as before): fast cross fire of questions and answers.

21. A pause; he glances hopelessly about as if about to be pushed over a cliff.

22. Prophetically, Oedipus dreads what the man might say, but he must hear. This line is the key to Oedipus in this scene, and perhaps in the entire play.

23. These are the words he must say and he knows what they will mean to everyone when he says them. This is a high dramatic moment of the scene. He is resigned, defeated, speaking as a doomed man.

24. With only a slight hope that the previous six words he has uttered will not seem so awful.

25. This interchange is not so fast, more labored and grim. These are questions that must be asked and answered.

26. Meaning the other old man, the Messenger.

27. Almost sobbing in grief. Very moved.

28. In awe.

29. This wellspring of emotion must be started by the actor playing Oedipus *before* this point is reached. *Then it bursts:* man crying out in anguish to the fates. *Suggestion:* Recall the cry of a trapped or dying animal, or a woman's wail at hearing her husband has been killed.

Chorus (First Strophe): O generations of man,
how I account your lives no better
than not living at all!
Where is to be found the man
who attains more happiness, than a mere seeming
and after the seeming, a falling away!   Yours is the fate that
warns me—
luckless, unhappy Oedipus!—
to call no creature living on earth enviable.

Aristophanes
(455–375 B.C.)

If your work on Oedipus has left you with the impression that the ancient Greeks were a baleful lot, remember that they enjoyed tragedy. They liked seeing their great heroes struggling against a remorseless and inevitable destiny, living courageously even though, like themselves, their heroes knew the futility of escape. They came away from the play exalted and inspired by the potentialities of their own natures, for they measured the stature of a man by how he withstood the buffeting of fate. Life was not all tragedy, because a man could laugh; the Greeks believed that this was part of man's courage.

THE BEGINNINGS OF COMEDY

During the great festivals of Dionysus, young men dressed as satyrs (half-men, half-goats) paraded through the streets amusing the spectators with derisive remarks.[3] Today we have night club comics who still carry on this tradition of the amusing insult. From this early custom grew the satyr play.[4] Later, these bits of nonsense were presented as after-pieces to the great tragedies. Some time around 486 B.C. the satyr plays were officially recognized, and comic poets were asked to submit comedies in competition for prizes. These satires retained the taunting, irreverent quality of the original satyrs. Gilbert and Sullivan followed this style, as do our own topical revues, which ridicule public figures and customs.

PREPARATION FOR *THE BIRDS*

In our next rehearsal you will see that the Greeks had a highly developed sense of humor, wild as it was. Aristophanes manages his satire with irony and a vivid imagination. He lampoons man's pe-

---

[3]In Greek legend, Dionysus was the god of fertility and wine, the patron of choral song and dance, and son of the god Zeus.

[4]The subject of satyr plays is fascinating, involved, and controversial. However, due to limitations of space, we cannot treat the subject in-depth here. For further study, see John Gassner, *Masters of the Drama*, 3rd rev. ed. (New York: Dover, 1954), pp. 80–81.

rennial discontent with his lot, and his desire to escape and create "the great society." Here we meet two defectors from the great city of Athens who retreat to the mountains to establish a utopia. Their scheme is a delightful madness: They propose that the King of the Birds establish a cloud cuckooland and support it by levying a tariff between men and gods. Even in naming his two con men, Aristophanes is satirical: Euelpides means hopeful and Pithetaerus means plausible.

In this scene, a great deal depends on the performer playing Epops. He must have great vitality, and must develop dances and a weird birdlike screech. The sounds and dances need to be as carefully developed as the sounds for the Woody Woodpecker cartoons or the comic motion routines of Charlie Chaplin in his film *Modern Times*. The character Epops is obviously the great-granddaddy of the Mad Hatter and every other kooky character created since his time.

Definite characterizations should also be created for the old men. As a suggestion, Euelpides might be a crafty, pompous, but blundering fool, who imagines himself as a leader of men. Pithetaerus, then, in contrast, might be slow-witted and shy, depending on his blustering partner to speak for him. However, once Pithetaerus achieves confidence in himself, he is irrepressible—and still a fool.

REHEARSAL

The Birds*

Aristophanes
An Excerpt

CAST: **Euelpides**   **Two Old Travelers**

Pithetaerus   **King of the Birds**

Epops

SCENE: *Exterior. Several platforms or steps of different heights. These can be masked by cardboard cutouts and painted to resemble jagged rocks. Discovered, Euelpides and Pithetaerus. They turn as they hear a blood-curdling screech from up and off.*

Epops: *(Off)* Open the thicket that I may go out!
                    (Enters, above)
Euelpides: Heracles save us! What creature is this? What plumage! *(Grasps Pithetaerus)* What means this triple crest?
Epops: Who wants me?[1]

1. They venture closer to inspect the bird-man.

*Excerpt from adaptation made by author.

2. Epops struts proudly.

Euelpides: ²The twelve gods have done you ill.

Epops: You twit me about my feathers? I—Epops,—who was once a man like you?

Euelpides: We laugh not at you—

Epops: At what then?

Euelpides: At your beak. It seems so strange to us.³

3. Epops runs to a high place, screeches, jumps, and ends by doing his peacock-strut dance before them.

Epops: I am a bird!

Euelpides: A peacock?

4. Epops will not be pinned down to specifics.

Epops: ⁴A bird.⁵

5. Again he screeches and does his dance.

Euelpides: Then where are your feathers?⁶
    I see none.

6. Inspecting Epops' short skirt.

7. Epops slaps his hand away indignantly, then struts away with great pomp and circumstance.

Epops: ⁷They have fallen off
    All birds moult their feathers,⁸ every winter
    And fresh ones grow in their place⁹
    But tell me—¹⁰ W-w-what-are-you?

8. He struts back menacingly.

9. Turns away, then jumps back to the attack, accusing them.

Euelpides: ¹¹We—? Mortals.

Epops: What brings you here?

Euelpides: To speak with you.

Epops: Yes, yes? What for—?

10. Pokes his finger at Euelpides' chest, accenting each word.

11. These next few lines are spoken very fast.

Euelpides: Because once you were a man like us
    Because you once had debts—like us
    And had no desire to pay them—

Epops: As you do not now.¹²

12. Euelpides holds up his hand as if to ask patience that he may continue and come to a conclusion with his prepared oratory.

Euelpides: And then you changed into a bird,
    And flew over land and sea. You know what men feel
    And how birds feel too. That's why we've come to you
    And ask you to direct us to some cozy town,
    Where we can snuggle down, and live, all soft and warm.

Epops: You're looking for a greater city than Athens?

Euelpides: One more pleasant to live in.

Epops: An aristocratic country—?

Euelpides: Not at all.

Epops: Then what sort of city would suit you best?

Euelpides: Why, one where our greatest care would be
　　Some friend knocking on our door at break of day
　　And saying "By Olympian Zeus, bathe early today,
　　Come to a wedding banquet at my house,
　　And bring the children too. I give a nuptial feast,
　　And must not be disappointed by my friends."

Epops: [13]I see you are fond of suffering
　　And—[14] noisy one, what say you?

Pithetaerus: [15]My tastes are similar.

Epops: There is a city of delights such as you want.
　　It's on the Red Sea.

Euelpides: Oh no! Not a seaport
　　Where some galley can appear carrying a process-server.
　　This[16]—this bird life here—
　　You should know full well,
　　What it's like to live with the birds—

Epops: It's not altogether disagreeable,
　　Not disagreeable at all.
　　In the first place one has no need of a purse.

Euelpides: See there! That does away with roguery!

Epops: For food the gardens yield white sesame,
　　Myrtle-berries, poppy, cress and mint.

Euelpides: By Zeus, you live a bridegroom's life![17]

Pithetaerus: Oh![18] Oh, O-O-O-h!
　　I have just been hit with the most incredible idea[19]
　　A plan to transfer supreme power to the birds.
　　Will you hear my advice?

Epops: Your advice? What advice?

Pithetaerus: Do not fly in all directions with open beaks.
　　It is not dignified.
　　Among us when we see a
　　thoughtless man, we ask,[20] "What sort of bird is this?"
　　A man with no brain is a bird, for he never remains in one place.

Epops: [21] This is your "advice"?

Pithetaerus: Hear me out. Stay in one place.
　　Found a city.

Epops: We birds—? What sort of city should we found?[22]

Pithetaerus: That's done it.
　　You have just made the most idiotic remark.
　　Look down there—[23]

Epops: [24]What?

Pithetaerus: Now—look up!

13. Sarcastically, with overdone sympathy.

14. This also is sarcastic, as Pithetaerus has been standing in silence and looking quite stupid.

15. Has trouble finding his voice as it has been in disuse so long. Tries different pitches on "my."

16. Unseen by Epops, Euelpides nudges Pithetaerus, clears throat, and speaks directly to Epops.

17. Poppyseed was used by Greeks on wedding cakes, myrtle berries for bridal wreaths; hence, "bridegroom's life."

18. Holding his head, he jumps up and down as if in pain.

19. Grasps Epops.

20. Although there is sense here, it must seem to be nonsense as it is spoken.

21. Complete disgust.

22. Pithetaerus throws up his hands in despair, walks away, thinks better of it, and returns to the attack.

23. Pointing to the floor.

24. Epops does not understand, but complies anyhow.

25. Still puzzled but receptive.

26. As he winks to Euelpides.

27. He gestures a circle in the air. Epops jerks his head around until he becomes unsteady.

28. Calms Epops by putting his hands on his shoulders. Here we have a standard comic situation, where the fool or clown is smarter than the smart men.

29. Epops leaps into the air with a screech.

30. The screech.

31. He flies about calling to the north, east, south, and west.

32. He uses the entire stage until he really seems to be flying. The last of his call should be offstage and seem to come from a distance.

Vase painting of actors dressed as birds. The artist may have witnessed a performance of Aristophanes' The Birds. (Courtesy of the Trustees of the British Museum.)

Eopos: All right—I'm looking.[25]

Pithetaerus: Now[26]—twirl your head around![27]

Again!

Epops: What? And wring my head off my neck?

Pithetaerus: Now tell me friend,[28]

What did you see?

Epops: I saw the clouds and sky.

Pithetaerus: And is this not the property of the birds?

Epops: Property? The air—?

Pithetaerus: Eggessactly!

The air between earth and heaven

Is the property of the birds.

When we mortals go to Delphi,

The Boeotians make us pay to pass over their land

In this way—when men pray to the Gods,

You must make the Gods pay tribute.

You but exercise the right of every nation toward strangers,

And forbid the smoke of sacrifice to pass the skies over your property.

Epops: By Earth! By snares and traps and cages![29]

Never have I heard of anything so neatly conceived.

If the other birds approve,

I'll build your city on our property.

Pithetaerus: Who will explain the plan to them?

Epops: None but you. Before I came they were ignorant

And knew not how to speak. I have amended that.

Pithetaerus: How can we gather them together?

Epops: Easily. I will arouse my messenger from the thicket.

The Nightingale will bring them on hot wings.

Pithetaerus: Dear bird, lose no time.

Epops: Epopopoi, popoi, popopopoi, popoi,[30] here, here,

quick, quick, my comrades of the air[31]

All you who pillage the fertile lands,

You numberless tribes who gather barley,

Whose gentle twitter resounds through the fields,

Tiotiotiotiotiotiotiotiotio![32]

And you who hop about the branches of the ivy

You mountain birds who feed on wild-olive berries,

Trito, trito, totobrix—

Hurry to my call!

You who snap the sharp-stinging gnats in the marshes

You who dwell on the plain of Marathon all damp with dew,

Come hither.

Let all the tribes of long-necked birds assemble here

And know what a clever old man has brought to us

In inspiration and reforms. Come—here, here, here![33]
Torotorotorotorotix, kikkabau, kikkabau, torotorotorolililix!
Pithetaerus: What a throat that bird possesses!
He has filled the thicket with honey-sweet melody!

33. The air is filled with the sounds of birds. If loudspeaker is available, use recordings of bird sounds. Otherwise, rehearse the class to make sounds with human voices and mechanical birdcalls. The noise must be deafening at the end of the scene.

The following is a short scene from the same author's great antiwar play.

REHEARSAL

Lysistrata*

Aristophanes
An Excerpt from Act I

CAST: **Lysistrata**
      Kalonika
      (These are two female characters. The roles may be played by two men as they were originally.)

SCENE: *Exterior. Platforms and steps may be used.*

SITUATION: *The war between Athens and Sparta seems endless. Lysistrata has decided that since the men can't end it, the women must do so. She is with her friend, Kalonika.*

Lysistrata: Kalonika, I tell you if Greece is to be saved, it is the *women* who must do it.[1]
Kalonika: The women? Why, then,[2] Greece will be a long time being saved.
Lysistrata: It will be saved by us—or be forever ruined.[3]
Kalonika: But, Lysistrata, even so, what makes you think that women can do what our great statesmen have failed to do? They always *try* for peace.[4]
Lysistrata: They *say* they try.[5]
Kalonika: They are men with great minds. They think of everything.[6]
Lysistrata: They make us believe they do.[7]
Kalonika: And when their great peace conferences fail, they can go to war. But we, Lysistrata, we know nothing about great affairs. We sit here waiting for the men to come to tell what they have done, dressed in transparent gowns of yellow silk, flowing about so that

1. Striking a heroic pose.
2. Not at all impressed.

3. Turns away and overdramatizes to make her point.

4. Overwhelmed by Lysistrata's idea.
5. Turns to her.
6. Misses the point.
7. Hands on hips, she leans toward Kalonika.

*From Aristophanes, *Lysistrata,* trans. Gilbert Seldes, in *A Treasury of the Theatre,* ed. John Gassner, pp. 1477–78. ©1935, 1940, 1950, 1951, 1953 by Simon and Schuster, Inc.

8. Turns and moves away, gesturing to indicate each thing she mentions.
9. Crosses to her to help her realize the point.
10. Turns to her.
11. Gesturing and pantomiming in an exaggerated and overly suggestive manner.

12. Crosses to her.

13. Completely sold on the idea. She moves about excitedly.

14. Happy that Kalonika finally got the point, she approaches her and puts an arm around her shoulder.

we can hardly walk, with flowers in our hair and embroidered slippers on our feet.[8]

Lysistrata: You have just recited the catalogue of our most powerful weapons.[9]

Kalonika: Weapons?[10]

Lysistrata: [11]The filmy yellow tunic. Yes.
The intoxicating perfume and
your dainty slippers.
Yes. Your lotions and your rouge and your provocative, flowing robe.

Kalonika: What about them?

Lysistrata: These are the weapons by which every woman can make the men of Greece lay down their arms.

Kalonika: If that were true I'd get myself a dress so thin I'd be embarrassed even before my husband.[12]

Lysistrata: I ask you now, if we have such power, should we not use it?

Kalonika: We should, indeed.[13] Why Lysistrata, you've hit upon a really grand idea. Each one of us will buy new clothes and jewels and lovely perfumes and seduce our husbands—and the war will end. Why, who'd have thought of it?

Lysistrata: [14]There's more than that to do, but to commence with— that is enough. I tell you, Kalonika, we can do it—just as I say— and ought not every honest Grecian woman come to help us?

FURTHER READING: GREEK DRAMA

The following list is, of necessity, selective. The conscientious actor should seek additional sources of information when researching a particular period, style, and playwright for an acting role. Individual playwrights are not listed. (See also "Further Reading: The Character and Acting Styles" in chapter 9, and the "Additional Reading" list at the end of the book.)

Arnott, Peter D. *An Introduction to the Greek Theatre.* Bloomington and London: Indiana University Press, 1967.

Baldry, H. C. *The Greek Tragic Theatre.* New York: W. W. Norton, 1971.

Butler, James H. *The Theatre and Drama of Greece and Rome.* San Francisco: Chandler, 1972.

Kitto, H. D. F. *Greek Tragedy.* New York: Doubleday, 1960.

Lattimore, Richmond. *The Poetry of Greek Tragedy.* Baltimore: Johns Hopkins University Press, 1958.

Lever, Kathrine. *The Art of Greek Comedy.* London: Methuen, 1956.

Renault, Mary. *The Mask of Apollo.* New York: Pantheon, 1966. An engrossing account of the life of a fictional actor in the fourth century B.C.

Webster, T. B. L. *Greek Theatre Production.* 2d ed. London: Methuen, 1970.

11
ROMAN DRAMA

After the premature death of Alexander the Great, Greek drama declined along with the civilization that created it. To the west, Rome was rising, and by A.D. 180 it controlled England and western Europe, as well as the Balkans, Asia Minor, Babylon, Egypt, and the entire coast of West Africa.

In their drama, however, the Romans were not leaders, but followers. Italian dramatic forms, no doubt, existed before 240 B.C. We have surviving evidence in art of some characters of these dramas, such as Maccus the stupid clown, Bucco the glutton or braggart, and others. These dramas were performed during festivals, triumphs, or dedications of temples on temporary wooden structures with no seating arrangements for the spectators. The authors and chief actors of such plays were frequently slaves. This gives us some idea of the lack of esteem in which these dramas were held.

Later, Italian writers began to translate and adapt the great Greek poets, especially Euripides and Menander. The most representative of these Roman playwrights were Plautus, Caecilius, and Terence. Unlike the Athenians, who wrote for an exclusive and sophisticated audience, these native Italians competed for the attention of a bawdy, earthy group of spectators accustomed to such diversions as boxing, wrestling, and gladiatorial combats.

Titus Maccius Plautus
(CA. 254–CA. 184 B.C.)

Foremost of these authors was Plautus, whose works bridge the gap between ancient Greek and the Renaissance dramaturgy. Over a hundred comedies are ascribed to him, some existing only in fragmentary condition. But at least twenty are accepted as being of his authorship. Plautus was not merely a translator. In *Miles Gloriosus,* he was facile enough to amalgamate plots of two different Greek originals. He is considered a master in the use of the vigorous, colloquial language of the Augustan age. His dialogue denies the platitude that Latin is a dry and uninteresting language; indeed, for his time he demonstrated a consummate knowledge of stagecraft.

His influence on subsequent dramaturgy is obvious. Molière, Corneille, Racine, Marlowe, Ben Jonson, and Shakespeare, all owe Plautus a debt of gratitude. The first known English comedy, *Ralph Royster Doyster* (acted before 1551), was undoubtedly founded on Plautus' *Miles Gloriosus*. The lost play, *The Historie of Error* (acted in 1577), was probably based on Plautus' *Amphitruo*. In writing *The Taming of the Shrew*, Shakespeare was certainly influenced by Plautus in several respects; he lifted the names "Tranio" and "Grumio." Thomas Heywood adapted the *Amphitruo* for his *Silver Age*; and John Dryden's *Amphitryon* (1690) is based partly on Plautus' *Amphitruo*, and Molière's adaptation of it. In our contemporary theatre, we have an adaptation of this play by Jean Giraudoux, *Amphitryon 38*, produced successfully on Broadway with Alfred Lunt and Lynn Fontanne playing the leading roles. Scenarios used by the Commedia dell'Arte were often developed from Plautus' *The Twin Menaechmi* since its comic concept lent itself to improvised situations. It is certain that Plautus' *The Twin Menaechmi* served as the basis for Shakespeare's *Comedy of Errors* (1592–93) which, in turn, served as the basis for Rodgers and Hart's musical comedy *The Boys from Syracuse* (1938). Among other adaptations of *The Twin Menaechmi* are Carlo Goldoni's eighteenth-century *The Venetian Twins*. Most recently, many different plots and characters from Plautus were welded together for the popular musical comedy *A Funny Thing Happened on the Way to the Forum* (1962).

PREPARATION FOR *THE TWIN MENAECHMI*

The play was first produced around 186 B.C. It is considered to be one of Plautus' most successful comedies, and calls for an "all-out anything goes" style, with much mugging and broad, physical acting.

REHEARSAL

The Twin Menaechmi*

Plautus
An Excerpt

CAST: **Menaechmus II, a young man from Syracuse**

Messenio, his slave

Désirée, a courtesan

---

*From Plautus, *The Menaechmi*, trans. Palmer Bovie, in *Roman Drama*, ed. Robert W. Corrigan (New York: Dell, 1966), pp. 53–57. ©1962 by Chandler Publishing Company. Reprinted by permission.

Another recent translation of this play, by Erich Segal, appears in his book *Plautus: Three Comedies* (New York: Harper & Row, 1969). This same excerpt appears on pp. 161–166.

SCENE: *A street in front of Désirée's house.*

One of a set of identical twins is lost as a child. The remaining twin is renamed in honor of his lost brother. He has been traveling with his slave, Messenio, and arrives in the city of Epidamnus, where, unknown to him, his lost twin lives. He has already been mistaken for his brother once and is becoming wary of the strange people who live in this town. As the following scene begins, he is about to be approached by Désirée, a courtesan with whom his brother has made a previous dinner engagement.

Désirée:[1] Oh my favorite fellow, my poor heart will burst
  If you keep standing here outside
  When the doors to our house are open wide
  To take you in. It's much more your place,
  This house, than your own home is, an embrace,[2]
  A bright smile on its face just for you, and a kiss
  On that most generous of mouths. This really is your house.
  And now all is prepared just the way you wanted
  And shortly we'll serve you your dinner and pour out the wine.
  (Pause.)[3]
  I said, the meal's all in order, just as you commanded;
  Whenever you're ready, come on in now, honey, any time.

Menaechmus II:[4] Who in the world does this woman think she's talking to?

Désirée: To you, that's who.

Menaechmus II:[5]   But what business have I with you
  At present, or what have I ever had to do with you up to now?

Désirée:[6] Heavens! It's you that Venus has inspired me to prize
  Over all the others, and you've certainly turned out to be worth it.
  Heavens above! You've set me up high enough with your gener-
  ous gifts!

Menaechmus II:[7] This woman is surely quite crazy or definitely drunk,
  Messenio, talking such intimate stuff to me
  A man she doesn't even know.

Messenio: I told you so![8]
  And now, it's only the leaves that are falling, just wait;
  Spend three more days in this town and the trees themselves
  Will be crashing down down on your head. The women are
  biased,
  Buy us this, buy us that, and buzzing around for your money.
  But let me talk to her. Hey, sweetie, I'm speaking to you.[9]

Désirée: You're what?[10]

Messenio: No, I'm not, I'm who. And while I'm at it, just *where*
  Did you get to know the man here who's with me so well?

Désirée: Why, right here in Epidamnus, where I've been for so long.

1. Comes out of the house and sees Menaechmus. She crosses to him, speaking all the while.

2. Menaechmus is looking back and forth from Désirée to Messenio who stands mouth agape.

3. Looks from Menaechmus to Messenio and back again. Then raises her voice as if he is deaf.

4. Startled, he crosses to Messenio trying to clear his ringing ears.

5. Turns and crosses to her.

6. She puts an arm around him and turns on the charm.

7. He crosses to Messenio. She turns away and pouts.

8. Aside to Menaechmus, he gesticulates broadly during this.

9. He crosses to her.

10. She turns to him.

11. Slight pause as she is taken aback, but recovers.

12. Crosses to Menaechmus and pulls him toward the house.

13. He pulls away and takes Messenio aside.

Messenio: Epidamnus? A place he never set foot in before today?

Désirée:[11] A *delicious* joke, you rascal.[12] Now, Menaechmus, darling,
Won't you come in? You'll feel much cozier and settled.

Menaechmus II:[13] By God, the woman's quite right to call me by my own name.
Still I can't help wondering what's up.

Messenio: She's got wind of your moneybag,
The one you relieved me of.

Menaechmus II: And damned if you didn't alert me
To that very thing. Here, you'd better take it. That way,
I can find out for sure whether she's after me, or my money.[14]

14. Gives him the money bag from his belt.

15. Very seductively.

Désirée:[15] *Andiam', O caro bene!* And we'll tuck right into that meal;
Mangiamo, igitur, et cetera.

Menaechmus II: Music to my ears,
And you're very nice to sing it, my dear. I only regret I cannot accept.

16. Crossing to him.

Désirée:[16] But why in the world did you tell me, a short while ago,
To have dinner ready for you?

Menaechmus II: I told *you* to have dinner ready?

Désirée: Of course, dinner for three, you, your parasite, and me.

Menaechmus II: Oh hell, lady, what the hell is all this parasite stuff?
God, what a woman![17] She's crazy as can be once again.

17. Moves and speaks directly to the audience.

18. Crosses to him.

Désirée:[18] Cookie duster Peniculus, C. D. Peniculus, the crumb devourer.

Menaechmus II: But I mean what kind of a peniculus? We all know that's a soft hair
Brush, but I don't know anyone *named* that. You mean my ridiculous
Little thing, the traveling shoebrush I carry for my suede sandals,
The better to buff them with? What peniculus hangs so close to me?[19]

19. Very suggestively.

Désirée: You know I mean that local leech who just now came by with you
When you brought me that sweet silk dress you stole from your wife.

Menaechmus II: I gave you a dress, did I? One I stole from my wife?
You're sure? I'd swear you were asleep, like a horse standing up.

20. Moves away from him and sulks.

21. Crosses to her.

Désirée:[20] Oh gosh, what's the fun of making fun of me and denying
Everything you've done?

Menaechmus II:[21] Just tell me what I'm denying.

Désirée: That you gave me today your wife's most expensive silk dress.

22. Enumerating each item on a finger of his hand.

Menaechmus II: All right, I deny that. I'm not married.[22] And I've never been married.

And I've never come near this port since the day I was born,
Much less set foot in it. I dined on board ship, disembarked,
And ran into you.

Désirée:[23] Some situation! I'm nearly a wreck. What's that ship
You're talking about?

23. Throws up her hands in despair and turns away.

Menaechmus II:[24]   Oh, an old prewar propeller job,
Wood and canvas, patched in a million places; transportation,
I guess, runs on force of habit. She's got so many pegs
Pounded in now, one right up against the next, she looks like the rack
You see in a fur-seller's store where the strips are hung all in a row.

24. Pantomimes this directly to the audience.

Désirée:[25] Oh, do stop now, please, making fun, and come on in with me.

25. Goes to him and takes his arm coaxingly.

Menaechmus II: My dear woman, you're looking for some other man, not me.[26]

26. Pulling his arm away and crossing to Messenio.

Désirée: I don't know you, Menaechmus?[27] the son of Moschus,
Born at Syracuse in Sicily, when Agathocles ruled,
And after him, Phintia; then Leporello passed on the power
After his death to Hiero, so that Hiero is now the man in control?

27. Enumerating each item on a finger of her hand.

Menaechmus II:[28] Well, that information seems certainly accurate, Miss.

28. A pause as he "registers" being dumbstruck and recovers.

Messenio:[29] By God Himself! Is the woman *from* Syracuse to have
This all down so pat?

29. Aside to the audience.

Menaechmus II:[30]   By the various gods, I don't see
How I can now really decline that offer she's making.

30. Aside to Messenio.

Messenio:[31] Please do, I mean *don't* step over that doorstep!
You're gone if you do.

31. Aside to Menaechmus as he grabs his arm and pleads.

Menaechmus II: Pipe down.[32] This is working out well.
I'll admit to anything she says, if I can just take advantage
Of the good time in store. Mademoiselle,[33] a moment ago
I was holding back on purpose, afraid that my wife might hear
About the silk dress and our dinner date. I'm all set
Now, anytime you are.

32. Calms him down.

33. Turns and crosses to her.

Désirée: You won't wait for Soft Hair?

Menaechmus II: No, let's brush *him* off; I don't care a whisker if he never, . . .
And besides, when he does, I don't want him let in.

Désirée: Heavens to Castor![34]

34. Throws up her hands, clasps them in prayer, and throws her arms around him.

FURTHER READING: ROMAN DRAMA

(See also "Further Reading: The Character and Acting Styles" in chapter 9, and the "Additional Reading" list at the end of the book.)

Arnott, Peter D. *The Ancient Greek and Roman Theatre.* New York: Random House, 1971.

Butler, James H. *The Theatre and Drama of Greece and Rome.* San Francisco: Chandler, 1972.

Duckworth, George E. *The Nature of Roman Comedy: A Study in Popular Entertainment.* 4th ed. Princeton, N.J.: Princeton University Press, 1967.

Segal, Erich W. *Roman Laughter: The Comedy of Plautus.* Cambridge, Mass.: Harvard University Press, 1968.

12
MEDIEVAL DRAMA

As the great Roman civilization began to decay, the art of acting in formal comedies and tragedies also declined. By the fifth and sixth centuries acting was almost a lost art. Roman theatres were demolished by invading armies or adandoned, and only the church remained, which was openly hostile to drama. In the Dark Ages, only the transient and ephemeral mime with his comedy routines and gymnastics kept the art alive. Although such performers were professional, theirs was a sorry life indeed, wandering from town to town all over Europe, acting in the streets or at festivals, and occasionally living high while performing at some castle for a feudal lord.

Oddly enough, it was the church, which had been so antagonistic toward the theatre, that was eventually instrumental in reviving it and the art of acting. It was the priests themselves, not the itinerant performers, who were the first actors of the Middle Ages. At the Christian feasts of Easter, the priests chanted and sang in Latin a liturgical drama of the discovery of Christ's resurrection on Easter morning. In time, the monks wrote and acted original dramas about biblical events. The church altar represented the empty tomb of Jesus; sections of the church were transformed into the Garden of Gethsemane, Pilate's palace, or Calvary by temporary structures of wood and cloth. These enactments became so popular that they could not accommodate the crowds, and were eventually moved into the churchyards and streets. Eventually, the sensual attitudes of the people began creeping into these plays, along with occasional irreverences and parodies of sacred religious rituals. This caused some of the church hierarchy to become disillusioned, feeling that these plays had strayed too far from their original religious intentions.

It was then that lay associations and craft guilds took over. What began as religious spectacles, devised by ecclesiastics for the edification of the laity, came to appeal to the deep-seated instincts of the people; they were an inexhaustible source of wonder and delight.

This deeply felt instinct for the magic of drama comes naturally to man, and he is not complete without it.

Although this lay activity in religious drama thrived all over middle Europe during the fourteenth and fifteenth centuries, a prosperous England contributed to the early development of popular, more secular, dramas. These were supported mainly by the workers' guilds or municipal governments. Shakespeare's portrayal of Bottom and his fellow craftsmen in *A Midsummer-Night's Dream* no doubt reflected a professional's scorn of these earlier rustic amateurs.

These honest little medieval plays were originally translated from the Latin into the vernaculars, and assumed some elements of characterization (although not comparable to modern standards). Actually, their crudeness and naiveté enhanced their effectiveness and made them entertaining to the public, while, at the same time, fortifying religious faith and vision. As John Gassner has said, medieval drama "affords the spectacle of an entire people growing and displaying its dramatic art as an act of communion."

THE PLAYS

The medieval plays are generally grouped into several different genres:

The *mystery plays* dealt with scriptural events, such as the Nativity, the Passion, and the Resurrection.

The *miracle plays* were concerned with the legends of the saints—St. George, St. Nicholas, etc.

The *morality plays* were abstract, illustrating and teaching moral truths allegorically, such as *Everyman, Mankind,* etc. Characters were personified virtues or qualities.

THE ACTORS

In England, trade companies or guilds performed the medieval plays, especially the moralities. The assignments were amusingly literal: The guild of bakers chose plays dealing with food, the guild of goldsmiths enacted the presentation of the gifts by the Magi, and the fisher's guild chose either the parable of loaves and fishes or Noah's flood. Generally, a prologue was spoken by a herald or narrator, and the actors frequently performed on movable stages. The mouth of hell might be shown (with or without fire), and with demons wearing hideous head masks and costumes.

The Devil had an attendant fool called Vice, Shift, or Fraud, whose job it was to tease the Devil, to the amusement of the crowd. Later, this domestic fool survived in regular drama, and is accepted to be a prototype of the clowns in Elizabethan dramas. The moralities and the mysteries were performed until, and often into, the Renaissance, when more traditional drama began. But these medieval plays found such favor with the public that some of the guild players left their crafts to wander into the hinterlands, writing and performing their own plays. In England, some moved into, and substantially influenced, the rich Elizabethan theatre.

Very few details can be gathered from the existing records, but one is a direction note in the Cornish plays. When a character first entered, it was customary for him to be introduced, whereupon he would strut about the stage in a circle before taking his place in the scene. In some English halls, this custom still exists. Evidently, the prompter was a functionary of some importance, often whispering the players' lines to them in a resounding stage whisper.

PREPARATION FOR THE *NOAH* REHEARSAL (14th TO 15th CENTURIES)

In rehearsing this short play, keep in mind the sincere dedication and the unsophistication of these people. E. K. Chambers writes that *Noah* was an activity of the guild of ship-wrights at York, and of the watermen's guild at Beverley, Newcastle, and York.[1]

REHEARSAL

Noah, a Morality Play*

An Adaptation

CAST: Narrator
Noah
Shem
Ham
Japheth
Shem's Wife
Ham's Wife
Japheth's Wife
Noah's Wife

[1]E. K. Chambers, *The Medieval Stage*, 2 vols. (New York: Oxford University Press, 1963), p. 118.

*An original of this play is in the British Museum, Harleian Manuscript M.S. 2124, as printed in *The Chester Plays*, Part 1, edited for the Early English Text Society by H. Deimling, 1892. I have modernized the spelling for easier interpretation, and have added stage directions.

1. Noah stands.

2. Noah's wife stands.

3. Shem, Ham, and Japheth stand.

4. The wives stand, each on individual cue.

5. To his family.

6. *Slitch:* viscous clay.

7. They all pantomime working.

Narrator: At first in some high place
Or in the clouds it may be
God speaketh unto Noah:—
"I God, that all the world have wrought,
Heaven and Earth, and all of nought,
I see my people, in deed and thought,
all set foully in sin.
Man that I made I will destroy,
Beast, worm, and fowl that fly.
Therefore, Noah, my servant free,[1]
That righteous man art, I see,
A ship soon that shalt make thee,
Three hundred cubits it shall be long,
And fifty of breadth, to make it strong.
With water I shall overflow,
Man that I did make.
Destroyed all the world shall be,
Save thou; thy wife,[2]
Thy sons three[3]
And all their wives also with thee[4]
Shall be saved, for thy sake."

Noah: Thy bidding, Lord, I shall fulfill,
And never more grieve nor grill,
That such Grace has sent me till
Among all mankind.
To work this ship, chamber and hall,[5]
As God hath bidden us do.

Shem: Father, I am all ready bound:
An axe I have, by my crown,
As sharp as any in this town.

Ham: I have a hatchet wondrous keen,
To bite well, as may be seen.

Japheth: And I can make a pin,
And with this hammer knock it in.

Shem's Wife: Here is a good hack stock;
On this you may hew and knock.

Ham's Wife: And I will gather slitch,[6]
[7]The ship to caulk and pitch.

Japheth's Wife: And I will gather chips here,
To make a fire for you here,
And for to make your dinner,
Against you come in.

Narrator: And so, all of Noah's family set to work,—
All but Noah's wife who saw no need.

Noah: Good wife, do now as I bid thee.

Noah's Wife: Not I, not ere I see more need.
  Though thou stand all the day and stare.

Noah: Lord, that woman be crabbed, ay,
  And never is meek, that I dare say.

Narrator: Again was heard the voice of God,—
  "Of clean beasts with thee thou take
  Seven and seven, ere thou slake;
  He and she, mate to mate,
  Quickly do thou bring
  [8]Of beasts unclean two and two,
  Male and female, and no more;
  Of clean fowls seven also,
  The he and she together:
  Of fowls unclean two and no more,
  As I of beasts said before
  These shall be saved through my love,
  Against I send the weather.
  This world is filled full of sin,
  And that is now well seen."

Noah: Sir, here are lions, leopards in.
  Horses, mares, oxen and swine,
  Goats, calves, sheep and kine
  Here sitten,—thou may see.

Noah's Wife: I will not out of this town,
  If I have not my gossips every one.
  They shall not drown by St. John,
  If I may save their lives.
  They loved me full well, I attest,
  Unless thou let them in thy chest;
  Row forth, Noah, wither thou list,
  And get thee a new wife.

Noah: Shem, son, lo! thy mother is wroth![9]

Shem: I shall fetch her in, by my troth,
  Without any fail.
  Mother, my father after thee sent,[10]
  And bids thee into yonder ship wend.

Noah's Wife: Son, go again to him, and say
  I will not come therein today.

Ham: Shall we all fetch her in?

Noah: Yea, sons, in Christ's blessing and mine.

Noah's Wife: That I will not, for all you call,
  But I have my gossips all.

Shem: In faith, mother, yet you shall,

8. Shem and wife, Ham and wife, Japheth and wife pantomime different beasts in pairs.

9. *Wroth:* angry.

10. Shem goes to his mother.

11. They carry her in.

12. Blackout. Thunder strikes. Lights flash on and off revealing actors swaying and clutching each other. Screams, rain effect, thunder and lightning. Ham and Shem roll a long length of blue-green cloth between them simulating great waves. Then all is calm. Noah pantomimes reopening windows.

Whether you will or nought.[11]

Narrator: Then Noah shutteth the windows of the ark.[12]

Noah: Now forty days are fully gone,

Send a raven I will anon,

This betokenth God has done us some Grace,

And is a sign of peace.

Narrator: And God spoketh again to his servant,—

"Noah, take thy wife anon,

And thy children every one;

Out of the ship thou shalt be gone,

And they all with thee,

Beasts and all that fly

Out anon they shall hie

On earth to grow and multiply."

NOTE ON INCIDENTAL MUSIC

Noye's Fludde, based on the Noah play in the Chester Cycle, by one of England's leading composers, Benjamin Britten, is played every four years at Lancing College in Sussex, England. See also André Obey's play *Noah.*

FURTHER READING: MEDIEVAL DRAMA

(See also "Further Reading: The Character and Acting Styles" in chapter 9, and the "Additional Reading" list at the end of the book.)

Chambers, E. K. *The Medieval Stage.* 2 vols. New York: Oxford University Press, 1963.

Craig, Hardin. *English Religious Drama of the Middle Ages.* New York: Oxford University Press, 1955.

Nagler, A. M. *The Medieval Religious Stage: Shapes and Phantoms.* New Haven, Conn.: Yale University Press, 1976.

Nicoll, Allardyce. *Masks, Mimes and Miracles.* New York: Harcourt Brace Jovanovich, 1931.

Woolf, Rosemary. *The English Mystery Play.* Berkeley: University of California Press, 1972.

13
THE COMMEDIA DELL'ARTE

It was not until some time in the latter part of the sixteenth century that a new and vital style of theatre became evident. The Commedia dell'Arte was so unique in concept that its influence exists to this day.

Various Italian troupes of itinerate actors began the style. It eventually spread all over the continent, where it reigned as the popular theatre for at least two hundred years. It was not until the eighteenth century that the style came to be known as the Commedia dell'Arte. It was both old and new in certain respects. It was new in its use of improvisation, but old in its use of masks and plots. Actual speeches were not written, but were left to the actor's impromptu wit and intelligence. Only the characters were known beforehand. A scenario describing the main developments in the story line was written and posted backstage, where actors might refer to it. This was known as "the plot"; it is interesting that later prompt books were also called "plots."

PLOTS AND ACTORS

Using stock characters, performances were a striking mixture of the grotesque, bitter irony, and boisterous, bawdy farce. In general, plots dealt with some variation of mistaken identity or love and intrigue: a young wife (the Amorosa) married to an old husband (Pantaloon), a clever but dishonest servant (Zanni or Harlequin), or a bragging warrior (Capitano) who usually proved cowardly during a crisis. Frequently, actors would choose one of these stock characters, design their own costumes, add their own personalities or special abilities, and become so famous that they continued to play the respective parts for the rest of their lives.

These actors were expected to supply not only set comedy routines—called *lazzi*—but juggling and acrobatics, while the actresses did the ballet or musical interludes. Some actors were accomplished gymnasts. One actor, at eighty-three years of age, could

Capitano

The works of Carlo Goldoni are frequently staged using Commedia dell'Arte characters, as was done in this production by the Tyrone Guthrie Theatre in Minneapolis. (Courtesy of the Minnesota Theatre Company.)

box another actor's ears with his foot. Another convulsed his audiences by doing a complete somersault while holding a glass of wine in his hand. Particular athletic skills often became an actor's specialty.

For the first time, women assumed an important part in theatrical history, performing female roles. In the beginning women's parts served mostly to further the plot by adding romance. Heroines were a sheltered lot of young things, disciplined by parents but ripe for love. Usually the heroine had a confidante, equally doll-like. Later, this confidante developed certain traits, thanks to the actresses who played her. She might be saucy, brazen, sly, but certainly more experienced in the ways of the world than the innocent heroine.

Free from the confinements of a written play and dialogue, these actors took full advantage of the opportunity; they made it, in every sense, an actor's theatre. The playwright and director were shadowy figures in this theatre, if they existed at all. Leading actors had their own set speeches for love scenes or situations common to most plots, such as denunciations, farcical panic, and so on. They were expert with a device known as *tirata della giostra*—or the use of gibberish, which modern actors are convinced is a late invention of their own. Topical jokes were favored by both actors and audiences. These masters of farce could always be counted on to make use of incidents occurring in the audience or in the news of the day. Troupes of four or five actors would take to the road, playing on makeshift stages during fairs or celebrations. Other, more elite, companies were often the favorites of royalty, playing at court, where they were held in great esteem.

For three hundred years these actors reigned supreme over the entire European theatre. They left their mark on the Shakespearean clowns, on Molière's plots and characters, and on our own vaudeville and nightclub comedians.

Although the style of acting of the Commedia contained some elements of what went before, these actors added enough of themselves so that the total effect was fresh and distinctive. They set the rules for playing farce. It is possible that the actors of the Commedia outdid even the Greeks in the physical qualities of their acting. Not content with graceful dances and pageantry alone, they developed skills in tumbling, juggling, and dangerous, involved horseplay. Released from the responsibilities of enacting great plays, their goal was to please the common man, and in so doing they found they also pleased some intellectuals. Several hundred years later, Charlie Chaplin, working with a new medium, used some of the same techniques as his professional ancestors.

ACTING TECHNIQUE

The word *comedy* is a generic term. As used by the Greeks, it denoted the form that was not tragedy. In France, all actors, comedians and tragedians, were referred to as *comédiens*. Over the years, many types of comedy have developed, each with its own specific technique. There is satire, comedy-romance, farce-comedy, high and low comedy, etc. *The Birds*, written as social criticism, is most effectively played as a farce. Pure comedy, as we know it today, is intellectual. It consists of the play on words, the witty remark, the amusing situation, even the lift of an eyebrow; for acting, it requires a bright mind and a feather touch.

Farce

Farce, on the other hand, is physical. In farce we use the sock on the head, the chase, the ridiculous fight, elaborate mechanical gadgets, all physical devices. In *Modern Times*, Chaplin was pitted against the towering machines of mass production. Circus clowns have machines that turn giants into dwarfs, or dogs into sausages. The makeup and costumes of farce are outlandish and absurd. The slapstick of our early "comedy" movies was, in reality, farce. The "comedy" of the Commedia dell'Arte is really farce. Characterizations are not symbolic, meaningful, or significant. They are one-dimensional, existing for their own sake. Situations may be normal, but reactions are off-center and improbable. Thought or reason is seldom used in farce. One of its chief characteristics is the accumulation of incredible events. Mack Sennett once said that farce must always have "a touch of madness" in it. It is only fitting that both actors and comedians recognize their debt to the first great actor's theatre—the Commedia dell'Arte.

Charlie Chaplin—the individual versus the machine—in Modern Times.

Clown vs. Comedian

"To be Othello," William Hazlitt wrote, "a man should be all passion, abstraction, imagination: To be Harlequin, he should have all his wits in his heels and in his fingers end."[1] It is important that the student-actor know the differences between acting comedy and acting farce. Comedians always react normally. They are indignant or angry when they have a reason, and happy at the same things we are. Indeed, they are motivated very much as we are ourselves, except that they are more incisive, more observant and acute in their feelings. They take an ordinary situation and underline its ridiculousness. Their comments are all part of their viewpoint, their special way of thinking.

But the clowns' reactions are untypical, improbable, often the complete antithesis of ours. They might jostle a harmless table and jump back, nervous and frightened. They are menaced by the inanimate. When a gun is pointed in a clown's face, he is calm. He may cry when another clown takes his balloon, but laugh when it bursts in his face. His innocence causes us to love him. His responses are not justified either physically or psychologically. Nor are his emotions predictable: He might pick flowers on a railroad track

Harlequin

[1]William Archer, ed., *Hazlitt on Theatre* (New York: Hill & Wang, 1958), p. 188.

and remain undisturbed by the approach of a train. Clowns are mentally undeveloped. They do not reason and are more childish than children. So children feel superior and protective, and therefore identify immediately with them. Clowns react slowly, but when they do, they cry louder and run faster than any of us. Clowns seldom show anger, though they are often frustrated. Clowns are never "real" people, but they must always be theatrically true to what they are inside, naive as it may be.

The sadness of Emmett Kelly, the circus hobo, is a mockery of sadness: He is so sad that he is funny. The wonderful bicycle clown, Joe Jackson, Sr., was constantly frustrated by his inability to master his machine, but he never got angry.[2] He bore his frustration with a sweet, almost silly, "Oh well, that's life" attitude. Watching Jackson perform told me more about man's fumbling through life than both acts of *Waiting for Godot*.

Let me illustrate the difference between the comedian and clown by citing two personalities. Alan King is considered one of our foremost monologuists and is the author of several books on humor. Let us assume that both Joe Jackson and Alan King start with the theme of frustration. The clown, Jackson, reacts to it physically, whereas King, the comedian, reacts mentally.

Exercise 125

Name your favorite funny man or funny woman and, after considering his or her method of working, decide if he or she is a clown or comedian.

---

[2]Joe Jackson, Jr., is now doing his father's act and has frequently appeared on television.

Joe Jackson, Sr. (left), and Joe Jackson, Jr. (right). (From the New York Public Library Theatre Collection.)

In the following Commedia dell'Arte scenario, we are going to act the parts of clowns. Later, when we have our first comedy, we will take up the study of comedy, which is a more complicated and subtle art to learn. But both can be considered high art forms.

PREPARATION FOR *THE TWINS*

Around 200 B.C., Plautus wrote a simple and even primitive little farce called *The Twin Menaechmi,* which you have encountered during your study of Roman drama. In it, identical twin boys from Syracuse are separated by a shipwreck, and then come together years later in the same town. By means of a series of mistakes in identity, they are once again united. Plautus was concerned not with exploring character, but with an accumulation of comic incidents.

In the sixteenth and seventeenth centuries, actors of the Commedia dell'Arte borrowed this plot and added to it their own special skills. They discarded the dialogue Plautus had written, preferring to speak extempore. Their own favorite characters were used, notably Pantaloon, the eccentric quack Dottore, the nagging wife, and the zany servant. No doubt, this story of the twins was one of their favorite scenarios. Even though the basic ideas of the Roman and the Commedia plots are similar, the difference in style gives the Commedia scenario an individuality of its own.

Later, Shakespeare profited by the Plautus original in writing *The Comedy of Errors* (1591), even naming some characters as Plautus had named them. But Shakespeare added more dimension to characters, and more significance to the plot. Undoubtedly, the Commedia actors achieved somewhat the same end by adding personalities and acting skills to the entertainment.

REHEARSAL

The Twins

A Scenario

CAST: **Captain**   **Doctor**

       Flavia   **Silvio**

       Pantaloon

Narrator: A Captain arrives in Parma in search of his long lost twin. Before his brother, Silvio, is found, the Captain is several times mistaken for him. Because Silvio has been drinking and associating with women other than his wife, Flavia, she has sent for her father, Pantaloon, in the hope that he can straighten out her husband.

Pantaloon mistakes the Captain for Silvio, curses him for his loose living and drinking. The Captain denies all, even knowing the old man. Pantaloon reluctantly informs his daughter that her husband is "possessed by demons" and leaves her to search for a physician.

Improvise the following scenario:

The Captain enters, and is followed on stage by an angry, shouting Flavia. She accuses him of being a poor provider, a philanderer, and a drunk. At first, the Captain tries to explain that she has mistaken him for someone else, but she begins striking him. Now convinced that she is a mad woman, he restrains her, but each time he does she releases herself and bursts out with more invective. When he denies that he ever saw her before, she tells him that she sees through his pretense and that he is trying to shed his legal responsibilities as a husband, and threatens him with the law.

Pantaloon enters with the Doctor, who is a little strange himself. Disregarding the Captain's violent protests, they try to take him into Silvio's house, where they can examine him. Believing that they are trying to murder him, the Captain tries to escape. The only way they can subdue him is by sitting on him; then the Doctor examines him. After several comic pieces of business with implements, the Doctor pronounces his opinion, "The man is mad!" He must be given a physic, bled, and confined. The Captain kicks and fights, shouting that they are thieves and murderers.

Silvio

At this point, Silvio enters. All turn to discover him. At first they believe they are seeing a ghost. But the Doctor, who is a specialist in this sort of thing, convinces them that what they are seeing is a supernatural phenomenon—and begins strange incantations. The Captain pushes them back and asks if Silvio ever had a twin. After several questions and answers, the Captain and Silvio decide that they are brothers and embrace. The old men cannot tell which brother is which, but Flavia assures them that she can tell. After ceremoniously kissing both, she picks Silvio as her husband, saying a wife certainly knows her husband's kiss. Silvio simpers in pride, but she tells him not to be a fool, that he never kissed her like the Captain.

▪ FURTHER READING: THE COMMEDIA DELL'ARTE

(See also "Further Reading: The Character and Acting Styles" in chapter 9, and the "Additional Reading" list at the end of the book.)

Disher, Maurice Willson. *Clowns and Pantomimes.* New York: Benjamin Blom, 1968.

Herrick, Marvin. *Italian Comedy in the Renaissance.* Urbana: University of Illinois Press, 1960.

Nicoll, Allardyce. *The World of Harlequin.* New York: Cambridge University Press, 1963.

Oreglia, Giacomo. *The Commedia dell'Arte.* New York: Hill & Wang, 1968.

Rolfe, Bari. *Commedia dell'Arte: A Scene Study Book.* Oakland, Calif.: Persona Products, 1976.

———. *Farces, Italian Style.* Oakland, Calif.: Persona Products, 1978.

Smith, Winifred. *The Commedia dell'Arte.* New York: Benjamin Blom, 1965.

14
SHAKESPEARE (1564–1616)

In Tudor and Elizabethan England, groups of strolling players wandered from town to town, without the protection of their guilds, and eking out a precarious living. In the opinion of the townspeople, such players were considered no better than beggars or thieves, for whom flogging was mandatory. In order to avoid such treatment, the players often sought the protection of some titled Englishman.

James Burbage, an actor in one of these troupes, and a former carpenter, became weary of his transient and precarious life. In 1576, he built a permanent structure for production of plays. Not surprisingly, this "plaiehowse" was called, *The Theatre*, and Burbage fashioned it after the inn yards in which he and his "fellowes" had been playing. Soon there were many other theatres, literally setting the stage for the luxuriant Elizabethan dramas.

After several years, the landlord refused to renew the ground lease on which the Theatre was built. James Burbage, his actor son

Moving the theatre.

Richard, and several actor-shareholders tore it down under cover of darkness and carried it piece by piece—literally on their backs—to a new location. This was done while the company was giving performances at court during the day. When they were finished, they could no longer call it the Theatre, as there were too many liens against that name. In honor of their Herculean task they called their little world *The Globe.*

THE ACTORS OF THE GLOBE

Kemp's "Nine Daies Wonder," dancing from London to Norwich.

To illustrate the physical condition of these actors, we know that Will Kemp, the much-loved comedian of the Globe Company, once wagered he could dance all the way from London to Norwich, over one hundred miles. He did this in nine days, accompanied by pipe and tabor, to the great delight of country people along the way. Is it any wonder that modern actors performing Shakespeare for the first time are amazed at the sheer physical stamina it requires?

Elizabethan actors always had the problem of maintaining sufficient breath to sustain the tone and then be ready for bursts of passion beyond that. It is interesting that eyewitnesses describing the acting of that time always allude first to the voice. Most of Shakespeare's characters are representative of royalty or nobility or are heroes of grandeur and spirit, not characters encountered in everyday life. The actors of the King's Company certainly realized that they were not speaking the words, phrases, or thoughts of ordinary people in everyday conversation.

These actors might well play thirty or more parts per season. Some were in new plays, which required more effort than plays already in the repertory. Usually actors performed a different play each time. Actors who could not read had to learn parts by ear, and those who could read were supplied little rolls, with their cues and speeches written on them. This roll could be worked through the fingers of one hand, leaving the other free for swordplay or "business" as the actors rehearsed. One such roll is still in existence at Dulwich College in England.

Until 1608, it was the rule that vacancies in the company left by the death of some senior member could only be filled by their own graduate apprentices. Twelve- or thirteen-year-old boys began by playing pages and children, while working under the tutelage of a senior shareholder. A Globe apprentice was little more than a slave: "He must do all servile offices about the house," Ben Jonson has recorded, "and be obedient to all his master's commandments and suffer such correction as his master shall meet . . . being bound only to . . . teach him his occupation."[1]

---

[1]Marchette Chute, *Ben Jonson of Westminister* (London: Penguin, 1960), p. 37.

When these apprentices became qualified, they were advanced to feminine roles and, as they matured, were made regular members of the company. Thus each new actor in the company was already a seasoned performer, familiar with the repertory, and in possession of impressive physical and vocal skills. We can assume from the way apprentices were trained that this was an excellent group of players. Many foreign visitors coming to London were struck by the quality of acting they saw. One traveler wrote, "Nothing quite like them has been known in Europe."

At first it might seem impossible to compare Shakespeare's friend and business partner Richard Burbage with the great actors who followed him. Their fame rests mainly on the excellence they displayed in one or two particular characters. But what an enormous range of acting talent Burbage must have had in order to create many if not all of Shakespeare's tragic heroes—Hamlet, King Lear, Macbeth, Richard III, and Othello—all most likely under the direction of Shakespeare himself. There can be little doubt that these two men created the standards for playwriting and acting as we know them today.

During the course of a Shakespearean play, the hero might experience more exceptional and dramatic events than do a dozen people in real life. Shakespeare gives no literal imitation of life. On occasion, he uses a lifelike gravedigger or a porter who serve to establish recognizable fact with the large-than-life protagonists. The complex characters of his heroes gain existence only through the use of poetry, which is studied, formal, and "true" insofar as it resembles the prose of daily speech. Perhaps you have been told that "people talked like that in those days." Not true; Shakespeare wrote poetry—words chosen for their beautiful sounds and their expressiveness, and then arranged these into melodic patterns to elucidate his meaning.

In everyday conversation we change pitch, hesitate, even make unpleasant sounds. We improvise. But poetry is planned. When speaking poetry the actor must use a sustained tone without resorting to chant. The trouble that Americans encounter in acting Shakespeare is due in great part to a disregard of these rules. We approach his plays as though they were realistic dramas. There is much proof of the error in this sort of thinking. As far back as the beginning of the twentieth century, André Antoine, the French leader of naturalism, tried unsuccessfully to produce Shakespeare using this approach at his Théâtre Libre. Stanislavski also tried it, and in despair wrote:

> Yet why can I express my perceptions of Chekhov but cannot express my perceptions of Shakespeare? . . . Apparently it is not the inner feeling itself, but the technique of its expression that prevents us from doing that in the plays of Shakespeare which we are able to do to a certain degree in the plays of Chekhov. That is the only solution. We have created a technique and methods for the

artistic interpretation of Chekhov, but we do not possess a technique for the saying of the artistic truth in the plays of Shakespeare.[2]

IMPORTANCE OF SHAKESPEARE

After four hundred years, Shakespeare's plays are produced more than those of any other playwright, living or dead. In nineteen years, he wrote thirty-seven plays; an amazing number of these "smash hits." If he could collect his royalties for current productions, they would exceed those of all present-day playwrights combined. As a "master-sharer" (one of the business partners) in the Globe playhouse, he had the responsibility of keeping the company busy in plays the public would pay to see. If a play was not "doing good business," another had to be ready.

AN ACTOR NAMED SHAKESPEARE

Some Elizabethan scholars have tended to depreciate Shakespeare the actor in favor of Shakespeare the poet. The impression has been given that he was no more than a small part actor, never entrusted with a part more important than the Ghost in *Hamlet*. Unfortunately, we have no programs and no critical reviews showing the parts he did actually play. But there are many legal documents in existence, such as grants, licenses, and royal commands for court performances, listing Shakespeare as one of the three most important actors of his company. The name of a mere "bit" player would hardly be listed immediately following the name of the leading actor of the Globe, Richard Burbage. When Ben Jonson supervised the printing of his play *Every Man in His Humour*, he listed the actors who first acted in this play in 1598. The name "Will. Shakespeare" heads the list at left and "Ric Burbage [sic]" the list at right. In publishing *Sejanus, His Fall*, Jonson listed actors Shakespeare and Richard Burbage as equally important. Several years after Shakespeare's death, two of his colleagues, who were the oldest "sharers" in the King's Company, prepared a dedication emphasizing that the plays were vehicles for actors. The dedication placed Shakespeare's name first in a list of "the names of the principall actors in all these playes."

However, the most convincing proof of Shakespeare's importance as an actor is so obvious that it seems to have been overlooked. The company to which he was so devoted, the Lord Chamberlain's Men (after 1603, the King's Men), had three levels of personnel. First there were the senior actors, or "fellowes," who contributed capital and as "sharers" received the profits or took the losses. They were responsible for the management, and were the "housekeepers," as well as playing all leading parts. The second group were the "hired

[2]From *My Life in Art* by Constantin Stanislavski, p. 350. Copyright 1924 by Little, Brown and Co., and 1948 by Elizabeth Reynolds Hapgood. Reprinted by permission of Theatre Arts Books, New York.

actors." The hired actors received a salary and were employed as needed, with no responsibilities other than acting. From this group the subordinate parts were cast. The third group were younger members who played pages, children, and women. When we remember that there were no managers, producers, directors, playwrights, or lawyers sharing in the company, Shakespeare's position as principal "sharer" is also strong testimony to his importance as an actor.

When Shakespeare was thirty-two, all of his worldly possessions were appraised at the equivalent of twenty-five dollars; when he retired at fifty, he was considered the Elizabethan equivalent of a millionaire. Was this sizable fortune accumulated by acting? Other Elizabethan actors had done so.[3] Certainly Shakespeare's fortune was not made from royalties from the immortal plays—there were no royalties. The plays were sold outright to the company. Shakespeare started his fortune as an actor, a "sharer," and by subsequent wise investments accumulated enough to retire to his beloved Stratford-upon-Avon and live his final years as the most distinguished and perhaps wealthiest gentleman in that community.

SHAKESPEARE THE DRAMATIST

Shakespeare began writing for the stage about the middle of 1591, a few years before the Globe was built. Eventually he wrote historical plays, tragedies, satires, light comedies, and farces—in fact, almost everything but a play dealing realistically with the London scene of his day.

No other playwright has ever surpassed him in characterization. He always managed to create his portraits, not in descriptive words, but in the dialogue itself. The characters express themselves with accuracy, brilliance, and deep emotion. They are written with careful regard for the play and the relationships to other characters in that play, so that the ultimate in character exploration is achieved by means of conflict. As an example, Hamlet, the thinker who cannot act, is juxtaposed with Laertes, who acts without thinking.

Because Shakespeare began as an actor and continued to act, he knew much better how to create drama than the better educated "university wits" of his time. It is evident in each of his plays that his was the output of a professional man of the theatre. No other writer in Elizabethan England wrote this way.

THE ELIZABETHAN AUDIENCE

Since he was a commercial playwright, we should examine the audience he tried to please. This will also give us some insight into the times, as well as being useful when acting his plays.

---

[3]At his death Burbage left £300 yearly in lands, and a rival actor, Ned Alleyn, bought a manor and endowed Dulwich College, which exists to this day.

During Shakespeare's early years in London, Elizabeth sat on the throne. It was an extremely creative period in the theatre. Most people could not read or write, but they had been awakened to developments in the sciences, the arts, and indeed to all things cultural. Entranced by the Italian Renaissance, which reached England by way of France, and by the invention of the printing press, they were eager for any sort of knowledge, and devoured it eagerly. A "plaiehowse" was a club, a social hall, and a school, in addition to being a place where one could be thrilled and entertained.

A typical audience might include nobles from Elizabeth's court, lowly apprentices, poets from the universities, and sailors just returned from the New World. It was an uninhibited, mixed crowd, drinking, eating, and smoking, very much like the people we see today at baseball games. If they showed a preference for history and kings, Shakespeare provided such plays. Whatever they wanted, comedy, tragedy, or romance, Shakespeare obliged. He never tried to give them what he thought they should have or what others thought would be good for them; and he never preached or tried to reform.

He knew that the average man liked a plot—some sort of story he could follow. Shakespeare thought so little of plots himself that he wasted no time inventing them. Instead he borrowed from history, from folklore, even from other plays. But he borrowed only when he

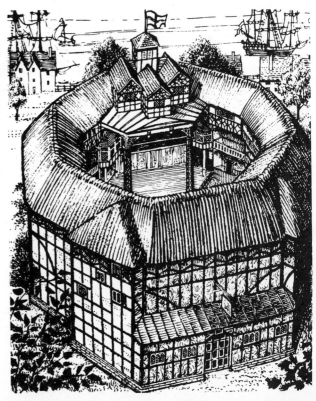

Artists' reconstructions of the Globe Playhouse, both interior and exterior. (Interior, from the Bettmann Archive; exterior, courtesy of the British Tourist Authority.)

could add other levels of interest. The Elizabethan man cared nothing about the seed when he was admiring a flower. For the spectators in the pit (the "groundlings"), Shakespeare had puns, coarse jokes, and plays on words. But even those were used with a professional's sure touch; he knew when and how much to use them.

To his contemporaries, Shakespeare was no towering immortal. No biography of him was published during his lifetime, nor for nearly one hundred years after his death. He was just one of a company of players, who worked with almost superhuman strength, playing in broad daylight to a noisy, unruly mob standing in the open air. Shakespeare's players had to compete with animal noises coming from the bull-baiting pits nearby. It required stamina and a big voice to capture and hold the attention of that audience. How many of our Academy Award winners of today could do that?

THE MUSIC OF SHAKESPEARE

While American children are taught to *read* Shakespeare, English children are taught to *speak* it. They learn to form the sounds of speech, to enunciate clearly and crisply, and to give melody to human communication by the use of Shakespeare's lines. Shakespeare's characterizations are so imbedded in the iambic and alliterative constructions that they seem to elude the American actor. But the Englishman, with Shakespeare such a part of him, accepts the unreality of blank verse, realizing that such eloquence is impossible for real people in real life situations.

While some playwrights preferred to use rhymes for their plays, Shakespeare chose blank verse. But by deviating from the metrical pattern, he obtained startling dramatic effects in sound, imagery, and emotion. His blank verse is, by definition, unrhymed iambic pentameter—"blank" because the listener can anticipate rhymes when the rhythmical pattern is at all regular. It also allows the actor to emphasize sounds he feels are essential for the revelation of character and emotion.

An *iambus* is a foot of two syllables—a short, or unaccented, one followed by a long, or accented, one. The human heart, for example, beats in iambs, two recurring strokes—brief, long; brief, long—and this is the fundamental rhythm of English poetry. Our breathing is also done in the iambic foot, out-breathing, in-breathing, with stress on the in-breathing because it takes longer and is more consciously done, whereas out-breathing is more automatic.

Exercise 126

Imagine that you are listening to a metronome ticking at about your usual heart rate. Indicate these beats by saying aloud, "tick," each time the pendulum swings right or left:

Tick —tick —tick —tick —tick
  1   2   3   4   5

The sound and movement of the metronome is measured, the rhythm never changing. Let us call each basic unit, each "tick," a *foot*. Now instead of the one word "tick," say two words, "to be," in the same time it took to say "tick." Ready?

To be —to be —to be —to be —to be
  1   2   3   4   5

Now let us stress or accent the second syllable, the "be."

Tó bē —tó bē —tó bē —tó bē —tó bē
  1   2   3   4   5

NOTE: The mark (´) indicates the short syllables or nonstress. The mark (¯) is the long, or accented, syllable. When we speak words arranged to make sense using *meter* and *stress* (or accent), we *scan*. The stresses should reveal not only meaning and feeling of the words, but also in many cases, proper pronunciation. Now instead of saying, "to be," say

Tó bē —ór nōt —to bē —thát īs —the quēst(ion)
  1   2   3   4   5

(The final syllable of the word *question* is unaccented, or slurred.)

Now let us review the terms. We have been working with a line consisting of five feet (or iambs), with an accent (or stress) on the second syllable of each foot. Each line should take from two to four seconds to speak. Such formalized lines taken together are called *iambic pentameter*. Shakespeare accustomed his listeners to this overall design, but he delighted in deviating from it for dramatic effects. So in the reading of blank verse the actor must be allowed liberty, but not license. The rhythm must remain underneath, no matter how the actor interprets.

Let us try another line.

Thé quāl í tȳ óf mēr ćy īs nót strain(ed)
  1   2   3   4   5

Obviously, this language is very different from everyday speech, in which we use trite images, repetitions, hesitations, and substitutions. The only purpose of everyday speech is to convey meaning, and we don't care how that is accomplished. If we need to use grunts, gestures, or facial contortions, we do so. But the poet designs and selects; each word must be the right word to express the meaning or emotion. The poet plans formally, using meter and managing an intensity of expression.

As an example, let's look at these lines from *Richard III*, Act V, Scene iii.

Come, bustle, bustle. Caparison my horse.
Call up Lord Stanley, bid him bring his power.
I will lead forth my soldiers to the plain,
And thus my battle shall be ordered.
My forward shall be drawn out in length,
Consisting equally of horse and foot.

Note how the *sounds* themselves express the excitement of the coming battle. Observe how the repetition of the word *horse* in the first and last lines prepares for the famous line to come, "A horse! A horse! My kingdom for a horse!" Note how the repetitions are designed and appropriate to the dramatic situation. Shakespeare was very clever about using surprises, using pauses in the lines, and in reversing the iambic beat now and then, especially in the third foot, to give an effect. This freedom to alter the pattern keeps his lines from ever sounding monotonous, and discourages an actor from intoning the lines like an old-time preacher. Declamatory delivery, while austere and dignified, is not dramatic, and must be avoided in speaking Shakespeare's lines.

Another device that Shakespeare frequently uses to make his dialogue active is the *half-line.* A speaker will end his speech in the middle of a metrical line and another will take it up and complete it. Here is an example from Act IV, Scene iii, of *Macbeth:*

MacDuff: How does my wife?
Ross: Why, well.
MacDuff: And all my children?
Ross: Well too.

If you read Shakespeare aloud, many reasons for the effects he uses will become obvious to you.

Exercise 127

Here is an exercise Peter Brook uses. All class members memorize a soliloquy or stanza of their choice, and divide the piece into three sections. Then, using no special expressive delivery, three individuals read the material aloud as a unit. The entire reading should be done in each of the following ways:

1. reading as quickly as possible
2. retarding the pace slowly
3. accenting certain previously selected words, using beats or silences for other words

NOTE: When speaking verse, there are mechanical beats that you must discover. The difference between "intoning" and speaking verse properly is in *adjusting the emphasis in accordance with the meaning.* The three main faults of the amateur in speaking verse are: (1) melodious or "stagey" reading; (2) academic singsong; and (3) colloquialism, which chops up the verse and is unforgivable. *Search out the meaning and the verse will appear automatically. Reality can be achieved only through the verse.*

ATMOSPHERE

Previously, we discussed the importance of *atmosphere,* which might be defined as the emotional tone created for a play or a scene. When the curtain rises on a proscenium stage, the setting usually makes the first impression. It sets the mood by its design and coloring. Next the audience notes the characters, and how they are grouped. If they are in symmetry and simply arranged, the audience will feel an atmosphere of serenity. But Shakespeare could not depend on settings or lighting. On his "unworthy scaffold," as he called his stage, actors could be revealed (or "discovered") only at the rear of the stage. His characters had to walk on. In order to create atmosphere he had to use sheer dramaturgy. Leaf through the first few pages of any of his plays and note how he establishes the mood for the play to follow: the lone soldier standing guard in *Hamlet,* his startled "Who's there?"; the unexplained fears of "Nay, answer me. Stand and unfold yourself"; and the bitter cold evidenced in the lines, the ghostly visitation. All these cause the audience to *feel* that sense of fate that permeates the play to come. Evil fills the air above the Witches in the opening scene of *Macbeth.* After this scene, the audience is receptive to the deep penetrations into human existence that follow.

Illusion, then, is one of the keys to Shakespeare's plays. He was not beyond criticism as a man; nor was he always a great artist. But one fact is irrefutable: At his best he was the most exciting creator of imaginative theatre who ever lived.

COLOR

Shakespeare always selected words or phrases which, when spoken by the actor, would produce calculated emotional reactions in an audience. Read aloud the following lines:

> *The devil damn thee black, thou cream-faced loon;*
> *Where gott'st thou that goose look?*

Note how the lines actually duplicate the sound of rage. In these two lines, we can feel the anger of the trapped Macbeth as his trembling "whey-faced" servant comes to report that the English soldiers are advancing. The sensual experience of that dramatic moment has been captured for us in the lines. Read some of Shake-speare's love scenes and note the soft syllables and liquid sounds. Find some scenes of mystery, and note the breathy sounds. Shake-speare was very skillful at finding the sounds that expressed the mood or emotion he wished to convey.

RHYTHM AND RESTS

The word *rhythm* is often used by actors when they are actually re-ferring to *meter*. As we have learned, meter deals with feet and stresses (as in iambic pentameter), but each line may have its own rhythm. Meter is set, *mechanical*; rhythm is *organic*, depending not on regularity, but on irregularity. Rhythm gives color, variety, and meaning to a line, and when so used it is called *cadence*.

No other playwright is so aware of actors as Shakespeare. He has generously provided proper breathing pauses and moments of rest for the actors before they have to continue. Such rests usually last the time it takes to speak ten syllables—plenty of time to catch a breath. Such pauses are called *caesuras*.

PROSE AND POETRY

Shakespeare wrote not only poetry, but also prose. As actors, let us examine the difference between poetry and prose. Will you agree that there is a kind of music in the lines of certain more modern playwrights? Think of the New York-Jewish cadences in the works of Clifford Odets and Arthur Miller.[4] What is the difference between their "music" and Shakespeare's? You simply cannot fool around with Shakespeare's words. His lines will not tolerate any insertions of "ah's" or incoherent mumblings to make the thoughts seem a sudden invention by the actor. Shakespeare, as an actor, was well aware of actors' devices; he wrote these devices into his lines. They must be spoken as written. You have no leeway in this; you are either right or wrong.

Let us examine the difference between poetry and prose by using an example. The following is a passage from one of Shakespeare's sources: Plutarch's *Life of Marcus Antonius,* as translated by Thomas North. In its rich Elizabethan prose it describes Cleopatra's retinue:

—*her barge in the river Cyndus, the poop whereof was of gold, the sails of purple, and the oars of silver, which kept stroke in rowing after the sound of the music of flutes, hautboys, cithers, viols, and such other instruments as they played upon in the barge. And now for the person of herself: she was laid under a*

---

[4]Clifford Odets is a playwright of the 1930s, and author of *Golden Boy, Awake and Sing, The Big Knife, The Country Girl,* and others. Arthur Miller is the author of *Death of a Salesman, The Crucible, After the Fall,* and others.—Ed.

pavillion of cloth-of-gold of tissue, apparelled and attired like the goddess Venus commonly drawn in picture. . . .

Now here is what flowed from Shakespeare's pen in *Antony and Cleopatra*, Act II, Scene ii:

The barge she sat in, like a burnish'd throne,
Burnt on the water: the poop was beaten gold;
Purple the sails, and so perfumed that
The winds were love-sick with them: the oars were silver,
Which to the tune of flutes kept stroke, and made

The water, which they beat, to follow faster,
As amorous of their strokes. For her own person,
It beggar'd all description: she did lie
In her pavillion—cloth-of-gold of tissue—
O'er-picturing that Venus, where we see
The fancy outwork of nature . . .

The source is prose; Shakespeare's lines are poetry.

SHAKESPEARE AND YOU

All actors are judged by their ability to play Shakespeare. It would be difficult to imagine this world without Shakespeare. As long as humans live, so also will "the Bard." If you continue acting, one day you will surely act in one of his plays. Shakespeare is the best possible training for actors just beginning. He is also the standard used to judge a master actor.

Hamlet, Lear, Lady Macbeth, Juliet—these remain the summit of achievement in the art of acting. Actors also find that a sense of pride comes when they are associated with Shakespeare. It is not just that he also was an actor. To be a Shakespearean actor gives self-esteem to a performer. It is as though some of the great man's genius rubs off. He lifted the "profession" to dignity by his art. When we forget or neglect him, as we did for a while after his death, actors and actresses sink back into the gutter where he found them—as mountebanks, fools, and bawds. With him, we gain the respect of our fellow man and ourselves. As his Players, we are extraordinary beings. Just to know his lines is an education, for they are some of the wisest words ever written.

ACTING STYLE FOR SHAKESPEARE

Shakespeare guides actors in the what, why, and how of his plays through the lines themselves, without stooping to condescending directions. If an actor understands the lines, he understands the character, the time, the place, and the dramatic situation of the play.

"Fine speaking is of the most crucial importance to the interpretation of Shakespeare in the theatre. A sense of style is almost equally essential." These are the words of Margaret Webster, in her excellent book *Shakespeare without Tears*.[5] Miss Webster continues:

> It has become the fashion to belittle the need for this much misinterpreted quality. "Style" is supposed to consist of a lot of outworn flourishes and mannerisms indicative of some dead and forgotten period when men wore long, curled hair and women encased their digestive apparatus in steel and whalebone. . . . This is a misconception. Style, to begin with, is much more than a harmonious visual effect. . . . You wear your sword so because otherwise the scabbard will get between your legs and you will fall over it; you take the weight of your cloak over the elbow and fling it thus around your shoulder because in this way it will keep you warm without tying you up in a cocoon; you swing your farthingale like this because otherwise, when you sit down, it will bounce up in front of you. You hold your shoulders back because they must carry the weight of armor; you keep your knees straight because, in tights, you would look knock-kneed if you didn't.
>
> But rightly used they will acquire rhythm and dignity. More than that, they will begin to belong to you and you will gain a feeling of reality. They will cease to be "costume" and become clothes.

Miss Webster then draws a parallel between the character and the actor:

> You cannot put his hands in your pockets, because he had none. Neither can you put your thoughts in his head. You cannot claim that this or that feels false or unreal to you because you yourself would feel it or say it differently. There is a style in thought as there is in speech or dress, a kind of inner breeding, and acting is the perfect fusion of these things.
>
> Shakespeare's characters, the major ones, are likely to be bigger in mental stature than the average modern actor, more perceptive in imagination, bolder and freer in action, sharper in wit, swifter in words. We have plenty of acting talent in America today. But they completely lack practice in their craft. They do not know, because they have never seen "stature" and "manner" in acting Shakespeare. They think of it as something exaggerated and "ham" and believe that the slip-shod speech and lazy, commonplace attitudes of the present day are, in some obscure way, more "real."[6]

PREPARATION FOR *HAMLET*

This play, written around 1600, is the product of a rich period in Shakespeare's writing. During a five-year span he wrote not only *Hamlet*, but *Julius Caesar*, *Othello*, *Macbeth*, and *King Lear*. *Hamlet* re-

---

[5]I traced the Websters back to 1797 and Benjamin Nottingham Webster, but when I found he was of theatrical parentage, I stopped, willing to accept the fact that there is a long association between the London Theatre and the Websters.

[6]Margaret Webster, *Shakespeare without Tears* (Greenwich, Conn.: Fawcett, 1942; paperback edition, 1955), pp. 296–97.

mains the supreme acting drama in the English language. Its history as a play is also the history of great actors and acting.

Exercise 128

Before attempting to stage this short scene from *Hamlet* you should read the play in its entirety. If you have studied well, you should have no difficulty answering the following questions.

1. There are various opinions as to Hamlet's sanity—to which do you subscribe?
   a. that he is neither mad nor pretends to be so
   b. that he pretends madness
   c. that he is mad at times and at other times pretends madness
   d. that he is really mad
   Can you give lines from the play to justify your conviction?
2. The enactment of the play before the court has been called the turning point of this play. Do you agree? If not, what in your opinion is the turning point?
3. What secret does Shakespeare share with just his audience and Hamlet?
4. What basic similarity has this play to Greek classical tragedy?
5. Give examples of Hamlet's procrastination and irresolution. Give examples of Hamlet's immediate action.
6. It has been said that in this play Shakespeare wrote of two worlds, the real and imaginary. Give examples of each. What are the consequences of the death of Polonius?
7. What do you understand to be Hamlet's inner conflict?
8. Do you think Hamlet ever loved Ophelia?
9. Do you see any evidence in the play that Hamlet is a Christian?
10. Why is Claudius able to enlist Laertes in his schemes?
11. Of what purpose is the Osric scene?
12. Hamlet finds the King alone in Act III, Scene iii, and has an opportunity to kill him but he does not. In the closet scene, however, he does kill Polonius. What are Hamlet's motivations for these seemingly opposing actions?
13. Does Hamlet ever become a man of supreme action?

Character Portrayals

Hamlet   The drive of the famous "closet scene" that follows is supplied by the play's protagonist, Hamlet. One element separates this play from a vulgar tale of brutal violence: Hamlet is a thinking man. He has a sense of justice—often mistaken for a lack of will, although Shakespeare gives much proof to the contrary. Hamlet does not lack will when he leaves the security of his friends to follow the Ghost. He is prompt in action when he kills Rosencrantz and Guildenstern, who planned to kill him. If Hamlet were merely a creature of blind and furious emotion, the play would be deprived of its deep insight into humanity. Hamlet *is* emotional, but he has

Richard Burton as Hamlet. (Courtesy of Zodiac.)

within him, as in every other man of intellect, a kind of self-restraint counseling him. Hamlet's instincts and impulses are tempered with justice, prudence, and conscience. This human versus animal struggle is within all of us, and it is this that gives the play its universal appeal. All of us hope we are human, but we are constantly being reminded that we are also animals. This is Hamlet's terrible dilemma—as it is ours.

Polonius A careless reader might envision Polonius as a doddering old clown. But as we consider the fatherly devotion he gives Laertes and Ophelia, we begin to appreciate admirable qualities in the old man. Once a shrewd and effective politician, he still maintains some knowledge and wisdom, but both are now in the process of atrophying. Samuel Johnson described Polonius in a single notable phrase, "dotage encroaching upon wisdom." Polonius has loved the past and chooses to live in it still. He does, however, realize that he is not as effective as he was and therefore overcompensates with frantic effort. This results in making him appear a meddlesome, pedantic bore.

Queen Shakespeare's genius for deep character exploration is obvious in his portrayal of Gertrude. As he unfolds the many layers of her character, we realize her many dimensions. We cannot overlook her sins as a wife, but this does not lessen our respect for her as a women of stature and gentleness. But it is in her tenderness toward Ophelia and her son that we find identification. We see her more as the victim of a horrible chain of consequences than as a direct accomplice in murder. Indeed, we cannot find that she had any suspicion of the fratricide. As Shakespeare reveals his Queen, we find her to be warm and vibrant, a gentlewoman buffeted by chance.

The Ghost Shakespeare uses this symbolic figure to personify the emotional undercurrent of the play. He limits the Ghost to a slow, stately walk, to measured speech in unearthly tones, and gives him a majestic solemnity. In this way, Shakespeare deprives him of the physical in order that we become more conscious of the emotional. It is through the Ghost that we feel the preternatural, the grandeur of the events, the accentuation of conscience as an active force. And it is no mistake that Shakespeare starts his play with the appearance of the Ghost, for by this means he creates early and efficiently the atmosphere for the entire play that follows. One of the most moving touches in the portrayal is the Ghost's tender solicitude toward his former Queen. We can well believe that Shakespeare loved this character. It is one of the few parts that we know with certainty he acted himself.

Background

You will remember from your study of the entire play that by this point in the play Hamlet has been interviewed by the King's

Edmund Kean as Hamlet. (Courtesy of the Henry E. Huntington Library and Art Gallery.)

1. The Queen is discovered at LC. She paces in anxiety, rubbing her hands together. As she returns to LC, Polonius tiptoes into view UR. He speaks in a husky whisper without moving from a point where he can still view the hall.

2. *Screened . . . and him:* she has protected Hamlet from the King's anger.

3. *I'll silence me:* I'll hide behind the curtain and be quiet.

3a. *Be round with him:* speak sharply to Hamlet.

4. Hamlet is excited, expecting anything. As he realizes his mother is alone, he stands defiantly with feet planted solidly far apart, grasping his sword in readiness. He speaks in a rude, challenging voice.

5. These four lines are snapped back and forth in anger.

6. The Queen is hurt and surprised at her son's manner, but it does not change.

7. Have you forgotten that I am the Queen and your mother?

8. *By the rood:* by the cross of Christianity.

9. He speaks these words with venom, but softens some on the last line.

sycophants, Rosencrantz and Guildenstern. Realizing that anything he says will be immediately relayed to his enemy, Hamlet does not disguise his aversion to their efforts or to them personally. Subsequently, on his way to obey a summons from his mother, he encounters the King at prayers. He is tempted to kill him, but then decides to await a more auspicious time. Hamlet feels that he could "drink hot blood" and could do "such bitter business as the day would quake to look upon." With his mother he decides "to be cruel—to speak daggers to her but use none." In this wild and defiant mood, he enters the following scene. (Hamlet should convey all this background as he comes before her.)

REHEARSAL

Hamlet

William Shakespeare
Act III, Scene iv

CAST: **Hamlet**   **Queen Gertrude**

Polonius   **Ghost**

SCENE: *The Queen's room. A chair ULC.*

(*Polonius enters to Queen*[1])

Polonius: He will come straight. Look you lay home to him.
  Tell him his pranks have been too broad to bear with,
  And that your Grace hath screened and stood between
  Much heat and him.[2] I'll silence me[3] even here.
  Pray you be round with him.[3a]

Hamlet: (*Within*) Mother, mother, mother!

Queen: I'll warrant you; fear me not. Withdraw; I hear him coming.
     (*Polonius hides U, behind a curtain.*
       Hamlet enters.[4])

Hamlet: Now, mother, what's the matter?[5]

Queen: Hamlet, thou hast thy father much offended.

Hamlet: Mother, you have my father much offended.

Queen: Come, come, you answer with an idle tongue.

Hamlet: Go, go, you question with a wicked tongue.

Queen: Why, how now, Hamlet?[6]

Hamlet: What's the matter now?

Queen: Have you forgot me?[7]

Hamlet: No, by the rood,[8] not so!
  You are the Queen, your husband's[9] brother's wife,
  And—would it were not so—you are my mother.

Queen: Nay,[10] then I'll set those to you that can speak.

Hamlet: Come, come, and sit you down, you shall not budge!
  You go not till I set you up a glass
  Where you may see the inmost part of you.

Queen: What wilt thou do? Thou wilt not murder[11] me? Help, help,
  ho!

Polonius: *(Behind)* What, ho! help, help, help!

Hamlet: [12]*(Draws)* How now? a rat? Dead for a ducat, dead!
          (Stabs through the arras and kills Polonius)

Polonius: *(Behind)* O, I am slain!

Queen: O me,[13] what hast thou done?

Hamlet: Nay, I know not.[14] Is it the King?

Queen: O, what a rash and bloody deed is this!

Hamlet: A bloody deed—[15] almost as bad, good mother,
  As kill a king, and marry with his brother.

Queen: As[16] kill a king?

Hamlet: Ay, lady, 'twas my word.
          (Pulls aside curtain and sees Polonius)
  Thou wretched,[17] rash, intruding fool, farewell!
  I took thee for thy better. Take thy fortune.
  Thou find'st to be too busy is some danger.—
  [18]Leave wringing of your hands. Peace! sit you down
  And let me wring your heart; for so I shall
  If it be made of penetrable stuff;
  If damned custom have not brazed[19] it so
  That it is proof and bulwark against sense.

Queen: What have I done[20] that thou dar'st wag thy tongue
  In noise so rude against me?

Hamlet: [21]Such an act
  That blurs the grace and blush of modesty;
  Calls virtue hypocrite; takes off the rose
  From the fair forehead of an innocent love,
  And sets a blister[22] there; makes marriage vows
  As false as dicers' oaths. O, such a deed
  As from the body of contraction[23] plucks
  The very soul, and sweet religion makes
  A rhapsody of words! [Heaven's face doth glow;
  Yea, this solidity and compound mass,
  With tristful visage, as against the doom,
  Is thought-sick at the act.]

Queen: Ay me, what act,
  That roars so loud and thunders in the index?

Hamlet: Look here upon this picture, and on this,
  The counterfeit presentment of two brothers.[24]
  See what a grace was seated on this brow;

---

10. She is indignant and starts UR, but he grabs her hand and forces her back into the chair at UL. He is at her R and still holds her.

11. Charlotte Cushman reportedly spoke this line "Thou wilt not kill me?" not only destroying the meter but substituting a weak word for a strong.

12. Hamlet springs impetuously to action, drawing his sword, and in a flash plunges it into the curtain. French actor-producer Jean-Louis Barrault has the theory that Hamlet could not draw a sword to kill a man. Therefore, his emotional reaction is to cry out, "a rat?"

13. The Queen stands in terror.

14. Almost hopefully.

15. Accusing her.

16. She separates the words, trying to understand.

17. Hamlet was fond of the old man who was to be his father-in-law; therefore he is sad. The Queen rubs her hands together, trying to dry the cold sweat.

18. He speaks and handles her harshly.

19. *Brazed:* like bronze metal.

20. Crying out in bewilderment.

21. Kneels at her R.

22. *Blister:* prostitutes were branded on the forehead.

23. *Contraction:* marriage contract.

24. Actors have interpreted these lines in different ways. Edwin Booth wore his father's medallion around his neck. He handled the cameo of his uncle worn around the neck of the Queen. Henry Irving represented the pictures in the "mind's eye." Notice that the lines describe a full figure, not a portrait bust, or cameo. Other actors have used the medallion of the father and the uncle on a string around Hamlet's neck. In this way Hamlet compares the two. (See [James] Branden Matthews and Ashley Horace Thorndike, *Shakespearian Studies* [New York: Columbia University Press, 1916].)

25. *Hyperion:* the standard of male beauty like our Apollo.
26. *Station:* posture.
27. Reverently.

28. *Mildew'd ear:* an ear of wheat that is rotten and worthless.

29. *Batten:* fatten.
30. *Moor:* barren upland.

31. *Heyday:* youthful high spirit.

32. *Rebellious hell:* Hamlet refers to the evil impulses rebelling against the good in humans.
33. *Mutiny:* Verb does not occur again in Shakespeare. Meaning here is "rebel."
34. Queen claps her hands over her ears. She is very moved by the attack.

35. *Grained:* ingrained.

36. *As will not leave their tinct:* lose color.
37. Undaunted and in order to better press his attack, Hamlet now stands. *Enseamed:* greasy.

Hyperion's²⁵ curls; the front of Jove himself;
An eye like Mars, to threaten and command;
A station²⁶ like the herald Mercury,
New lighted on a heaven-kissing hill:
A combination and a form indeed²⁷
Where every god did seem to set his seal
To give the world assurance of a man.
This was your husband. Look you now what follows.
Here is your husband, like a mildew'd ear²⁸
Blasting his wholesome brother. Have you eyes?
Could you on this fair mountain leave to feed,
And batten²⁹ on this moor?³⁰ Ha! have you eyes?
You cannot call it love; for at your age
The heyday³¹ in the blood is tame, it's humble,
And waits upon the judgment; and what judgment
Would step from this to this? [Sense sure you have,
Else could you not have motion; but sure that sense
Is apoplexed: for madness would not err;
Nor sense to ecstasy was ne'er so thralled
But it reserved some quantity of choice
To serve in such a difference. What devil was't
That thus hath cozened you at hoodman-blind?
Eyes without feeling, feeling without sight,
Ears without hands or eyes, smelling sans all,
Or but a sickly part of one true sense
Could not so mope.]
O shame! where is thy blush? Rebellious hell,³²
If thou canst mutiny³³ in a matron's bones,
To flaming youth let virtue be as wax
And melt in her own fire.³⁴ [Proclaim no shame
When the compulsive ardor gives the charge,
Since frost itself as actively doth burn,
And reason panders will.]

Queen: O Hamlet, speak no more!
Thou turn'st mine eyes into my very soul,
And there I see such black and grained³⁵ spots
As will not leave their tinct.³⁶

Hamlet: ³⁷Nay, but to live
In the rank sweat of an enseamed bed
Stewed in corruption, honeying and making love
Over the nasty sty!

Queen: O speak to me no more!
These words like daggers enter in mine ears.
No more, sweet Hamlet!

Hamlet: A murderer and a villain![38]
A slave,[39] that is not twentieth part the tithe[40]
Of your precedent lord; a vice of kings;[41]
A cutpurse[42] of the empire and the rule,
That from a shelf the precious diadem stole
And put it in his pocket!

Queen: No more!

(Ghost appears)

Hamlet: A king of shreds and patches!—[43]
Save me and hover o'er me with your wings,
You heavenly guards! What would your gracious figure?

Queen: Alas,[44] he's mad!

Hamlet: [45]Do you not come your tardy son to chide,
That, lapsed in time and passion, lets go by
The important acting of your dread command?
O, say!

Ghost: Do not forget. This visitation
Is but to whet thy almost blunted purpose.
But look,[46] amazement on thy mother sits.
O, step between her and her fighting soul!
Conceit[47] in weakest bodies strongest works.
Speak to her, Hamlet.

Hamlet: [48]How is it with you, lady?

Queen: [49]Alas, how is't with you,
That you do bend your eye on vacancy,[50]
And with the incorporal air[51] do hold discourse?
[Forth at your eyes your spirits wildly peep;
And, as sleeping soldiers in the alarm,
Your bedded hairs, like life in excrements,
Start up and stand on end.] O gentle son,
Upon the heat and flame of thy distemper
Sprinkle cool patience! Whereon do you look?

Hamlet: On him! on him!—Look you how pale he glares!
His form and cause conjoined,[52] preaching to stones,[53]
Would make them capable.—Do not look upon me,
Lest with this piteous action you convert
My stern effects. Then what I have to do
Will want true color—tears perchance for blood.

Queen: To whom do you speak this?

Hamlet: Do you see nothing[54] there?

Queen: Nothing at all;[55] yet all that is I see.

Hamlet: Nor did you nothing[56] hear?

Queen: No,[57] nothing but ourselves.

(Ghost moves)

38. A piteous cry from Gertrude.

39. His attack is savage now. He "speaks daggers" to her.

40. *Tithe:* one tenth, not one two-hundredth.

41. *Vice of kings:* roguish clown in old plays, usually wore torn clothes, hence "shreds and patches" also.

42. *Cutpurse:* a pickpocket.

43. Hamlet has now reached the top of his savagery and hate; but all breath leaves him as he sees the Ghost, drops to his knees, and crosses himself, eyes transfixed upon the apparition. *Note:* In an effort to intensify this moment of shock for the audience, Garrick is supposed to have used a mechanical device, which shattered the Queen's chair.

44. Sadly the Queen must admit to herself that her son is mad as all have been saying.

45. Possessed by the apparition, he whispers to it. *Lapsed in time and passion:* wasted time and impulse.

46. Gently, lovingly, the Ghost refers to the pathetic, terror-struck creature he once called his Queen.

47. *Conceit:* A word often used by Shakespeare meaning imagination.

48. Now, softened by the Ghost's reference to the Queen, Hamlet reaches back for her without taking his eyes from the Ghost.

49. She takes the outstretched hand and kneels beside him as she strokes the hand, then caresses it.

50. Crying now, she touches him with a motherly tenderness. Remember, she does not see anything but her son, and she is sure he is now experiencing the manic state.

51. *Incorporal:* bodiless.

52. *Conjoined:* united.

53. Hamlet fears that the "piteous action" of the Ghost will soften his resolve to deal in revenge and blood. Queen rises slowly, hand on his shoulder.

54. For the first time since the appearance of the Ghost, Hamlet ventures a quick glance back at his mother, then back to the vision as he asks, "Do you see nothing there?" pointing to the Ghost.

55. Attempting to comfort her poor, mad son.

56. Accents "hear."

57. Warm tones, soothing, comforting, like a lullaby.

58. Springs to his feet with a cry as he points to the moving "illusion" and turns to follow it, holding the pose.

59. Hamlet stands frozen looking after the Ghost. Gertrude steps back in amazement. After the outbreak of emotion, this silence should be thrilling.

60. Sadly, as she tries to reassure him.

61. *Ecstasy:* madness.

62. Impetuously he turns, repeating the word in contempt, as if it were preposterous. He then steps to her to make points to prove his sanity.

63. *Reword:* repeat.

64. Again returning to the deep shame he feels because of her conduct.

65. *Unction:* salve, soothing.

Hamlet: [58]Why, look you there! Look how it steals away!
My father, in his habit as he lived!
Look where he goes even now out at the portal![59]
(Exit Ghost)

Queen: [60]This is the very coinage of your brain.
This bodiless creation ecstasy[61]
Is very cunning in.

Hamlet: [62]Ecstasy?
My pulse, as yours, doth temperately keep time
And makes as healthful music. It is not madness
That I have utt'red. Bring me to the test,
And I the matter will reword;[63] which madness
Would gambol from. Mother, for love of grace,[64]
Lay not that flattering unction[65] to your soul,
That not your trespass but my madness speaks.
[It will but skin and film the ulcerous place,
Whilst rank corruption, mining all within,
Infects unseen.] Confess yourself to heaven;
Repent what's past; avoid what is to come;
[And do not spread compost on the weeds
To make them ranker. Forgive me this my virtue;
For in the fatness of these pursy times
Virtue itself of vice must pardon beg—
Yea, curb and woo for leave to do him good.]

Richard Burton as Hamlet speaking the lines: "But go not to my uncle's bed." (Courtesy of Friedman-Abeles, Inc., Photographers, New York City.)

Queen: O Hamlet,[66] thou hast cleft my heart in twain.

Hamlet: O, throw away[67] the worser part of it,
  And live the purer with the other half.
  [68]Good night—but go not to my uncle's bed.
  Assume a virtue, if you have it not.
  [69][That monster, custom, who all sense doth eat
  Of habits evil, is angel yet in this
  That to the use of actions fair and good
  He likewise gives a frock or livery,
  That aptly is put on.] Refrain tonight,
  And that shall lend a kind of easiness
  To the next abstinence; the next more easy;
  For use almost can change the stamp of nature,
  And master thus the devil, or throw him out
  With wondrous potency. Once more, good night;
  And when you are desirous to be blest,[70]
  I'll blessing beg of you.—For this same lord,
  I do repent; but heaven hath pleased it so,
  To punish me with this, and this with me,
  That I[71] must be their scourge and minister.
  I will bestow him, and will answer well
  The death I gave him.[72] So again, good night.
  I must be cruel, only to be kind;
  Thus bad begins, and worse remains behind.[73]

66. The anguish she is feeling inside makes her shriek.

67. He makes a move to kiss her, but is repelled as he remembers her intimacy with his uncle, the "bloated king." At this point, Sarah Bernhardt (who played Hamlet with great success) is said to have taken a strand of the Queen's long hair, and bent to kiss it.

68. Unlike his previous accusing tone, Hamlet now speaks to her with pity and compassion for her frailty.

69. Suggested cuts.

70. Hamlet means that when he finds his mother praying for absolution, he will kneel and ask her forgiveness.

71. He feels that he is Heaven's instrument of punishment for all their sins.

72. He starts to lift the body, then turns up to speak to her.

73. *Remains behind:* a prophecy that more is to come and that it will be worse.

FURTHER READING: SHAKESPEARE

Every page in this book might be filled listing the thousands of books on the various aspects of Shakespeare. We have space for only a few. For aspects other than acting, consult bibliographies, concordances, and indexes. (See also "Further Reading: The Character and Acting Styles" in chapter 9, and the "Additional Reading" list at the end of the book.)

Jaggard, William. *Shakespeare Bibliography*. New York: Ungar, 1959. Lists 36,000 entries. Both this and the following are expensive; consult your librarian.

Smith, Gordon Ross. *A Classified Shakespeare Bibliography*. University Park: Pennsylvania State University Press, 1963. Lists some 20,000 books on Shakespeare.

Elizabethan Background

There are many books that will give you the look and feel of Elizabethan times. The first listing below is good; the second is more complete.

Chute, Marchette. *Shakespeare of London.* New York: E. P. Dutton, 1949. Now in paperback.

Raleigh, Walter, et al., eds. *Shakespeare's England: An Account of the Life and Manner of His Age.* London and Oxford: Clarendon Press, 1916–62. Vol. I, religion, court, army, navy, travel, education, handwork, law, commerce, medicine, sciences, etc.; Vol. II, fine arts, heraldry, costume, home, London, books, actors and acting, playhouses, masques, court entertainment, sports, Shakespeare's English, ballads, games, and index of passages cited from Shakespeare.

Dictionaries

Abbott, E. A. *A Shakespearian Grammar.* London: Macmillan, 1874. Old, but none quite like it; studies differences between Elizabethan and modern English.

Bartlett, John. *A Complete Concordance of Shakespeare.* London: St. Martin's, 1960. Index of words, phrases, and passages.

Irvine, Theodora. *A Pronouncing Dictionary of Shakespearian Proper Names.* New York: Barnes and Noble, 1947.

Kokeritz, Helge. *Shakespeare's Names: A Pronouncing Dictionary.* New Haven, Conn.: Yale University Press, 1959.

———. *Shakespeare's Pronunciation.* New Haven, Conn.: Yale University Press, 1953.

Variorums

Granville-Barker, Harley. *Prefaces to Shakespeare.* Princeton, N.J.: Princeton University Press, 1947. The famous variorums in 4 vols.

Hazlitt, William. *The Characters of Shakespeare's Plays.* New York: E. P. Dutton, 1929. Essays of 1817.

General Information

Bentley, Gerald E. *Shakespeare, A Biographical Handbook.* New Haven, Conn.: Yale University Press, 1961. A good buy in paperback.

Chambers, E. K. *The Elizabethan Stage.* Oxford and London: Clarendon Press, 1923. Expensive, in 4 volumes, but it is *the* generally accepted authority. Consult library.

Acting Style for Shakespeare

Brown, John Russell. *Shakespeare in Performance.* New York: Harcourt Brace Jovanovich, 1976.

Clurman, Harold. "Actors in Style and Style in Actors." *New York Times Magazine,* December 7, 1952. An excellent article that should be reprinted.

Joseph, Bertram. *Acting Shakespeare.* New York: Theatre Arts Books, 1969.

————. *Elizabethan Acting.* 2d ed. New York: Oxford University Press, 1964.

Sprague, A. C. *Shakespearean Players and Performances.* Cambridge, Mass.: Harvard University Press, 1953.

Webster, Margaret. *Shakespeare without Tears.* New York: Fawcett, 1955. Paperback.

15
MOLIÈRE (1622–1673)

To the French, Molière is the best loved of all French authors, and is to them what Shakespeare is to us. A strange comparison? Until the nineteenth century the French considered Shakespeare a barbarian who mixed cruelty, comedy, and tragedy into a single play. But Molière had that gay, debonair French touch. Unlike Shakespeare, he was neither a philosopher nor a dramatic poet. But there are interesting similarities between the two playwrights. Molière was born six years after Shakespeare's death and both died in their fifties. Both were actors attached to permanent companies of players. Both borrowed plots from other sources to revolutionize the drama of their day. Shakespeare wrote thirty-seven plays to Molière's thirty —and both are immortals.

We need not theorize or assume anything in adopting an acting style for Molière's plays. We could have no better instructor than Molière himself, for he was also a great teacher of acting. One of his contemporaries, de Vise, felt that Molière could teach a stick to act. This was probably because Molière had to work hard to acquire his skill as an actor. He understood how "all the pieces fit."

MOLIÈRE AS AN ACTOR

In France during the seventeenth century, an obscure young actor, who was an even more obscure author, was playing in barns, racquet courts, inn yards—anywhere his little company could find an audience. Molière first learned the job of utility actor, then supporting player, and finally how to "carry a show" himself, taking the leading parts. To the latter task, he added the job of management and authorship. He had been well educated at a Jesuit school. A good part of his fourteen-year apprenticeship was spent under the tutelage of several great Commedia dell'Arte players. This was to make an indelible impression on all his future work as both actor and playwright.

Nature did not fashion Molière in the accepted mold of the actor. He was not tall, did not have a fine voice, and never had that romantic look.[1] All his life he tried to cure himself of a habit of speaking too quickly. When he tried to overcome it, he was seized by uncontrollable hiccoughs. He also had difficulty in making his eyebrows behave; they were thick, black, and kept darting all over his forehead. But he studied the actors of the Commedia dell'Arte troupe, which he had joined. This troupe included at least three performers who were the best of their time.

APPRENTICESHIP

Molière watched the fine actors of his troupe acting behind their masks, and saw them achieve effects by the use of gesture, posture, and bodily movement alone. He practiced tirelessly. There was time; he was still in his twenties. He tried to use his square, unresponsive body to make only the most necessary and telling gestures. He decided to turn to his advantage the shortcomings nature had given him: He displayed the wide-set eyes, short legs, and peasant face proudly to his audiences. Always alert to the audience, he studied what they wanted. He began to try different ideas; some were not good and came to nothing; but others got response.

When he found himself slipping into his old habit of rushing his speeches, he stopped dead, and then changed the tone and tempo of his voice. This, he found, created a comic effect in itself, so he developed it. One of the actors he worked with wrote later that Molière "seemed to have several voices." The wandering eyebrows, which had given him such concern at first, were reserved for making specific points. "No one has ever been so good at rearranging his face," wrote a Parisian when Molière had become recognized as a virtuoso of mime.

There is an object lesson for all young actors in the career of Molière. It is plain that he took inventory of himself, developed what was effective with audiences, then studied to turn his liabilities into assets. Obviously, to work and study as he did meant that Molière wanted to entertain. The critic Sarcey quotes Molière as saying, "There is no other rule of the theatre than that of pleasing the public."[2]

MOLIÈRE'S STYLE

When Molière finally reached Paris, he seemed to hold up a mirror in which Frenchmen could see themselves. He showed how extravagant and effete they had become. He laughed at their clothes,

---

[1]Talma had the romantic look, as did Molière's pupil, Baron. Edwin and J. W. Booth, and Mounet Sully all had it—and in the last generation, John Barrymore.

[2]Francisque Sarcey (1827–99), the most important French dramatic critic of his time, was author of *Comediens et Comediennes*.

their manners, and society; he ridiculed their politics, speech, religion—and even French "amour." But it was a gentlemanly and cultured laughter, more like an indulgent smile. It never stung, but always was "of gay disposition."

Molière calls the individuals he writes "types"; Chekhov wrote "characters." The miser, the invalid, the hypocrite, the noble, the pedant, the bore, and the coquette are types. Molière depended on the actors to supply the personality and flesh and blood, to make the types into people. Tartuffe is sketched in broad outlines. I have seen the part developed as an unctuous little con man, and I have seen him portrayed as a threatening cadaver with hypnotic eyes; each interpretation was interesting.

Authorities seem amazed that Molière, as an actor, relied so much on his body in the interpretations of his characters—his use of posture or silhouette to express a point—when he could have written lines to accomplish it. Having been trained in the great Commedia school, Molière knew that such a moment would be more memorable if shown by action rather than words. So we must remember that in Molière's plays there are places where the author expects the actor to enrich the moment by the acting skill Molière presupposed as part of every actor.

Molière developed the comedy techniques that he learned from the Commedia school. As you study his plays, you will find that he borrowed and used such comedy techniques as the cumulative repetition (of lines or business), the malaprop, the echo-reply, the comic business of peeling off layer after layer of clothing, the double take, the fast transition of speech or action, and pomposity's pratfall. When these techniques are used most effectively, they should seem natural. But we can be sure that Molière devised them and worked on them repeatedly until they had the neatness and precision needed in playing farce-comedy.

Precision of movement, speech, and gesture—so necessary to the successful playing of comedy—can also be seen in the sweep of a brush across a canvas, the painter leaving his deft, sure mark for all time. It can be seen during those measured seconds as the Olympic champion prepares for his attempt. Great dancers have precision, and indeed it can be seen in many fields of endeavor. Wherever you find the expert you find precision.

THE STAMP OF THE COMMEDIA

The lessons Molière learned from the Commedia are sealed forever in his plays: the precision of the Italian performers, and the clear-cut substance of a comedy moment. In *Precious Damsels*, some characters wear Commedia masks while others are in clown white. In *The Would-Be Gentleman*, two girls chase two boys around the room; then, at a given signal, the chase reverses, and the boys chase the girls—pure Commedia dell'Arte!

The actor Coquelin became world-renowned for his interpretation of Cyrano de Bergerac, but for many years he made a specialty of the comic heroes of Molière. Here he is pictured as Sganarelle in Les Precieuses Ridicules. (Courtesy of the Henry E. Huntington Library and Art Gallery.)

In most of Molière's great comedies, the skillful execution of comedy routines seems more important than plot. Like Shakespeare, he seems to have considered plot as merely the cord tying the parts together to make a package. And what attractive packages they made! Molière's special gift was in adding refinement to the wonderfully theatrical Commedia technique. He did so with his wit, his light satiric touch, and his love and understanding of all the human frailties. The Commedia actors took a comedy situation and crystallized it into one hilarious moment by means of a ''piece of business'' (or as they called it, a *lazzi*). Molière gave these isolated bits an order, a design—and a quality of literature. He made each comedy unit dependent on previous units, these in turn contributing to those to come. Then all were set into a pattern, which contributed to the overall comedic effect.

ZEST IN PLAYING FARCE-COMEDY

When an audience becomes convinced that the actors themselves are enjoying playing in a comedy, then the audience's enjoyment is increased. This contagious quality, which is so essential in comedy or farce, has been described in various ways. Some refer to it as enthusiasm. It is a kind of ''bubbling over,'' the display of a zest for life. This joyous spirit comes down to us directly from the Commedia dell'Arte; it is the essence of their style. A Molière play produced without this quality becomes merely an interesting museum piece. It was a foregone conclusion with Molière that actors and directors would supply life for his plays so that they could sparkle with brilliance and wit. However, in planning your approach to his plays, always remember that he refined and gave sophistication to the uninhibited farcical antics of the Commedia clowns.

MOLIÈRE AS DIRECTOR

In directing the members of his company, Molière was often accused of being a martinet. On the subject of the proper accentuation of a line, he would tolerate no difference of opinion. The verse he wrote was the *Alexandrine iambic hexameter*—a line of twelve syllables, sometimes divided in the middle and with a rhyme at the end.[3] The Alexandrine is the traditional line of French poetry (so named because early romances about Alexander the Great were written in this form). In addition, Molière's justly celebrated prose was devised so that the proper meaning of the line is best expressed when correctly accented. It is no wonder he was so determined that actors speak his lines correctly!

[3]There is an adaptation of *Tartuffe* by Richard Wilbur that attempts the almost hopeless task of putting the Alexandrine into similar English verse, still retaining the sense of the play.

PREPARATION FOR *GEORGE DANDIN*

Read the full play carefully before attempting this excerpt. It has some of the typical characteristics of farce: the jealous husband who locks his erring wife out of their home, the importance of some physical prop (in this case, a door), and lines spoken directly to the audience.

A rich peasant, George Dandin, has married the daughter of a noble but impoverished family. Dandin learns that a young neighbor has been making love to his wife and complains to his wife's parents. They confront the young lovers and both deny the accusations. The parents then reprove Dandin for his jealousy. Each time he sees the lovers together he complains to the noble family, but the daughter is clever enough to convince her parents that Dandin is wrong. The situation is made difficult because the parents believe that the exchange of Dandin's money for their noble strain was to his advantage. The third time Dandin discovers his wife with her lover, Dandin locks her out of the house and sends for her parents so they will be convinced of her ways by seeing for themselves.

As with all farce, the following scene must be played with spirit and speed. Note the short, repetitive words for comic effect, the "clipped" speeches, and the "build" to a comic line.

REHEARSAL

George Dandin

Molière
An Adaptation from Act III, Scene viii

CAST: **George Dandin** *("Dandin" means "Ninny"; Rabelais was the first to use the word as a proper name.)*
Angélique *Young wife of Dandin and daughter of M. de Sotenville.*

SCENE: *In front of George Dandin's house.*

TIME: *After midnight. Moonlight bathes the stage in half-light.*

AT RISE: *Angélique enters and moves surreptitiously to the house, looking from side to side. She wears a cape. George Dandin is in a long, red, striped nightgown and stocking cap. Angélique carefully tries to open the door and is surprised that it is bolted from inside.*

George Dandin: [1]*Ah ha!* So, I've caught you playing your pranks because you think me sound asleep. Well, wife, I'm glad to see you out there at this time of night.

1. As he appears at the window.

2. Again she tries the door.
3. Mocking her.
4. An accusation.

5. Hard, firm delivery.

6. Genuinely shocked.

7. He claps his hands together.

8. Smugly.

9. Sincerely.

10. This is a true confession.

11. A pause. She decides upon a change of attitude, almost "baby talk."

12. His conciliatory tone gives her hope, but this is changed with his next speech. From a blubbering self-pity he changes quickly to an austere firmness on "Your promises—"

13. Acting out the innocent.

Angélique: There's no harm in my going out for a breath of cool night air.[2]

George Dandin: [3]"There's no harm in my going out for a breath of cool night air." No, No! After midnight is the proper time to be getting fresh air. You must think I'm stupid.[4] I know all about your rendezvous with that—that—Don Juan! I saw you! I overheard everything you said.[5] This time your mother and father can't help being convinced of how right I was. This time they'll believe that I've been right about you all along. I've sent for them. They'll be here any minute now!

Angélique: [6]Oh heavens—

George Dandin: Now comes my triumph![7] Yes, Yes! Until now you have denied everything, fooled your parents and whitewashed your evil ways. No matter what I said I saw you were very clever in the way you twisted my facts, and put me in the wrong. Yes, yes! But now the truth is going to be plain—

Angélique: Oh, please—open the door.

George Dandin: Ah, no! We'll just quietly wait for your parents. What a delight it's going to be when they see you outside at this time of night.[8] While you're waiting why don't you think up some clever way of getting out of this!

Angélique: [9]What could I possibly say—

George Dandin: *Nothing!* There's nothing you can invent this time that I can't prove false.

Angélique: [10]All right, it's true! I've been wrong and you have good reason to complain. But I ask you, please, don't let my parents see me standing out here. Please? Open the door?

George Dandin: No.

Angélique: [11]Oh, my poo-o-r little husband—

George Dandin: Yes, I'm a "poor little husband" because you are caught.[12] Never once have you ever said such a sweet thing to me before.

Angélique: I promise you, I'll never, never—

George Dandin: Your promises have nothing to do with it. I want your parents to know once and for all what your behavior has been—

Angélique: You have every right to be angry.[13] But you ought to forgive a young girl of my age who has seen nothing of the world she has just entered; who has used her liberty without thinking of the harm she might be doing to others. I won't try to excuse myself for the wrong I've done you. I only ask you to forget and spare me the angry reproaches of my father and mother. I give you my word that in the future you will find me the best of wives and I'll show you such love and devotion that you'll never have cause to mistrust me again.

George Dandin: No.

Angélique: Be generous.[14]

George Dandin: No.

Angélique: Please, please—

George Dandin: *Never!* I am determined that your mother and father see you for what you are, a shameful—

Angélique: All right then![15]

I warn you that a woman in my situation might do anything! I'll do something to make you sorry—

George Dandin: [16]What will you do?

Angélique: See this knife?[17] *I'll kill myself!*

George Dandin: Good, good—Ha, ha—

Angélique: Not so good—*for you!* Everyone knows how we quarrel, how you shout at me. When I'm found dead, no one will have any doubt but that you killed me and my parents will see that you're punished for murder. You'll pay the full penalty—the guillotine!

George Dandin: Nonsense, you can't fool me with that—

Angélique: George Dandin, if you don't open this door at once you'll find out what a woman will do when she's desperate!

George Dandin: [18]You're only trying to frighten me.

Angélique: Oh, I am, am I?[19]

Since I must, this will end it and show if I am deceiving you or not—[20]

[21]I hope they punish you in full, George Dandin, for my death—and—and—your cruelty—ah-h-h—

George Dandin: [22]Oh, my goodness!

[23]can she be so malicious as to kill herself just to get me hanged? I'll take a light and see.

(He unbolts door, then opens it furtively.[24] He holds the candle high and looks about, but she is not in sight. As he opens the door, Angélique slips quietly behind it.)

George Dandin: [25]No one here! Or here! I thought so. She's run off. She's run off. She couldn't get anywhere with me with her tears and threats. Well, that makes it worse for her. Her parents will now be *convinced* that she runs around at night!

(He tries the door)

It's *locked!* It must have blown shut.

(He beats on the door)

Hey! Someone—! The door is locked.

I'll wake the servants. You in there—hear me?

The door—open it—open up—

(He beats furiously)

Open this door at once—!

Ludwig Brekmann as George Dandin, in an amusing production of this play, at the Municipal Theatre, Hamburg, Germany. Director Ernest Matray conceived and staged the farce in the style of the Commedia dell'Arte. (Photo by Rose-Marie Clausen, Hamburg. From The Theatre in Germany. *Reprinted by permission of F. Bruckmann Verlag.)*

14. The next four lines should be spoken quickly and with "build" to "All right then—"

15. A pause. Then she quietly threatens him.

16. Laughing derisively.

17. She holds it high like a heroine in a melodrama.

18. His laughter is a little hollow now.

19. Weakening.

20. Now that she realizes she can convince him, she drives on.

21. Again the melodramatic heroine. Pretends to stab herself.

22. He cannot believe it has happened—but it may be true.

23. Thinking only of the effect of her death on him. Spoken directly to the audience.

24. Door must open onstage.

25. Holding candle high and peering into the darkness R and L.

26. She speaks sweetly at first then as she pretends to recognize her husband, she barks with a shrewish rage.

27. Completely subdued. Pleads.

28. As he glances offstage, he becomes frantic and returns to beating on the door. Angélique shouts over the noise.

(Angélique appears at the window, all smiles and pretending she was asleep.)

Angélique: [26]W-w-hat? Who is it? Who's there? Oh, it's you. You dirty old drunkard, out all night in your nightshirt! Is this a proper hour to be coming home? Why, it's nearly daylight. Is this the sort of life a decent man leads?

George Dandin: Let me in.[27]

Open up—pl-e-e-a-se?[28]

Your father and mother are coming!

Quick! Let me in!

Angélique: Ah, no. I'm tired of you staying out all night. I want them to see just what I've been putting up with—!

PREPARATION FOR *TARTUFFE*

Exercise 129

Read the entire play carefully so that you are able to answer the following questions.

1. Can you give some reasons why *Tartuffe* is the most often produced of all Molière's plays?
2. In as few words as possible, describe what this play is about.
3. Does the theme of this 300-year-old play apply to today's society?
4. Name the conflicting forces in *Tartuffe*.
5. In *Tartuffe*, which group is Molière writing about: (1) St. Eustache peasants, (2) the French bourgeoisie, (3) nobility of Louis XIV's court?
6. Molière is considered to be the champion of which form of playwriting: (1) comedy-drama, (2) farce, (3) tragedy, (4) romance?
7. Describe Mariane, Dorine, Orgon, and Tartuffe from lines in the play.
8. In your opinion, which author has most influenced present-day comedy: (1) Aristophanes, (2) Molière, (3) Shakespeare?
9. It has been said that Molière's solutions to his plays do not follow the lines of comedy. Can you think of other endings more in keeping with the comic spirit of this play?
10. Molière hides Orgon under a table while a scene is played that might not otherwise be comic. Is this device one that might be used by the Commedia actors?
11. Molière acted the part of Orgon. Do you see any evidence in the play that the author knew acting and actors? Give examples.
12. What was Molière's outstanding contribution to the theatre?
    a. his use of stock Commedia characters
    b. the construction of his plays
    c. adaptation of old Roman plots
    d. memorable characterizations
    e. the follies and absurdities of mankind

13. A rule of old-time comedians was to "rehearse slow—play fast." Why would this advice be valuable in preparing our scene from *Tartuffe?*

14. This scene has been called "brilliant." Check the qualities you believe essential to a successful performance of this scene:
    a. the pert, irrepressible characterization of Dorine
    b. the pompous, but futile, exasperation of Orgon when provoked by Dorine
    c. the running comic threat of a slap

REHEARSAL

Tartuffe

Molière
An Adaptation by Robert Bruce Wallace*
Act II, Scene ii

CAST: **Orgon**

Dorine

Mariane

SETTING: *Required: a stool at C, a double door L. At rise, Mariane is DC seated on a high stool. Her father, Orgon, has evidently been lecturing her; he is stopped in the middle of a gesture to listen. He puts his finger to his lips, motioning her to be silent, points to the door DL, tiptoes to it, and opens it suddenly. Dorine, who has been leaning against the door, stumbles into the room, trying to regain her balance as she screams loudly and fearfully.*

Orgon: Ah hah![1] What were you doing?[2] Spying? [3]That must be a big bump of curiosity you have there—to make you eavesdrop on us this way.

Dorine: I heard some gossip[4]—guesswork—a lie, I'm sure, about a marriage. But I didn't believe it.

Orgon: Indeed?[5] Is it so far beyond belief?

Dorine: I wouldn't believe a word of it, sir, even if it came from you!

Orgon: I know how to make you believe it, though—[6]

Dorine: Of course! You'll concoct some clever explanation—

Orgon: I'm telling you[7] exactly what will happen—very soon.

Dorine: Nonsense![8]

Orgon: What I am speaking of, my girl, is not a subject to be joked about.

1. As Dorine staggers headfirst past Orgon and Marianne, Orgon shouts victoriously, "Ah hah!"
2. Orgon runs to Dorine.
3. He takes her ear with one hand and with his upstage hand indicates that she has a bump on her head. Positions: Dorine DR, Orgon to her L, and Mariane on stool.
4. In an attempt to cover her embarrassment, she assumes an officious manner.
5. Orgon nods, forcing a smile, pretending to agree.
6. The strained smile fades quickly. He has had enough and is suddenly serious.
7. Spoken as a dictate.
8. She has been shaking her head "no," shrugging, and chuckling steadily.

*This adaptation by Robert Bruce Wallace makes no attempt to reproduce the Alexandrine in English, but rather to keep Molière's characterizations and comedy rhythms intact.

9. Addressing Mariane.

10. Positions at this point: Mariane on stool C, Dorine to her R, Orgon to Dorine's R. Dorine shakes her head, "no." Her body should express self-confidence and sureness—feet apart, planted firmly, arms folded.

11. Soothing him as she places her hand on his chest, gently patting him. On his speech, he pushes her hand away.

12. Again patting his chest. Same business for Orgon on her line, "this scheme of yours."

13. Dorine turns to Mariane and puts a protecting arm on her.

14. On her last line, Dorine begins the patting business, but Orgon sees it coming and brushes her away with his line ending "in your position." Dorine steps menacingly to him, eyes narrowing, chin jutting out. Orgon grabs her and thrusts her easily to his right. Positions: Dorine R, Mariane at C, Orgon between them.

15. On "So he says," she again strides threateningly to him. Orgon starts for her, and she ducks in front of both to L of Mariane.

16. Positions at this point: Mariane at C, Orgon at her R, Dorine ranging freely up and down LC during this speech. One minute she is bold and shouting at him, the next darting about, avoiding his mounting anger.

17. As they snarl at each other, Mariane becomes a shield to protect Dorine and an obstacle preventing Orgon from getting to Dorine. Mariane's head goes from right to left—as if at a tennis match. *Note:* This must be carefully drilled—a certain word, a certain movement.

18. The quarrel is getting more heated and louder.

Dorine: *(Crossing to Mariane)* Go on—! [9]Don't believe a word your father says—He's only joking.

Orgon: I'm telling you—[10]

Dorine: No, no, no,—no—no—. No matter what you say, no one would believe you.

Orgon: I'm—getting—angry—!

Dorine: All right.[11] You are believed—! So much the worse for you. I don't understand—you *look* like an intelligent man with that beard and all. Then how can you be idiot enough to want—

Orgon: *What?* Now you listen to me, young woman,—you have taken certain liberties in this house which I don't like—

Dorine: Please, Monsieur,[12] let's talk without getting angry. You must be fooling with this scheme of yours. Your daughter[13] has nothing in common with that bigot! He has other things to think about, besides—how would you benefit by the match? You have all the money you need so why take on a beggar as a son-in-law?

Orgon: You are far too free with that tongue of yours—[14]far too free—for anyone in your position! If he has nothing—all the more reason to respect him. His poverty is noble. It raises him beyond desire for worldly goods. He lost his fortune because he cared nothing for earthly things while he was striving for the blessings of eternity. My help may be the means of getting him out of trouble and restoring his property to him. His vast estates were well known in his own district where he is still regarded as a gentleman.

Dorine: [15]So he says. But, sir, such pride is not compatible with piety. If he embraces the simplicity of a holy life, he shouldn't boast of his fine and noble birth. Why such pride? But this discussion is offending you.[16] Let's talk about him as a person and forget his noble state. Can you have the heart to give a girl like this to a man like him? Shouldn't you, in all decency, foresee the outcome of such a marriage? It's hard enough to be a faithful wife, but he who gives his daughter to a man she hates must someday answer to heaven for her missteps. Think, sir, of the chances you take![17]

Orgon: You presume to tell me how to live— You—you a servant girl?

Dorine: You could do worse than follow my advice.

Orgon: Daughter, we'll waste no more time on this nonsense. I know what's best for you. I'm your father! [18]Oh, I know I once promised you to Valère, but he's a gambler and I suspect him of being a free thinker. And I never see him in church.

Dorine: You expect him to be there at certain times when you are—to make sure you see him?

Orgon: Who asked your advice on this matter? Are you the family lawyer or a maid? Tartuffe is on the best of terms with heaven

Mariane pleads with Orgon in a scene from Molière's Tartuffe, *produced at the Repertory Theatre of Lincoln Center, New York. (Photo by Barry Hyams.)*

and that means more than anything else.[19] This marriage will fulfill all your hopes and dreams. It will be full of pleasure and joy. You will live together in faithful love like two young children, like two turtle doves. There will never be a harsh word between you—.[20] Don't interrupt! Hold your tongue![21] Don't stick your nose into what doesn't concern you!

Dorine: [22]I only speak for your own good, Monsieur—

Orgon: [23]Very nice of you. Now be quiet!

Dorine: If I didn't like you—

Orgon: Spare me that, please. I don't need your affection—

Dorine: All right then, I'll like you—in spite of yourself—

Orgon: Damn!

Dorine: Your good name means a great deal to me. I don't want people making fun of you.

Orgon: Silence—silence—silence!

Dorine: It would be a crime to permit such a marriage.

Orgon: [24]Will you shut up? You—you—*serpent with a poisonous tongue!*

Dorine: What?[25] You—a religious man, losing his temper?

Orgon: Yes, I must get better control of myself—but you infuriate me with your talk. Once more, will you be quiet?

Dorine: Very well.[26] But if I can't speak, I'll go on thinking all the more.

Orgon: Think all you like,[27] just don't let us hear what you're thinking. Or!

(*To his daughter*) Now, child.[28] I'm not a stupid man and I've looked carefully into every angle of—

Dorine: (*Aside*) It drives me wild when I can't talk!

19. On "anything else," Orgon takes a pinch of snuff. He has become so angry and nervous he hopes this will conceal his frustration, but we can see his hands tremble. He then paints a beautiful romantic picture and uses honey tones.

20. This is too much for the practical little Dorine—she can stand no more and tries to jump in, but Orgon anticipates her and raises his fervor and his voice.

21. Dorine tries again, and again the same business by Orgon.

22. Now meek and sweet, she steps in front of Mariane to face Orgon.

23. Almost automatically, he passes Dorine to his right, facing his daughter again. Orgon speaks quickly and quietly, but we see he is trying to control his feelings. Dorine is using her charm, but she is throwing darts at him. Neither are showing anger at this point, but it begins to build from here on.

24. Stamps his foot in frustration on "Will you shut up?" Then he hunts for some horrible name to call her.

25. Still not angry, she shames him for his outburst as if he were a six-year-old.

26. Shrugging. Cheerfully resigned.

27. Passes his left hand back at her as if shooing a pesky fly. *Note:* It may help Orgon to get the feeling of this scene if he imagines he is intent on some work and a persistent fly is bothering him.

28. He wags his finger at her with a harsh, threatening tone. Then, in sudden contrast, turns to Mariane again with his soft, warm tones.

29. Orgon darts a quick murderous glance at Dorine. She cringes, then shrugs it off with a mischievous smile. Orgon resumes his pompous lecture to Mariane.

30. Straight front.

31. From a high perch of outraged dignity.

32. Looks at him with wide-eyed innocence.

33. Now suddenly all his control vanishes—he storms at her. Orgon starts a gesture to slap her, but she sees it coming and slaps the hand back. The force of his turned body sends it on its way again. This time she bends slightly, the blow barely missing her. She smiles with satisfaction. This must be rehearsed in slow motion and allowed to increase in speed as it becomes automatic. In performance it must be fast to be funny.

34. Raises his right hand to threaten her and with his left coaxes her to speak.

35. This is an order!

36. He dashes to her with hand raised, all control gone now. She avoids him, they circle once around Mariane. Then Dorine runs off R, screaming with laughter.

37. He looks fearfully at his outstretched hands.

38. Looking at his shaking fingers—they even frighten him.

39. Orgon starts walking to L.

40. He is off by now.

41. Mariane, who has sat without uttering a sound during the entire scene, now begins to titter to herself; it grows louder and louder. If this is done imaginatively, it can be almost startling to an audience who has become accustomed to Mariane's silence.

Orgon: [29]I admit that Tartuffe isn't handsome, still his looks are—

Dorine: Like a bulldog's! [30]

Orgon: Even if one cannot appreciate his other qualities—

Dorine: She's getting a bargain, all right. (*Orgon turns to Dorine, crossing his arms and staring at her*) If I were in her place, no man would marry me without risking the consequences. He'd soon learn that a woman always has a way to get even.

Orgon: So—(*To Dorine*) No matter what I say, it makes no difference?[31]

Dorine: [32]Who said anything to you?

Orgon: What were you doing then?

Dorine: Just talking to myself.

Orgon: [33]That does it! (*To Mariane*) I'll just give her the back of my hand for such insolence—Daughter, you should approve of my plans and accept the husband I have chosen for you—(*Looks to Dorine*) Well—? Aren't you going to say something to yourself?

Dorine: I have nothing to tell myself.

Orgon: Just—one—more—word[34]

Dorine: I don't feel like it!

Orgon: Oh, come now—I'm waiting—

Dorine: I'm not such a fool! (*Now satisfied, he faces Mariane and speaks firmly*)

Orgon: Daughter! This is final.[35] You will obey my wishes and accept my choice.

Dorine: I wouldn't accept him if he were the last man on earth![36]

Orgon: Child, that maid of yours is a pestilent little hussy. She made me forget myself—[37] Just look—how I'm trembling![38] I can't continue the discussion—[39] I must calm down—Yes—some fresh air—a walk—a walk—some fresh air[40]

Mariane: (*Titters*)[41]

FURTHER READING: MOLIÈRE

(See also "Further Reading: The Character and Acting Styles" in chapter 9, and the "Additional Reading" list at the end of the book.)

Fernandez, Ramon. *Molière: The Man Seen Through the Plays.* New York: Hill & Wang, 1958. Paperback.

Gossman, Lionel. *Men and Masks: A Study of Molière.* Baltimore: Johns Hopkins University Press, 1963.

Palmer, John. *Molière.* New York: Benjamin Blom, 1970.

Schwartz, Isidore A. *The Commedia dell'Arte and Its Influence on French Comedy in the Seventeenth Century.* Paris: H. Samuel, 1933.

Wilcox, John. *The Relation of Molière to Restoration Comedy.* New York: Benjamin Blom, 1964.

16
THE RESTORATION AND THE EIGHTEENTH CENTURY

The magnificent repertory of drama identified with the Elizabethan (or Renaissance) period declined into a period of decay and disintegration. The decline was slow, taking almost a quarter of a century, but the theatre's doom was irrevocable. The Puritans, who had opposed the stage since Elizabeth's day, gathered support year by year. The civil war began in 1642, and soon all London theatres were officially closed. Authorities were instructed to treat stage players as rogues and pull down all stage galleries, seats, and boxes. Nevertheless, not all public interest in theatre disappeared. Actors scattered to the provinces or performed surreptitiously in London. There are numerous records of recurrent raids and the seizure of actor's property. Evidently these actors were a tenacious group; they survived floggings, jailings, and social ostracism.

In 1660, with the return of Charles II from exile in France, the Restoration period began. Soon two theatrical companies were active in London. Enchanted by what he had seen on French stages, the new king sponsored the theatre. He remembered the lovely female charms he had seen displayed by the French actresses—charms that no boy actor could provide. In addition, boy actors had grown mature, and a new generation had not been trained to take their places. Therefore, the first actresses began appearing on the London stage. Paradoxically, they were most popular as boys, in "breeches parts." They must have been light, airy, and saucy to attract the royal patrons as they did.

All entertainments were aimed at pleasing the aristocracy, unlike Shakespeare's theatre, which had been an institution for all classes of people. Few of the plays written during the Restoration are performed today. The small leisure-class audience found pleasure in the comedies of Sir George Etherege, William Wycherley, George Farquhar, Sir John Vanbrugh, John Dryden, Thomas Otway, and later in the more brilliant work of William Congreve. These plays have been called comedies of manners. In the writing of Dryden and Congreve, *manners* had a different connotation than we give it today.

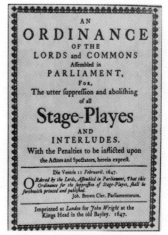

Notice dated 1647 ordering abolishment of all stage plays.

A Typical Restoration audience is the subject of this eighteenth century engraving by William Hogarth. (From the Henry E. Huntington Library and Art Gallery. Reproduced by permission.)

When Lady Froth in Congreve's *Double Dealer* is asked what "manner" is, she replies, "Some distinguishing quality . . . something . . . a little *jene-scay-quoysh*." These comedies show the influence of Molière, the Commedia, and especially Ben Jonson.[1] But instead of the earthy Jonsonian flavor, they had a more intellectual quality, a style and a grace totally lacking in Jonson's more brutal, "realistic" plays. Elements of the comedy of manners are, as Allardyce Nicoll phrases them, "At least one pair of witty lovers, the woman as emancipated as the man, their dialogue free and graceful, an air of refined cynicism over the whole production, the plot of less consequence than the wit."[2]

[1]During the years 1660–1700, Jonson was a more admired playwright than Shakespeare. At least it was said that Jonson's work needed no "improvements." In contrast, *Romeo and Juliet* was given a happy ending, and the *Macbeth* witches were suspended on strings. Even songs and dances were added to Shakespeare.

[2]Allardyce Nicoll, *History of the English Drama, 1660–1900* (London: Cambridge University Press, 1961), p. 197.

Audiences enjoying such plays were mostly court followers and
aristocrats. They sat (often on stage) in their elegant silks and bro-
cades under the glow of a hundred candles, and were more vocif-
erous than the actors whom they applauded, cursed, interrupted,
and judged. They argued, fought, drank stout, and ate fruit bought
from orange girls who wandered at their peril among the benches
(there were no aisles). One of these orange girls later became a
popular actress, "Mrs." Nell Gwyn.[3]

It is obvious what sort of plays this rakish audience demanded.
Some of the titles are revealing: *She Wou'd if She Cou'd, The Lady of
Pleasure* , *Love in a Tub*, and *Virtue Betrayed*. Plays had low moral standards, as did most actors of the time. Although plays dealt with
illicit love and intrigue, playwrights zealously avoided indelicacy
and coarseness in dialogue, as if saying, "We do as we please, but
hide it."

CHARACTERISTICS OF RESTORATION COMEDY

Playwrights of this time catered to libertine audiences made up
mostly of the upper classes. Manners of the time were conventionalized on the stage as a social game with self-conscious gestures
in which each movement was observed. Characters were types,
serving much the same purpose as the symbolic face-painting of the
Chinese actors. Restoration types might be classified: the gallant reluctant to marry, the testy duchess, the plain citizen, the philander-
ing wife, the gossip, the rich husband or uncle, the country maid,
the fop, and the cuckold. Such characters were placed in painted
settings and framed inside a proscenium arch. Plays were full of
bustling actions and intrigue, and the dialogue was spiced with a
lively wit.

FIRST ENGLISH BOOKS ON ACTING

The first two books in English on the subject of acting appeared
early in 1700. Previously, there had been instruction books printed
on oratory and declamation. The earliest book was attributed to a
celebrated actor of the Restoration, Thomas Betterton.[4] A writer,
Charles Gildon (1665–1724), collected the actor's thoughts and published these posthumously. Some of these thoughts are worthy of
note. Betterton held that the actor "must be Master of Nature in all
its appearances which can only be drawn from Observation." He

David Garrick (right) greets his
friend William Hogarth (left).
Hogarth was the brilliant
caricaturist of the eighteenth
century and Garrick was the
greatest actor of his day. (From
a contemporary silhouette
owned by the Henry E. Huntington Library and Art Gallery
and reprinted with their permission.)

---

[3]Single girls did not use the "Miss" prefix as it had unsavory connotations. "Mrs." was pronounced "Mistress," and Nell Gwyn surely became mistress of Charles II, bearing him several
children to whom he gave titles.

[4]Charles Gildon, *The Life of Mr. Thomas Betterton, The Late Eminent Tragedian. Wherein the Action
and Utterances of the Stage, Bar and Pulpit are Distinctly Consider'd* (London: printed for Robert
Gosling, 1710). See also T. Cole and H. K. Chinoy, eds., *Actors on Acting* (New York: Crown,
1949), pp. 97–102.

added that "in all good speech there is a sort of Music with Respect to its Measure, Time and Tune." His other advice is reminiscent of earlier books on oratory and later books on Victorian elocution: "When you speak of yourself, the Right not the Left hand must be apply'd to the Bosom."

A few years later another acting book appeared, authored solely by an actor. Luigi Riccoboni, a former Commedia player, was an actor of experience and intelligence. For those who believe that creative acting is the exclusive knowledge of our century, read what Riccoboni wrote in 1728: "The actor must show nature, yes; but in an Elevated and Noble form, the Trivial being reserved for the streets."

Riccoboni gave a timely warning:

> *There are Some who say that on a Stage we should Imitiate Real Life—they are Fools who do not Seek, and who Deny, that there is any thing Further or Better.*
>
> *If a man enters Strongly into a proper Enthusiasm and Speaks in the Accents of the Soul, his Features will naturally form themselves into an agreement.*
>
> *The great business of the Stage is to Enchant the Spectators into a Persuasion that the Tragedy they are beholding is no Fiction, and that they who speak and act are not Players but real Heroes.*[5]

David Garrick. (Henry E. Huntington Library and Art Gallery.)

The great David Garrick, prodded no doubt by James Boswell, planned to write a book on acting. What a treasure that would have been to us! He mentions it in a letter to William Powell, dated 1766.[6] If he did write it, it was never found and never published. But "Little Davy" was a very busy man in the theatre.[7] Not only was he manager-actor-author-director, but also an inventor of stage devices and lighting, a costume designer, a socialite, and a rake.

Garrick is thought to be the acting model described by his friend, Denis Diderot, in *The Paradox of Acting* (1830).[8] The "paradox," according to Diderot, was that an actor should move an audience, never himself—not much of an innovation. James Boswell accepts this in his *On the Profession of a Player* (1770), calling it "a kind of double feeling,"[9] a duality in which the actor's own character is placed into the recesses of his mind as he allows the character to take possession. Diderot's "paradox" was later to cause a tempest in

[5]Luigi Riccoboni, *Riccoboni's Advice to Actors*, translated and paraphrased from dell'Arte representative (1728) by Pierre Rames, Florence, Italy: *Mask Magazine*, vol. 3, April 1911, pp. 175—80. See also Cole and Chinoy, eds., *Actors on Acting*, pp. 59–63.

[6]David M. Little, et al., eds., *Letters of David Garrick* (Cambridge, Mass.: Belknap Press of Harvard University Press, 1963), p. 488. Letter to William Powell dated 1766. James Boswell also speaks of discussing such an acting book with Garrick.

[7]So-called because David Garrick was 5 feet, 4 inches tall.

[8]Denis Diderot, *The Paradox of Acting*, and William Archer, *Masks and Faces* (both New York: Hill & Wang, 1958).

[9]James Boswell, *On the Profession of a Player*, reprinted from *The London Magazine* by Elkin, Mathews and Marrot, Ltd., London, 1929.

a teapot between Coquelin and Irving. Evidently it was not clear to these gentlemen that Diderot was speaking of control, and not recommending a cold, mechanical approach to a part. Certainly no actors of the status of Irving and Coquelin would deny that emotion must be used at some time in the acting process. In this book we have spent much time on that point.

ACTORS WITHOUT PLAYS

The teacher making lesson plans might wish that there were less congestion of great names in this section. History, not our wishes, must be arbiter in this. While few good plays were written during the eighteenth century, this period produced a rich harvest of great actors and actresses. Names that would echo forever in green rooms and theatre foyers were first whispered in these candlelit playhouses: Mr. and Mrs. Betterton, Colley Cibber, Quin, Wilks and Mrs. Barry, Macklin, Garrick, the lovely actress with that fascinating name of Mrs. Bracegirdle, Mrs. Oldfield, Kitty Clive (who almost married Garrick), Nell Gwyn, Peg Woffington, Sarah Siddons, Edmund Kean; and on the continent, the romantic-looking Talma, Luigi and Francesco Riccoboni, the great German actor Schröder, the Russian Shtchepkin, whom Stanislavski called "our great lawgiver," and the devastating Rachel in Paris. All of these thrilled and awed audiences of their day. Most of them came from humble beginnings, and through the magic of theatre were transformed into intimates of kings and queens. Great literary minds like Dr. Samuel Johnson, James Boswell, Samuel Pepys, Oliver Goldsmith, William Hazlitt, and Leigh Hunt wrote of them. Sir Joshua Reynolds, Thomas Gainsborough, and William Hogarth immortalized them with brush and pen. They were the toasts of their age, the darlings of society. With little that was distinguished in plays, they popularized theatre and created some of the finest traditions in drama.

DAVID GARRICK

Among this constellation of stars, one—David Garrick—seems brighter than all the others. It has been claimed that Garrick completely reformed the art of acting by refusing to engage in artificiality and cant.

This is somewhat refuted as our knowledge increases of Thomas Betterton and Charles Macklin. Macklin prepared his Shylock interpretation by methods we have erroneously come to believe as exclusive to our time. He visited in the Jewish ghetto of London, absorbing attitudes, gestures, and inflections peculiar to Jews. His Shylock was the sensation of London. Alexander Pope declared, "This is the Jew that Shakespeare drew." In an effort to eliminate any bombast from his work, Macklin began rehearsals by merely

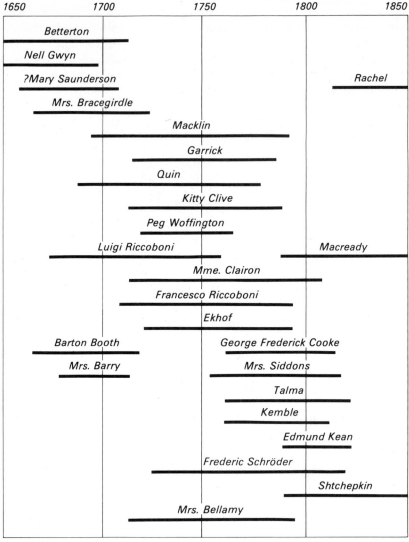

	1650	1700	1750	1800	1850

Betterton

Nell Gwyn

?Mary Saunderson

Rachel

Mrs. Bracegirdle

Macklin

Garrick

Quin

Kitty Clive

Peg Woffington

Luigi Riccoboni

Macready

Mme. Clairon

Francesco Riccoboni

Ekhof

Barton Booth

George Frederick Cooke

Mrs. Barry

Mrs. Siddons

Talma

Kemble

Edmund Kean

Frederic Schröder

Shtchepkin

Mrs. Bellamy

The life spans of some great theatre personalities, 1650–1850. (The birth date of Mary Saunderson is unknown.)

reading, getting the sense of the lines, and allowing them to be absorbed; then slowly and carefully, as convictions grew, so did his enlargement of the character.

Although Garrick's acting book has been denied us, we do know a good deal of his acting methods. He came from a nontheatrical family. In fact, he thought his brother might disown him for following the life of a player. The Garrick brothers had a little wholesale wine business and David had dabbled in amateur theatricals as a hobby. When he applied to Drury Lane and Covent Garden as an actor, he was quickly rejected. He finally hired himself to the Goodman's Field Theatre where, between acts of a concert, he performed *Richard III*. Billed as a "Young Gentleman who never appeared on any stage," Garrick was suddenly, unexpectedly, catapulted overnight into fame. Pope wrote that this new, young man "never had been equalled as an actor" and that he "will never have a rival." Obviously, Garrick was in the right place at the right time. Within the next seven months he played eighteen widely different parts. Six short years later, he was not only the leading player, but also an entrepreneur of Drury Lane, where he stayed for thirty years. Yes, Davy had luck—but also an indomitable will.

Garrick seemed equally adept at comedy and tragedy. Audiences howled with laughter at his Abel Drugger in *The Alchemist* and then cried at his King Lear. In fact, Garrick was the first to say that comedy was the proper schooling for tragedy. The Garrick Lear was carefully created, starting with his observation of a mentally ill old man. He was convinced that a good actor should always be in sympathy with the feelings of his character and be transformed beyond himself. Garrick also contended that in the warmth of playing, with involvement in the character and the situation, the great actor might produce an electric inspirational moment, surprising even himself. Garrick was scholarly, thorough, and a very hard worker, with apparently boundless energy. He would not tolerate any slipshod or slovenly habits in himself or in the casts he worked with. Declamation "revolted" him, and he believed that in an actor "affectation should be marked as the blackest of all sins against nature." When bombastic old Quin saw Garrick act, he said, "If the young fellow is right, I and the rest of the players have been all wrong."

It is strange that Garrick never performed in any play by his contemporary, Richard Brinsley Sheridan. But by the time *School for Scandal*, and *The Rivals* appeared, Garrick had wearied of his many responsibilities and retired. Sheridan succeeded him as manager of Drury Lane.

Dr. Johnson wrote of Garrick:

Garrick as Macbeth. (Courtesy of Harvard College Library Theatre Collection.)

> *It is amazing that anyone should be so ignorant as to think that an actor will risk his reputation by depending on the feelings that shall be excited in the presence of two hundred people—no, sir, Garrick left nothing to chance; every gesture, every expression of countenance and variation of the voice, was settled in his closet before he set foot upon a stage.* [10]

There is an oft-repeated remark of Garrick's to the effect that an actor should be able to make love to a table or chair as well as to a Juliet. I cannot take this seriously. Davy was a vain little man, fond of boasting and fun, and this remark was probably tossed off to amuse some people who expected the great entertainer to entertain. The sober record of his meticulous work habits and his brilliant

[10]Mrs. Clement Parsons, *Garrick and His Circle* (New York: G. P. Putnam's, 1906).

achievements seems a better foundation on which to determine his theories of acting than this single flippant remark.

An actor in Garrick's estimable position was bound to have envious detractors. One was no less than the King of England, who thought David "a great fidget"; but Americans will discount this remark because the king's name was George III. However, there may have been some truth in it. Others accused Garrick of using too many gestures and being forever busy while onstage. In a death scene, someone disliked the way he writhed about the floor clutching at the carpet. Others noted how he kicked over a chair at the appearance of the Ghost in the Queen's Closet Scene of *Hamlet*. But remember that when such actions are coldly set down on paper, the essential element is eliminated—the life and personality of the actor. I believe that the way Garrick performed these pieces of business made them thrilling to most spectators. If we consider them just as mechanical actions, we deny the art of the actor; and Garrick was a great actor.

SARAH SIDDONS

Unlike Garrick, Sarah Siddons (the former Sally Kemble) was of a theatrical family. Eldest of twelve children, she trouped the little country towns with her family, who were strolling players. Often they would encounter a sign on the outskirts of a town, "No monkeys, marionettes, or actors," and they would have to detour. Mr. and Mrs. Kemble had plans; their children would not be players. John Phillip, two years younger than Sally, studied for the priesthood. They planned to find a good husband for Sally, and she would settle down to a quiet, comfortable life far away from the turmoil of the stage. But at eighteen Sally married one of the actors in her father's company, William Siddons, who was twelve years her senior.

Mr. and Mrs. William Siddons continued to act in the provinces. News of Sally had come to Garrick's ear, and he sent a scout to witness a performance of the young actress. At fifty-eight, Garrick no longer had the patience to endure the constant bickerings of his three leading ladies, one of whom was the redoubtable Mrs. Abington. "Every one of them," he wrote, "considers herself at least equal to the queenly heroines she personates." He felt that a fresh young competitor would settle them. "If any lady begins to play tricks, I will immediately play off my masked battery of Siddons against them." Sarah, as she was now called, was twenty and in the final months of her second pregnancy. By now her brother John had given up all thoughts of the priesthood and had returned to acting. After bearing a little girl, Sarah Siddons opened in her first play in London at Drury Lane, *The Merchant of Venice*.

As Portia she was dressed atrociously; the other actresses had had the pick of the wardrobe before her. She seemed awkward, her Por-

tia had no humor, and there was something rural about her manner.
But worst of all, she was not accustomed to such a big house. She
could not be heard. The critics were unimpressed. "On the stage
there is nothing so barren as cold correctness," one critic wrote. The
others seemed to agree that the country actress was not for the city
of London. But Garrick tutored her, and when she was not working
she sat in front, watching the great actor. Even so, when she played
Lady Anne to his Richard III, she moved a critic to say that her
performance was "lamentable." Her contract at Drury Lane was not
renewed. Her former rival, Mrs. Abington, now became her de-
fender. "You are all fools," she told the management and proph-
esized that they would regret the action.

The young actress wrote:

Sarah Siddons. (Henry E. Huntington Library and Art Gallery.)

> *It was a stunning and cruel blow. It was very near destroying me. My
> blighted prospects, indeed, induced a state of mind that preyed upon my health,
> and for a year and a half I was supposed to be hastening to a decline. For the
> sake of my poor children, however, I roused myself to shake off this despon-
> dency, and my endeavors were blessed with success, in spite of the degradation
> I had suffered in being banished from Drury Lane as a worthless candidate for
> fame and fortune.*[11]

By sheer determination she was able to pull herself out of her
depression. She would show London and Drury Lane what they
had rejected. For five years she played every part that came her
way. Suddenly, in a little watering place called Bath, her reputation
skyrocketed.

In 1782, when she was twenty-seven, Sarah Siddons and her family again made the trip to London. On her opening night, terror
clutched her. "The awful consciousness that one is the sole object of
attentions to that immense space—may perhaps be imagined but
cannot be described," she wrote of her opening. But this night was
more than just another opening. She had tasted bitter defeat on this
very stage seven years before. The play she was to act was *Isabella or
The Fatal Marriage*, which she had played successfully at Bath. But
London was not Bath. On the night before the opening, her voice
disappeared, only to reappear miraculously "on the day."

The year 1782 became "the year of the Siddons." People remembered only one other debut to equal hers, the night young Garrick
had brought an audience to its feet shouting his praises. The next
day Sarah found that "the enthusiasm she excited had something
idolatrous about it; she was regarded less with admiration than with
wonder, as if a being of superior order had dropped from another
sphere, to awe the world with the majesty of her appearance."[12] Sir
Joshua Reynolds painted her as *The Tragic Muse* and signed his name

The Tragic Muse *by Sir
Joshua Reynolds. (Photo of the
original painting now in the
Huntington collection and used
by permission of the Henry E.
Huntington Library and Art Gallery.)*

[11]Thomas Campbell, *The Life of Sarah Siddons* (New York: Harper Brothers, 1834), p. 35. By
permission.
[12]William Archer and Robert Lowe, eds., *Hazlitt on Theatre* (New York: Hill & Wang, 1958).

on the border of the skirt. "I have resolved," he told her, "to go down to posterity upon the hem of your garment."

How did this shy, country actress, so limited in acting range (she could not play comedy), convince all London that she was "a superior being"—a goddess? Mrs. Siddons possessed an incredible beauty—hawklike nose, piercing black eyes, and great strands of glinting auburn hair.[13] She moved slowly, majestically, molded in the grand, romantic style of acting, and she acted it both onstage and off. They joked about the way she spoke to waiters in iambic pentameter, "You've brought me water, boy; I asked for beer." She is supposed to have patronized Edmund Kean who, like Garrick, was a small man, by saying, "You are a fine actor, but it's a pity there's so little of you." But Kean's name was to be linked with her own and Garrick's as one of the three greatest acting talents of the century.

EDMUND KEAN

Almost everything we know of Kean's acting is based on the writings of two critics who were the first to practice dramatic criticism as we know it today. "I have all along spoken freely of Mr. Kean's faults," Hazlitt wrote, "or what I considered such, physical, as well as intellectual."[14] This seems to bear out what we know of the actor's life. He had little or no schooling, which was not unusual for the time. But there is no evidence of Kean's interest in any learning beyond his study of Shakespeare. We know that he suffered an injury to his leg when he fell from a horse as a circus performer, and thereafter walked with a limp. His voice was an unpleasant and unreliable instrument. Hazlitt said it was "somewhat between an apoplexy and a cold." Like Garrick, he was not at all a handsome man, as was Kemble. Kean was addicted to drink—"my old complaint," he called it—and was plagued all of his life by guilt because of his illegitimate birth.

How then is it possible to class him with Garrick and Siddons? Mrs. Siddons's niece offered an explanation of Kean's magic in rousing an audience:

Edmund Kean. (Courtesy of the Henry E. Huntington Library and Art Gallery.)

> *Kean is a man of decided genius, no matter how he neglects or abuses nature's good gift, he has it. He has the first element of greatness—power. No taste perhaps and no industry, perhaps; but, . . . he has the one atoning faculty that compensates for everything else, that seizes, rivets, electrifies all who see and hear him, and stirs down to their very springs the passionate elements of our nature. Only genius can do this.*[15]

---

[13]"My God, Madame, is there no end to your nose?" Reynolds asked as he painted her portrait.

[14]Archer and Lowe, *Hazlitt on Theatre*, p. xxxv.

[15]Frances Ann Kemble, *Records of a Girlhood* (New York: Henry Holt & Co., 1879).

This undoubtedly indicates he was capable of amazing emotional surges that came to him on the spur of the moment, and gave him the power to transport audiences along with him. Previously, we discussed the hazards of emotions taking control of the actor; this was possibly Kean's great fault. Also, he was not intellectually equipped to plan an overall design in his work. He was all fire, an exciting slapdash of bits and pieces, lacking the patience of the true artist. He could not discipline himself, onstage or off. As Hazlitt said, "We miss in Kean, not the physiognomy, or the costumes, as much as the architectural building up of the part."

HIGH COMEDY

In the years preceding the French Revolution, France was arbiter for the world in cultural matters. There was a general shift toward lighter, gayer, more decorative types of expression in all the arts. In the English plays of this time, the acting was typically French. Its quintessence was a kind of elaboration, a rococo flare. It had tempo, smartness, and a precision reminiscent of a minuet. Old actors called this "the manner," and indeed it is just that. Propriety is woven into the very texture of plays by Congreve and Sheridan. They are not properly acted without it. It gives color and authenticity to these pieces. It is properly artificial, bright, and vivacious.

To probe the inner life of a Mr. Tattle, a Mrs. Candour, a Lady Sneerwell, or a Charles Surface is to diffuse the bold outlines used in creating them. Searching such parts for "spine" and "truth" is to deny their distinctiveness. They are clean-cut, superficial *types*—and as such they are delightful.

Eighteenth-century actors depended a great deal on their bodies, their grace, their personal magnetism, and their powers of expression. They used their voices as biting, precise instruments to articulate the author's waxed and polished wit. No author of this time wrote with naturalism as a goal. Fashionable plays of the day were frivolous reflections of the mores of the upper class. Capable actors brightened them with a style that had high gloss and sophistication. Stark Young describes this style:

> The voice (would) be clear, finished, the lips expert, the tongue striking well on the teeth; the tone would go up and down but always be sure of its place in the throat, be crisp, shining, in hand, like the satin and gold of the furniture and costumes, the rapier at the wrist, the lace over it, the worldliness and the wit. [16]

Preceding the Commedia scenario, we investigated the clown and his physical approach to playing farce. Now we approach a type of comedy that is mostly intellectual. This style is known as high com-

---

[16]Stark Young, *The Flower in Drama* (New York: Charles Scribner's, 1923), p. 88.

edy or drawing-room comedy. In serious plays, the actors attempt to move the emotions of the audience by re-creating a similar emotional experience in themselves. But comedy is not supported by, and indeed has no affinity with, emotion. This style of playing is more cerebral than visceral. To be effective, both comedy and farce require highly developed discipline and skill. Each movement, stance, and inflection must be precise and studied. *Comedy is style at its height!* It should be easy, graceful—and, above all, rehearsed to a technical precision. Nothing can be left to the inspiration of the moment. Wit is inspirational; it is a sudden, ingenious arrangement of words that produce merriment. But wit is not comedy. Comedy must be planned beforehand.

The Detachment Principle   In playing high comedy, the actors should not always stay within the confines of their characters. In fact, they are most successful when they take an attitude of standing outside them. By detaching themselves from the character, they gain perspective from which they can share the joke with the audience.

For instance, let us take the old example of the man who slips on a banana peel and falls. It is far from comedy to the man, but to us, standing safely on the sidelines, it is comic. It is cruel perhaps, but then to a very sensitive person, all laughter may be cruel. Someone must always be the butt of a joke. The next time you hear a good storyteller delighting people with a joke, notice how he assumes a character for a particular gesture or effect, and then figuratively steps outside the character to make comments *in his own identity.* From this viewpoint, he is able to editorialize, to share the joke with his listeners.

In playing comedy, actors are both involved in their characters and detached. By another process, the actor attempts to cause the audience to laugh *at* the character. In using this approach, the actor stays within his character at all times, but this does not produce a true comic effect. Other elements enter into it. The audience may feel sorry for the character, or hate him.

The Audience-Actor Relationship   In comedy, the detachment of actor from character requires a more friendly relationship with the audience than is needed even for tragedy. The actor of comedy is, in a way, part of the audience. He confides in them and is their contact with all that is happening. He is sharing the joke with them. The great clowns and comedians are always likable, while some of our greatest tragic figures are despicable. Macbeth and Richard III are murderers and villains to the audience, but this does not destroy the excitement of the tragedies. Older actors knew that they must always "keep their heads in comedy and lose their hearts in tragedy."

Distortion   As in tragedy, characters should be designed, created—but with an important difference. One particular facet of the character must be selected, then enlarged and distorted. Yet in the playing this exaggeration must seem almost unconsciously done.

The comedic spirit is rooted in this overdrawn or underdrawn aspect of character. We know that Molière's invalid is hale and hearty, and we laugh because his hypochondria is distorted out of proportion.

One of the favorite stunts used in college musicals is to dress up the burly football team as chorus girls. The more they try to imitate dainty femininity, the more awkward they seem and the greater are the laughs. It is all off-balance, distorted. But if a womanly man dresses as a woman, this is not so off-balance and is therefore less amusing. We may laugh out of embarrassment, but it is not pure comedy, because other elements enter into it.

This distortion we have been speaking about must always be rooted in the character. It is wrong to perform extraneous "bits" (such as slipping, voice tricks, or stumbling over one's feet) just for the purpose of getting laughs. But if your character is otherwise known as tipsy, clumsy, or awkward, then such "bits" are connected and may very well fit into your characterization.

In playing farce, the overemphasis of an aspect of the character can be unreal, even completely absurd. A farce character can leave the stage to go some distance and pop back seconds later with mission accomplished. We accept such ridiculousness in farce, but in comedy everything must be made theatrically real and believable.

The Comedic Spirit   To summarize then, the successful playing of comedy calls for a principle of detachment, a closer audience-actor relationship, distortion of some facet of the character, and theatrical truth. Perhaps the most important task for the comedy actor is to convince the audience that the actor, too, is enjoying his character's eccentricities. This must be done genially; it must never seem rude, bitter, or mean. The best rule is: Never attempt to play a comedy character unless you can find something in him to love.

REHEARSAL

The Way of the World

William Congreve
An Adaptation from Act IV, Scene i

CAST: Mirabell
          Mrs. Millamant

Mirabell:[1] Do you lock yourself up from me to make my search more curious? Or is this pretty artifice contrived to signify that here the chase must end, and my pursuits be crowned? For you can fly no further.

Mrs. Millamant: There is not so impudent a thing in nature as the saucy look of an assured man, confident of success. The pedantic

1. Mrs. Millamant enters from USL in a huff. Mirabell follows her on, but stops as she takes a position DC.

2. Mrs. Millamant turns upstage.

arrogance of a very husband has not so pragmatical an air.[2] Ah!, I'll never marry, unless I am first made sure of my will and pleasure.

Mirabell: Would you have 'em both before marriage?

Mrs. Millamant: Mirabell, I'll lie abed in a morning as long as I please.

Mirabell: Then I'll get up in a morning as early as I please.

Mrs. Millamant: I won't be called names after I'm married.

Mirabell: Names?

3. Turns back, facing him directly.

Mrs. Millamant: [3]Aye, as wife, spouse, my dear, joy, love, sweetheart, and the rest of the nauseous cant in which men and their wives are so fulsomely familiar. Mirabell, don't let us be familiar or fond, nor kiss before folks, nor go to Hyde Park together the first Sunday in a new chariot, to provoke eyes and whispers, and then never to be seen together again; as if we were proud of one another the first week and ashamed of one another ever after. Let us never visit together, nor go to a play together; but let us be very strange and well-bred; let us be as strange as if we had been married a great while; and as well-bred as if we were not married at all.[4]

4. Walks upstage, as if she is finished with her requests.

Mirabell: Have you any more conditions to offer?

5. Again turns to him as if taking advantage of his receptivity.

Mrs. Millamant: [5]Liberty to pay and receive visits to and from whom I please; to write and receive letters without interrogatories or wry faces on your part; to wear what I please; and choose conversations with regard only to my own taste; to have no obligation upon me to converse with wits that I don't like, because they are your acquaintance; or to be intimate with fools, because they are your relations. Come to dinner when I please; dine in my dressing gown when I'm out of humor, without giving a reason. To have my closet inviolate; to be sole empress of my tea-table, which you must never pressure to approach without first asking leave. And lastly, wherever I am you shall always knock at the door before you come in. These articles subscribed, if I continue to endure you a little longer, I may by degrees dwindle into a wife.[6]

6. These are her terms. She turns away with a "take it or leave it" attitude.

Mirabell: Have I liberty to offer conditions—that when you are dwindled into a wife, I may not be beyond measure enlarged into a husband?

Mrs. Millamant: You have free leave. Speak and spare not.

7. *Imprimis* means "In the first place."
8. *Covenant* means "stipulate."

Mirabell: I thank you. Imprimis[7] then, I covenant,[8] that your acquaintance be general; that you admit no sworn confidant, or intimate of your own sex; no she-friend to screen her affairs under your countenance, and tempt you to make trial of a mutual secrecy. No decoy-duck to wheedle you a fop scrambling to the play in a mask—then bring you home in a pretended fright, when you think you shall be found out—and rail at me for missing the play.[9] Item I article, that you continue to like your own face, as long as I shall; and while it passes current with me, that you endeavor not to re-coin it. To which end, together with all vizards for the day, I prohibit all masks for the night, made of oil-skins, and I know not what,—hog's bones, hare's gall, pig water, and the marrow of roasted cat.[10] I denounce against all strait lacing, squeezing for a shape, till you mold my boy's head like a sugar-loaf. Lastly, to the domination of the tea-table I submit—but with proviso, that you exceed not in your province; but restrain yourself to native and simple tea-table drinks,[11] as tea, chocolate, and coffee: as likewise to genuine and authorized tea-table talk—such as mending of fashions, spoiling reputations, railing at absent friends, and so forth—but that on no account you encroach upon the men's prerogative, and presume to drink healths, or toast fellows. These provisoes admitted in other things I may prove a tractable and complying husband.

Mrs. Millamant: [12]I hate your odious provisoes!

Mirabell: Then we are agreed! Shall I kiss your hand upon the contract?

Mrs. Millamant: I shall never say it![13]

If Mirabell should not make a good husband—I am a lost thing, for I love him violently. I think I must have him.[14]

Well . . . I think . . . I'll endure you.

9. On hearing his first demand, she starts for UL, crossing in front of Mirabell, but he stops her.

10. Again she starts for UL. He crosses before her, blocking her exit.

11. As he takes a step forward on each point, she steps back R.

12. Pushing him aside, she starts quickly for UL.

13. She hesitates. A faint smile of satisfaction as she turns front to audience.

14. He smiles and then takes her hand and kisses it. They both laugh and embrace.

No collection of classic dramatic literature would be representative without Richard Brinsley Sheridan's masterpiece *The School for Scandal*. Sheridan had been a dramatist only two years when he wrote what has been called the greatest comedy in the English language. The famous screen scene in this play is thought to be the most skillfully constructed comedy scene ever written in our language. This play, which was George Washington's favorite, has outlived its own time and has consistently maintained its popularity. It is an archetype of high comedy and wit. Polished and dazzling, it moves swiftly to its climax.

PREPARATION FOR *THE SCHOOL FOR SCANDAL*

The abridged version used here differs from the one you will find in your library. It is an acting version—that is, it has been arranged by theatre practitioners and inspired comedians—to extract the most out of its lines and situations after playing it before hundreds of audiences.

Richard Brinsley Sheridan
(1751–1816)

All the actors in this play should work to develop precision both in movement and diction. There should be no trace of localized accents. The cast must be rehearsed tirelessly in order to achieve that teamwork known as ensemble playing.

The Character of Lady Teazle

The eminent drama critic of the 1890s, Mr. William Winter, has written of Ada Rehan's performance as Lady Teazle and in so doing has described what other actresses have achieved in the part. He sets forth a concise blueprint for the character that might be of value to any young actress preparing the part.

> *Mrs. Abington,*[17] *the original representative of the part, made Lady Teazle entirely artificial, that being the temperament of the actress, and therein she obtained a brilliant success. Elizabeth Farren, who succeeded Mrs. Abington, embodied her with a natural refinement, making her an aristocrat by birth. Dora Jordan, who followed Elizabeth Farren, depicted her as a tantalizing compound of affectation and nature; the robes and manner were artificial; but the brown cheek, the cherry lips, the mischievous laughter, and the rustic freedom of the country girl were deliciously perceptible through the customs, airs, and trappings of fashion. This would seem to be the right method of playing the part, and this was the method pursued by Ada Rehan. Her impersonation of Lady Teazle pleased by its brilliancy, but it was her noble dignity and tender grief, at the close of the screen scene, that made the performance deeply impressive and commended it to an exceptional place in remembrance. She embodied Lady Teazle as a woman of self-respecting mind and tender heart—a sweet woman deeply touched and sharply wounded with a sense of misconduct and shame. The moral nature of the thoughtless young wife is aroused to the knowledge of duty, and she perceives her ingratitude and perverse unkindness, and she suffers in a spirit of profound contrition. Lady Teazle was shown to be a person of frank, downright moral sense, such as the insidious Joseph's sophistries were powerless to contaminate, and at the climax of the comedy every shred of dissimulation fell away from her and she stood forth an honest, natural, affectionate woman, humble, contrite, and more than ever lovely.*[18]

In characterizing Lady Teazle, the actress should not forget that Lady Teazle's sophistication and polish are acquired. At heart she is a country girl. The "tease" of Teazle may not be Sheridan's pun, but it would explain her visit to Joseph's flat.

Other Characters

Joseph Sheridan uses this character to represent the society he is lampooning. Joseph is witty, quick, and malicious. He pretends to be pious, but in reality is a hypocrite. (Contrast this character with Tartuffe.)

---

[17]This is the same Mrs. Frances Abington previously referred to as defending Mrs. Siddons at Drury Lane. Regarding Mrs. Abington's performance as Lady Teazle, a contemporary, Tom King, wrote that her "every word stabbed."

[18]William Winter, *Ada Rehan, A Story* (privately printed for Augustin Daly, 1898), p. 123.

Charles   He is the opposite of his brother Joseph, being frank, honest, and basically good while pretending to be a rake.

Sir Peter Teazle   Although rich, Sir Peter is generous, but believes in getting value. He is warm-hearted and loyal, although inclined to be somewhat cantankerous.

REHEARSAL

The School for Scandal

Richard Brinsley Sheridan
Act IV, Scene iii *(the famous "Screen Scene")*

CAST: **Joseph Surface**   **Charles Surface**
       Servant   **Lady Teazle**
       Sir Peter Teazle

SCENE: *The library in Joseph Surface's home. Necessary furniture: a divan, a screen covered with maps, and a chair. Divan is a little to right of dead center. Joseph is discovered. He turns to greet Lady Teazle as she enters.*

Lady Teazle: Have you been very impatient? I vow I couldn't come before.[1]

Joseph: O Madam, punctuality is very unfashionable in a lady of quality. *(Gestures to a place on divan.)*

Lady Teazle: Do you know, Sir Peter is grown so ill-natured of late, and so suspicious, when I know the integrity of my own heart—indeed 'tis monstrous![2]

Joseph: My dear Lady Teazle, when a husband entertains a groundless suspicion of his wife, she owes it to the honor of her sex to outwit him.

Lady Teazle: [3]The best way of curing his jealousy is to give him reason for it?

Joseph: Once make a trifling faux pas, and you can't conceive how cautious you would grow—[4]

Lady Teazle: This is the oddest doctrine—

Joseph: Prudence,[5] like experience, must be paid for. Heaven forbid I should persuade you to do anything you thought wrong. I have too much honor to desire it.

Lady Teazle: [6]We may as well leave honor out of the argument.

Joseph: Ah,[6a] the ill effects of your country education still remain with you.

Lady Teazle: I doubt they do indeed; and I will own to you that if I could be persuaded to do wrong,[7] it would be by Sir Peter's ill humour—sooner than your *honourable* logic.

1. Lady Teazle crosses in front of Joseph to divan. When she is seated he comes level.

2. Removes her gloves and settles herself.

3. Joseph reacts politely to her every remark.

4. Still standing but in a position to ease onto divan next to her. She pauses as if weighing his advice.
5. Joseph sits, putting his right arm back of divan.

6. Rising slowly, Lady Teazle smiles and looks knowingly at him. Ethel Barrymore made a memorable moment of this.
6a. Feeling his bird is escaping, Joseph rises.
7. She crosses to left toward door. Positions at this point: Joseph, URC, Lady Teazle, ULC.

8. Servant exits, leaving door open.

9. Looks about, moving R.

10. Servant reenters, picks up book from divan, and hands it to Joseph, who then comes down to divan and reclines on it with his back toward upstage. Servant returns to place above entrance door.

11. Joseph pretends to be absorbed in the book, his back to Sir Peter, who taps him gently with his walking stick.

12. Servant is now arranging books and papers.

13. Sir Peter takes spectacles out of case and holds them out to see maps.

14. Joseph leads Sir Peter away from screen and motions that he sit on the divan as Joseph crosses back of it to DR.

15. Sir Peter glances at Servant and Joseph dismisses him with a nod as he walks front of divan to chair at L.

16. Sir Peter replaces glasses in case, then in pocket.

17. Joseph moves chair close so that he sits facing Sir Peter.

18. Puts hand on Joseph's knee.

19. Offers his hand and Joseph shakes it briefly.

20. Wags his finger at Joseph.

21. Sir Peter stamps his stick to make his point.

22. Takes out kerchief from sleeve and sniffs at it. He is feeling very sorry for himself.

Joseph: Then, by this hand, which he is unworthy of—(*Taking her hand, about to kiss it as Servant enters.*) Blockhead! What do you want?

Servant: I beg your pardon, Sir, but I thought you would not choose Sir Peter to come up without announcing him.[8]

Joseph: Sir Peter! The devil—?

Lady Teazle: Sir Peter![9] I'm ruined,—ruined! Now, Mr. Logic—Oh! mercy, he's on the stairs—I'll get behind here—and if I'm so imprudent again—

(She goes behind screen)[10]

Joseph: Give me that book. (*Sits, R of divan as Sir Peter enters*)

Sir Peter: Ah! [11]There he is—ever improving his mind—Mr. Surface,—Mr. *Surface!*

Joseph: (*Pretending to be startled, gets up, throws the book on divan*) O, my dear Sir Peter, I beg your pardon, I have been dozing over a stupid book.[12] (*Sir Peter looks about, circling above divan.*)

Sir Peter: Very neat indeed.[13] (*Stops at screen.*) Well, well,—and you even make your screen a source of knowledge—hung, I perceive, with maps.

Joseph: Oh yes, I find great use for that screen.[14] Here's a chair, Sir Peter—

(But Sir Peter sits on divan. Joseph places chair near him and sits)

[15]*(Servant leaves)*

Sir Peter: There is a subject, my dear friend, on which I wish to unburden my mind.[16] Lady Teazle's conduct of late has made me very unhappy. I have pretty good authority to suppose that she has formed an attachment. I think I have discovered the man.[17]

Joseph: You alarm me.

Sir Peter: My dear friend—[18]

Joseph: Sir Peter, such a discovery would hurt me just as much as it would you.[19]

Sir Peter: Have you no guess who I mean? What do you say to Charles?

Joseph: My brother? Impossible.

Sir Peter: Oh, my dear friend,[20] the goodness of your own heart misleads you. You judge of others by yourself.

Joseph: Certainly, Sir Peter, the heart that is conscious of its own integrity is ever slow to credit another's treachery.

Sir Peter: What noble sentiments![21] Ah Joseph—your brother has no sentiment—you never hear him talk so.

Joseph: Yet I can't but think Lady Teazle has too much principle.

Sir Peter: What is principle against the flattery of a handsome, lively young fellow? And then, you know, the difference in our ages—If I were to make it public, why the town would only laugh—at the foolish old bachelor,[22] who had married a young girl.

Joseph: You must never make it public.

Sir Peter: That the nephew of my old friend, Sir Oliver, should be the person to attempt such a wrong, hurts me.

Joseph: If it should be proved on Charles,[23] he is no longer a brother of mine. The man who can tempt the wife of his friend, deserves to be branded as a pest of society.

Sir Peter: What sentiments! What noble sentiments! What a difference there is between you.

Joseph: Yet I cannot suspect Lady Teazle's honor.[24]

Sir Peter: I'm sure I wish to think well of her! She has lately reproached me with no settlement on her—Here,[25] my friend, are two deeds, by one she will enjoy eight hundred a year independent while I live, and by the other, the bulk of my fortune at my death.

Joseph: This conduct, Sir Peter, is truly generous.

(Enter Servant)

Servant: Your brother, Sir,[26] is speaking to a gentleman in the street, and says he knows you are within.

Joseph: I'm not within—I am out for the day!

Sir Peter: Stay. A thought has struck me; you shall be at home.[27] *(Joseph nods to Servant, who leaves.)* Let me conceal myself somewhere, then you tax him on the point we have been talking.

Joseph: Would you have me join in so mean a trick?

Sir Peter: You do him the greatest service by giving him an opportunity to clear himself. *(Looks at screen)* Here, behind the screen—Hey! What the devil! There seems to be one listener here already—I'll swear I saw[28]—a *petticoat!*

Joseph: Ha! ha! ha! Harkee![29]—'tis a little French milliner that having some character to lose, on your coming, Sir, she ran behind the screen.

Sir Peter: Here's a closet will do as well. Oh, you naughty boy! "A little French milliner," eh? *(Starts for screen; Joseph stops him and guides him to closet)* Oh, you sly rogue![30] *(Goes into closet.)*

Joseph: A curious situation I'm in,—to part man and wife in this manner.

Lady Teazle: *(Peeping around screen)* [31]Couldn't I steal off?

Joseph: Keep close, my angel!

Sir Peter: [32]Joseph, tax him home!

Joseph: Back, my dear friend.[33]

Lady Teazle: *(Peeping)*[34] Couldn't you lock Sir Peter in?

Joseph: Be still, my life.

Sir Peter: [35]The little milliner won't blab?

Joseph: In, in, Sir Peter.

(Enter Charles)[36]

Charles: Holla! *(Looking about)* What has made Sir Peter steal off?

23. Joseph rises and goes back of divan, placing hands on Sir Peter's shoulders as if to comfort him.

24. Joseph now moves DL in thought as he pretends to be defending Lady Teazle.

25. Sir Peter produces two deeds from inner pocket, and buries face in kerchief as he reads. Joseph sits on his right and also produces a kerchief. They grope for hands, shake, turn heads to look at each, and shake again. This business must be set and gauged to Sir Peter's lines.

26. At entrance of Servant, Joseph rises turns R and up behind divan to him. Sir Peter rises and goes to Joseph on his line.

27. Positions: Servant, UL; Joseph, ULC; Sir Peter, ULC (to Joseph's R).

28. Joseph is fearful that Sir Peter is going to say "Lady Teazle."

29. Relieved, Joseph laughs nervously, regains his poise and passes it off as a man-to-man joke.

30. Wagging his finger at Joseph.

31. Pokes her head out one side of screen.

32. Sir Peter opens closet door a little.

33. Closes door.

34. Pokes her head out the other side of screen.

35. Same business with door.

36. A breezy entrance. Charles moves easily and naturally. He punches Joseph on the shoulder as he passes him entering the room.

Sir John Gielgud as Joseph Surface in The School for Scandal. *(Radio Times Hulton Picture Library.)*

37. Charles has ended at divan. Joseph comes down to him.

38. Charles sits CL of divan.

39. These three lines may be repeated to heighten the comedy.

40. Charles rises.

41. Joseph goes to him and leads him to L away from closet. Speaks *sotto voce.*

42. The three are all above the divan and before the screen: Sir Peter, R; Charles, C; Joseph, L.

43. Like a child caught in the act, Sir Peter cannot look into Charles's eyes.

44. Back of Charles, to Servant.

45. Leads Sir Peter DL.

46. Joseph now leads Sir Peter DL to Charles. Positions: Joseph, UL, then exits; Sir Peter, DCL; Charles, DL.

47. The "sentiment" line should be made important, as it is repeated later.

Joseph: Hearing you were coming, he did not choose to stay.

Charles: What! [37]Afraid I wanted to borrow money of him?

Joseph: He thinks you are endeavouring to gain Lady Teazle's affections.

Charles: So the old fellow has found out that he has got a young wife, has he?[38]

Joseph: This is no subject to jest on, brother—

Charles: I never had the least idea of what you charge me, but if a pretty woman was purposely to throw herself in my way—and that pretty woman married to a man old enough to be her father—

Joseph: Well?

Charles: Why, I believe I should be obliged to—[39]

Joseph: What—?

Charles: To borrow a little of your morality,[40] that's all. But brother, I always understood *you* were her favorite.

Joseph: Brother, brother, a word with you[41]—Sir Peter has overheard all we have been saying—

Charles: Sir Peter? Where is he? *(Points to screen)* Here?

Joseph: *(Pointing to closet)* There!

Charles: Sir Peter, come forth![42] *(Opens door)*

Joseph: No, no—

Charles: *(Pulling in Sir Peter)* What! My old guardian! what—turn inquisitor?

Sir Peter: Give me your hand, Charles[43]—I believe I have suspected you wrongfully, but what I have heard has given me great satisfaction.

Charles: Then 'twas lucky you didn't hear any more. Wasn't it, Joseph? You might as well have suspected him, as me, mightn't he, Joseph?

(Re-enter Servant and whispers to Joseph)

Servant: Lady Sneerwell is below, and says she will come up.

Joseph: She must not come here.[44] *(Exit Servant)* *(Aside)* They must not be left together—*(Aloud)* I'll send Lady Sneerwell away, and return directly. *(As Sir Peter approaches the screen)* Sir Peter! *(Charles takes a step toward him)* Not you, Charles. Sir Peter—

Charles: Oh! *(Charles goes to screen and examines it)*

Joseph: *(Leading Sir Peter away from the screen)* Not a word of the French milliner.[45] *(Sir Peter laughs slyly. Then Joseph sees Charles at the screen and brings him to Sir Peter.)* Charles! Entertain Sir Peter—*(Exits)*

Sir Peter: Ah, Charles, if you associated more with your brother, one might indeed hope for your reformation. [46]There is nothing in the world so noble as a man of sentiment.[47]

Charles: Pshaw! He is too moral by half.

Sir Peter: Joseph is no rake—but he's no saint either. *(Chuckles as he whispers)* He had a girl with him when I called.

Charles: Joseph?

Sir Peter: Sh-h-h-h! A little French milliner. She's in the room now.

Charles: The devil she is—! There—? [48] *(Sir Peter makes a hissing sound three times, as he points to the screen)* What do you mean, s-ist, s-ist, s-ist—?[49] *(Sir Peter repeats sounds and gestures)* Behind the screen—? [50]Let's have her out—

Sir Peter: *(Trying to stop him)* No, no,—Joseph's coming—

Charles: Oh, we'll have a peep at the little milliner—

Sir Peter: Here he is![51] *(Just as Joseph re-enters, Charles throws down the screen)*

Charles: [52]Lady Teazle! By all that's wonderful.

Joseph: Lady Teazle! By all that's horrible.

Sir Peter: Lady Teazle! By all that's damnable!

Charles: Sir Peter, this is one of the smartest French milliners I ever saw.[53] You seem all to have been diverting yourselves at hide and seek and I don't see who is out of the secret. Shall I beg your ladyship to inform me? Not a word? Brother, will you be pleased to explain? What, is morality dumb too? Sir Peter, though I found you in the dark, perhaps you are not so now! All mute? Well, I suppose you perfectly understand one another—so I'll leave you to yourselves.[54] *(Going)* Sir Peter, there's nothing in the world so noble as a man of sentiment. *(Exit)*

Joseph: Sir Peter,[55] I confess that appearances are against me—but I shall explain everything to—

48. Pointing to closet as he crosses to Sir Peter.

49. Pulls Charles close to him and speaks *sotto voce.*

50. A step toward screen. In panic, Sir Peter runs in front of divan to R.

51. Charles, UCL; Sir Peter, UCR; Joseph, UL.

52. They open up to reveal Lady Teazle.

53. Faces each as he questions them and waits in silence for their answers.

54. Crosses up to door L. Others "dress" stage. Sir Peter moves down before divan at R, motivated by his embarrassment.

55. Joseph moves down L, but on a line with Sir Peter.

A contemporary print of the famous screen scene from original production of The School for Scandal. *(Victoria and Albert Museum.)*

Sir Peter: If you please, Sir!

Joseph: The fact is—Lady Teazle, knowing my pretensions to your ward, Maria—and knowing my friendship to the family—she, Sir, called here—in order that I explain these pretensions—but on your coming, being apprehensive of your jealousy, withdrew—and this, you may depend on it, is the whole truth of the matter.

Sir Peter: A very clear account, upon my word; and I dare swear the lady will vouch for every article of it.

Lady Teazle: [56]For not one word of it, Sir Peter. There is not one syllable of truth in what the gentleman has told you.

Sir Peter: I believe you, upon my soul, ma'am!

Joseph: *(Aside to her)* Madam, will you betray me?

Lady Teazle: Good Mr. Hypocrite, I'll speak for myself.

Sir Peter: Ay, let her alone, sir. She'll make out a better story than you, without prompting.

Lady Teazle: I came here on no matter relating to your ward. I came to listen to his pretended passion, if not to sacrifice your honour.

Sir Peter: I believe the truth is coming indeed!

Joseph: The woman's mad!

Lady Teazle: No, Sir; she has recovered her senses. Sir Peter, the tenderness you expressed for me,[57] when you could not think I was witness to it, has so penetrated to my heart, that had I left the place without the shame of discovery, my future life should have spoken the sincerity of my gratitude.[58] As for that smooth-tongued hypocrite, I behold him now so truly despicable that I shall never again respect myself for having listened to him.[59] *(Exit)*

Joseph: Sir Peter[60]—Heaven knows—

Sir Peter: That you are a villain! And so I leave you to your conscience.

Joseph: You are too rash, Sir Peter. The man who shuts out conviction by refusing to—[61]

Sir Peter: Oh, damn your sentiments!

(Exit Sir Peter, still talking. Joseph collapses on the divan)

56. Lady Teazle moves down between the men and takes stage at center in front of divan.

57. Joseph has moved DL a little on this speech.

58. Lady Teazle now steps to Joseph.
Note: Be certain characters are not bunched or crowded, and all moves are properly motivated by the actors.

59. Sir Peter, now quite broken, uses kerchief to dab his eyes. This is comedy but must be done sincerely by the actor. Lady Teazle turns to Sir Peter as if to take his hands or to make some affectionate gesture—thinks better of it—bows dutifully near the door, then exits quickly.

60. As he steps to Sir Peter in defense of himself.

61. Sir Peter holds up his hand as if saying "no more" as he walks in front of Joseph to door; turns for last line, then exits.

FURTHER READING: THE RESTORATION AND THE EIGHTEENTH CENTURY

(See also "Further Reading: The Character and Acting Styles" in chapter 9, and the "Additional Reading" list at the end of the book.)

Brown, J. R., and Harris, B. *Restoration Theatre.* New York: G. P. Putnam's, 1967.

Dobree, Bonamy. *Restoration Comedy: 1660–1720.* New York: Oxford University Press, 1962.

Downer, Alan S. "Nature to Advantage Dressed: Eighteenth Century Acting," *PMLA* (1943), 58:4 (part I), pp. 1002–37.

Fujimura, Thomas H. *Restoration Comedy of Wit*. Princeton, N.J.: Princeton University Press, 1952.

Hinshaw, N. W. "Graphic Sources for a Modern Approach to Acting Restoration Comedy," *Educational Theatre Journal*, May 1968, pp. 157–70.

MacCollum, John I., Jr. *The Restoration Stage*. Boston: Houghton, Mifflin, 1961.

Muir, Kenneth. *The Comedy of Manners*. London: Hutchinson University Library, 1970.

Palmer, John. *The Comedy of Manners*. New York: Russell, 1962.

Perry, Henry T. *Comic Spirit in Restoration Drama*. New York: Russell, 1962.

17
NINETEENTH-CENTURY DRAMA

NINETEENTH-CENTURY MELODRAMA

Melodrama was the most popular form of theatre in the nineteenth century. The very name conjures up images of black-caped villians in porkpie hats, twirling their mustaches as curly headed, pink-cheeked heroines plead for their lives or those of their handsome, noble-souled heroes. It is a form often dismissed as trivial, despite its long and popular life on the stage in the last century.[1] This is perhaps due to the recent popularity of the *meller*, an exaggerated style of play written to satirize the old drama during the heyday of camp and nostalgia. Because of this, there is a temptation to play legitimate melodrama with all the stops out—to "ham it up." The fact is that when played seriously today, the old melodramas still work their magic.

PREPARATION FOR *THE OCTOROON*[2]

Read the play carefully. Note that the clearly defined characters are drawn in bold strokes. This is an idealized world, similar to that of romantic drama, except that the characters are not royalty but common people. This is life as it ought to be, with clear-cut issues and moral choices. There is no doubt at all concerning which character is to be loved, which is to be hated, and which is to be laughed at. Play the scene earnestly. Don't play for laughs; play for tears and/or applause. Think of each moment as a living picture, or *tableau*. Moves should be bold and definite. Melodrama has no place for the small, fussy details of today's Method. A great deal of the charm of this style has to do with the almost dance quality of movement, the

[1]For an excellent discussion of melodrama and its modern counterparts, see Robert W. Corrigan, *The World of the Theatre* (Glenview, Ill.: Scott, Foresman, 1979), pp. 103–13.

[2]*The Octoroon* can be found in John Gassner, ed., *Best Plays of the Early American Theatre from the Beginning to 1916* (New York: Crown, 1967), p. 185; or in A. H. Quinn, ed., *Representative American Plays*, 7th ed. (New York: Appleton, Century, Crofts, 1957), p. 429.

delicately timed pause at propitious moments, and the carefully chosen gesture used as a recognizable indication of emotion. When these are present, together with playing scenes straight, the rhythm is wonderful.

REHEARSAL

The Octoroon

Dion Boucicault
An Excerpt from Act II

CAST: **Zoe**

George

SCENE: *A wharf on the river.*

BACKGROUND: *The play was written in 1859 and takes place at about that time. George Peyton owns Terrebone Plantation, but, through bad fortune and the machinations of Jacob M'Closky, is about to lose it. He is in love with the beautiful Zoe, but has never revealed the fact to her. She, of course, is secretly in love with him. However, the wealthy Dora Sunnyside has just told Zoe that she is in love with George, that she is an heiress, and that her fortune "would release this estate from debt." Not knowing that Zoe also loves him, Dora has asked Zoe to inform George of her love and to encourage George to propose to Dora.*

1. Looking offstage in the direction that Dora and Scudder have just exited.

2. Looking at her. In both cases it is a stage convention (understanding) that they are speaking their thoughts and that neither can hear the other.

3. Looking toward the audience, but speaking her thoughts aloud rather than addressing them directly.

4. Taking tentative steps toward her.

5. Toward the audience. (Her thoughts again.)

6. To him.

7. He moves toward her slowly, steadily, and is next to her by the end of the speech.

8. Facing the audience.

9. Facing him.

10. He means his love for Zoe, of course.

Zoe: [1]They are gone!—*(Glancing at George.)* Poor fellow, he has lost all.

George: [2]Poor child! how sad she looks now she has no resource.

Zoe: How shall I ask him to stay?[3]

George: Zoe, will you remain here?[4] I wish to speak to you.

Zoe: *(Aside.)* Well, that saves trouble.[5]

George: By our ruin you lose all.

Zoe: O, I'm nothing; think of yourself.[6]

George: I can think of nothing but the image that remains face to face with me;[7] so beautiful, so simple, so confiding, that I dare not express the feelings that have grown up so rapidly in my heart.

Zoe: *(Aside.)*[8] He means Dora.

George: If I dared to speak!

Zoe: [9]That's just what you must do, and do it at once, or it will be too late.

George: Has my love been divined?[10]

Zoe: It has been more than suspected.[11]

George: Zoe, listen to me, then.[12] I shall see this estate pass from me without a sigh, for it possesses no charm for me; the wealth I covet is the love of those around me—eyes that are rich in fond looks, lips that breathe endearing words; the only estate I value is the heart of one true woman, and the slaves I'd have are her thoughts.

Zoe: George, George, your words take away my breath![13]

George: The world, Zoe, the free struggle of minds and hands is before me;[14] the education bestowed on me by my dear uncle is a noble heritage which no sheriff can seize; with that I can build up a fortune, spread a roof over the heads I love, and place before them the food I have earned; I will work—

Zoe: Work![15] I thought none but colored people worked.

George: Work, Zoe, is the salt that gives savor to life.

Zoe: [16]Dora said you were slow; if she could hear you now—

George: [17]Zoe, you are young; your mirror must have told you that you are beautiful. Is your heart free?

Zoe: Free? of course it is![18]

George: [19]We have known each other but a few days, but to me those days have been worth all the rest of my life. Zoe, you have suspected the feeling that now commands an utterance—you have seen that I love you.

Zoe: Me! you love *me*?[20]

George: [21]As my wife,—the sharer of my hopes, my ambitions, and my sorrows; under the shelter of your love I could watch the storms of fortune pass unheeded by.

Zoe: *My* love! my love?[22] George, you know not what you say![23] I the sharer of your sorrows—your wife! Do you know what I am?

George: [24]Your birth—I know it. Has not my dear aunt forgotten it—she who had the most right to remember it? You are illegitimate, but love knows no prejudice.[25]

Zoe: (*Aside.*)[26]Alas! he does not know, he does not know! and will despise me, spurn me, loathe me, when he learns who, what, he has so loved.—(*Aloud.*)[27] George, O, forgive me! Yes, I love you—I did not know it until your words showed me what has been in my heart; each of them awoke a new sense, and now I know how unhappy—how very unhappy I am.[28]

George: Zoe, what have I said to wound you?[29]

Zoe: Nothing;[30] but you must learn what I thought you already knew. George, you cannot marry me; the laws forbid it!

George: Forbid it?[31]

Zoe: [32]There is a gulf between us, as wide as your love, as deep as

11. She means his love for Dora.

12. He is "walking on air." He may move around, but must be next to her, facing her at the end.

13. She turns away, hands to her breast.

14. He should, of course, gesture freely, but the gestures must be bold, definite, selective.

15. She turns to him.

16. She moves away, excited that he is speaking so openly to her.

17. Following her.

18. Not knowing his intent. Puzzled by the question.

19. Slowly and sincerely.

20. Takes a couple of tentative steps backward, hands to her throat.

21. Moves toward her.

22. A couple more tentative steps backward.

23. Turns away from him, hands to her breast.

24. Moving to her.

25. Spoken *toward* but not *to* the audience. Find the right gesture and pose. Perhaps moving both hands downward, palms facing the floor, chest forward on the last word.

26. Moving toward the audience a step or two. Once again the lines are addressed *toward,* but not *to,* the audience.

27. Turns and moves to him.

28. Face and eyes downcast, avoiding his gaze.

29. Very concerned. Taking her hands in his.

30. Pulling her hands away from his, reluctantly.

31. Faces the audience.

32. Moving away, facing the audience. She cannot look at him. At the end of the speech one hand is extended toward him.

33. Moves to her, takes her hand in both of his.
34. Turns to face him.
35. Turns away again.
36. Turns to him again.

37. Examines her fingers.

38. He does. He cannot take his eyes from hers.

39. She turns away again, toward the audience.

40. An *Octoroon* is a person of one-eighth Negro ancestry.
41. He moves to her side.

42. Turns to him.

43. He turns his head away, confused.

44. She moves away from him.
45. He follows her.
46. She faces him for "Yes" then directs the rest of the line toward the audience, chin up.
47. Turns her head sadly toward him.
48. Crestfallen.
49. Touched by his sincerity and pain.
50. Slowly, sadly.

51. She runs off.

52. He follows her.

my despair; but O, tell me, say you will pity me! that you will not throw me from you like a poisoned thing!

George: Zoe, explain yourself—your language fills me with shapeless fears.[33]

Zoe: [34]And what shall I say? I—my mother was—[35] no, no—not her! Why should I refer the blame to her?[36] George, do you see that hand you hold? look at these fingers; do you see the nails are of a bluish tinge?

George: Yes, near the quick there is a faint blue mark.[37]

Zoe: Look in my eyes;[38] is not the same color in the white?

George: It is their beauty.

Zoe: Could you see the roots of my hair you would see the same dark, fatal mark. Do you know what that is?

George: No.

Zoe: That is the ineffaceable curse of Cain.[39] Of the blood that feeds my heart, one drop in eight is black—bright red as the rest may be, that one drop poisons all the flood; those seven bright drops give me love like yours—hope like yours—ambition like yours— life hung with passions like dew-drops on the morning flowers; but the one black drop gives me despair, for I'm an unclean thing —forbidden by the laws—I'm an Octoroon![40]

George: [41]Zoe, I love you none the less; this knowledge brings no revolt to my heart, and I can overcome the obstacle.

Zoe: But *I* cannot.

George: We can leave this country, and go far away where none can know.

Zoe: And your mother,[42] she who from infancy treated me with such fondness, she who, as you said, has most reason to spurn me, can she forget what I am? Will she gladly see you wedded to the child of her husband's slave?[43] No! she would revolt from it, as all but you would; and if I consented to hear the cries of my heart, if I did not crush out my infant love, what would she say to the poor girl on whom she had bestowed so much? No, no![44]

George: [45]Zoe, must we immolate our lives on her prejudice?

Zoe: [46]Yes, for I'd rather be black than ungrateful! [47]Ah, George, our race has at least one virtue—it knows how to suffer!

George: Each word you utter makes my love sink deeper into my heart.[48]

Zoe: [49]And I remained here to induce you to offer that heart to Dora!

George: [50]If you bid me do so I will obey you—

Zoe: No, no! if you cannot be mine, O, let me not blush when I think of you.[51]

George: Dearest Zoe![52]

(Exit George and Zoe.)

FURTHER READING

(See also "Further Reading: The Character and Acting Styles" in chapter 9, and the "Additional Reading" list at the end of the book.)

Birdoff, Harry. *The World's Greatest Hit: "Uncle Tom's Cabin."* New York: S. F. Vanni, 1947.

Booth, Michael R. *English Melodrama.* London: Herbert Jenkins, 1965.

Cross, Gilbert. *Next Week East Lynne: Domestic Drama in Performance, 1820–1874.* Lewisburg, Pa.: Bucknell University Press, 1976.

Downer, Alan S. "Players and the Painted Stage: Nineteenth Century Acting," *PMLA,* 61 (1946): 522–76.

Grimsted, David. *Melodrama Unveiled: American Theatre and Culture, 1800–1850.* Chicago: University of Chicago Press, 1968.

Mammen, Edward W. *The Old Stock Company School of Acting.* Boston: The Public Library, 1945.

Moody, Richard. *America Takes the Stage: Romanticism in American Drama and Theatre, 1750–1900.* Bloomington: Indiana University Press, 1955.

Wilson, Garff. *A History of American Acting.* Bloomington: Indiana University Press, 1966.

———. *Three Hundred Years of American Drama and Theatre.* Englewood Cliffs, N.J.: Prentice-Hall, 1973.

The brilliant stage writing exemplified by Sheridan lay dead until Oscar Wilde brought the comedy of manners to life again in just three weeks' writing time. In 1900 Oscar Wilde was also dead, but not without a gibe: "If another century began and I was still alive it would be more than the English could stand." Wit has been called "educated insolence," and Wilde abounded in it.

Oscar Wilde
(1854–1900)

PREPARATION FOR *THE IMPORTANCE OF BEING EARNEST*

This superfarce gives an audience nothing to think about, but a great deal to enjoy. It is a triumph of artificiality. Beginning with lies, entanglements pile one on another until it seems the whole structure will fall. Wilde's precarious plot contrasts amusingly with his precise, urbane, overcivilized characters who move politely among the snarls of deception and misunderstanding. It is all style, extravagantly absurd and amusing. This is the way an audience will enjoy it—and the way actors should play it.

The characters are not "real," but they are very much alive. Usually, when young actors are asked to enact sophistication, they tend to assume a bored, unattractive attitude. In contrast, the people of this play are devoted to polite, gracious manners. They are always charming, even when saying disagreeable things.

They follow a definite pattern of behavior accepted as the correct way to live in a civilized society; any other way would be barbaric. Charm was greatly valued. Imagine a girl of today asking another's permission to look at her—and the other being refreshing enough to admit that she loves being looked at. In the comedy of manners, all pretend that life is made up of the most exquisite demeanor. All men are wits and the ladies are engrossed with social amenities. Then, unexpectedly, the social masks drop and we see the ordinary, and even quite primitive, human beings who have been wearing them. Some of the delight an audience finds is in witnessing this contrast between the ideal and the reality. In a comedy of manners people are typically dressed beautifully in the mode of the day. They are free of the economic pressures of making a living, and they skirmish over trifles.

REHEARSAL

The Importance of Being Earnest

Oscar Wilde
An Excerpt from Act II

Cast: Cecily   **Algernon**

Gwendolen   **Jack**

SCENE: *Garden of the Manor House. There is a metal table DRC and chairs with tea service set. There is a door to the interior UC.*
Discovered, Cecily sitting at table making an entry in her diary. Gwendolen enters from L and Cecily rises.

1. Cecily rises and advances to meet Gwendolen, offering her hand.

Cecily: Pray let me introduce myself to you.[1]
My name is Cecily Cardew.

2. Moving to Cecily and shaking hands.

Gwendolen: Cecily Cardew?[2] What a very sweet name. Something tells me that we are going to be great friends. I like you already more than I can say. My first impressions of people are never wrong.

Cecily: How nice of you to like me so much after we have known each other such a comparatively short time.[3] Pray sit down.

3. Indicating chair R of table.

Gwendolen: I may call you Cecily, may I not?

4. Still standing: waits for Gwendolen to be seated.

Cecily: With pleasure.[4] .

Gwendolen: And you will always call me Gwendolen, won't you?[5]

5. Gwendolen sits at chair R of table.

Cecily: If you wish.

Gwendolen: Then that is all quite settled, is it not?

Cecily: I hope so.[6]

Gwendolen: Perhaps this might be a favorable opportunity for my mentioning who I am. My father is Lord Bracknell. You have never heard of papa, I suppose?

Cecily: I don't think so.

Gwendolen: Outside the family circle, papa is entirely[7] unknown. I think that is quite as it should be. Cecily,—mama, whose views on education are remarkably strict, has brought me up to be extremely short-sighted; it is part of her system; so do you mind my looking at you through my glasses?

Cecily: Oh, not at all Gwendolen. I am very fond of being looked at.

Gwendolen: [8]You are here on a short visit, I suppose?

Cecily: Oh, no, I live here.

Gwendolen: Really? [9]Your mother, no doubt, or some female relative of advanced years, resides here also?

Cecily: My dear guardian, with the assistance of Miss Prism, has the arduous task of looking after me.

Gwendolen: Your guardian?

Cecily: Yes, I am Mr. Worthing's ward.

Gwendolen: Oh! [10]It is strange he never mentioned to me that he had a ward. He grows more interesting hourly. I am not sure, however, that the news inspires me with feelings of unmixed delight. I am very fond of you Cecily; I have liked you ever since I met you. But I am bound to state that now that I know you are Mr. Worthing's ward, I cannot help but expressing a wish you were—well, just a little older than you seem to be—and not quite so very alluring in appearance. In fact, if I may speak candidly—

Cecily: Pray do! I think that whenever one has anything unpleasant to say, one should always be candid.

Gwendolen: Well, to speak with perfect candor, Cecily, I wish that you were fully forty-two, and more than usually plain for your age.[11] Ernest has a strong, upright nature. He is the very soul of truth and honor. But even men of the noblest possible moral character are extremely susceptible to the influence of physical charms.[12]

Cecily: I beg your pardon, Gwendolen, did you say Ernest?

Gwendolen: Yes.

Cecily: Oh, but it is not Mr. Ernest Worthing who is my guardian. It is his brother—his elder brother.

Gwendolen: Ernest never mentioned to me that he had a brother.[13]

Cecily: They have not been on good terms—

Gwendolen: Ah! That accounts for it. [14]And now that I think of it, I have never heard any man mention his brother. The subject seems distasteful to most men. Of course you are quite, quite sure that it is not Mr. Ernest Worthing who is your guardian?

6. Cecily sits, chair L of table.

7. All through this speech, Gwendolen's eyes have been examining Cecily's dress, complexion, hands, manner, etc.

8. Using her lorgnette, Gwendolen has verified her worst fears that Cecily is young, attractive, and charming. There is a pause as she swallows the knowledge, then she speaks.

9. Rising, she walks a step to R in thought, then back to place.

10. She now saunters back of Cecily's chair to center, then turns to her.

11. Gwendolen walks in front of table to R.

12. Cecily rises, walks left, and turns back to Gwendolen for question.

13. Gwendolen sits in Cecily's chair (R of table).

14. Looking front.

15. Cecily walks in front of table to R, turns, and leans over table to face Gwendolen.
16. Speaking shyly and confidentially; then sits in chair R of table.
17. Gwendolen rises politely.
18. Cecily also rises politely, then shows diary.

19. Examines Gwendolen carefully through her lorgnette.
20. Producing her diary from her bag, holds it during the next move, but leaves bag on floor near chair R.

21. Meditating, she walks several steps to L.

22. Thoughtfully and sadly.

23. Satirically. Gwendolen now at LC, Cecily R of table.
24. ''Thank you'' is spoken with elaborate politeness. She then turns straight front for ''Detestable girl.''
25. Sweetly.
26. Superciliously Cecily looks angrily at her, takes up tongs, and puts four lumps of sugar into the cup.
27. As she moves in front of table to R, she returns diary to her bag. During this, Cecily is cutting a large piece of cake, which she puts on Gwendolen's plate on table R.
28. Gwendolen smiles sweetly at her, sits R of table, takes up tea, sips, makes a grimace, puts down cup at once, reaches out her hand for bread and butter, looks at it and finds it is cake, rises in indignation—*then* speaks. (All this silent business should be done calmly and deliberately. It will hold the audience's attention without lines.)

Cecily: Quite sure. In fact,[15] I am going to be his.

Gwendolen: I beg your pardon?

Cecily: Dearest Gwendolen, there is no reason why I should make a secret of it to you.[16] Mr. Ernest Worthing and I are engaged to be married.

Gwendolen: My darling Cecily, I think there must be some slight error.[17] Mr. Ernest Worthing is engaged to me.

Cecily: [18]I am afraid you must be under some misconception. Ernest proposed to me exactly ten minutes ago.

Gwendolen: It is certainly very curious, for he asked me to be his wife yesterday afternoon at 5:30. If you would care to verify the incident, pray do so.[19] I never travel without my diary. One should always have something sensational to read in the train.[20] I am so sorry, my dear, but I am afraid *I* have the prior claim.

Cecily: It would distress me more than I can tell you, dear Gwendolen, if it caused you any mental or physical anguish, but I feel bound to point out that since Ernest proposed to you, he clearly has changed his mind.

Gwendolen: [21]If the poor fellow has been entrapped into any foolish promise I shall consider it my duty to rescue him at once, and with a firm hand.

Cecily: [22]Whatever unfortunate entanglement my dear boy may have got into, I will never reproach him with it after we are married.

Gwendolen: Do you allude to me, Miss Cardew, as an entanglement? You are presumptuous. On an occasion of this kind it becomes more than a moral duty to speak one's mind. It becomes a pleasure.

Cecily: Do you suggest, Miss Fairfax, that I entrapped Ernest into an engagement? How dare you? This is no time for wearing the shallow mask of manners. When I see a spade, I call it a spade.

Gwendolen: I am glad to say that I have never seen a spade.[23] It is obvious that our social spheres have been widely different.

Cecily: May I offer you some tea, Miss Fairfax?

Gwendolen: [24]Thank you. *(Aside)* Detestable girl! But I require tea!

Cecily: [25]Sugar?

Gwendolen: No thank you. [26]Sugar is not fashionable, any more.

Cecily: Cake, or bread and butter?

Gwendolen: Bread and butter, please. [27]Cake is rarely seen at the best houses nowadays.

Cecily: Miss Fairfax—

Gwendolen: [28]You have filled my tea with lumps of sugar and though I asked most distinctly for bread and butter, you have given me cake. I am known for the extraordinary sweetness of my nature, but I warn you, Miss Cardew, you may go too far.

Cecily: [29]To save my poor, innocent, trusting boy from the machinations of any other girl, there are no lengths to which I would not go.

29. Rising.

Gwendolen: From the moment I saw you I distrusted you. I felt that you were false and deceitful. My first impressions of people are invariably right.

Cecily: It seems to me, Miss Fairfax, that I am trespassing on your valuable time. No doubt you have many other calls of similar character to make in the neighborhood.

(Jack enters)[30]

30. From garden L, and seeing only their smiling faces, is blissfully unaware of the mayhem the faces conceal.

Gwendolen: Ernest! My own Ernest!

Jack: Gwendolen! Darling!

Gwendolen: A moment![31] May I ask if you are engaged to be married to this young lady?

31. Cecily gives to L on his entrance. He walks between girls, and offers to kiss Gwendolen. She draws back, holding up a restraining palm, then points to Cecily.

Jack: To dear little Cecily?[32] Of course not! What could have put such an idea into your pretty little head?

32. Laughing as if the very idea were preposterous.

Gwendolen: [33]Thank you. You may.

33. Gwendolen now offers her cheek.

Cecily: I knew there must be some misunderstanding, Miss Fairfax.[34] The gentleman whose arm is at present around your waist is my dear guardian, Mr. John Worthing.

34. Sweetly. Really relieved.

Gwendolen: I beg your pardon?

Cecily: This is Uncle Jack.

Gwendolen: Jack! Oh![35]

35. Receding DL, Jack follows her.

(Enter Algernon)

Sir John Gielgud, Dame Edith Evans, and Margaret Leighton in The Importance of Being Earnest. *(Radio Times Hulton Picture Library.)*

36. From L.

37. Goes straight to Cecily DL without noticing anyone else, offering to kiss her. She repeats business of Gwendolen (as identically as possible). At this point, Gwendolen is DR with Jack to her L. Cecily is DL with Algernon to her R.

38. Looks about, sees that Gwendolen is the only other girl present, and laughs at the absurdity of it.

39. Repeats business of Gwendolen.

40. Gwendolen crosses Jack to front of table, then to C.

41. Algernon is now between the girls.

42. She moves in front of Algernon to Gwendolen at C.

43. The girls put their arms around each other's waists, as if for protection. Jack is now DL of table. Gwendolen is at C, Cecily to her L, and Algernon is DLC.

44. Coming up L, swings chair left of table and leans over it. He speaks slowly, hesitatingly.

45. Surprised.

46. Very pleased to say it.

47. More seriously.

48. More pleased than ever.

49. The girls are gloriously noble and proud through their tears.

Cecily: Here is Ernest![36]

Algernon: My own love![37]

Cecily: A moment, Ernest! May I ask you—are you engaged to be married to this young lady?

Algernon: To what young lady? Good heavens! [38]Gwendolen!

Cecily: Yes, to good heavens, Gwendolen, I mean to Gwendolen.

Algernon: Of course not! What could have put such an idea into your pretty little head?

Cecily: Thank you.[39] You may.

Gwendolen: I felt there was some slight error, Miss Cardew. [40]The gentleman now embracing you is my cousin, Mr. Algernon Moncrieff.

Cecily: Algernon Moncrieff! Oh!

Algernon: [41]I cannot deny it.

Cecily: Oh!

Gwendolen: Is your name really John?

Jack: I could deny it. But my name is certainly John. It has been John for years.

Cecily: [42]A gross deception has been practiced on both of us.

Gwendolen: [43]My poor wounded Cecily!

Cecily: My sweet, wronged Gwendolen!

Gwendolen: You will call me sister, will you not?

Cecily: There is just one question I would like to be allowed to ask my guardian.

Gwendolen: An admirable idea! Mr. Worthing, there is just one question I would like to be permitted to put to you. Where is your brother Ernest? We are both engaged to be married to your brother Ernest, so it is a matter of some importance to us to know where your brother Ernest is at present.

Jack: [44]Gwendolen—Cecily—it is very painful for me to be forced to speak the truth. It is the first time in my life that I have ever been reduced to such a painful position, and I am really quite inexperienced in doing anything of the kind. However, I will tell you quite frankly that I have no brother Ernest. I have no brother at all. I never had a brother in my life, and I certainly have not the smallest intention of having one in the future.

Cecily: [45]No brother at all?

Jack: [46]None!

Gwendolen: [47]Had you never a brother of any kind?

Jack: [48]Never! Not even of any kind.

Gwendolen: I am afraid it is quite clear, Cecily, that neither of us is engaged to be married to anyone.

Cecily: [49]It is not a very pleasant position for a young girl suddenly to find herself in, is it?

Gwendolen: Let us go into the house.[50] They will hardly venture to come after us there.

Cecily: No, men are so cowardly, aren't they?

(The girls exit)

FURTHER READING

Harris, Frank. *Oscar Wilde.* New York: Dell, 1960.

Holland, Vyvyan. *Oscar Wilde, A Pictorial Biography.* New York: Viking, 1960.

Minney, Rubleigh James. *The Edwardian Age.* Boston: Little, Brown, 1965.

Pearson, Hesketh. *Oscar Wilde, His Life and Wit.* London: Grosset's, 1946.

NATURALISM, REALISM, AND THE FOURTH WALL[3]

Although the eighteenth-century actors, Talma, Garrick, and even Sarah Siddons, were said to be "realistic," we must accept the term not as we use it today, but in relation to the accepted standard of acting that preceded it. During the latter part of the nineteenth century, new attitudes toward realism in the theatre began to appear. This influence became the groundwork for much twentieth-century drama. Amateurs again stepped into prominence. André Antoine, a clerk in a gas company, joined an evening class in "Recitation and Diction," which inspired him to form an amateur group called the Théâtre Libre, devoted to a new style of acting in a new style of play. They let it be known that they wanted to perform only unpublished plays dealing with everyday subjects.

The quest for realism spread. It was established in Germany by Otto Brahm's Freie Büehne, and in England by the Independent Theatre (which found a new author with new ideas, George Bernard Shaw). Later, the Abbey Theatre was established in Ireland. In Russia, a rich man's dilettante son took the stage name of Stanislavski so as not to disgrace his family, and with Vladimir Danchenko began the Moscow Art Theatre. All were amateurs. The professional actor could not, or cared not, to change his way of working. The amateurs, knowing little of acting (except that they wanted to act), set about the task of training themselves in a style suitable to the plays being submitted to them. Emile Zola was busy in France writing novels and plays about common people. Although Henrik Ibsen began in romanticism with such plays as *Peer Gynt,* he later became the cornerstone of the realistic movement. When Ibsen was com-

---

50. They cast scornful looks at their respective beaux, and with arms around waists, retire into the house. The boys join each other at C and watch them disappear.

---

[3]This was so-called because the proscenium arch was considered as the "fourth wall" of a room, open to provide the audience with a view.

pared to Zola, he readily admitted a similarity; "but with this difference," he added, "Zola descends into the cesspool to take a bath, I to cleanse it." In Russia, Nicolai Gogol, Ivan Turgenev, Leo Tolstoy, Anton Checkhov, and Maxim Gorki were creating a new type of drama. With all this activity of fine minds working on plays that were different not only in development but also in conception, it was obvious that the old, flamboyant, declamatory style of acting had to be replaced by a new acting method.

Down through the centuries, we have seen how representative actors used the basic essentials in building characterization. Not only do we have their own words to that effect, but we have eyewitness accounts of these things in their work. No one will deny that in this century we have made some developments in acting out of our particular needs, and we have given new terminology to old processes, but we did not invent creative acting, and neither did Antoine or Stanislavski.

The plays of Sophocles, Shakespeare, and Molière, while having certain intellectual content, do not attempt to alter radically the intellectual concepts of an audience. The plays written by Ibsen, Chekhov, and their contemporaries, however, do just that. This was an innovation of the "new" playwrights, and their plays required an intrinsically different type of acting. There was a need for acting that would more deeply probe the hidden depths of character, exploring internal values rather than accenting the previously accepted values of style, elegance, and theatricality. Voice and enunciation were no longer as important as they had been. These new playwrights wrote the language of ordinary people, the speech heard in the marketplaces and streets. They did not use carefully selected and beautiful words, nor did they set them to meter.

The action in these plays was confined to that of ordinary men and women. Such plays could be understood by the butcher and baker. The action no longer involved the daring of larger-than-life heroes facing insurmountable odds. Instead of fighting fate or an invading army, these new heroes fought existing social or economic mores.

Standards of acting based on magnetism, stage presence, and a trained body and voice were practically discarded because the butcher and baker had none of these. They did not want to admire an artistic ideal; they wanted to look in a mirror. Stress was placed on the "real-life" aspects—the inner, not the outer, man. Freudian theories were translated into acting terms. What appeared on the surface was only a part of, or perhaps unrelated to, the "real" meaning hidden beneath. No longer could an actor pick up a manuscript and swiftly interpret a character. It required time to get inside such characters. It was not wise to make snap judgments or depend solely on the tested and reliable devices of voice, gesture, or timing. The need had arrived for a new acting style. Once developed, this same method would serve for subsequent plays written by twentieth-century playwrights such as Eugene O'Neill, Clifford Odets, Arthur Miller, and Tennessee Williams.

Henrik Ibsen's influence on the theatre since his day has been monumental. His unique gift was in creating the so-called well-made play, which stated in dramatic terms a number of social problems of significance to his generation. Many of these problems no longer concern us, but his dramatic skill was so great that his plays live on because of other qualities.

We can hardly imagine today just what a play was before Ibsen began writing them. Early nineteenth-century plays were written to a set formula something on this order:

Act I. Exposition, introduction of protagonists, and a struggle suggested.

Act II. Act III. Situations, given over to mounting tensions.

Act IV. Spectacular ball or fête, stage filled with people, magnificent costumes and games, dances, etc., with an outburst, a quarrel, and a challenge. This was the climax. All must look bad for the hero.

Act V. Everything resolved, all loose ends tied together (denouement).

Before Ibsen, no one expected a hero to be motivated by anything but heroic impulses. Ibsen discarded the fancy ornaments used in earlier plays, the strutting, posturing, ranting tirades, and the climactic scenes so loved by actors. It was Ibsen who won the first decisive victories for realism. He is particularly known for his profundity and imagination, his special use of characterizations, his dialogue, and his play construction.

Along with August Strindberg, Ibsen revolutionized play writing. Existing drama was too sweet a confection for their tastes. Both worked in naturalism, and later both experimented with new forms. In 1880 the study of psychology was just beginning to interest authors. Ibsen used this knowledge to give depth to characters. He shifted emphasis to internal examination, in a search aimed not so much at greater realism, but at greater truth. Before he dominated the stage, no one went to the theatre expecting to witness similar experiences to those they had in everyday life.

In *The Master Builder*, Ibsen was experimenting with symbolism. In the scene that follows, we see the furthest limit of his venture from realism into symbolism. We shall see later how Strindberg went far beyond Ibsen in this field, how he explored the hidden recesses of the soul, probing into dreams, even madness. Ibsen saw the road ahead, but was unable to follow it because his time was running out. In one of his last letters he wrote, "I shall not be able to absent

Henrik Ibsen
(1828–1906)

myself from the old battlefields. But if I return, I shall come forward with new weapons and new equipment." He was never to return to the battle. It was for younger men. But they would benefit by the old Norwegian's victories.

The following lines are from Ibsen's *Collected Poems*, 1871:

I will build me a cloud castle—Through the North its light shall fall.
With two wings will I build it—a great wing and a small.
In the larger shall inhabit a bard of deathless power;
The lesser shall be given to be a maiden's bower.

PREPARATION FOR *THE MASTER BUILDER*

Exercise 130

After studying *The Master Builder* in its entirety, you should be able to answer the following questions:

1. This play has many symbols. Name three and specify what they mean to you. Why was the Master Builder convinced he must climb the tower? Is his fall symbol, fact, or both? Explain.

2. What price has Solness paid for success and what threatens that success? Why does Solness refuse Ragnar a chance to be on his own? Solness believes he is mad; does anyone in this play agree with him?

3. Perform an improvisation in which Hilda stops to ask directions to Solness's house, where she hopes to "claim her kingdom."

4. How does the scene between Solness and the Doctor contribute to Hilda's dramatic entrance?

5. Which character in this play is called "a bird of prey"? Who are "the helpers and servers"?

6. Frequently Ibsen uses a key word to describe Aline's character. What is that word? The author portrays a grown woman grieving over the loss of dolls. What do you think were his reasons for doing this? Mrs. Solness has been called "one of the living dead." Why?

7. What is the theme of this play? Can you write the plot development in two or three sentences? What is the climax? How does Kaia contribute to the plot?

8. Hilda comes to stay forever with Solness, then decides to leave. What causes her to change her mind? Do you believe it a wise decision? Do you believe Solness is a religious man? Give reasons.

9. When Ibsen was writing this play, he was advising a wife who believed her husband had been hypnotized by another woman. Do you find any evidence of hypnosis in this play?

10. Hilda forces Solness to climb the tower, even though she knows there is a chance he may fall to his death. Obviously Ibsen wanted his audience to admire his leading woman, yet he has her gamble with another's life. If you were playing Hilda, what ways would you devise to make this acceptable to your audience?

11. Ibsen gives a word picture of Solness climbing the steeple. Work out an improvisation of this action using Ibsen's dialogue as a guide.

12. Can you think of any reasons why the playwright would bring Solness back on stage in act III, after he had taken him off carrying the wreath?

13. As there is so little physical action and so much talk, on what do you think the actors should concentrate in order to make this play absorbing to an audience?

CHARACTERIZATION

Hilda Wangle   Hilda is not the typical girl of Ibsen's century. Here, Ibsen wrote almost prophetically of the girl of today. We now have many Hilda Wangles. They swoon over their latest crush, from Rudy Vallee to Frank Sinatra to Elvis Presley. To some adults, such child-women may appear brash and undisciplined. Even so, none could deny that these Hildas live in an enchanted period of life.

But Ibsen's Hilda never grew up. She denies age, she is the eternal fresh breeze—so raw at times that we shudder; but she is forever invigorating us and renewing our own youth. Hilda is a romantic. She has that rare gift for believing and accepting. Life has not had time to teach her the bitter lessons of skepticism. She is brash, mercurial, unpredictable, generous, perhaps even foolish in giving of herself and her devotion. But whatever Hilda does impulsively, she also does with an open and trusting heart. She has the eagerness of youth, and the impatience to get on with life and living, to drain the cup *now*, with no thought of tomorrow. This requires courage. An audience will excuse a dozen flaws of character if a protagonist has courage.

Halvard Solness   Halvard Solness is the opposite of everything Hilda represents. Hilda comes into Halvard's life when he is beginning to feel the sour inactivity of age, and he basks in her youthful glow. It is neither her fault nor his that she has arrived late. The gallant effort they make to rise above time is the courageous and admirable element of this play. While we sense their defeat, we admire the indomitable human spirit in them that permits them even to dare. Solness knows he is no hero. He is even somewhat of a villain to himself. He regrets the many dishonorable actions he has taken in order to get ahead. But because Hilda believes him a hero, he tries to fulfill her dream of him—and dies in the attempt.

Nevertheless, Hilda's Master Builder lives on. Although this play is all too rarely performed, it should be a great favorite in high schools, for it tells us of the creative powers of youth, and pleads with us to respect, to hold onto, that power. Although Ibsen called his play "a tragedy," it is in reality a hymn to youth.

REHEARSAL

The Master Builder

Henrik Ibsen
An Excerpt from Act I
Translated by John C. Pearce, Ph.D.

CAST: Halvard Solness, Master Builder
Hilda Wangle

SCENE: *Interior, Solness's house. Required: a table and chairs. At rise, Hilda is seated at table LC wearing a traveling suit. The student-actress should find a way to show the audience that she is a guest here, not a hostess. (Something might be done with her handbag, showing that she is carrying her necessities with her.) Solness is bringing a tray to the table RC. It contains two cups. As he places one on the table before Hilda, she speaks.*

Hilda: Mr. Solness!

Solness: Yes?

Hilda: Are you very forgetful?

Solness: Forgetful?[1] No, not so far as I know.

Hilda: Then have you nothing to say to me about what happened—up there?

Solness: *(In momentary surprise)*[2] Up at Lysanger? *(Indifferently)* Why—there's nothing much to talk about, it seems to me.

Hilda: *(Looking reproachfully at him)* How can you sit there and say such things?

Solness: Well, then, why don't you tell me about it.

Hilda: [3]When the tower was finished, we had such a wonderful celebration in the town.

Solness: Yes,[4] that day I'll never forget.

Hilda: *(Pleased)* You won't? How kind of you.

Solness: Kind?

Hilda: There was music in the cemetery—[5]and many, many hundreds of people. We school-girls were dressed in white and we all had flags.

Solness: Oh yes, those flags.[6] I certainly remember those.

Hilda: So then you climbed right up on the scaffolding—right up to the very top. And then you had a big wreath with you, and you hung that wreath right up on top of the weathervane . . .

Solness: *(Interrupting)* Yes, I always used to do that—then. That's an old custom.

1. He smiles, places the other cup at his place, pulls out the chair, and sits.

2. As he sips from the cup, he hesitates, then looks up at her.

3. She rises, strides deliberately upstage. Throughout the coming scene she ranges about as if she were unconsciously separating her dream of Solness from the reality of the man sitting with her.

4. Musing pleasantly as he sips from his cup.

5. She begins to be caught up in her fantasy. She uses great sweeping, heroic gestures and movements.

6. To Solness, this story has no glamor, it is merely a recall of dear days past.

Hilda: It was so terribly thrilling—[7]to stand below and to look up at you! Just think. If he should fall—he—the Master Builder himself!

Solness: (*As if to change the subject*) [8]Yes, yes, yes—it might very well have happened too, because one of those little imps in white made such a commotion—shouting and screaming up at me . . .

Hilda: (*Sparkling with pleasure*) [9]"Hurrah for Master Builder Solness!" Yes!!

Solness: And waved—and swung that flag around—that I—Well, I got giddy when I looked down at her.

Hilda: (*Seriously*) That little imp—[10]that was I.

Solness: (*Looking steadily into her eyes*) I am sure of that now. It must have been you.

Hilda: (*Lively again*) Oh, it was so gloriously thrilling! [11]I couldn't imagine that there was a builder in the whole world who could build such a tremendously high tower. And there you stood, right on the very top of it big as life! And that you didn't even get dizzy, not the least bit.[12] I just tremble when I think of it!

Solness: You're quite sure I wasn't . . .

Hilda: (*Preposterous idea*) No, indeed! No! Oh, *no!* I knew that instinctively. If you *had* been, you never could have stood up there—and sung!

Solness: (*Astonished*) [13]Sung? I sang?

Hilda: You certainly did.

Solness: I've never sung a note in my life.

Hilda: You sang then. It sounded like harps in the air.

Solness: (*Thoughtfully*) [14]That's strange, that is.

Hilda: (*She is silent for a little, then looks at him and speaks in a low voice*) But then—it was afterwards—that the real thing happened.

Solness: [15]The real thing?

Hilda: (*Again sparkling*) Oh come now, I surely don't have to remind you of that, do I?

Solness: Well, just remind me a little.

Hilda: You don't remember that they gave a big lunch in your honor at the Club?

Solness: [16]Yes,—but it was dinner for me. I left next morning.

Hilda: And from the Club you were invited to our house for supper.

Solness: You're right, Miss Wangle. It's wonderful how all these [17]little details impressed you.

Hilda: [18]Little details! Well, I like that! Was it also just a little detail that I was alone in a room afterward when you came in?

Solness: You were—[19]alone?

Hilda: (*Ignoring his question*) You didn't call me a little imp then.

Solness: No? I didn't?

7. Hilda is acting it all out—she is the wreath, the steeple, the hero—and all just as romantic as they were in King Arthur's day.

8. Pushing the cup away, he settles back contentedly in his chair. The actor might transmit this mood of comfort and mild amusement to us by smoking.

9. She comes down to him, leans over the table looking closely at him, somehow hoping he will recognize her.

10. As he does not, she must tell him.

11. Resuming her walk up and down.

12. Solness knows that he *was* dizzy.

13. He remembers some of her tall tale as fact, but *this* is preposterous.

14. Although he believes all this a complete fabrication, he is nevertheless flattered and amused.

15. Just a bit suspicious.

16. He is relieved.

17. "Little details" should be colored into insignificance.

18. Moving back of him to his L and leaning over, her face near his, she forces him to look squarely at her.

19. Very apprehensive.

20. Again resuming the walk.

21. She is now at C, and above the table, lost in her own dream. It will be quite effective if she can show us (without her own realization, of course) that her dream is hers alone and only remotely a part of the man seated at the table.

22. The realist.

23. A little upset with him because he has not accepted her enthusiasm. *"Orangia"* should be said as if it were Heaven. Oranges were then very rare in Norway and considered a great delicacy.

24. Back to her fantasy, straight front.

25. Pouting.

26. An awkward pause as Solness gathers his senses. This is what he has feared all along—that he has misbehaved in some way.

27. As she throws up her hands in impatience and strides away from him.

28. Again leaning over the table and almost shouting into his face.

29. Very quickly but innocently.

30. Making her point even more definitely than before.

31. He slowly rises from the chair.

32. A fast turn away from him in utter disgust.

33. He approaches her timidly in voice and manner as she stands, her back to him, her feet far apart, and hands clasped behind in anger.

Hilda: You said I was beautiful in my white dress,[20] and you said I looked like a little princess—

Solness: And I'm sure you did, Miss Wangle—and—besides, we were all feeling so gay and free that day.

Hilda: And that's when you said that when I grew up[21] I should become your princess.

Solness: (*Laughing a little*) Dear, dear, did I say that too?

Hilda: Yes you did! And when I asked how long I should have to wait, you said that you would come again in ten years, like a troll, and carry me off—to Spain—or some fabulous place. And you promised you would buy me a kingdom there.

Solness: Yes. Well, after a good meal one doesn't leave a small tip. (*With disbelief*) [22]Did I really say all that?

Hilda: You did. You even told me what the kingdom would be called.

Solness: What was that?

Hilda: It was to be called "The Kingdom of Orangia."[23] That's what you said.

Solness: That's an appetising name.

Hilda: Well, I didn't like it a bit.[24] It seemed as if you were making fun of me.

Solness: Oh, I'm sure I didn't intend to do that.

Hilda: [25]Well, I should hope not—considering what you did next.

Solness: (*With some trepidation*) [26]What did I do next?

Hilda: Well, that's just the end![27] If you've forgotten that too! I should have thought that no one could help remembering a thing like that!

Solness: Why not give me just a hint, then—

Hilda: (*Looks steadily at him*) [28]You grabbed me and kissed me, Mr. Solness!

Solness: (*Shocked*) [29]I did?

Hilda: [30]Indeed you did. You grabbed me with both your arms and you bent my head way back—and you kissed me—*many* times.

Solness: [31]My dear, kind Miss Wangle!

Hilda: Surely you could never deny that?

Solness: Ah, but I do! I feel I must deny it.

Hilda: (*Scornfully*) Oh, you wouldn't[32]—oh—how can you?
(*She turns, walks away, stands with her back to him angrily*)

Solness: (*Pleadingly*)[33] Miss Wangle . . .

FURTHER READING

Gassner, John. *Masters of the Drama*. New York: Simon & Schuster, 1945, pp. 354–86.

————. *A Treasury of the Theatre*. Vol. 2. New York: Simon & Schuster, 1951, pp. 10–14, 40–41.

Ibsen, Henrik. *Six Plays*. Translated by Eva LeGallienne. New York: Modern Library, 1957. Introduction.

Tennant, P. F. D. *Ibsen's Dramatic Technique*. London: Albert Saifer, 1962.

Weigand, Hermann. *The Modern Ibsen: A Reconstruction*. New York: E. P. Dutton, 1960.

Anton Chekhov
(1860–1904)

Anton Chekhov's style of play writing brought out the quiet, uneventful character probing that has become synonymous with Stanislavski and the Moscow Art Theatre. Some theatregoers complain that Chekhov's plays are aimless and depressing. But Chekhov's goals were not centered on plots, strong-willed characters, or prepared climaxes. His remarkable achievement was that he was able to construct plays of enduring vitality without such aids. Although his plays are dramatically understated, the acting can reveal complex themes and counterthemes, concluding with a crescendo of masterful orchestration. But if the acting fails to reveal the buried emotions and the hidden thoughts of the characters, then the dialogue may appear confusing, gloomy, or even boring.

The typical Chekhovian character has *charm,* a word we would hardly use to describe a character from Strindberg. Indeed Chekhov thought of his characters affectionately. They amused him. (See marginal notes in the excerpt.) They exist in a half-world between a nostalgic past and an illusory future.

The Three Sisters, the most frequently performed of Chekhov's plays, has been called a "most richly textured play." In it we find examples of the celebrated Chekhovian dialogue, seemingly unimportant, even trivial, on the surface, and yet revealing inner thoughts that expose the very souls of the characters.

PREPARATION FOR *THE THREE SISTERS*

The following scene is not simple to act because there is so much that must be contributed by the actors. Begin your preparation by reading the entire play not once but several times.

Exercise 131

When you feel you *know* the people of the Prozoroff household, test yourself by answering the following questions dealing with atmosphere, theme, and characterization:

1. Describe the atmosphere of this play as you imagine it.
2. Chekhov gives the ages of the three sisters in the dialogue. How old is Irina? Masha? Olga?

3. Masha is fond of quoting, "A green oak ..." Finish the sentence and state its significance.
4. Contrast the Solony-Irina scene in act II with the Vershinin-Masha scene in act I. Both are love scenes. Yet how do they differ?
5. In act I, Masha cries constantly, but in act II she says she has been laughing all day. Why?
6. What sort of life does Vershinin picture for his children's children?
7. What is Masha's philosophy of life?
8. What do you understand to be the theme of this play? Does the play have a protagonist?
9. Chekhov uses songs and music in acts I and II, but in act III he indicates a fire offstage. What is the dramatic use of each?

Stanislavski as Vershinin. (Courtesy of Sov-Photo.)

In your study of *The Three Sisters* you have come to know fourteen people. In our scene we shall concentrate on only three, but our knowledge of the others and our feeling of the play's atmosphere will help with the short scene.

Even in the following short scene, we can appreciate the engrossing picture Chekhov paints of Russian life in a small town. If the people who frequent the Prozoroff living room are not cheerful, they are lively, friendly, and talkative. Even if their talk is only "whistling in the dark," it provides them with the courage to go on. One of Chekhov's characters talks about the migration of birds in the autumn: "They will always go on flying. It doesn't matter what thoughts they are thinking, high thoughts or low ones, they just go on flying, not knowing where they are going, or why. They just go right on flying."

It was for the plays of Chekhov that Stanislavski's system was developed and no method is more effective when producing a play of realism such as *The Three Sisters*. Begin by placing yourself in the atmosphere of the play, remembering that it is Russia in the late nineteenth century. An immediate consideration for this scene is to become conscious of the social levels existing in Russia at that time.

REHEARSAL

The Three Sisters*

Anton Chekhov
An Excerpt from Act III

CAST: **Olga**

Irina

Masha

(The character of NATASHA *can be imagined in this excerpt.)*

*From Anton Chekhov, *Four Great Plays by Chekhov* (New York: Bantam Books, 1958).

SCENE: *The bedroom shared by Olga and Irina. There are two beds surrounded by screens. There is a table for each bed, a sofa by one wall, and a couple of chairs. Reread the beginning of act III to establish the mood and situation at the start of this excerpt.*

Irina: [1]Yes, how petty our Andrey has grown, how dull and old he has become beside that woman! At one time he was working to get a professorship and yesterday he was boasting of having succeeded at last in becoming a member of the Rural Board. He is a member, and Protopopov is chairman. . . . The whole town is laughing and talking of it and he is the only one who sees and knows nothing. . . . And here everyone has been running to the fire while he sits still in his room and takes no notice. He does nothing but play his violin. . . . *(nervously)* Oh, it's awful, awful, awful! *(Weeps)* I can't bear it any more, I can't! I can't!, I can't![2]

(Olga comes in and begins tidying up her table)

Irina: *(sobs loudly)* Turn me out, turn me out, I can't bear it any more!

Olga: *(alarmed)* What is it? What is it, darling?[3]

Irina: *(sobbing)* Where?[4] Where has it all gone? Where is it? Oh, my God, my God! I have forgotten everything, everything . . . everything is in a tangle in my mind. . . . I don't remember the Italian for window or ceiling. . . . I am forgetting everything; every day I forget something more and life is slipping away and will never come back, we shall never, never go to Moscow. . . . I see that we shan't go. . . .

Olga: Darling, darling[5] . . .

Irina: *(restraining herself)*[6] Oh, I am wretched. . . . I can't work, I am not going to work. I have had enough of it, enough of it! I have been a telegraph clerk and now I have a job in the town council and I hate and despise every bit of the work they give me. . . . I am nearly twenty-four, I have been working for years, my brains are drying up, I am getting thin and old and ugly and there is nothing, nothing, not the slightest satisfaction, and time is passing and one feels that one is moving away from a real, fine life, moving farther and farther away and being drawn into the depths. I am in despair and I don't know how it is I am alive and have not killed myself yet. . . .

Olga: Don't cry, my child, don't cry. It makes me miserable.[7]

Irina: I am not crying, I am not crying. . . . It's over. . . . There, I am not crying now. I won't. . . . I won't.[8]

Olga: Darling, I am speaking to you as a sister, as a friend, if you care for my advice, marry the baron!

(Irina weeps)

Sir John Gielgud as Lt. Col. Alexander Vershinin in Gielgud's production of Chekhov's The Three Sisters, *London, 1935. (Radio Times Hulton Picture Library.)*

1. Standing by the doorway, looking out. Masha is lying on the sofa. Is she asleep, or lost in her thoughts?
2. Moves to a chair, sits, and pulls a handkerchief from her sleeve.
3. Moves to Irina.
4. Takes Olga's hands in hers.
5. Strokes her hair.
6. Stands. Then walks agitatedly around the room.

7. Crosses to Irina.

8. Moves away from Olga, controlling herself, dabbing at her eyes with the handkerchief, and then collapses on her bed.

A scene from The Three Sisters *with Irina (Marianne Faithful, center) trying to coax brother Andrey Prozorov (George Cole) to have some fun. The other sisters are Olga (left), played by Avril Elgee, and Masha, played by Glenda Jackson. (Courtesy of Her Britannic Majesty's Consulate-General.)*

9. Moves slowly toward Irina and kneels by the side of the bed.

Olga: *(softly)*[9]You know you respect him, you think highly of him. . . . It's true he is ugly, but he is such a thoroughly nice man, so good. . . . One doesn't marry for love, but to do one's duty. . . . That's what I think, anyway, and I would marry without love. Whoever proposed to me I would marry him, if only he were a good man. . . . I would even marry an old man. . . .

Irina: I kept expecting we should move to Moscow and there I should meet my real one. I've been dreaming of him, loving him. . . . But it seems that was all nonsense, nonsense. . . .

10. They must be facing toward the audience.

Olga: [10]*(puts her arms round her sister)* My darling, lovely sister, I understand it all; when the baron left the army and came to us in a plain coat, I thought he looked so ugly that it positively made me cry. . . . He asked me, "Why are you crying?" How could I tell him! But if God brought you together I should be happy. That's a different thing, you know, quite different.[11]

11. Pause. Olga sees that Irina is calm. She stands up in time to see Natasha.

(Natasha with a candle in her hand walks across the stage from door on right to door on left without speaking)

Masha: *(sits up)* She walks about as though it were she had set fire to the town.

12. Moving to Masha, she ruffles Masha's hair.

Olga: Masha, you are silly.[12] The very silliest of the family, that's you. Please forgive me *(a pause)*.

Masha: I want to confess my sins, dear sisters. My soul is yearning. I am going to confess to you and never again to anyone. . . . I'll tell you this minute *(softly)*. It's my secret, but you must know everything. . . . I can't be silent . . . *(a pause)*.[13] I am in love, I am in love. . . . I love that man. . . . You have just seen him. . . . Well, I may as well say it straight out. I love Vershinin.

13. Takes Olga's hands in hers.

Olga: (*going behind her screen*) Leave off. I don't hear anyway.

Masha: But what am I to do?[14] (*Clutches her head.*) At first I thought him queer . . . then I was sorry for him . . . then I came to love him[15] . . . to love him with his voice, his words, his misfortunes, his two little girls. . . .

Olga: (*behind the screen*) I don't hear you anyway. Whatever silly things you say I shan't hear them.

Masha: Oh, Olya, you are silly. I love him—so that's my fate. It means that that's my lot. . . . And he loves me. . . . It's all dreadful. Yes?[16] Is it wrong? (*Takes Irina by the hand and draws her to herself.*) Oh, my darling . . . How are we going to live our lives, what will become of us? . . . When one reads a novel it all seems stale and easy to understand, but when you are in love yourself you see that no one knows anything and we all have to settle things for ourselves. . . . My darling, my sister[17] . . . I have confessed it to you, now I'll hold my tongue. . . . I'll be like Gogol's madman[18] . . . silence . . . silence. . . .

14. Standing.
15. Crosses to Olga's screen.

16. Irina rises from her bed. Masha crosses to her.

17. Steps back to arm's length, still holding Irina's hands.
18. Drops Irina's hands and turns away.

FURTHER READING

Buford, W. H. *Chekhov and His Russia.* London: Keegan Paul, 1947. Social and intellectual life of the late nineteenth century in Russia.

Krutch, Joseph Wood. *"Modernism" in Drama.* Ithaca, N.Y.: Cornell University Press, 1953. See chapter headed (of all things!) "Pirandello."

Magarshack, David. *Chekhov the Dramatist.* New York: Hill & Wang, 1950.

Simmons, Ernest J. *Chekhov, A Biography.* Boston: Little, Brown, 1962.

REVOLUTION IN THE MAKING

August Strindberg
(1849–1912)

Although August Strindberg may have lacked Ibsen's self-control, accuracy of detail, and skill at play making, he had a more penetrating insight into underlying experiences that almost bordered on mysticism and the occult. The difference between the characters of Ibsen and Strindberg is the difference between a photograph and an X ray.

Strindberg shared with both Ibsen and Chekhov a mastery at probing the human soul. But Strindberg was able to take reality and spin it through the air until it seemed more like an exciting theatrical illusion than reality. Strindberg referred to his characters as "my souls"; they were not people to him, but the substance inside people. His "souls" had the look of people—they ate and loved— but they existed in a rarefied Strindbergian atmosphere, and they

had the power and vigor of madness. Strindberg seems nearer to Poe than to Ibsen.

Fame came to Strindberg as a result of his realistic plays, *Miss Julie* and *The Father.* The master Antoine produced his plays. But today interest seems to focus on the plays of his later period, for in these he delved into a deeper reality. They have the validity of dreams. This involvement with dreams and the dream state later became known as surrealism. The plays have a contagion of death about them, but Strindberg treated pain and death as healing agents, which purify like fire. They were written with a conscious naïveté, but still maintain a kind of sophistication. They are what is called in painting "primitives." These are very personal plays, written to release the author's own tortures.

Others, such as Maurice Maeterlinck, Gerhart Hauptmann, and even Ibsen, worked for a time with symbolism, but Strindberg has far more influence today.

In *The Dance of Death* Strindberg placed two people in an old tower. Although utterly weary of each other, they are nevertheless bound together forever by time and custom. The old man is maddened because he has never been promoted. These two failures try to live out their days by creating for themselves an illusionary world of glamor and status. This play, written in 1901, has certain similarities to *The Chairs* by Eugene Ionesco, written in 1952; both are referred to as "tragic farces."

Ibsen closed the door on nineteenth-century realism. He said masterfully all there was to say in the "peephole theatre."[4] But Strindberg opened another door: He is the rightful father of the theatre of illusion. As Eugene O'Neill wrote, "Strindberg still remains among the most modern of moderns, the great interpreter in the theatre of the characteristic spiritual conflicts which constitute drama."

There are three distinct periods of dramatic activity in the works of August Strindberg. He began by writing traditional, little romantic dramas. Then about 1887, with *The Father* and *Miss Julie,* he entered into a period in which he produced ultrarealistic plays, which established him as a serious playwright. But the plays of his later period, after the turn of the century, strike our generation as the most portentous and relevant to our times—the esoteric and symbolic pieces like *The Dream Play* and *The Ghost Sonata.*

In *The Ghost Sonata,* Strindberg pioneered a style of drama never before attempted in the theatre. Luigi Pirandello, Michel de Ghelderode, Bertolt Brecht, Samuel Beckett, Jean Genet, and many lesser-known, latter-day playwrights are Strindberg's beneficiaries. In *The Theatre of the Absurd,* Martin Esslin writes, "The first to put on stage a dream world in the spirit of modern psychological thinking

---

[4]"Peephole theatre" refers to productions in which the playwright peeks into the privacy of the characters' lives. This term is applied only to realistic theatre.

was August Strindberg. The three parts of *To Damascus* (1898–1904), *A Dream Play* (1902), and *The Ghost Sonata* (1907), are masterly transcriptions of dreams and obsessions and direct sources of the Theatre of the Absurd."

PREPARATION FOR *THE GHOST SONATA*

It is significant, in the writing of *The Ghost Sonata*, that Strindberg digressed from many traditional rules of dramaturgy and evolved a style in which theme and images in motion prevailed over plot and characterizations. *The Ghost Sonata*, considered the most famous of the Chamber Plays, was written in 1907 from the pit of Strindberg's private inferno, demonstrating his scorn for the world, but also showing his deep sympathy for the deluded creatures who are born into it. The play abounds in striking visual and aural effects. It is set in a kind of limbo or purgatory, where humans are doomed to exist before they reach the peaceful realm of the dead.

The plot, slight as it is, begins with an evil Old Man enlisting the aid of an idealistic young Student to gain entry into a mystery house, where the Old Man seeks vengeance on its inhabitants. The scenes of the play have been compared to the movements of a sonata, the first scene an allegro, the second the largo. The following excerpt from the second scene will be incomprehensible without knowing how it fits into the entire play. In this scene, known as the "Ghost Supper," the Old Man exposes the deceit and betrayal of the other guests, and he demolishes them by showing how he has them all in his power. But the mood changes quickly when the Old Man is proved to be a murderer and is left defenseless.

REHEARSAL

The Ghost Sonata*

August Strindberg
An Excerpt from Scene ii

CAST: The Colonel   **The Old Man**

The Mummy   **Bengtsson**

SCENE: *UL is a porcelain stove; its mantle holds a mirror, a pendulum clock, and a candelabrum. In the rear wall is a door to the hyacinth room and above that is concealed a door to a closet. UR leads to a hallway, and*

---

*From the book *The Chamber Plays* by August Strindberg. Trans. by Evert Sprinchorn and Seabury Quinn, Jr. Copyright © 1962 by Evert Sprinchorn and Seabury Quinn, Jr. Published by E. P. Dutton & Co., Inc. and used with their permission.

down from that is a statue with a curtain that can be drawn to conceal it. Baron Skanskorg and The Fiancée are already seated, but they have no lines in this excerpt. Chairs are arranged in a semicircle.

1. In the doorway to the hyacinth room. Speaks off.
2. *The Mummy* enters.

3. They seat themselves in a semicircle. Silence.

4. Pause.

5. Slowly, deliberately, and with frequent pauses.

The Colonel: Polly!¹

The Mummy: ²Cluck, Cluck! Dumb-cluck!

The Colonel: Shall we invite the young people, too?

The Old Man: No! Not the young people! They shall be spared.³

The Colonel: Shall I ring for the tea?

The Old Man: Why bother? No one cares for tea. Why play games?⁴

The Colonel: Then perhaps we should start a conversation?

The Old Man: About the weather? Which we know. ⁵Ask each other how we're feeling? Which we also know. I prefer silence . . . in which one can hear thoughts and see the past. Silence cannot hide anything—which is more than you can say for words. I read the other day that the differences in languages originated among the primitive savages who sought to keep their secrets from the

The Ghost Sonata *as produced by Ira Zukerman for North Carolina School of the Arts. Costumes and settings are by Christina Giannini. (Courtesy of North Carolina School of the Arts.)*

other tribes. Languages are therefore codes, and he who finds the key can understand all the languages of the world. But that doesn't mean that secrets cannot be discovered without a key. Especially in those cases where paternity must be proved. Legal proof is of course another matter. Two false witnesses provide complete proof of whatever they agree to say. But in the kind of escapades I have in mind one doesn't take witnesses along. Nature herself has planted in man a blushing sense of shame, which seeks to hide what should be hidden. But we slip into certain situations without intending to, and chance confronts us with moments of revelation, when the deepest secrets are revealed, the mask is ripped from the imposter and the villain stands exposed. . . .[6]

Extraordinary, how silent you all are![7]

Take this house, for example. In this estimable house, in this elegant home, where beauty, wealth, and culture are united . . .[8] All of us sitting here, we know who we are, don't we? . . . I don't have to tell you. . . . And you know me although you pretend ignorance. . . . Sitting in that room is my daughter,[9] yes mine, you know that too . . . She has lost all desire to live, without knowing why . . . She was withering away because of the air in this house, which reeks of crime, deception, and deceits of every kind. . . . That is why I had to find a friend for her, a friend from whose very presence she would apprehend the warmth and light radiated by a noble deed. . . .[10] That was my mission in this house. To pull up the weeds, to expose the crimes, to settle the accounts, so that these young people might make a new beginning in this home, which is my gift to them![11]

Listen to the ticking of the clock, like a deathwatch beetle in the wall!

Listen to what it's saying: . . . "time's-up, time's-up! . . ."

When it strikes—in just a few moments—your time is up. Then you may go—not before. But the clock raises its arm before it strikes. [12]—Listen! It's warning you: "Clocks can strike!"—[13] And I can strike too! Do you understand?

The Mummy: [14]But I can stop time in its course. I can wipe out the past, and undo what is done. Not with bribes, not with threats—but through suffering and repentance.[15]

We are poor miserable creatures, we know that. We have erred, we have transgressed, we, like all the rest. We are not what we seem to be. At bottom we are better than ourselves, since we abhor and detest our misdeeds. But when you, Jacob Hummel,[16] with your false name, come here to sit in judgment over us, that proves that you are more contemptible than we! And you are not

6. Pause. All look at each other in silence.

7. Long silence.

8. Another long silence.

9. Pointing to the hyacinth room.

10. He refers to the fire and how the *Student* saved many lives.

11. Pause.

12. The clock can be heard preparing to strike the hour.

13. *The Old Man* strikes the table with his crutch.

14. *The Mummy* goes over to the clock and stops its pendulum; then speaks in her normal voice, seriously.

15. Approaches *The Old Man.*

16. Pointing to *The Old Man.*

17. He has tried to rise and speak, but has collapsed in his chair and shriveled up. Like a dying insect, he shrivels more and more during the following dialogue.

18. She rings the bell on the table.

19. She rings again. The little *Milkmaid* appears in the door to the hall, unseen by all except *The Old Man,* who shies in terror. The *Milkmaid* disappears when Bengtsson enters.

20. *Sponger:* one who lives off others.

21. Approaches *The Old Man,* and passes her hand over his face.
22. Johansson appears in the door to the hall, knowing his slavery to *The Old Man* is ended. *The Old Man* produces a bundle of papers, which he throws on the table. *The Mummy* strokes *The Old Man's* back.
23. Like a parrot, then crows like a rooster.
24. Making clucking noises.
25. Imitates a cuckoo clock.
26. *The Mummy* opens the concealed door to the closet.
27. *The Old Man* goes into the closet as *The Mummy* closes the door.
28. *Bengtsson* places the screen in front of the door.

the one you seem to be! You are a slave trader, a stealer of souls! You once stole me with false promises.[17] You murdered the Consul who was buried today, you strangled him with debts. You have stolen the student and shackled him with an imaginary debt of his father's, who never owed you a penny . . .

But there is one dark spot in your life, which I'm not sure about—although I have my suspicions . . . I think that Bengtsson might help us.[18]

The Old Man: No! Not Bengtsson! Not him![19]

The Mummy: Then it is true? He does know!

Bengtsson, do you know this man?

Bengtsson: Yes, I know him and he knows me. Life has its ups and downs, as we all know, and I have been in his service, and once he was in mine. To be exact, he was a sponger in my kitchen for two whole years. Since he[20] had to be out of the house by three o'clock, dinner had to be ready at two, and those in the house had to eat the warmed-up food left by that ox. Even worse, he drank up the pure soup stock and the gravy, which then had to be diluted with water. He sat there like a vampire, sucking all the marrow out of the house, and turned us all into skeletons. And he nearly succeeded in putting us into prison, when he accused the cook of being a thief. . . . Later I met this man in Hamburg under another name. He had become a usurer or bloodsucker. And it was there that he was accused of having lured a young girl out onto the ice in order to drown her, for she was the only witness to a crime which he was afraid would come to light. . . .

The Mummy: [21]That is the real you! Now empty your pockets of the notes and the will![22] Pretty bird! Where's Jacob!

The Old Man: Jacob's here![23]

The Mummy: Can clocks strike?

The Old Man:[24] Clocks can strike!

Coo-coo! Coo-coo! Coo-coo! . . .[25]

The Mummy: [26]Now the clock has struck! Stand up, and enter the closet where I have sat for twenty years, crying over our misdeeds. You'll find a rope in there, which can represent the one you strangled the Consul with, and with which you intended to strangle your benefactor. . . . Go in![27]

Bengtsson! Put up the screen! The death screen![28] It is over!—May God have mercy on his soul!

All: Amen!

FURTHER READING

Bjorkman, Edwin. *Introductions to Plays by August Strindberg.* New York: Charles Scribner's, 1928. 4 vols. *The* authority.

Clark, Barrett, and Freedley, George. *A History of Modern Drama.* New York: Appleton-Century-Crofts, 1947.

Gassner, John. *Masters of the Drama.* New York: Simon & Schuster, 1945, pp. 388–95.

Mortensen, Brita, and Downs, Brian. *Strindberg, An Indroduction to His Life and Work.* New York: Cambridge University Press, 1949. Paperback.

Sprigge, Elizabeth. *The Strange Life of August Strindberg.* New York: Macmillan, 1949. Excellent.

Valency, Maurice. *The Flower and the Castle.* New York: Macmillan, 1963. About Ibsen and Strindberg.

18
TWENTIETH-CENTURY DRAMA

It might be said that George Bernard Shaw straddled both the nineteenth and twentieth centuries like a colossus. G.B.S. has been criticized for peopling his plays with characters who were little more than speakers for Shavian wit and raillery. However, Shaw could develop characterizations that were vivid and highly entertaining, such as Caesar, Androcles, Major Barbara, Higgins, Liza, and Candida.

When Shaw began to write plays he was unable to get producers to read them, and so he published them himself. In substituting books for theatre, he assumed somewhat more than the playwright's rightful function. Shaw took on the jobs of scene designer, director, actors, and, at times, producer and audience. Sometimes there seem to be more directions than lines in his plays. I have known actors who automatically started work on a Shaw play by running a blue pencil through every word of narrative so that they might better concentrate on the job at hand; namely, *to contribute to the character themselves as creative artists.* Shaw does explore the background and goals of his characters rather imaginatively. If this exploration inspires you as an actor or can be blended into your conception, it is well and good to use his comments.

George Bernard Shaw
(1856–1950)

PREPARATION FOR *PYGMALION*

In *Pygmalion,* we are concerned with a specific English dialect spoken by a particular class in a certain section of London. Cockney, like American, is a localized version of English. Nothing upsets an Englishman more than to be told by an American that he speaks "with an English accent." In *Pygmalion,* Shaw uses the subject of phonetics as a bond to hold his story together. Eliza speaks a "gutter language," and Professor Higgins sets about to reform her speech. When he does so, the play is over, the story told—except for showing the audience how Eliza's character changes with her change in speech. In the excerpt we are to use, Eliza's cockney is not so important as it is earlier in the play. However, she reverts to it when she is off-guard, tired, or angry, as she is in our scene.

REHEARSAL

Pygmalion*

George Bernard Shaw
An Excerpt from Act IV

CAST: Eliza
      Higgins

SETTING: *Higgins's study, midnight. Required for this exercise: sofa at LC. On the floor in front of it are some men's soft slippers. At RC is Higgins's desk and chair. Door UL.*

Immediately preceding this moment we have had a long scene of very high spirits. The characters have all returned from the Embassy Ball, which has been a triumph. Higgins and Pickering have been elated, complimenting each other, as Eliza has sat silently and inconspicuously waiting for someone to admit she had some part in the success. From a first amazement, her mood has grown to anger, and now she is fighting back her tears of rage. Pickering has just left, as has Mrs. Pearce. Higgins is in stocking feet, very smug and content with his victory.

At rise, Higgins is walking from his desk at L to door L, intending to call Mrs. Pearce. Eliza is on the sofa, looking like a beaten puppy.

1. Not looking at her; she is just a part of the furniture.

Higgins: *(Following Pickering to the door)* Goodnight. *(Over his shoulder, at the door)* Put out the lights, Eliza;[1] and tell Mrs. Pearce not to make coffee for me in the morning: I'll take tea. *(He goes out.)*
    Eliza tries to control herself and feel indifferent as she rises and walks across to the hearth to switch off the lights. By the time she gets there she is on the point of screaming. She sits down in Higgins's chair and holds on hard to the arms. Finally she gives way and flings herself furiously on the floor, raging.

Higgins: *(In despairing wrath outside)* What the devil have I done with my slippers? *(He appears at the door)*

---

*The award-winning stage musical and film *My Fair Lady* was based on this play. Excerpt by permission of The Public Trustee and The Society of Authors, London.

Liza: *(Snatching up the slippers, and hurling them at him one after the other with all her force)* There are your slippers.[2] And there. Take your slippers; and may you never have a day's luck with them![3]

Higgins: *(Astounded)* [4]What on earth—! *(He comes to her.)* What's the matter? Get up. *(He pulls her up)* Anything wrong?

Liza: *(Breathless)* Nothing wrong—with you. I've won your bet for you, havnt I? Thats enough for you. I dont matter, I suppose.

Higgins: You won my bet! You! Presumptuous insect! *I* won it. What did you throw those slippers at me for?

Liza: Because I wanted to smash your face.[5] I'd like to kill you, you selfish brute. Why didnt you leave me where you picked me out of—in the gutter? You thank God it's all over, and that now you can throw me back again there, do you? *(She crisps her fingers frantically.)*

Higgins: *(Looking at her in cool wonder.)* The creature is nervous, after all.

Liza: *(Gives a suffocated scream of fury, and instinctively darts her nails at his face)!!*

Higgins: *(Catching her wrists)* Ah! would you? [6]Claws in, you cat. How dare you shew your temper to me? Sit down and be quiet. *(He throws her into the easy-chair)*

Liza: *(Crushed by superior strength and weight)* Whats to become of me? Whats to become of me?

Higgins: How the devil do I know whats to become of you?[7] What does it matter what becomes of you?

Liza: You dont care. I know you dont care. You wouldnt care if I was dead. I'm nothing to you—not so much as them slippers.

Higgins: *(Thundering)* T h o s e slippers.

Liza: *(With bitter submission)* Those slippers. I didnt think it made any difference now.

A pause. Eliza hopeless and crushed. Higgins a little uneasy.

Higgins: *(In his loftiest manner)* Why have you begun going on like this? May I ask whether you complain of your treatment here?

Liza: No.

Higgins: Has anybody behaved badly to you? Colonel Pickering? Mrs. Pearce? Any of the servants?

Liza: No.

Higgins: [8]I presume you dont pretend that *I* have treated you badly?

Liza: No.

Higgins: I am glad to hear it. *(He moderates his tone.)* Perhaps youre tired after the strain of the day. Will you have a glass of champagne? *(He moves toward the door)*

Liza: No.[9] *(Recollecting her manners)* Thank you.

Higgins: *(Good-humored again)* This has been coming on you for some

2. Pitches them at him, not so hard that they cannot be found later.

3. She beats on the floor like a child in a tantrum.

4. He starts back to get the slippers, but stops as she speaks.

5. Eliza standing at C, Higgins at LC. She is in a towering rage, alternately crying and storming.

6. He wheels her upstage before him and into the sofa, not the "easy-chair." Higgins is now C facing her.

7. He paces up and down back of sofa, stopping to throw questions at her like a prosecuting attorney.

8. Stops suddenly, then asks incredulously. Resumes his pacing. Now patronizing her.

9. She moves L to sofa and eases into it as she sniffles.

10. Back of sofa.

11. Eliza moves to UR and he follows her on his line.

12. He breaks the mood by walking to back of desk. He does not sit. (He is too interested in what he has to say.)

13. This business with the apple is excellent for the comedy points as it is audible as well as visual and also it shows his insensitivity to others. In a subtle way it is matching "the action to the words."

days. I suppose it was natural for you to be anxious about the garden party.[10] But thats all over now. (*He pats her kindly on the shoulder. She writhes.*) Theres nothing more to worry about.

Liza: No. Nothing more for you to worry about. (*She suddenly rises and gets away from him by going to the piano bench, where she sits and hides her face*) Oh God! I wish I was dead.[11]

Higgins: (*Staring after her in sincere surprise*) Why? In heaven's name, why? (*Reasonably, going to her*) Listen to me, Eliza. All this irritation is purely subjective.

Liza: I don't understand. I'm too ignorant.

Higgins: It's only imagination. Low spirits and nothing else. Nobodys hurting you. Nothings wrong. You go to bed like a good girl and sleep it off. Have a little cry and say your prayers: that will make you comfortable.

Liza: I heard your prayers. "Thank God its all over!"

Higgins: (*Impatiently*) Well, dont you thank God it's all over? Now you are free and can do what you like.

Liza: (*Pulling herself together in desperation*) What am I fit for? What have you left me fit for? Where am I to go? What am I to do? Whats to become of me?

Higgins: (*Enlightened, but not at all impressed*) Oh, thats what's worrying you, is it? [12](*He thrusts his hands into his pockets, and walks about in his usual manner, rattling the contents of his pockets, as if condescending to a trivial subject out of pure kindness*) I shouldnt bother about it if I were you. I should imagine you wont have much difficulty in settling yourself somewhere or other, though I hadnt quite realized that you were going away. (*She looks quickly at him: he does not look at her, but examines the dessert stand on the piano and decides that he will eat an apple*) You might marry, you know.[13] (*He bites a large piece out of the apple and munches it noisily.*) You see, Eliza, all men are not confirmed old bachelors like me and the Colonel. Most men are the marrying sort (poor devils!); and youre not bad-looking: its quite a pleasure to look at you sometimes— not now, of course, because youre crying and looking as ugly as the very devil; but when youre all right and quite yourself, youre what I should call attractive. That is, to the people in the marrying line, you understand. You go to bed and have a good nice rest; and then get up and look at yourself in the glass; and you wont feel so cheap.

Eliza again looks at him, speechless, and does not stir.

The look is quite lost on him: he eats his apple with a dreamy expression of happiness, as it is quite a good one.

Higgins: (*A genial afterthought occurring to him*) I daresay my mother could find some chap or other who would do very well.

Liza: We were above that at the corner of Tottenham Court Road.[14]

Higgins: (*Waking up*) What do you mean?

Liza: I sold flowers. I didnt sell myself. Now youve made a lady of me and I'm not fit to sell anything else. I wish youd left me where you found me.

Higgins: (*Slinging the core of the apple decisively into the grate*) Tosh, Eliza.[15] Dont you insult human relations by dragging all this cant about buying and selling into it. You neednt marry the fellow if you dont like him.

Liza: What else am I to do?

Higgins: Oh, lots of things. What about your old idea of a florist's shop? Pickering could set you up in one: he's lots of money. (*Chuckling*) He'll have to pay for all those togs youve been wearing today; and that, with the hire of the jewellery, will make a big hole in two hundred pounds. Why, six months ago you would have thought it the millennium to have a flower shop of your own.[16] Come! youll be all right. I must clear off to bed.[17] I'm devilish sleepy. By the way, I came down for something. I forget what it was.

Liza: Your slippers.

Higgins: Oh, yes, of course. You shied them at me.[18] (*He picks them up, and is going out when she rises and speaks to him*)

Liza: Before you go, sir—

Higgins: (*Dropping the slippers in his surprise at her calling him Sir*) Eh?

Liza: Do my clothes belong to me or to Colonel Pickering?

Higgins: (*Coming back into the room as if her question were the very climax of unreason*)[19] What the devil use would they be to Pickering?

Liza: He might want them for the next girl you pick up to experiment on.

Higgins: (*Shocked and hurt*) Is that the way you feel toward us?

Liza: I dont want to hear anything more about that. All I want to know is whether anything belongs to me. My own clothes were burnt.

Higgins: But what does it matter? Why need you start bothering about that in the middle of the night?

Liza: I want to know what I may take away with me. I dont want to be accused of stealing.

Higgins: (*Now deeply wounded*) Stealing! You shouldnt have said that, Eliza. That shews a want of feeling.

Liza: I'm sorry.[20] I'm only a common ignorant girl; and in my station I have to be careful. There cant be any feelings between the like of you and the like of me. Please will you tell me what belongs to me and what doesnt?

Higgins: (*Very sulky*) You may take the whole damned houseful if you

14. With some bitterness.

15. Moves to the R where we pretend there is a fireplace, and in passing tosses the core into it.

16. Crossing up to door UL.

17. Moves to door, stops, turns, and over shoulder, he asks.

18. Finds slippers, repeats business of going and the over-the-shoulder question.

19. She is now facing upstage before the sofa. Before his line regarding Pickering, he takes a deliberate walk down to her R.

20. The scene should now begin to build in emotion.

21. To UL.
22. He is now at her L, as she has "given" a few steps to her R as he has moved.

like. Except the jewels. Theyre hired. Will that satisfy you?[21] (*He turns on his heel and is about to go in extreme dudgeon*)

Liza: (*Drinking in his emotion like nectar, and nagging him to provoke a further supply*) Stop, please.[22] (*She takes off her jewels.*) Will you take these to your room and keep them safe? I dont want to run the risk of their being missing.

Higgins: (*Furious*) Hand them over. (*She puts them into his hands*). If these belonged to me instead of the jeweller, I'd ram them down your ungrateful throat. (*He perfunctorily thrusts them into his pockets, unconsciously decorating himself with the protruding ends of the chains*)

23. She holds it out to him. There is a moment as he looks at it silently. Then he steps to·her, snatches it, and throws it at her feet. (Remember, Eliza must be able to find it quickly later on.)
24. She is in mortal terror and covers her head to avoid the blows she fully expects.

Liza: (*Taking a ring off*) This ring isnt the jeweller's: its the one you bought me in Brighton.[23] I dont want it now. (*Higgins dashes the ring violently into the fireplace, and turns on her so threateningly that she crouches over the piano with her hands over her face and exclaims*) Dont you hit me![24]

Higgins: Hit you! You infamous creature, how dare you accuse me of such a thing? It is you who have hit me. You have wounded me to the heart.

Liza: (*Thrilling with hidden joy*) I'm glad. Ive got a little of my own back, anyhow.

25. Higgins is indignant.

Higgins: (*With dignity, in his finest professional style*) You have caused me to lose my temper: a thing that has hardly ever happened to me before.[25] I prefer to say nothing more tonight. I am going to bed.

26. Like a child.

Liza: (*Pertly*) Youd better leave a note for Mrs. Pearce about the coffee; for she wont be told by me.[26]

27. Each "damn" should be timed with some movement.

Higgins: (*Formally*) Damn[27] Mrs. Pearce; and damn the coffee; and damn you; and damn my own folly in having lavished hard-earned knowledge and the treasure of my regard and intimacy on a heartless guttersnipe. (*He goes out with impressive decorum, and spoils it by slamming the door savagely.*)

28. Eliza is pleased at the way things have gone. She struts about in satisfaction, decides to find the ring, does so, and puts it on with admiration.

Eliza smiles for the first time.[28]

FURTHER READING

Henderson, Archibald. *George Bernard Shaw, Man of the Century*. New York: Appleton-Century-Crofts, 1956. The authorized biography.

Eugene O'Neill
(1888–1953)

The high cultural standards Eugene O'Neill set for himself as a playwright were different from those of other playwrights of his time. "Most modern plays," he said, "are concerned with the rela-

tion between man and man, but this does not interest me at all. I am interested in the relation between man and God." For the first time in American dramaturgy, O'Neill made it possible that plays written by an American deserved to be compared with other literature, even to the great plays of the past written by Sophocles and Shakespeare. This had always been an ambition of O'Neill's and he fulfilled it with *Lazarus Laughed, Strange Interlude,* and *Mourning Becomes Electra.* By the use of masks, he was able to revive in contemporary form, the use of the Greek chorus and the Restoration aside. During the ten-year period of his retirement, beginning in 1935, he disavowed some of these earlier ambitions and returned to the use of modern realism, which resulted in two major works: *The Iceman Cometh* and *Long Day's Journey into Night.*

Although Bernard Shaw once called O'Neill, "a banshee Shakespeare," he left us a priceless legacy in American drama by consistently demonstrating how human destiny affects an individual. His dedication to his chosen art and his driving ambition eventually gained O'Neill four Pulitzer Prize awards and he remains America's only Nobel Prize dramatist.[1]

PREPARATION FOR *LONG DAY'S JOURNEY INTO NIGHT*

This autobiographical play, written in 1940, was not produced until 1956, after O'Neill's death. It is a play of "old sorrow, written in tears and blood," according to his dedication, in which he was able "to face my dead at last" and to "write it with deep pity and understanding and forgiveness for all the four haunted Tyrones."

Working with a conventional family premise, O'Neill was able to permeate his play with more profound dimensions by comparing youthful dreams and ambitions with the tragic realities of life. In this play, family relationships are not stable, but alternate between love and sharp painful condemnations. Characters are masterfully drawn and developed. Critic Henry Hewes has said, "Each of the quartet [the Tyrones] advances from morning's surface jocularity into evening's soul-shaking revelations of self-truth."[2] *Long Day's Journey into Night* may be Eugene O'Neill's finest play, and some believe it the greatest tragedy ever written by an American playwright.

The following excerpt from act III is revealing of the mother character in this play. Mary is described by O'Neill as fifty-four, of medium height, and still in possession of her young, graceful figure, although her hair has turned white. Her hands are never still;

---

[1]Pulitzer prizes were awarded to O'Neill for *Beyond the Horizon* (1920), *Anna Christie* (1921), *Strange Interlude* (1928), and *Long Day's Journey into Night* (1956). The Nobel Prize for literature was awarded to him in 1936.

[2]From *Saturday Review,* November 24, 1956.

rheumatism has knotted her fingers and she is sensitive about them. Her voice is soft and musical, contributing to her simple unaffected charm, as well as to her unworldly innocence brought about by being isolated and bereft of all but conventional wifely protection. As a child she was sheltered and convent-schooled. It was not until after her marriage that she was exposed to a world of cheap hotel rooms, alcohol, tobacco; her husband's drunken cronies, his penuriousness, and his former mistress.

O'Neill conferred on this character (for which his own mother served as model) a kind of pathetic and tragic dignity. From the agonies of childbirth, increased because of her husband's stinginess in hiring a cheap doctor, she experiences her first release—through morphine. Dope is her way back into her girlish dreams and the security of the convent life.

The other character in this excerpt is the serving girl, Cathleen. She is ignorant and bumptious, although cheerful, hearty, and loyal.

REHEARSAL

Long Day's Journey into Night*

Eugene O'Neill
An Excerpt from Act III

CAST: Cathleen

      Mary

SCENE: *Cathleen stands left of the table, which is just off center stage, an empty whiskey glass in her hand. She shows the effects of her drinks. Mary is pale, but her eyes shine with an unnatural brilliance. As she sits at the table RC, she alternates a mood of gay youthfulness with a dark introspective detachment. They have returned from town, where they have made an important purchase.*

Cathleen: The way the man in the drugstore acted when I took in the prescription for you.
                       Indignantly.
The impidence of him!
Mary: *With stubborn blankness.*
What are you talking about? What drugstore? What prescription?
      Then hastily, as Cathleen stares in stupid amazement.

Oh, of course, I'd forgotten. The medicine for the rheumatism in my hands. What did the man say?[1]

1. Mary walks to screen door at R.

Then with indifference.

Not that it matters, as long as he filled the prescription.

2. Puts down glass.

Cathleen: [2]It mattered to me, then! I'm not used to being treated like a thief. He gave me a long look and says insultingly, "Where did you get hold of this?" and I says, "It's none of your damned business, but if you must know, it's for the lady I work for, Mrs. Tyrone, who's sitting out in the automobile." That shut him up quick. He gave a look out at you and said, "Oh," and went to get the medicine.

Mary: *Vaguely.*

[3]Yes, he knows me.

3. Looking out the screen door.

She sits in the armchair at right rear of table. She adds in a calm, detached voice.

I have to take it because there is no other that can stop the pain—*all* the pain—I mean, in my hands.

She raises her hands and regards them with melancholy sympathy. There is no tremor in them now.

Poor hands! You'd never believe it, but they were once one of my good points, along with my hair and eyes, and I had a fine figure, too.

Her tone has become more and more far-off and dreamy.

They were a musician's hands. I used to love the piano. I worked so hard at my music in the Convent—if you can call it work when you do something you love. Mother Elizabeth and my music teacher both said I had more talent than any student they remembered. My father paid for special lessons. He spoiled me. He would do anything I asked. He would have sent me to Europe to study after I graduated from the Convent. I might have gone—if I hadn't fallen in love with Mr. Tyrone. Or I might have become a nun. I had two dreams. To be a nun, that was the more beautiful one. To become a concert pianist, that was the other.

She pauses, regarding her hands fixedly. Cathleen blinks her eyes to fight off drowsiness and a tipsy feeling.

I haven't touched a piano in so many years. I couldn't play with such crippled fingers, even if I wanted to. For a time after my marriage I tried to keep up my music. But it was hopeless. One-night stands, cheap hotels, dirty trains, leaving children, never having a home—

She stares at her hands with fascinated disgust.

See, Cathleen, how ugly they are! So maimed and crippled! You would think they'd been through some horrible accident!

She gives a strange little laugh.

Long Day's Journey into Night, an outstanding success of the National Theatre of Great Britain. Laurence Olivier starred as James Tyrone. (Photo by Zoe Dominic, courtesy of the National Theatre.)

So they have, come to think of it.

She suddenly thrusts her hands behind her back.

I won't look at them. They're worse than the foghorn for reminding me—

Then with defiant self-assurance.

But even they can't touch me now.

She brings her hands from behind her back and deliberately stares at them—calmly.

They're far away. I see them, but the pain has gone.

Cathleen: *Stupidly puzzled.*

4. Cathleen walks a step UL, then returns as an afterthought.

You've taken some of the medicine? It made you act funny, Ma'am.[4] If I didn't know better, I'd think you'd a drop taken.

Mary: *Dreamily.*

It kills the pain. You go back until at last you are beyond its reach. Only the past when you were happy is real.

She pauses—then as if her words had been an evocation which called back happiness she changes in her whole manner and facial expressions. She looks younger. There is a quality of an innocent convent girl about her, and she smiles shyly.

If you think Mr. Tyrone is handsome now, Cathleen, you should have seen him when I first met him. He had the reputation of being one of the best looking men in the country. The girls in the Convent who had seen him act, or seen his photographs, used to rave about him. He was a great matinee idol then, you know. Women used to wait at the stage door just to see him come out. You can imagine how excited I was when my father wrote me he and James Tyrone had become friends, and that I was to meet him when I came home for Easter vacation. I showed the letter to all the girls, and how envious they were![5] My father took me to see him act first. It was a play about the French Revolution and the leading part was a nobleman. I couldn't take my eyes off him. I wept when he was thrown in prison—and then was so mad at myself because I was afraid my eyes and nose would be red. My father had said we'd go backstage to his dressing room right after the play, and so we did.

5. Cathleen chuckles from interest and sympathy.

She gives a little excited, shy laugh.

I was so bashful all I could do was stammer and blush like a little fool. But he didn't seem to think I was a fool. I know he liked me the first moment we were introduced.

Coquettishly.

I guess my eyes and nose couldn't have been red, after all. I was really very pretty then, Cathleen. And he was handsomer than my wildest dream, in his make-up and his nobleman's costume that was so becoming to him. He was different from all ordinary men, like someone from another world. At the same time he was simple, and kind, and unassuming, not a bit stuck-up or vain. I fell in love right then. So did he, he told me afterwards. I forgot all about becoming a nun or a concert pianist. All I wanted was to be his wife.

She pauses, staring before her with unnaturally bright, dreamy eyes, and a rapt, tender, girlish smile.

Thirty-six years ago, but I can see it as clearly as if it were tonight! We've loved each other since. And in all those thirty-six years, there has never been a breath of scandal about him. I mean, with any other woman. Never since he met me. That has made me very happy, Cathleen. It has made me forgive so many other things.

REHEARSAL

Long Day's Journey into Night*

Eugene O'Neill
An Excerpt from Act II, Scene 1

CAST: **Edmund**
      Jamie

SCENE: *The living room around 12:45 P.M. Read the opening description of the setting. Reread the beginning of act II, scene 1 to review what has transpired just before the excerpt starts. Edmund is alone in the room, standing at the table.*

He grabs the bottle and pours a drink, adds ice water and drinks. As he does so, he hears someone coming in the front door. He puts the glass hastily on the tray and sits down again, opening his book. Jamie comes in from the front parlor, his coat over his arm. He has taken off collar and tie and carries them in his hand. He is wiping sweat from his forehead with a handkerchief. Edmund looks up as if his reading was interrupted. Jamie takes one look at the bottle and glasses and smiles cynically.

Jamie: Sneaking one, eh? Cut out the bluff, Kid. You're a rottener actor than I am.

Edmund: *Grins.*
Yes, I grabbed one while the going was good.

Jamie: *Puts a hand affectionately on his shoulder.*
That's better. Why kid me? We're pals, aren't we?

1. Throwing his coat over a chair.

Edmund: I wasn't sure it was you coming.

Jamie: I made the Old Man look at his watch.[1] I was halfway up the walk when Cathleen burst into song. Our wild Irish lark! She ought to be a train announcer.

Edmund: That's what drove me to drink. Why don't you sneak one while you've got a chance?

Jamie: I was thinking of that little thing.

He goes quickly to the window at right.

The Old Man was talking to old Captain Turner. Yes, he's still at it.

He comes back and takes a drink.

And now to cover up from his eagle eye. He memorizes the level in the bottle after every drink.

He measures two drinks of water and pours them in the whiskey bottle and shakes it up.

There. That fixes it.

He pours water in the glass and sets it on the table by Edmund.

And here's the water you've been drinking.

2. Smiling at Jamie.

Edmund: Fine! You don't think it will fool him, do you?[2]

Jamie: Maybe not, but he can't prove it.

Putting on his collar and tie.

I hope he doesn't forget lunch listening to himself talk. I'm hungry.

He sits across the table from Edmund—irritably.

That's what I hate about working down in front. He puts on an act for every damned fool that comes along.

Edmund: *Gloomily.*

3. Puts book on table, stretches, sits back.

You're in luck to be hungry.[3] The way I feel I don't care if I ever eat again.

Jamie: *Gives him a glance of concern.*

4. Leans forward.

Listen, Kid.[4] You know me. I've never lectured you, but Doctor Hardy was right when he told you to cut out the redeye.

Edmund: Oh, I'm going to after he hands me the bad news this afternoon. A few before then won't make any difference.

Jamie: *Hesitates—then slowly.*

I'm glad you've got your mind prepared for bad news. It won't be such a jolt.

He catches Edmund staring at him.[5]

5. Sits back.

I mean, it's a cinch you're really sick, and it would be wrong dope to kid yourself.

Edmund: *Disturbed.*

6. Rises and paces nervously to window, keeping his back to Jamie.

I'm not. I know how rotten I feel, and the fever and chills I get at night are no joke.[6] I think Doctor Hardy's last guess was right. It must be the damned malaria come back on me.

Jamie: Maybe, but don't be too sure.[7]

Edmund: Why?[8] What do you think it is?

Jamie: Hell, how would I know? I'm no Doc.[9]

> *Abruptly.*

Where's Mama?[10]

Edmund: Upstairs.

Jamie:
> *Looks at him sharply.*[11]

When did she go up?

Edmund: Oh, about the time I came down to the hedge, I guess. She said she was going to take a nap.

Jamie: You didn't tell me—[12]

Edmund:
> *Defensively.*

Why should I? What about it? She was tired out. She didn't get much sleep last night.

Jamie: I know she didn't.[13]

> *A pause. The brothers avoid looking at each other.*

Edmund: That damned foghorn kept me awake, too.[14]

> *Another pause.*

Jamie: She's been upstairs alone all morning, eh? You haven't seen her?[15]

Edmund: No. I've been reading here. I wanted to give her a chance to sleep.[16]

Jamie: Is she coming down to lunch?

Edmund: Of course.

Jamie:
> *Dryly.*

No of course about it. She might not want any lunch. Or she might start having most of her meals alone upstairs. That's happened, hasn't it?

Edmund:
> *With frightened resentment.*[17]

Cut it out, Jamie! Can't you think anything but—?

> *Persuasively.*

You're all wrong to suspect anything. Cathleen saw her not long ago. Mama didn't tell her she wouldn't be down to lunch.

Jamie: Then she wasn't taking a nap?

Edmund: Not right then, but she was lying down, Cathleen said.

Jamie: In the spare room?

Edmund: Yes. For Pete's sake, what of it?[18]

Jamie:
> *Bursts out.*

You damned fool! Why did you leave her alone so long? Why didn't you stick around?[19]

Edmund: Because she accused me—and you and Papa—of spying on her all the time and not trusting her.[20] She made me feel ashamed. I know how rotten it must be for her. And she promised on her sacred word of honor—

7. Staring at him with concern.

8. Turning to face Jamie.

9. Smiles and shrugs, attempting to feign unconcern.

10. A slight pause as Jamie seems to think of something.

11. Rises quickly, moves to the hall door, and looks up the stairway.

12. Turns to look at Edmund.

13. Looking back to stairway.

14. Moves to window. Looks out.

15. Crosses to Edmund.

16. Continues looking out window, avoiding Jamie's gaze.

17. Turning to Jamie.

18. Crossing to table.

19. Following him.

20. Sits at the table.

21. Moves around the table to his chair.
22. Pounds on the table for emphasis.
23. Sits in his chair.

Jamie: *With a bitter weariness.* [21]

You ought to know that doesn't mean anything.

Edmund: [22]It does this time!

Jamie: That's what we thought the other times. [23]

He leans over the table to give his brother's arm an affectionate grasp.
Listen, Kid, I know you think I'm a cynical bastard, but remember I've seen a lot more of this game than you have. You never knew what was really wrong until you were in prep school. Papa and I kept it form you. But I was wise ten years or more before we had to tell you. I know the game backwards and I've been thinking all morning of the way she acted last night when she thought we were asleep. I haven't been able to think of anything else. And now you tell me she got you to leave her alone upstairs all morning.

Edmund: She didn't! You're crazy!

Jamie: *Placatingly.*

All right, Kid. Don't start a battle with me. I hope as much as you do I'm crazy. I've been as happy as hell because I'd really begun to believe that this time—

He stops—looking through the front parlor toward the hall—lowering his voice, hurriedly.

She's coming downstairs. You win on that. I guess I'm a damned suspicious louse. [24]

They grow tense with a hopeful, fearful expectancy. Jamie mutters.
Damn! I wish I'd grabbed another drink.

Edmund: Me, too.

24. They both sit back in their chairs.

FURTHER READING

Alexander, Doris. *The Tempering of Eugene O'Neill.* New York: Harcourt, 1962.

Clark, Barrett. *Eugene O'Neill, The Man and His Plays.* New York: Dover, 1947.

Gelb, Arthur, and Gelb, Barbara. *O'Neill.* New York: Harper, 1962. Recommended.

Leech, Clifford. *Eugene O'Neill.* New York: Grove Press, 1963.

Bertolt Brecht
(1898–1956)

It may seem that just as we are getting an acting style established in our minds, someone comes along who says, "No, no, that's not the way to act. I will show you how." We have gone from Classical to Commedia, to Elizabethan, to Restoration, to Realism, to—will it never end? Probably not; an art cannot remain static and live.

EXPRESSIONISM

Early in this century, the theatre was almost completely dominated by naturalism. There was Stanislavski in Russia, André Antoine in France, Granville Barker in England, and, in middle Europe, George II, duke of Saxe-Meiningen and Otto Brahm. But after the First World War, a revolt began against this style. In such expressionistic plays as Ernst Toller's *Man and Masses,* Georg Kaiser's *Morn to Midnight,* Elmer Rice's *Adding Machine,* and O'Neill's *The Hairy Ape* and *Emperor Jones,* naturalism was replaced by a style that was frankly theatrical. In writing, acting, and producing, the aim was to express certain impressions; for instance, in *The Hairy Ape,* there was no attempt to make people walking along Fifth Avenue look or behave like real people. They walked like automatons and wore masks; they were created to express a thought and not imitate nature. However, the emotional content was similar to the realistic theatre.

At the end of the Second World War, there appeared the "lost generation" of disillusioned young artists, among them a German poet named Bertolt Brecht. Realism was all wrong for his day, Brecht maintained. His would be a "scientific" theatre, for a scientific age. It was his belief that the lives of individuals could no longer be portrayed on the stage apart from social and economic conditions. He contended that the theatre should dispense with vulgar emotionalism and that it should be a "learning theatre."

Brecht was a Marxist, but he was openly denounced by the U.S.S.R. To make matters worse, the Russian theatre officially approved and adopted the Stanislavski system that represented everything of which Brecht disapproved: that is, the transfigured actor, the emotionally moved audience, and the naturalism of the presentation.

BRECHTIAN THEORIES

Brecht's theory of acting was based on the concept of *Verfremdung* or "alienation," the so-called A effect, which today is more commonly called "estrangement." (The German word *Verfremdung* might be translated as "seeming odd to.") This did not imply that he wanted the audience to be alienated from the play or the players. Rather, he wished to create in the audience and actors a detached attitude toward the performance. He proposed the opposite of the realistic theory, which sought to create an empathy between actor and audience, and between audience and play.[3]

In preparing one of Brecht's plays using his acting theories, our first step will be to purge our minds of every effort to reproduce

[3]Peter Demitz, *Brecht* (Englewood Cliffs, N.J.: Prentice-Hall, 1962), pp. 106–16.

reality.[4] Our accent must be on how events happen, and not on the emotions of the people they happen to. The acting approach needs to be abstract and objective, with only one timid finger touching reality.

The "A effect" eliminates the magic, along with what Brecht calls the "hypnotic tensions" of emotionalism. In our attitude toward our audience, we must try not to create any empathy. We must dehumanize our bodies and personalities. We don't want the audience to "feel" for our characters; indeed, as actors, we are not going to feel for them ourselves. We are going to stand back and observe them. We must keep in mind that his plays are "learning plays," that his is a theatre of instruction. As actors we are going to be surprised at our characters. Always there will be the shock of recognition. As Brecht himself explains, "To see one's mother as a man's wife, one needs the 'A effect'—for instance, when one acquires a stepfather."[5]

Actors are to become *demonstrators*, such as an eyewitness describing an event who does not become personally involved in it. In Brecht's theatre, the actors are reporters. It is the difference between seeing a riot on television and hearing a newscaster tell about it. The *newscaster* is Brecht's actor.

Brecht often attempted to make this point clear by giving an illustration. Let us try to find his meaning by means of an experience.

Exercise 132

One of our players pretends that he has been an eyewitness to an accident. Two other players are to be police officers questioning him about the circumstances.

The incident: An old man was standing on the curb, apparently trying to decide whether or not he would cross the street. A passing motorist saw him, but the old man, perhaps because of poor eyesight, did not see the approaching car. The driver of the car thought perhaps the old man had decided not to cross and proceeded ahead at the same time as the old man crossed. There was an instant when both seemed to know what was going to happen, but nothing could be done to prevent the tragedy. The old man was killed and the driver has been taken away for emergency treatment.

Attitude of the eyewitness: He has not been actively involved in the accident, being merely a spectator. He speaks of it in the past tense. The dramatic moment has passed. Therefore he is in a position to relate and make comment without bias. He demonstrates by acting out the limping old man, the moment of terror, the motorist's subsequent disturbances, what was said by each man, *all as he remembers them.* It has not been *his* tragedy. *He himself has not been or is not now emotionally involved.*

---

[4]John Willet, *Brecht on Theatre* (New York: Hill & Wang, 1959), p. 136.
[5]Ibid., p. 144.

Attitude of policemen: The accident and the report are simply in their line of duty. Questions are asked according to a set form. One policeman fills out this form as answers are given. They do not suspect the man of being involved and do not accuse him. They are polite but insistent.

Our three actors should improvise dialogue for this exercise after becoming familiar with the above facts.

As we rehearse a play by Brecht, we study our characters critically, not in a sympathetic way. We see the character's folly or virtue, but we do not become involved; *we do not identify with him.*

As practical working actors, we begin by reading his play. Brecht asks us to be astounded and question not only the incidents in the play, but the behavior of the character we are to play.[6] The actor must never *be*; he must *show* the character. To aid us, Brecht suggests that we:

1. transpose our characters into the third person
2. reset the action and incidents from present to past tense
3. speak aloud all of our stage directions during rehearsals

From the start we have been seeking a method of detachment, or "alienation." Asides are to be spoken directly to the audience. We will not try for any illusion that these asides are anything but information we are frankly giving to the audience. We will *show*, not *re-create*, a particular incident, and we must above all avoid being "universally human."[7]

Assume that we have prepared our play earnestly and sincerely along these lines and are now ready to show it to an audience. Remember, from the first we have taken great pains to prevent our audience from any empathy toward the play or the characters. What happens? They cry for *Mother Courage*; their hearts break for the plight of *The Jewish Wife;* they are deeply moved![8]

If the "alienation effect" is to be given a fair chance, it may be that we will need plays that do not involve everyone so much. To the end of his life, Brecht lamented that his plays were being misunderstood, that spectators should not be emotionally involved. But Bertolt Brecht was a brilliant man of the theatre. He filled the stage with his originality in lighting, projections, signs, symbols, poetry, music, masks. He had a genius for creating theatre. Although he tried to avoid the beautiful, the lyrical, or anything directly moving, we are fortunate that he failed. The English theatrical critic, Kenneth

---

[6]Ronald Gray, *Brecht* (Edinburgh and London: Oliver and Boyd, 1961), pp. 65–70.

[7]See Martin Esslin, *Brecht, The Man and His Work* (New York: Doubleday, 1960), pp. 141–42, for comparison to the villain in old melodramas.

[8]Esslin, *Brecht*, p. 234.

Tynan, was "unmoved by what Brecht had to say but overwhelmed by the way in which he said it."[9]

PREPARATION FOR *THE GOOD WOMAN OF SETZUAN*

In this play, Brecht uses a device that served Robert Louis Stevenson years ago when writing *The Strange Case of Dr. Jekyll and Mr. Hyde.* In most dramas, conflict is expressed by a hero struggling against a villain, fate, "the system," or some other force. But in *Dr. Jekyll* and *Good Woman* the conflict is within one character. The evil alter ego becomes an *actual physical embodiment.* In both these plays, the physical transference from good to bad and from bad to good is witnessed by the audience.

Duality in characters has become a favorite device of the so-called avant-garde playwright. Such roles are challenging to an actor. Actual physical changes must be made so that there is no confusion in the minds of the audience as to which character is occupying their immediate attention. And yet the change must not seem pat or contrived. There is a constant danger that an audience will recognize the device *as a device*—and if they do, the tendency is to laugh.

It is easy—too easy—to characterize a hard, practical businessman by relying on memories of other actors in similar parts. There is only one solution—personal observation. Find a man you know who is more interested in money than in his fellow man, and observe firsthand how he behaves. His greed will be shown in some way. Similarly, does a "good woman" really talk in saccharine tones and mince about with hesitant steps? Learn from your own *observation*—then *select, adapt, and develop these two characterizations imaginatively.*

Shen Te, the "Good Woman" of Setzuan, befriends three shabby little gods and is rewarded with riches. But Shen Te cannot bear the sight of human suffering and begins to share her good fortune. Her unselfishness does not come from any sense of moral obligation, but is a spontaneous expression of her kind nature. However, others take advantage of it, and she is surrounded by a wolf pack of spongers, so that she cannot continue. It is painful for her to be unkind to others, and so she invents a male "cousin," Shui Ta, a calculating profit-minded businessman. The theme according to John Willet is "that in a competitive society goodness is often suicidal."[10] But time after time, Brecht's expressed intentions are defeated by his extraordinary gift for writing vivid and moving drama; the "message" is lost. We find only admiration for Shen Te's courage and her devotion toward her fellow man.

Reread the play to make certain that you understand the style and how this excerpt fits into the plot.

[9]Kenneth Tynan, *Curtains* (New York: Atheneum, 1961), p. 389.
[10]John Willet, *Brecht on Theatre.*

REHEARSAL

The Good Woman of Setzuan*

Bertolt Brecht
Translated by Eric Bentley
An Excerpt from Scene 3

CAST: Yang Sun

Shen Te

SCENE: *A park at evening. A large willow tree center. Yang Sun stands beneath it with a rope in his hands. He was about to hang himself when he was interrupted by two prostitutes whom he insulted. They have just left. Shen Te stands nearby.*

Yang Sun: [1]Even in the farthest corner of the park, even when it's raining, you can't get rid of them! (*He spits.*)

Shen Te (*overhearing this*): And what right have you to scold them?[2] (*But at this point she sees the rope.*) Oh!

1. Staring off after the prostitutes.

2. He turns at the sound of her voice.

---

*Excerpt from Bertolt Brecht's *The Good Woman of Setzuan*. English version by Eric Bentley. Copyright © 1947, 1948, 1956, 1961 by Eric Bentley. Used by permission of the publisher, the University of Minnesota Press, Minneapolis.

The Good Woman of Setzuan, *as performed at the Studio Theatre, Munich. Produced by Hans Schweikart, settings by Casper Neher. (From* The Theatre in Germany. *Reprinted by permission of F. Bruckmann Verlag.)*

3. Defiantly.
4. Pointing to his head.
5. He turns away from her and coils the rope in his hands.

6. He turns quickly to her.

7. Turns his back to her.

8. Looking over his shoulder at her. Pause.

9. Another pause. She stares at him. He avoids her eyes.

10. He turns on her.

11. He is very agitated and animated during this speech. It should move very quickly.

12. Directly into her face.

13. Turns away from her.

14. She speaks very quietly and simply, not looking at him.

15. He turns to her. He is moved but refuses to show it.

Yang Sun: Well, what are you staring at?[3]

Shen Te: That rope. What is it for?

Yang Sun: Think! Think![4] I haven't a penny. Even if I had,[5] I wouldn't spend it on you. I'd buy a drink of water.

(The rain starts.)

Shen Te *(still looking at the rope)*: What is the rope for? You mustn't!

Yang Sun: What's it to you? Clear out![6]

Shen Te *(irrelevantly)*: It's raining.

Yang Sun: Well, don't try to come under this tree.[7]

Shen Te: Oh, no. *(She stays in the rain.)*

Yang Sun: Now go away. *(Pause.)* For one thing, I don't like your looks, you're bow-legged.

Shen Te *(indignantly)*: That's not true!

Yang Sun: Well, don't show 'em to me.[8] Look, it's raining. You better come under this tree.

(Slowly, she takes shelter under the tree.)[9]

Shen Te: Why did you want to do it?

Yang Sun: You really want to know? *(Pause.)* To get rid of you![10] *(Pause.)* You know what a flyer is?

Shen Te: Oh yes, I've met a lot of pilots. At the tearoom.

Yang Sun: You call *them* flyers? Think they know what a machine is?[11] Just 'cause they have leather helmets? They gave the airfield director a bribe, that's the way *those* fellows got up in the air! Try one of them out sometime. "Go up to two thousand feet," tell him, "then let it fall, then pick it up again with a flick of the wrist at the last moment." Know what he'll say to that? "It's not in my contract." Then again, there's the landing problem. It's like landing on your own backside. It's no different, planes are human. Those fools don't understand. *(Pause.)* And I'm the biggest fool for reading the book on flying in the Peking school and skipping the page where it says: "we've got enough flyers and we don't need you." I'm a mail pilot and no mail. You understand that?[12]

Shen Te *(shyly)*: Yes. I do.

Yang Sun: No, you don't. You'd never understand that.[13]

Shen Te: [14]When we were little we had a crane with a broken wing. He made friends with us and was very good-natured about our jokes. He would strut along behind us and call out to stop us going too fast for him. But every spring and autumn when the cranes flew over the villages in great swarms, he got quite restless. *(Pause.)* I understand that. *(She bursts out crying.)*

Yang Sun: Don't![15]

Shen Te *(quieting down)*: No.

Yang Sun: It's bad for the complexion.

Shen Te *(sniffing)*: I've stopped.

(She dries her tears on her big sleeve. Leaning against the tree, but not looking at her, he reaches for her face.)

Yang Sun: You can't even wipe your own face. *(He is wiping it for her with his handkerchief. Pause.)*

Shen Te *(still sobbing)*: I don't know *anything!*[16]

Yang Sun: You interrupted me! What for?

Shen Te: It's such a rainy day. You only wanted to do[17] . . . *that* because it's such a rainy day.

(To the audience.)[18]

In our country
The evenings should never be somber
High bridges over rivers
The grey hour between night and morning
And the long, long winter:
Such things are dangerous
For, with all the misery,
A very little is enough
And men throw away an unbearable life.

(Pause.)

Yang Sun: Talk about yourself for a change.[19]

Shen Te: What about me? I have a shop.

Yang Sun *(incredulous)*: You have a shop, do you? Never thought of walking the streets?

Shen Te: I *did* walk the streets. Now I have a shop.

Yang Sun *(ironically)*: A gift of the gods, I suppose!

Shen Te: How did you know?[20]

Yang Sun *(even more ironical)*: One fine evening the gods turned up saying: here's some money!

Shen Te *(quickly)*: One fine morning.

Yang Sun *(fed up)*: This isn't much of an entertainment.[21]

(Pause.)

Shen Te: I can play the zither a little.[22] *(Pause.)* And I can mimic men. *(Pause.)* I got the shop, so the first thing I did was to give my zither away. I can be as stupid as a fish now, I said to myself, and it won't matter.

I'm rich now, I said[23]
I walk alone, I sleep alone
For a whole year, I said
I'll have nothing to do with a man.

Yang Sun: And now you're marrying one![24] The one at the tearoom by the pond?

(Shen Te is silent.)

Yang Sun: What do you know about love?

Shen Te: Everything.[25]

16. She pulls away and continues using her sleeve.

17. Indicating the rope.

18. This is recited very simply, but with feeling.

19. He sits beneath the tree.

20. Moves to his side and kneels.

21. Looks in the opposite direction.

22. She tries unsuccessfully to get his interest.

23. Looking up at the sky.

24. He turns to her. She continues looking at the sky.

25. She looks him straight in the eye.

26. He turns his eyes away from her again.

27. He sighs loudly.

28. He looks at her, then looks away.

29. She leans back against the tree next to him.

Yang Sun: Nothing. *(Pause.)*[26] Or d'you just mean you enjoyed it?

Shen Te: No.

Yang Sun *(again without turning to look at her, he strokes her cheek with his hand)*: You like that?

Shen Te: Yes.

Yang Sun *(breaking off)*: You're easily satisfied, I must say. *(Pause.)*[27] What a town!

Shen Te: You have no friends?

Yang Sun *(defensively)*: Yes, I have![28] *(Change of tone.)* But they don't want to hear I'm still unemployed. "What?" they ask. "Is there still water in the sea?" You have friends?

Shen Te *(hesitating)*: Just a . . . cousin.[29]

Yang Sun: Watch him carefully.

Shen Te: He only came once. Then he went away. He won't be back.

(Yang Sun is looking away.)

But to be without hope, they say, is to be without goodness!

(Pause.)

Yang Sun: Go on talking. A voice is a voice.

Shen Te: Once, when I was a little girl, I fell, with a load of brushwood. An old man picked me up. He gave me a penny too. Isn't it funny how people who don't have very much like to give some of it away? They must like to show what they can do, and how could they show it better than by being kind? Being wicked is just like being clumsy. When we sing a song, or build a machine, or plant some rice, we're being kind. You're kind.[30]

30. She looks at him. His eyes are closed.

31. She brushes it away.

Yang Sun: You make it sound easy.

Shen Te: Oh, no. *(Little pause.)* Oh! A drop of rain![31]

Yang Sun: Where'd you feel it?

Shen Te: Between the eyes.

Yang Sun: Near the right eye? Or the left?

Shen Te: Near the left eye.

Yang Sun: Oh, good. *(He is getting sleepy.)* So you're through with men, eh?

32. She sits up, kneels, and studies him closely. His eyes remain closed.

Shen Te *(with a smile)*: [32]But I'm not bow-legged.

Yang Sun: Perhaps not.

Shen Te: Definitely not.

(Pause.)

Yang Sun *(leaning wearily against the willow)*: I haven't had a drop to drink all day, I haven't eaten anything for *two* days. I couldn't love you if I tried.

(Pause.)[33]

33. She leans back against the tree next to him. She smiles.

Shen Te: I like it in the rain.

FURTHER READING

Brecht, Bertolt. *Parables for the Theatre.* Translated by Eric Bentley. Minneapolis: University of Minnesota Press, 1961.

Esslin, Martin. *Brecht, the Man and His Work.* New York: Doubleday, 1960.

Gray, Ronald. *Brecht.* New York: Grove Press, 1961.

Munk, Erica, ed. *Stanislavski and America.* New York: Hill & Wang, 1966. See Eric Bentley's article "Stanislavski and Brecht," pp. 116–23.

Weideli, Walter. *The Art of Bertolt Brecht.* New York: New York University Press, 1963.

Willet, John. *Brecht on Theatre.* New York: Hill & Wang, 1959.

19
THEATRE TODAY

The "new theatre" is known by many names. Some call it the theatre of the Absurd, the Underground theatre, while others refer to it as off-off Broadway, the theatre of Protest, or the New Wave. Those who do not care for it call it just another art fraud. Playwrights connected with it subscribe to none of these labels, preferring to have their work considered individually, apart from any movement or trend. Harold Pinter has been called the leading British playwright of the Absurd school and yet, in this connection, he has said, "I don't see any placards on myself, and I don't carry any banners. Ultimately, I distrust any definitive labels."[1]

Whatever name modern playwrights go by, their plays seem influenced by the nineteenth-century existentialist Sören Kierkegaard and the subsequent writings of Franz Kafka and James Joyce. The movement's association with the theatre might be said to have begun with Strindberg's "dream plays"; certainly Strindberg influenced these new playwrights. A closer relationship is perhaps found in the Ubu plays by Alfred Jarry, produced in 1896. But the theatre of the Absurd got off to a real start in 1950 when Eugene Ionesco's *The Bald Soprano* opened in Paris.

The leading characters in these plays are in marked contrast to the protagonists of old. Ibsen's heroes had goals to reach, or they wanted dignity; but the undignified characters of the Absurd can find nothing to attain. They drag aching feet as they move listlessly through a mental vacuum. Unlike O'Neill's ape-man, they do not even want "to belong." Samuel Beckett's vagrant "heroes" in *Waiting for Godot* subject an audience to two hours of despair and self-pity, and the play ends exactly as it began, with nothing gained, nothing lost. How many of us could sit in that existential hell of a hotel room with the characters Sartre has invented for his *No Exit* and not feel a little ashamed of being human? Where other plays we have studied seek to free the spectators' minds of the petty or mean

[1]Harold Pinter, "Writing for Myself," *Twentieth Century* 169, no. 1008 (February 1961): 172–75.

The Theatre of the Absurd: Pantomime of Places, *improvisation by the Bauhaus Stage, Weimar, 1924. (Courtesy of Frau Oskar Schlemmer.)*

and elevate their thoughts by lofty themes and heroic achievements, the absurd theory of play writing seems to depend on the element of shock and sensation, rather than morality and human stature. Would you consider it enlightening to spend an evening with people who live in garbage cans and spout case histories from Jung and Freud? As Esslin has pointed out, these playwrights have done what Brecht failed to do: they have succeeded in alienation.

WHY "ABSURD"?

With advances in science and technology and the subsequent decline in formerly respected moral values, man seems more and more lost in the smog of the jet age. He feels estranged, separated from the standards of yesterday. Having lost all rapport with the world and himself, he is beset with a feeling of isolation and futility. He sits, waiting for someone to help, to give him answers; he is "waiting for Godot." The playwrights of this "school" ask that we see the utter ridiculousness of this absurd situation. Perhaps they are even trying to "laugh us out of it," just as the would-be suicide in *Luv* is laughed out of his intention. They seem to be telling us that nothing can ever be fully explained and that this is the mystery of life. So we should relax and learn to accept things as they are; this is the only way we will find out who we are and what we are doing here. The danger in this philosophy of disengagement is that the cure might become part of the disease.

After examining the theatre of the Absurd, we might conclude that these plays deal with dehumanized characters set into plays that are not plays at all, and that they offer themes based on variations of a philosophy of futility. But if we are to be consistent in our policy of considering the pros and cons of each of our subjects, we shall be required to explain the reasons for the loud acclaim given these plays in every theatrical capital of the world—except New York. Even after admitting that there is a certain intellectual snob appeal toward anything new in art, we shall need to find other reasons for such popularity.

PREPARATION FOR *WAITING FOR GODOT*

Samuel Beckett
(b. 1906)

Like most contemporary playwrights, Samuel Beckett was influenced by Bertolt Brecht. His *Waiting for Godot* is an acknowledged masterpiece, which will remain in the repertoire of world theatre. Who is Godot? Audiences often assume that Godot is God. But the author has stated that Godot is a common French name, which attracted him when he was writing the play. And so, people must torment themselves wondering what the play means. In truth, *Waiting for Godot* is not to be explained; it is a metaphor of life by a great author.

As a piece for the theatre it is, in Harold Clurman's words, ''a poetic harlequinade—tragicomic as the traditional Commedia dell'Arte usually was: full of horseplay, high spirits, cruelty, and a great wistfulness.''

This best suggests the style for its production. Since its Broadway premiere in 1956, this metaphysical farce has challenged many talented comedic actors.[2]

There is a great deal of literature on *Waiting for Godot*. One can read it all; yet the enigma will remain because the play has been conceived as an unsolvable mystery about the human condition. It contains unanswerable questions, pitiful wondering, and ridiculous effort. The play is comic in its futile attempts to arrive at some conclusion, and tragic in its circular movement that arrives nowhere.

It is a metaphysical contemplation theorizing about the nature of existence. Beckett often gives his characters lines that suggest the meaning of the play. One example appears in the following words spoken by Estragon in *Waiting for Godot:* ''We always find something, eh Didi, to give us the impression we exist?''[3]

[2]These three paragraphs were written especially for this text by Dr. William Melnitz, Dean Emeritus, College of Fine Arts, University of California, Los Angeles.
[3]Samuel Beckett, *Waiting for Godot* (New York: Grove Press, 1952), p. 44a.

There seem to be as many points of view as there are critiques concerning the meaning of the play, and how it should be performed; the significance of the characters, and how they should be portrayed. In this excerpt, you are expected to try to add your own interpretation to those that already exist.

The parts may be played by either men or women. In general, it appears to be agreed that the characters are clowns dressed as tramps with derby hats. Although each has an individuality, we ask nothing of their backgrounds because they are actually caricatures—representatives of man . . . Everyman. It is up to us to furnish background information according to the results of our own participation in the drama. Beckett poses the questions. It is up to each player and each member of the audience to supply whatever answers are possible. It, therefore, follows that depth of appreciation depends on one's ability to relate to Beckett's philosophy.

The following excerpt concerns the two main characters, Vladimir (Didi) and Estragon (Gogo). There is a tenderness between them. They are forever dependent on each other. The thought of separating occurs to them, but never seems possible. They are not tragic to themselves. They are calmly dispassionate. They talk, joke, weep, and move about a bit, always *enduring* the endless waiting. They are like circus clowns, using tumbling, juggling, baggy pants, and hat routines. They are archetypes, like those of the Commedia dell'Arte. They present Beckett's comments tinged with vaudeville and burlesque techniques. Beckett has apparently indicated them as clowns because their only function is simply to mirror mankind.

Beckett's characters do not speak from their own inner compulsion. Rather, they speak words supplied by the author. They seem somewhat like manipulated puppets. This strange technique is often difficult for the audience to grasp. It is Beckett's way of presenting his own philosophy. Characters with definite traits would have hindered Beckett.

The character's interminable discussions result in no decisions. They simply introduce the audience to its own state of anxiety, foolishness, anticipation, patience, hope, resignation, and boredom.[4] At the finish of each interchange and of each act the audience is left without answers. The people in the audience, having used their time to sit expectantly in the theatre—exactly as Vladimir and Estragon have done—have spent their time to arrive at nothing.

It is difficult to accept completely the miserable state of existence Beckett sets forth. But *Waiting for Godot* has taken a permanent place in historical dramaturgy partly because it reflects the social disruption and anxiety surrounding the atomic age.

Perhaps a little game can help to illustrate the state of mind pro-

---

[4]Alfonso Sastre, "Seven Notes on *Waiting For Godot*," no. 6. "Toward a Metaphysics of Boredom," in *Casebook on Waiting for Godot*, ed. Ruby Cohn (New York: Grove Press, 1967), pp. 105–6.

Donald Moffat, Bruce French, Dana Eclar, and Ralph Waite in the Los Angeles Actors' Theatre production of Waiting for Godot, *1977, directed by Gwen Arner. (Photo by Craig Dietz. Courtesy of Gwen Arner.)*

duced by *Godot.* Stand six feet from a wall. Walk three feet toward the wall. Stop. You are halfway there. Walk again, this time one and a half feet toward the wall. Stop. Again you are halfway there. It is now obvious that if you continue this process, always walking halfway to the wall, you will never reach it.

Ludovic Janvier says, "Godot is a name for nothing." He quotes Samuel Beckett's reply when questioned about the meaning of the word *Godot,* "If I had known, I would have said so in the play."[5]

The following excerpt occurs at the end of the first act. Vladimir and Estragon are still on the same road, at the same place, by a mound, near a barren tree. This is their "space." Day becomes night in a short moment. The moon rises swiftly and stands still in the sky replacing the sun. This is their "time." Space and time remain constant in *Waiting for Godot,* one of the techniques Beckett uses to express his thinking. There is no yesterday or tomorrow, only the present.

During this act Vladimir, the more intellectually oriented, seems to be watching out for Estragon, who is more physically oriented. Earlier a child has appeared to confirm that Godot will keep the

---

[5]Ludovic Janvier, "Cyclical Dramaturgy," in *Casebook on Waiting for Godot,* ed. Ruby Cohn, p. 166.

appointment. Estragon's boots have been hurting and he has been struggling throughout the act to remove them. Your success in this scene will depend on immersing yourself in the feeling and meaning of the total play. Beyond the included stage directions, the interaction between the two clowns should be improvised. This improvisation will be less action than a realization of the empathy of the clowns for each other. The marginal notes are only suggestions. If you can improvise your own, the scene will become a more valuable exercise.

REHEARSAL

Waiting for Godot*

Samuel Beckett
An Excerpt from Act I

CAST: Vladimir

       Estragon

SCENE: *The light suddenly fails. In a moment it is night. The moon rises at back, mounts in the sky, stands still, shedding a pale light on the scene.*

1. Spoken as if to say, "Now we're getting somewhere." This refers to the coming of night and infers the hope that surely there *will* be a to-morrow.

Vladimir: At last![1] *(Estragon gets up and goes toward Vladimir, a boot in each hand. He puts them down at edge of stage, straightens and contemplates the moon.)* What are you doing?[2]

Estragon: Pale for weariness.

2. Critically. The next few lines are like a Laurel and Hardy comedy. Vladimir is aggressive; Estragon is naively explaining.

Vladimir: Eh?

Estragon: Of climbing heaven and gazing on the likes of us.

3. Vladimir can't believe his eyes.

Vladimir: Your boots, what are you doing with your boots?[3]

4. Quietly explains.

Estragon: *(Turning to look at the boots.)* I'm leaving[4] them there. *(Pause.)* Another will come, just as . . . as . . . as me, but with smaller feet, and they'll make him happy.

Vladimir: But you can't go barefoot!

Estragon: Christ did.

Vladimir: Christ! What has Christ got to do with it? You're not going to compare yourself to Christ![5]

5. Increase of pace and sound.

Estragon: All my life I've compared myself to him.

Vladimir: But where he lived it was warm, it was dry!

Estragon: Yes. And they crucified quick.

Silence.[6]

6. Another pointless discussion ended.
7. On—to the next thing. (A pretense at progress.)

Vladimir: We've nothing more to do here.[7]

Estragon: Nor anywhere else.

Vladimir: Ah Gogo, don't go on like that. To-morrow everything will be better.

Estragon: How do you make that out?

Vladimir: Did you not hear what the child said?

Estragon: No.

Vladimir: He said that Godot was sure to come to-morrow. *(Pause.)* What do you say to that?

Estragon: Then all we have to do is wait on here.[8]

8. Taking courage at the thought.

Vladimir: Are you mad? We must take cover. *(He takes Estragon by the arm.)* Come on.

(He draws Estragon after him. Estragon yields, then resists. They halt.)

Estragon: *(Looking at the tree.)* Pity we haven't got a bit of rope.[9]

9. It is obvious the tree is too weak and useless to be used for hanging.

Vladimir: Come on. It's cold.

(He draws Estragon after him. As before.)

Estragon: Remind me to bring a bit of rope to-morrow.[10]

10. Useless, of course, but nevertheless it's an idea.

Vladimir: Yes. Come on.

(He draws him after him. As before.)

Estragon: How long have we been together all the time now?[11]

11. A new thought? (A bit of increase in pace and excitement.) Memories? Can they help?

Vladimir: I don't know. Fifty years maybe.

Estragon: Do you remember the day I threw myself into the Rhone?

Vladimir: We were grape harvesting.

Estragon: You fished me out.

Vladimir: That's all dead and buried.

Estragon: My clothes dried in the sun.

Vladimir: There's no good harking back on that.[12] Come on.

12. Useless.

(He draws him after him. As before.)

Estragon: Wait![13]

13. Removes his derby in order to think.

Vladimir: I'm cold!

Estragon: Wait![14] *(He moves away from Vladimir.)* I sometimes wonder if we wouldn't have been better off alone, each one for himself. *(He crosses the stage and sits down on the mound.)* We weren't made for the same road.

14. Replaces his derby in order to speak.

Vladimir: *(Without anger.)* It's not certain.[15]

Estragon: No, nothing is certain.[16]

15. As if explaining patiently to a child.

16. Agreeing heartily—that at least is a certainty!

(Vladimir slowly crosses the stage and sits down beside Estragon.)

Vladimir: We can still part, if you think it would be better.[17]

17. A bit sorry.

Estragon: It's not worth while now.[18]

18. With a shrug.

(Silence.)

Vladimir: No, it's not worth while now.[19]

19. Having considered deeply.

(Silence.)[20]

20. Both slowly nodding in comfortable agreement.

Estragon: Well, shall we go?[21]

Vladimir: Yes, let's go.

21. With a sigh and the sound of determination.

(They do not move.)

Curtain

Eugene Ionesco
(b. 1912)

PREPARATION FOR *THE BALD SOPRANO*

France has always been receptive to, and led the world in, art inno-vations. Several years ago Parisian audiences showed their disin-terest in theatre as it was being presented. Thirty-two theatres closed, and box office receipts dropped to nearly two-fifths. But one small theatre was "packing them in." A new author, Eugene Ionesco, had a fresh kind of theatre. Realism was not enough for him.

Ionesco has been called an anti-playwright. He disliked the theatre but, while learning English, he copied out phrases from a copy book and arranged some of these fossilized words into a "play" and read it to some friends. He thought he was writing a tragedy of the breakdown in communication for which people sub-stitute hollow slogans, dreary social clichés, and status phrases. To Ionesco's horror, his friends thought his play very funny.

In the excerpt we are using from this same play, *The Bald Soprano*, two people are trying to find identity. By use of embalmed speech, Ionesco is able to add an absurdity, a special rhythmic brightness, to the surface of what is basically a very human and comic situation. The scene becomes a caricature of reality, pointing up the ridicu-lousness of our everyday social conversation. It is a paradox, absurd, and a classic example of avant-garde play writing.

The Bald Soprano is certainly not a well-made play. It is not even a play in the traditional sense but it is a startling piece of theatre. This play, and particularly the following scene, was one of the opening salvos of the avant-garde revolution.

You will note in the author's directions that he frequently asks that his actors appear bored. He states, "The dialogue which follows must be spoken in voices that are drawling, monotonous, a little singsong without nuances." He wishes to convey to the audience the thought that communication between humans is difficult. Fine. The author's wish should also be the actor's. But since the play-wright has written monotony into his lines, it would seem to belabor the point to ask the actors to act bored. How much better it would be had he explained to his actors what he wished, and then been respectful enough to permit them the means of accomplishing it! It is one thing to convey boredom and another thing to become boring to an audience.

But then Ionesco is not an actor, and never was. An actor knows that his primary goal is to interest his audience, and that the audi-ence is accustomed to being reached by use of movement and word coloring. This is the language they understand. It would make an interesting exercise to first play the scene as Ionesco directs, and then to play it again by coloring lines with everything that can be added by the players' imaginations and individualities. There is so little physical movement in the scene than an actor may "feel" the necessity of finding some means to interest the audience. One suggestion would be to show the thought process that precedes a certain line that is spoken—the reasons for saying the line.

REHEARSAL

The Bald Soprano*

Eugene Ionesco
Translated by Donald M. Allen
An Excerpt

CAST: **Mrs. Martin**

   Mr. Martin

SETTING: *"A middle-class English Interior." Needed: two chairs placed at center stage, set at angles to give proper sight lines and a clock chime that can be loud or soft.*

At rise: Mr. and Mrs. Martin sit facing each other without speaking. They smile timidly at each other.

Mr. Martin: Excuse me, madam, but it seems to me, unless I'm mistaken, that I've met you somewhere before.

Mrs. Martin: I, too, sir. It seems to me that I've met you somewhere before.

Mr. Martin: Was it, [1]by any chance, at Manchester that I caught a glimpse of you, madam?

Mrs. Martin: That is very possible. I am originally from the city of Manchester. But I do not have a good memory, sir. I cannot say whether it was there that I caught a glimpse of you or not!

Mr. Martin: Good God, that's curious! I, too, am originally from the city of Manchester, madam!

Mrs. Martin: That is curious!

Mr. Martin: Isn't that curious![2] Only I, madam, I left the city of Manchester about five weeks ago.

Mrs. Martin: That is curious! What a bizarre coincidence! I, too, sir, I left the city of Manchester about five weeks ago.

Mr. Martin: Madam, I took the 8:30 morning train which arrives in London at 4:45.

Mrs. Martin: That is curious! How very bizarre! And what a coincidence! I took the same train, sir, I too.

1. *Suggestion:* Try awkward pauses between each new thought as Mr. Martin tries to think of something to make conversation.

2. By beginning this scene slowly and filling it with embarrassed looks and hesitations, the audience will become interested. Remember, this play's asset is its novelty.

3. As Mrs. Martin agrees, Martin nods and smiles his approval, but then when she fails to recall, he immediately is crestfallen.

Mr. Martin: Good Lord, how curious! Perhaps then, madam, it was on the train that I saw you?

Mrs. Martin: It is indeed possible; that is, not unlikely. It is plausible and, after all, why not!³—But I don't recall it, sir!

Mr. Martin: I travelled second class, madam. There is no second class in England, but I always travel second class.

Mrs. Martin: That is curious! How very bizarre! And what a coincidence! I, too, sir, I travelled second class.

Mr. Martin: How curious that is! Perhaps we did meet in second class, my dear lady!

Mrs. Martin: That is certainly possible, and it is not at all unlikely. But I do not remember very well, my dear sir!

4. Martin hopefully attacks each fresh new thought.

Mr. Martin: ⁴My seat was in coach No. 8, compartment 6, my dear lady.

Mrs. Martin: How curious that is! My seat was also in coach No. 8, compartment 6, my dear sir!

Mr. Martin: How curious that is and what a bizarre coincidence! Perhaps we met in compartment 6, my dear lady?

Mrs. Martin: It is indeed possible, after all! But I do not recall it, my dear sir!

Mr. Martin: To tell the truth, my dear lady, I do not remember it either, but it is possible that we caught a glimpse of each other there, and as I think of it, it seems to me even very likely.

Mrs. Martin: Oh! truly, of course, truly, sir!

5. At first crestfallen, then thinks of another possibility.

Mr. Martin: How curious it is!⁵ I had seat No. 3, next to the window, my dear lady.

Mrs. Martin: Oh, good Lord, how curious and bizarre. I had seat No. 6 next to the window, across from you, my dear sir.

Mr. Martin: Good God, how curious that is and what a coincidence! We were then seated facing each other, my dear lady! It is there that we must have seen each other!

Mrs. Martin: How curious it is! It is possible, but I do not recall it, sir!

Mr. Martin: To tell the truth, my dear lady, I do not remember it either. However, it is very possible that we saw each other on that occasion.

Mrs. Martin: It is true, but I am not at all sure of it, sir.

Mr. Martin: Dear madam, were you not the lady who asked me to place her suitcase in the luggage rack and who thanked me and gave me permission to smoke?

Mrs. Martin: But of course, that must have been I, sir. How curious it is, how curious it is, and what a coincidence!

6. This has now become a refrain. It is spoken because there is a silence which should be filled with some sound.

Mr. Martin: How curious it is, how bizarre, what a coincidence!⁶ And well, well, it was perhaps at that moment that we came to know each other, madame?

Mrs. Martin: How curious it is and what a coincidence! It is indeed possible, my dear sir![7] However, I do not believe that I recall it.

Mr. Martin: Nor do I, madam. *(A moment of silence. The clock strikes twice, then once.)* Since coming to London, I have resided in Bromfield Street, my dear lady.

Mrs. Martin: How curious that is, how bizarre![8] I, too, since coming to London, I have resided in Bromfield Street, my dear sir.

Mr. Martin: How curious that is, well then, well then, perhaps we have seen each other in Bromfield Street, my dear lady.

Mrs. Martin: How curious that is, how bizarre! It is indeed possible, after all! But I do not recall it, my dear sir.

Mr. Martin: I reside at No. 19, my dear lady.

Mrs. Martin: How curious that is. I also reside at No. 19, my dear sir.

Mr. Martin: Well then, well then, well then, well then, perhaps we have seen each other in that house, my dear lady?

Mrs. Martin: It is indeed possible but I do not recall it, dear sir.

Mr. Martin: My flat is on the fifth floor, No. 8, my dear lady.

Mrs. Martin: How curious it is, good Lord, how bizarre! And what a coincidence! I too reside on the fifth floor in flat No. 8, dear sir!

Mr. Martin: *(Musing)* How curious it is, how curious it is, how curious it is, and what a coincidence! You know, in my bedroom there is a bed, and it is covered with a green eiderdown. This room, with the bed and the green eiderdown is at the end of the corridor between the w.c.[9] and the bookcase, dear lady!

Mrs. Martin: What a coincidence, good Lord, what a coincidence! My bedroom, too, has a bed with a green eiderdown and is at the end of the corridor, between the w.c., dear sir, and the bookcase!

Mr. Martin: How bizarre, curious, strange! Then, madam, we live in the same room and we sleep in the same bed, dear lady. It is perhaps, there that we have met!

Mrs. Martin: How curious it is and what a coincidence! It is indeed possible that we have met there, and perhaps even last night. But I do not recall it, dear sir!

Mr. Martin: I have a little girl, my little daughter, she lives with me, dear lady. She is two years old, she's blond, she has a white eye and a red eye, she is very pretty, her name is Alice, dear lady.

Mrs. Martin: What a bizarre coincidence! I, too, have a little girl. She is two years old, has a white eye and a red eye, she is very pretty, and her name is Alice, too, dear sir!

Mr. Martin: *(In the same drawling, monotonous voice)* [10]How curious it is and what a coincidence! How bizarre! Perhaps they are the same, dear lady!

Mrs. Martin: How curious it is! It is indeed possible, dear sir. *(A rather long moment of silence. The clock strikes 29 times. Mr. Martin, after*

7. *Warn clock.*

8. The refrain again, but once the pattern is established, it may be amusing to the audience to alter the reading. For instance, this time it could be read as if what she said solved everything and was indeed a great discovery.

9. *w.c.:* English expression for water closet, or bathroom.

10. Again the author reminds us that he expects the scene to be flat and colorless.

11. And again.

having reflected at length, gets up slowly and, unhurriedly, moves toward Mrs. Martin, who, surprised by his solemn air, has also gotten up very quietly.)

Mr. Martin: *(In the same flat, monotonous voice, slightly singsong)* [11]Then, dear lady, I believe that there can be no doubt about it, we have seen each other before and you are my own wife . . . Elizabeth, I have found you again! *(Mrs. Martin approaches Mr. Martin without haste. They embrace without expression. The clock strikes once, very loud. This striking of the clock must be so loud that it makes the audience jump. The Martins do not hear it.)*

Mrs. Martin: Donald, It's you, darling! *(They sit together in the same armchair, their arms around each other, and fall asleep. The clock strikes several more times . . .)*

Harold Pinter
(b. 1930)

PREPARATION FOR *THE HOMECOMING*

Harold Pinter began his theatrical career as an actor. That is probably why he is so much an "actor's playwright." Few, if any, dramatists write plays that depend so heavily on subtext. His dialogue, on the surface, either seems to say nothing or, at best, something superficial. It demands that the actor take it and *use* it to achieve an objective, to get a response from the other character in the scene. An implicit menace frequently lurks beneath the surface of these scenes, which frequently involve a "power play" of sorts: two people vying for the upper hand, but using the most commonplace dialogue. *Implication* is the key word in playing the scene that follows. Control is everything here, but the air must crackle with tension. Lenny loses control of himself, and therefore loses control of the "power" in this scene.

Read the play carefully. Try to discover the motivating forces that drive Ruth and Lenny. This is a crucial scene because it is their first meeting and it sets the stage for what is to follow in the plot.

REHEARSAL

The Homecoming*

Harold Pinter
An Excerpt from Act I

CAST: Lenny

Ruth

*From *The Homecoming* by Harold Pinter. (New York: Grove Press, 1967), pp. 38–40. Copyright ©1965 and 1966 by H. Pinter Ltd. Reprinted by permission of Grove Press, Inc.

SCENE: *Evening. A living room. Ruth sits by a table with a glass of water in her hand. Lenny stands by another table with his glass of water on it.*

Lenny: Excuse me, shall I take this ashtray out of your way?[1]

Ruth: It's not in my way.[2]

Lenny: It seems to be in the way of your glass. The glass was about to fall. Or the ashtray. I'm rather worried about the carpet. It's not me, it's my father. He's obsessed with order and clarity. He doesn't like mess. So, as I don't believe you're smoking at the moment, I'm sure you won't object if I move the ashtray.

He does so.[3]

And now perhaps I'll relieve you of your glass.

Ruth: I haven't quite finished.[4]

Lenny: You've consumed quite enough, in my opinion.

Ruth: No, I haven't.

Lenny: Quite sufficient, in my own opinion.

Ruth: Not in mine, Leonard.

Pause.

Lenny: Don't call me that, please.

Ruth: Why not?

Lenny: That's the name my mother gave me.

Pause.

Just give me the glass.[5]

Ruth: No.[6]

Pause.

Lenny: I'll take it, then.[7]

Ruth: If you take the glass . . . I'll take you.

Pause.

Lenny: How about me taking the glass without you taking me?

Ruth: Why don't I just take you?

Pause.

Lenny: You're joking.

Pause.

[8]You're in love, anyway, with another man. You've had a secret liaison with another man. His family didn't even know. Then you come here without a word of warning and start to make trouble.[9]

She picks up the glass and lifts it towards him.[10]

Ruth: Have a sip. Go on. Have a sip from my glass.

He is still.

Sit on my lap. Take a long cool sip.[11]

She pats her lap. Pause.

She stands, moves to him with the glass.[12]

Put your head back and open your mouth.

Lenny: Take that glass away from me.[13]

Ruth: Lie on the floor. Go on. I'll pour it down your throat.[14]

---

1. He moves to her table and reaches for it.

2. She puts her free hand on his hand as he reaches for the ashtray. He does not move his hand from hers.

3. He crosses and puts the ashtray on his table. She watches him intently. He then turns and moves back to her.

4. The next several lines are spoken as they stare determinedly at each other. Neither moves.

5. He reaches for it.

6. She moves it away from him.

7. He reaches again. She blocks him with her free hand and moves the glass farther away in the other hand. The next four lines are spoken with neither person moving.

8. He turns and moves away.

9. He turns to face her.

10. She moves and speaks very deliberately and slowly.

11. Seductively.

12. For the rest of the scene she speaks and moves slowly, deliberately, seductively.

13. Backing away from her.

14. Moving toward him.

15. Backing away nervously.

16. He has been staring at her in disbelief. He does not move until she is gone. Then he moves quickly.

17. Obviously shaken.

Lenny: What are you doing, making me some kind of proposal?[15]

She laughs shortly, drains the glass.

Ruth: Oh, I was thirsty.

She smiles at him, puts the glass down, goes into the hall and up the stairs.

He follows into the hall and shouts up the stairs.[16]

Lenny: What was that supposed to be? Some kind of proposal?

Silence.

He comes back into the room, goes to his own glass, drains it.[17]

EXPERIMENTAL THEATRE IN AMERICA

In *Theatre of Protest and Paradox*, published in 1964, George Wellwarth remarks that the avant-garde movement has failed to produce any coherent body of work in America.[6] However, exciting new playwrights and directors have more recently appeared. While it is yet early to detect coherence among contemporary works, several strong groups are devoting much of their time to new concepts. In Los Angeles, theatre-goers have supported the Center Theatre Group's Mark Taper Forum, which works closely with smaller theatre groups on experimental writing and productions. In New York, producer Joseph Papp has given much time to new ideas in the theatre. In San Francisco, the American Conservatory Theatre (ACT) offers experimental theatre, as well as traditional. Collaboration between theatrical producers in the eastern, midwestern, and western United States is beginning to appear. The seedlings are sprouting now; the actor must be ready.

While our actors, directors, and producers are not indifferent to new developments, producing costs here are much higher than in Europe. Productions are always a gamble, even in the best of circumstances; American audiences support only the plays they wish to see. If *Waiting for Godot* and *Rhinoceros* had been commercial successes on Broadway, there would have been an avalanche of plays of the Absurd. But they were not.

When costs made it impossible to experiment with untried plays on Broadway, smaller theatres were engaged in lower-rent districts, mostly in Greenwich Village. This movement became known as "Off Broadway." There were regularly scheduled performances in licensed theatres, employing union actors and stage hands and inviting newspaper and magazine critics. In other words, it was a little Broadway, complete with box office and regular ticket sales. Then, after it became established, rents were raised, unions became more demanding, and ticket prices soared.

[6]George Wellwarth, *Theatre of Protest and Paradox* (New York: New York University Press, 1964).

Experimental theatre: The world premiere of Michael Christofer's Ice, *with Ron Rifkin and Cliff DeYoung, produced at the Mark Taper Forum, Los Angeles, 1976. (Courtesy of Mark Taper Forum, Los Angeles.)*

This change created a need for another movement, which became known as "off-off Broadway." These groups operate in lofts, cellars, churches, and libraries but, because of restricitons, are not allowed to sell tickets. So they must rely on "membership fees" or grants to support their work. Usually, the actors are theatre students, novices, or those with other means of support. On off-off Broadway, a play's "run" is restricted by the unions to no more than nine performances.

With the question of economics solved, these groups allow new playwrights the opportunity to see their plays performed before audiences. If not directly influenced by the plays of the Absurd, the work of the American playwrights of the 1960s might, at least, be considered of the same genre. They are certainly not structured plays in a traditional sense. They often reject plot, and deal only in situation. Out of the hundreds produced, I know of only one play that presents a memorable character. The characters are *types*—often identified only as General, Second Protestor, or Man—following Ionesco's example of calling his leading actors Berenger. Dialogue is undistinguished, given over to nonsequiturs. When a theme is apparent it is usually pessimistic, expressing dissent from life or society. Many playwrights of the 1970s decade seem to have taken a more inquisitive attitude toward the human condition. In their works we find somewhat less pervading pessimism. More drama has appeared that allows the audience to make personal evaluation.

Off-off Broadway has opened doors for aspiring playwrights.

These groups have also mounted the first full-scale attack on realism, which has for too many years stifled fresh, new forms and ideas in the theatre. These devoted professional-amateurs attempt to say things in a different way, choosing metaphors, not only authentic to interior and exterior patterns but also theatrically true. In many productions, startling effects have been achieved—by improvisation, through multimedia (films, swirling lights, blatant sounds, gigantic mannequins, masks, acrobatics), and using stylization, imagination, and an impudent but exciting theatricality.

But the most important contribution of all the new movements is the return to older, purer forms of theatre. These movements have recaptured the marvelous, the illusion, that spirit of Shakespeare, Molière, and the Commedia dell'Arte. Once again we may pay homage to the clown, that ancient symbol of man, bumbling about in a world he never seems to understand. Once again the stage has become an enchanted place, Alice's Wonderland, the abode of dwarfs, monsters, and divine nonsense. This new theatre has given other dimensions to language. Characters speak gibberish or say what they do not mean, or mean what they never say because they distrust ordinary language as a means of communication. It has been called a theatre of reflecting mirrors, where reality blends almost imperceptibly into fantasy.

This style of theatre has proved that illusion does exist, and that it cannot thrive in a climate of rationality and naturalism. But most important, from an acting standpoint, these theatres have demonstrated that characters can be vividly alive without any human emotion or motivation.

These playwrights have the avowed intent of tearing down realism and once again giving us theatre. For this we can only admire their courage. If their work shocks us into realizing that it is not in man's nature to quit, but to survive, to meet every challenge, and to re-create values—then it has been a most worthwhile venture.

ACTING IN THE EXPERIMENTAL THEATRE

The foregoing discussion has aimed at providing the actor with a few definitions and objectives. It is important to be aware of the pros and cons of Theatre of the Absurd and the other kinds of theatre that have evolved since. It is an essential part of the actor's preparation to be informed about the aims of the author.

The question is often asked, "How does one apply 'the method' to the plays of the avant-garde, to the poetic theatre of Shakespeare, to the 'epic' theatre of Brecht, and to the Restoration theatre?" The question itself presupposes that the Stanislavski system is a kind of Lydia E. Pinkham cure-all.[7] In fact, it evolved from requirements of

[7]Quite a difference has developed between "the method" and Stanislavski's system. Two actresses highly publicized as being Method have never read Stanislavski. See Lewis Funke and John E. Booth, *Actors Talk about Acting* (New York: Random House, 1961), pp. 169, 453.

the *realistic* theatre. If accepted in its entirety, it is only applicable to that theatre. But Stanislavski based his work on tested creative processes of older actors he had studied. This process includes an in-depth understanding of play and period, observation, concentration, motivation, imagination, a trained body and voice, and an examination of the inner drives of character. These are parts of Stanislavski's system, and also part of the working technique of many fine actors long before he was born. But the developments made for the particular requirements of realism obviously serve little purpose in other types of drama.

It is not generally known that in 1905, Stanislavski predicted the break with realism when he wrote:

> *Realism, and [depicting] the way of life have outlived their age. The time has come to stage the unreal. Not life itself, as it occurs in reality, must be depicted, but rather life as it is vaguely perceived in fantasies and visions at moments of lofty emotion. This is the spiritual situation that must be transmitted scenically, in the way that painters of the new school use cloth, musicians of the new trend write music, and the new poets, poetry. The works of these painters, musicians, and poets have no clear outlines, definite and finished melodies, or precisely expressed ideas. The power of the new art lies in its combinations of colors, lines, musical notes, and the rhyming of words. They create general moods that carry over to the public unconsciously. They create hints that make the most unobservant person create with his own imagination.* [8]

It is much easier to explain how *not* to act the new plays than how to act them. The texture of each play is so different that it is impossible to generalize. Not only is each author unlike any other, but each play he writes may approach the absurd thesis from a different point of view. The creative acting process for Michel de Ghelderode's *Women at the Tomb* would be different from the approach to the same author's *Pantagleize.* The first might be called a modern morality play; the second is more in the spirit of the Commedia. The actors and director must translate the particular author's conception of a play into acting terms.

Perhaps you are by now convinced that today's actors need to know many different sytles of acting. Most actors resist this thought. But all acting cannot be rolled into one single miracle pill. Indeed, this is the great dilemma of today's actors. They have learned how to be intense with inner values, to explore minutiae, and have learned their lessons well. But now they see that playwrights and audiences are moving away from the depressing little rooms of realism in which they have specialized. Only the most insensitive will deny that audiences have become bored with the constant diet of box sets and "just plain folks." Broadway moves within the periphery of its own private world so much that perhaps it cannot

---

[8] Konstantin Stanislavski, *Moia zhizn' v iskusstve*, p. 501, as quoted in Nikolai A. Gorchakov, *The Theatre in Soviet Russia*, trans. Edgar Lehrman (New York: Columbia University Press, 1957), p. 44.

see what is happening in the rest of the world and indeed in other cities of its own country. Another theatrical revolution has begun, and it is no longer practical for an actor to be a specialist in a single acting technique. The new actors must have an integrated knowledge of basic creative fundamentals from which they can adapt as changes occur.

This makes us wonder if older actors, trained and practiced for three decades in naturalism, can ever meet the challenge of today and tomorrow. It is difficult to abandon settled working habits once they become firmly entrenched. But it is not so difficult for younger minds and bodies to acquire new techniques; they have nothing to unlearn. Antoine could not get established professionals to abandon their old romantic style of acting and had to train amateurs in realism. Conditions today may represent a pendulum swing in the opposite direction.

These new plays need people who can project an idea more than an emotion, who know that there is a difference between style and "stylistic." The Theatre of the Absurd demands acting that is conventionalized in form and actors who do not need to rely on emotion or spontaneity. Where are such actors to be found today?

The American commercial stage, television, and films are such costly and ponderous industries that they seldom venture into ex-

Anita Gilette and David Dukes in Travesties *by Tom Stoppard (left); Nicholas Hammond and Jean Marsh in* The Importance of Being Earnest *by Oscar Wilde (right). These two plays appeared in tandem at the Mark Taper Forum, Los Angeles, 1977. According to Jack Richardson in* Commentary *(vol. 61, no. 1, 1976), Stoppard used the structure and style of* The Importance of Being Earnest, *weaving into* Travesties *Wilde's methods and the character of Algy. The investment of the trivial with significance and vice versa is present in both plays. (Photos courtesy of Mark Taper Forum, Los Angeles.)*

perimentation. As a result, new plays along with new actors have been finding their initial hearings on the low-budget stages or in the educational theatres, which are carefully watched by the professional and commercial producers. It would seem to follow that a beginning actor, with some experience in acting the plays of Ionesco, van Itallie, or Pinter, might find an open door in the experimental theatres.

PREPARATION FOR "INTERVIEW" FROM *AMERICA HURRAH!*

In our next excerpt, from *America Hurrah!*, you will notice the author's use of short repetitious dialogue, the cliché, and the constant defensive apology. Quite apart from the obvious comic effect these produce, they are typical devices found in the plays of Ionesco, Beckett, and the most successful of the absurdists, Pinter. Such repetition demonstrates the preoccupation of the characters with themselves and their own thoughts.

Itallie's "Interview" is reminiscent of one of Pinter's early revue sketches called "Applicant," except that in Pinter's writing the roles are somewhat characterized.[9] The lack of any background, coloration, or personality kinks prevents Itallie's First Interviewer or Second Applicant from being anything but *types*. This makes it difficult for actors to begin even the most basic development of characters. The excerpt has been chosen because it can be an effective exercise in the use of timing and ensemble playing, which has become so important in working in contemporary plays.

REHEARSAL

"Interview"*

Jean-Claude van Itallie
An Excerpt from *America Hurrah!*

CAST: First Applicant   First Interviewer

Second Applicant   Second Interviewer

Third Applicant   Third Interviewer

Fourth Applicant   Fourth Interviewer

---

[9]Harold Pinter, "Applicant," in *The Dwarfs and Eight Revue Sketches* (New York: Dramatists Play Service, 1965).

*Reprinted by permission of Coward, McCann & Geoghegan, Inc. From *America Hurrah!* by Jean-Claude van Itallie. Copyright ©1966, 1967 by Jean-Claude van Itallie. *America Hurrah!* (including *Interview*) is the sole property of the author and is fully protected by copyright. It may not be acted either by professionals or amateurs without written consent. Public readings, radio and television broadcasts likewise are forbidden. All inquiries concerning these rights should be addressed to Ashley-Famous Agency, Inc., New York, New York.

SCENE: *The First Interviewer for an employment agency, a young woman, sits on stage as the First Applicant, a Housepainter, enters.*

1. Standing.

2. Sitting.

3. The characters will often include the audience in what they say, as if they were being interviewed by the audience.

4. Pointedly.

5. Standing again quickly, afraid to displease.

6. Busy with imaginary papers, pointing to a particular seat.

7. Pointing.

8. Sitting.

9. Suspicious, but writing it down.

10. Second Applicant, a female floorwasher, enters.

11. Sitting.

12. Standing.

13. Pointing.

14. Sitting.

15. Third Applicant, a banker, enters.

First Interviewer:[1] How do you do?

First Applicant:[2] Thank you, I said, not knowing where to sit.[3]

First Interviewer:[4] Won't you sit down?

First Applicant:[5] I'm sorry.

First Interviewer:[6] There. Name, please?

First Applicant: Jack Smith.

First Interviewer: Jack what Smith?

First Applicant: Beg pardon?

First Interviewer: Fill in the blank space, please. Jack blank space Smith.

First Applicant: I don't have any.

First Interviewer: I asked you to sit down.[7] There.

First Applicant:[8] I'm sorry.

First Interviewer: Name, please?

First Applicant: Jack Smith.

First Interviewer: You haven't told me your MIDDLE name.

First Applicant: I haven't got one.

First Interviewer:[9] No middle name.[10]

First Interviewer: How do you do?

Second Applicant:[11] Thank you, I said, not knowing what.

First Interviewer: Won't you sit down?

Second Applicant:[12] I'm sorry.

First Applicant: I am sitting.

First Interviewer:[13] There. Name, please?

Second Applicant:[14] Jane Smith.

First Applicant: Jack Smith.

First Interviewer: What blank space Smith?

Second Applicant: Ellen.

First Applicant: Haven't got one.

First Interviewer: What job are you applying for?

First Applicant: Housepainter.

Second Applicant: Floorwasher.

First Interviewer: We haven't many vacancies in that. What experience have you had?

First Applicant: A lot.

Second Applicant: Who needs experience for floorwashing?

First Interviewer: You will help me by making your answers clear.

First Applicant: Eight years.

Second Applicant: Twenty years.[15]

First Interviewer: How do you do?

Second Applicant: I'm good at it.

First Applicant: Very well.

Third Applicant:[16] Thank you, I said, as casually as I could.

First Interviewer: Won't you sit down?

Third Applicant:[17] I'm sorry.

Second Applicant: I am sitting.

First Applicant:[18] I'm sorry.

First Interviewer:[19] There. Name, please?

First Applicant: Jack Smith.

Second Applicant: Jane Smith.

Third Applicant: Richard Smith.

First Interviewer: What *exactly* Smith, please?

Third Applicant: Richard F.

Second Applicant: Jane Ellen.

First Applicant: Jack None.

First Interviewer: What are you applying for?

First Applicant: Housepainter.

Second Applicant: I need money.

Third Applicant: Bank president.

First Interviewer: How many years have you been in your present job?

Third Applicant: Three.

Second Applicant: Twenty.

First Applicant: Eight.[20]

First Interviewer: How do you do?

Fourth Applicant: I said thank you, not knowing where to sit.

Third Applicant: I'm fine.

Second Applicant: Do I have to tell you?

First Applicant: Very well.

First Interviewer: Won't you sit down?

Fourth Applicant: I'm sorry.

Third Applicant:[21] Thank you.

Second Applicant:[22] I'm sorry.

First Applicant:[23] Thanks.

First Interviewer:[24] There. Name, please?[25]

All Applicants: Smith.

First Interviewer: What Smith?

Fourth Applicant: Mary Victoria.

Third Applicant: Richard F.

Second Applicant: Jane Ellen.

First Applicant: Jack None.

First Interviewer: How many years' experience have you had?

Fourth Applicant: Eight years.

Second Applicant: Twenty years.

First Applicant: Eight years.

Third Applicant: Three years four months and nine days not counting vacations and sick leave and the time both my daughters and my wife had the whooping cough.

16. Sitting.
17. Standing again.
18. Standing again.
19. Pointing to a particular seat.

20. Fourth Applicant, a lady's maid, enters.

21. Sitting again.
22. Standing again.
23. Sitting.
24. Pointing to a particular seat.
25. Fourth Applicant sits.

26. Second Interviewer, a young man, enters and goes to inspect Applicants. With the entrance of each Interviewer, the speed of the action accelerates.

27. Standing.

28. Sitting.

29. Standing.

30. Sitting.

First Interviewer: Just answer the questions, please.

Fourth Applicant: Yes, sir.

Third Applicant: Sure.

Second Applicant: I'm sorry.

First Applicant: That's what I'm doing.

Second Interviewer:[26] How do you do?

First Applicant:[27] I'm sorry.

Second Applicant:[28] Thank you.

Third Applicant:[29] I'm sorry.

Fourth Applicant:[30] Thank you.

Second Interviewer: What's your name?

First Interviewer: Your middle name, please.

First Applicant: Smith.

Second Applicant: Ellen.

Third Applicant: Smith, Richard F.

Fourth Applicant: Mary Victoria Smith.

First Interviewer: What is your exact age?

Second Interviewer: Have you any children?

First Applicant: I'm thirty-two years old.

Second Applicant: One son.

Third Applicant: I have two daughters.

Fourth Applicant: Do I have to tell you that?

First Interviewer: Are you married, single, or other?

Second Interviewer: Have you ever earned more than that?

First Applicant: No.

Second Applicant: Never.

Third Applicant: Married.

Fourth Applicant: Single, now.

31. Third Interviewer, a woman, enters.

32. Sitting.

33. Standing.

34. Sitting.

35. Standing.

36. Fourth Interviewer, a man, appears on the heels of the Third Interviewer.

37. Standing.

38. Sitting.

39. Standing.

40. Sitting.

Third Interviewer:[31] How do you do?

First Applicant:[32] Thank you.

Second Applicant:[33] I'm sorry.

Third Applicant:[34] Thank you.

Fourth Applicant:[35] I'm sorry.

Fourth Interviewer:[36] How do you do?

First Applicant:[37] I'm sorry.

Second Applicant:[38] Thank you.

Third Applicant:[39] I'm sorry.

Fourth Applicant:[40] Thank you

PREPARATION FOR *MARIGOLDS*

This play was the critics' choice for the Best American Play award in 1970, as well as a Pulitzer Prize winner in 1971 and a winner of the Obie Award. The play's theme parallels the effects of Cobalt 60 on marigold seeds with the effects of a flighty and self-indulgent mother on her daughters. The character of this acid-tongued Beatrice dominates not only her daughters but the action of this fine comedy-drama.

Having survived her own childhood poverty and an unhappy marriage, she remains indomitable and ambitious. The family lives in genteel squalor, which Beatrice supports by caring for an old lady who lives with her and her daughters, Ruth and Tillie. Ruth is subject to mental seizures and Tillie is a vague and indeterminate child whose high school teacher has encouraged her to experiment with atomic energy on marigold seeds.

REHEARSAL

The Effect of Gamma Rays
on Man-in-the-Moon Marigolds*

Paul Zindel
An Excerpt from Act 1

CAST: **Ruth**
      Beatrice
      Tillie

SCENE: *As the scene begins, Beatrice is sitting watching her daughter, Tillie, fondle her beloved rabbit. Ruth enters at a gallop, throwing her books down and babbling a mile a minute.*

Ruth: Can you believe it? I didn't until Chris Burns came up and told me about it in Geography, and then Mr. Goodman told me him-

New York Television Theatre's production of Marigolds, with Eileen Heckart (standing) as Beatrice and Judith Lowry as her boarder. (Courtesy of WNET, Educational Broadcasting Corp.)

1. To Tillie.

2. The telephone rings.

3. Ring.

4. Ring.

5. Ruth grabs the phone.

6. Aside to Beatrice.

7. Covering the mouthpiece.

8. Beatrice gets up and shuffles slowly to the phone.

9. Finally, into the phone.

self during the eighth period in the office when I was eavesdropping. Aren't you so happy you could bust? Tillie? I'm so proud I can't believe it, Mama. Everybody was talking about it and nobody . . . well, it was the first time they all came up screaming about her and I said, "Yes, she's my sister!" I said it, "She's my sister! My sister! My *sister!*" Give me a cigarette.

Beatrice: Get your hands off my personal property.

Ruth: I'll scratch your back later.

Beatrice: I don't want you to touch me!

Ruth: Did he call yet? My God, I can't believe it, I just can't.

Beatrice: Did who call yet?

Ruth: I'm not supposed to tell you, as Mr. Goodman's private secretary, but you're going to get a call from the school.

Beatrice: [1]What is she talking about?

Tillie: I was in the Science Fair at school.

Ruth: Didn't she tell you yet? Oh, Tillie, how could you? She's fantastic, Mama! She's a finalist in the Science Fair. There were only five of them out of hundreds and hundreds. She won with all those plants over there. They're freaks! Isn't that a scream? Dr. Berg picked her himself. The principal! And I heard Mr. Goodman say she was going to be another Madam Pasteur and he never saw a girl do anything like that before and . . . so I told everybody, "Yes, she's my sister!" Tillie, "You're my sister!" I said. And Mr. Goodman called the Advance and they're coming to take your picture. Oh, Mama, isn't it crazy? And nobody laughed at her, Mama. She beat out practically everybody and nobody laughed at her. "She's my sister," I said, "She's my sister!"[2]

That must be him! Mama, answer it—I'm afraid.[3]

Answer it before he hangs up![4]

Mama! He's gonna hang up![5]

Hello? . . . Yes . . .[6]

It's him! . . . Just a minute, please . . .[7]

He wants to talk to you.

Beatrice: Who?

Ruth: The *principal!*

Beatrice: Hang up.

Ruth: I told him you were here! Mama![8]

Beatrice:[9] Yes? . . . I know who you are, Dr. Berg . . . I see . . . Couldn't you get someone else? There's an awfully lot of work that has to be done around here, because she's not as careful with her home duties as she is with man-in-the-moon marigolds . . .

Me? What would you want with me up on the stage? . . . The other mothers can do as they please . . . I would have thought you had enough in your *history* without . . . I'll think about it . . . Goodbye, Dr. Berg . . .[10]

I said I'd think about it![11]

Ruth: What did he say?

Beatrice:[12] How could you do this to me? How could you let that man call our home!

I have no clothes, do you hear me? I'd look just like you up on that stage, ugly little you!

Do you want them to laugh at us? Laugh at the two of us?

Ruth:[13] Mother . . . aren't you proud of her? Mother . . . it's an *honor.*[14]

Tillie:[15] But . . . nobody laughed at me.

Beatrice:[16] Oh, my God . . .[17]

PREPARATION FOR *AMERICAN BUFFALO*

David Mamet's *American Buffalo* received the Drama Critics Award for Best American Play of 1977. It emerges as a comment on a segment of society that has been "massaged by the message of the media." The three men, Don, Teach, and Bob, who hang out in Don's junk shop, are planning to rob a coin collector. They behave as if this were a perfectly normal venture, naively proceeding to play out their big business. Their limited language is now and then punctuated mistakenly by words undoubtedly picked up from television or gangster films. It is both comic and tragic. We laugh at their ridiculous seriousness. We know it is true, yet it seems like the make-believe of children at play. There is a kind of tenderness in the interaction of the three personalities. They are fond of each other. Loyalty, jealousy, love, and suspicion are all present, as they would be within a close family.

If it is played absolutely straight, the audience perceives the pathos with tremendous impact. One senses that, regardless of the social status of the characters, these are the essential emotions and behavior patterns in life. No matter how seriously we work at them, dreams don't always come true.

REHEARSAL

American Buffalo*

David Mamet
An Excerpt from Act II

1. They are lounging around.

SCENE: *Teach and Don are involved in an argument about Fletcher.*[1]

Teach: The man is a cheat, Don. He *cheats* at cards—Fletcher, the guy that you're waiting for.[2]

Don: Where do you get this?

Pause

2. Teach tries to maintain a position of superiority with Don. This is his self-image. Don accepts it even though it never really influences him one way or the other.

You're saying Fletcher cheats at cards.

Pause

You've seen him. You've *seen* him he cheats.

Pause

You're *telling* me this?

Teach: You live in a world of your own, Don.

3. The habit of repeating a statement is actually a way of commenting and keeping the conversation going. It relieves Don of having to make an intellectually based contribution.

Don: Fletch cheats at cards.[3]

Teach: Yes.

Don: I don't believe you.

Teach: Ah, you can't take the truth.

4. The use of earthy language is as natural as eating or sleeping. Words originally used as expletives have long lost their meanings.

Don: No. I am sorry. I play in this fucking game.[4]

Teach: And you don't know what goes on.[5]

5. Don rises to pace a bit as he gives this his deep consideration.

Don: I leave Fletcher alone in my store . . . He could take me off any time, day and night.

What are you telling me, Walt? This is nothing but poison, I don't want to hear it. *(Pause)*

Teach: And that is what you say.

Don: Yes. It is.

Pause

6. Teach assumes the attitude of an instructor with a backward child. He remains comfortably seated.

Teach: Think back, Donny.[6] Last night. On one hand. You lost two hundred bucks.

Pause

You got the straight, you stand pat. I go down before the draw.

Don: Yeah.

Teach: He's got what?

Don: A flush.

Teach: That is correct. How many did he take?

7. Don has been concentrating.

Don: What?[7]

Teach: How many did he take?

Pause

Don: One?

Teach: No. Two, Don. He took two.

Pause

8. Don is recalling clearly now.

Don: Yeah. He took two on that hand.[8]

Teach: He takes two on your standing pat, you kicked him thirty bucks? He draws two, comes out with a *flush*?

Don: *(Pause)* Yeah?[9]

Teach: And spills his fucking Fresca?

Don: Yeah?[9]

Teach: Oh. You remember that?[10]

Don: *(Pause)* Yeah.

Teach: And we look down.

Don: Yeah.

Teach: When we look back, he has come up with a king-high flush.

> *Pause*

After he has drawed two.

> *Pause*

You're better than that, Don. You know you had him beat, and you were right.

> *Pause*

Don: It could happen.[11]

9. Mounting disbelief at what he is hearing.

10. Teach begins increasing his pace and voice tone as he pounds the advantage home.

11. He sits again slowly, trying to evaluate.

FURTHER READING: THEATRE TODAY

No period in the history of the theatre has had more material published about it than the modern/contemporary. Below are listed a few of the many interesting and useful books dealing with today's theatre. (See also "Further Reading: The Character and Acting Styles" in chapter 9 and the "Additional Reading" list at the end of the book.)

Abel, Lionel. *Metatheatre.* New York: Hill & Wang, 1963.

Artaud, Antonin. *The Theatre and Its Double.* Translated by Mary Caroline Richards. New York: Grove Press, 1958.

Esslin, Martin. *The Theatre of the Absurd.* Rev. ed. Garden City, N.Y.: Doubleday, 1969.

Foreman, Richard, et al. *The Theatre of Images.* Edited by Bonnie Maranca. New York: Drama Book Specialists, 1977.

Schechner, Richard. *Environmental Theatre.* New York: Hawthorn, 1973.

———. *Public Domain: Essays on the Theatre.* Indianapolis: Bobbs-Merrill, 1969.

Critical Opinions

Adelman, Irving, and Dworkin, Rita. *Modern Drama—A Checklist of Critical Literature.* Metuchen, N.J.: Scarecrow Press, 1967.

Breed, Paul F., and Sniderman, Florence M. *Drama Criticism Index.* Detroit: Gale Research Co., 1972.

Palmer, Helen H., and Dyson, Anne Jane, eds. *European Drama Criticism.* Hamden, N.J.: Shoestring Press, 1968.

Pownall, David. *Articles on Twentieth Century Literature.* New York: Kraus-Thomson, 1973. Several volumes.

20
YOUR FUTURE IN THE THEATRE

(Photo by Bill Ganslen.)

PRACTICAL CONCERNS

1. Talent, Instinct, and Drive

For several hundred years theatre people have tried to discover whether it is possible to teach acting. The consensus of opinion is that acting cannot be taught; that an actor can be trained, but that talent is a gift. I agree that an actor can be trained, but that part about "gift" and "talent" is ambiguous for a journeyman actor.

There was a time when I considered myself an infallible judge of acting talent. I relinquished that avocation during the filming of a George Arliss picture in which I was playing opposite a young actress whom Universal had "let go" as a stock player. This left her free-lancing, and at the time we were making this picture she was not at all sure of a Hollywood future. Although I found her attractive personally, I remember also thinking that she had little chance of reaching any notable success. Her eyes were too large, and she had affected speech and mannerisms. If anyone had asked me "Will she make it?" I would certainly have answered in the negative. The young lady's name was Bette Davis, future winner of ten Academy Award nominations.

Even Mr. Arliss could make an error in judging "talent." During the tryout of *Green Goddess*, he decided that one of his supporting players was ineffectual, and he gave Ronald Colman his notice. Shirley Booth was almost replaced in *Come Back, Little Sheba* because she was "shuffling through the part, giving a stock company performance," according to the author, William Inge, and the director, Daniel Mann.[1] Miss Booth's characterization was acclaimed and is still considered one of the classics of modern acting. During rehearsals of *Death of a Salesman*, it was doubtful if Lee Cobb would ever be allowed to open in the part.

---

[1]Richard Maney, *Fanfare, The Confessions of a Press Agent* (New York: Harper & Row, 1957), p. 86. Quoted by permission.

Bette Davis and Hardie Albright in the movie So Big. *(With permission of Creative Management Associates.)*

The decision you must make as to whether or not to become an actor should not depend entirely on the opinions given by those in, or on the fringes of, the theatre. Even critical judgments of professionals are notoriously poor. This may be explained if we accept that our emotions are completely independent of our critical faculties. In your own experience, you know that often when viewing a poor television show or reading a trashy novel, you somehow get caught up and are moved in spite of the fact that your critical judgment is constantly telling you that the material is trash.

So much for "talent" and judgments of it. If you can recognize it, you are more perceptive than I—or less experienced. As for that other word, *gift*, the dictionary describes it as "endowed with talent" and so by circuitous reasoning, if you know "talent," you will have no difficulty in knowing who is "gifted."

David Garrick had no training at all. One day he was a wine salesman, and the next the outstanding actor of his generation. But let's not overlook some other qualities he had. Garrick, the wine merchant, believed wholeheartedly in Garrick, the actor. If you believe as much in yourself as Garrick did, you too can become a fine actor. Sarah Bernhardt believed, "Will-power is a fundamental condition of success for every man; for the actor it is a condition to which all others are subordinate."[2]

Naturally, you'll have moments of doubt when you'll think seriously of giving up the idea and settling down to a nice, steady, unglamorous job. Just be positive that you want to act so much that you can survive a sense of ineptitude, bitter criticism, and long periods of apparent failure. You'll not be the first with doubts or

[2]H. J. Stemming, trans., *The Art of Sarah Bernhardt* (New York: Dial Press, 1925).

reasons for them. Here is a notice about a young lady's first appearance in a good part in a great city:

> *On before us tottered, rather than walked, a very pretty, delicate, fragile-looking creature dressed in a most unbecoming manner in a faded salmon-colored sack and coat, and uncertain whereabouts to fix either her eyes or her feet. She spoke in broken, tremulous tone and at the close of her sentences her words generally lapsed into a horrid whisper that was absolutely inaudible.* [3]

That's enough to put anyone out of show business, isn't it? It was written by a London critic reporting the first appearance there of Sarah Siddons. And she was not rehired for the next season. As we have seen, this failure in London made such a scar that she very nearly gave up the theatre. But she went back to the provinces and saturated herself in work. Work seems to be the magic ingredient of outstanding acting. In my research on great actors of the past, and in professional association with the best of my time, I cannot think of one who did not earn his fame by love of the art and indomitable labor. And labor it is; it entails years of tedious craft training, conditioning of body and voice, development of instinct and intellect, plus constant execution of the art. How much easier it would be to be "gifted" and thus avoid all this back-breaking effort. Yes, Garrick was "gifted," but he also exhausted everyone around him—*working!*

Another attribute of the fine actor is the possession of an indomitable drive to be great. Sarah Bernhardt's motto was *quand même* ("inspite of everything"), which she kept constantly before her. Although she entered the Conservatoire at sixteen, she was twenty-two before her career really began and twenty-five before her first success. This should be a useful lesson to those who expect overnight stardom. In his book *Seven Daughters of the Theatre* Edward Wagenknecht tells of the celebrated American actress, Julia Marlowe, who, as a girl,

Julia Marlowe as Juliet. (From the Katherine Grey Collection.)

> *studied in seclusion for three solid years the five roles in which she had decided to prepare herself. To keep her body supple she took up fencing. She was willing to practice half a day if necessary on the tone quality of a single word. Her texts she studied in the light of all commentaries, reading as widely as possible in the backgrounds of the period involved. She made herself a miniature theatre, with dolls for actors, so that she might visualize the entire production from start to finish, giving it actual body before her eyes. In all this she was aided notably by unusual powers of concentration, frequently becoming so absorbed in her task that she would be oblivious to everything else going on around her.* [4]

[3] W. Clarke Russell, *Representative Actors* (London: Frederick Warne and Co., 1888).
[4] From *Seven Daughters of the Theatre,* by Edward Wagenknecht. Copyright 1964 by the University of Oklahoma Press.

Like Julia Marlowe, you must plan your work intelligently. Work is the *only* way to develop body and voice. Reading will not accomplish this; neither will sitting around discussing "show biz." *And no one can do it for you!* It requires regular and systematized planning; so much time for dancing—folk, ballet; so much for fencing—broadswords and foil; then singing—classical, modern; breath control; diction—and so on.

Edwin Booth wrote, "I have barely time to swallow my dinner hastily and go to work—work. Never since I began my theatrical career did it seem so truly to resemble downright bodily, mental, and spiritual "hammer and tongs."[5]

If you live in a small town and feel you have no place to study such things, or couldn't afford all those lessons, remember that if you want something badly enough, you'll work out your problems. If not—it's wiser to stop wishing now! There is a library in your town. Get some books with exercises in them. (See end of chapter.) Anything you do to prepare yourself will be helpful so that when your chance comes, nothing will be able to resist that power within you. Dedicated study and training should be considered as your investment in your future.

2. Luck

I'm afraid it must be admitted that luck has quite a bit to do with success. Hardly anyone who has been around show business for any length of time will deny the importance of being in the right place at the right time. To an actor, it can mean the difference between stardom and being a good reliable player the rest of his life. This whole area of "luck" is not a premise to which I subscribe easily; I have never believed in rabbits' feet or "never whistle in a dressing room," or "never wish anyone good luck on an opening," or any such theatrical superstitions. But I do believe in the lucky break.

Yet I say again, when that chance comes, an actor had better be ready. It may never come again. The actor who will benefit from that lucky break will be the one who can carry on, who is equipped to follow one success with another. No matter how handsome or magnetic an actor may be, he must never neglect his training. Training and experience will sustain him when his youthful appearance is gone.

3. Appearance

Some thirty years ago, looks were very important. There were 900 to 1,000 players under contract to studios.[6] A few were "types," but the majority were handsome youngsters, chosen because they were photogenic. The box office names at that time were all glamorous

---

[5]Edwina Booth Grossman, *Edwin Booth.* Copyright 1894 by D. Appleton-Century Co., p. 161.

[6]Today there are very few contract players and, for the most part, these are contracted for certain television series. When the show is finished, so is the contract.

women and handsome men. With the advent of the gangster pictures came the elevation of the "mug." Even the pretty boys began
talking out of the sides of their mouths, trying to be tough. Mugs
were box-office successes, and the uglier they were, the more tickets
they sold. Thus ended an old movie tradition.

Today, a girl may have a shape like a banana, but if she can act or
is skilled at comedy she is given consideration, especially if she has
been a success on the stage or in nightclubs. Although physical requirements are not what they were, there are other positive qualities
aspiring actors must have—particularly training and experience.
Each year thousands of hopefuls with no training and no experience
come to Hollywood and New York and try to break into the profession. Then, finally broke and disillusioned, they return home without once entering a casting office. A straight line is not always the
shortest distance to Broadway or Vine Street. Keep away from the
big time until you have an education and some experience. When
they want you they will surely find you.

4. Experience

In previous centuries the theatre trained its own by the time-
honored apprentice method, and this system survived until the de-
mise of repertory and stock companies. This was on-the-job training
consisting of much practice and only such theory as an apprentice
might obtain when some older member of the company volunteered
information. There were, of course, certain advantages: Pupils could
communicate by that unique language that is only fully understood
by actors. The apprentice could also watch his master practice what
he preached. But the process was instruction by osmosis: At best,
instruction was more incidental than planned or systematically pro-
gressive.

Today the amateur will find much activity in community theatres.
The locations of these, and of summer theatres and the relatively
new 99-seat theatres, can be found by contacting Actor's Equity Association offices in New York or in Los Angeles. Any activity with
these theatres that use nonprofessionals is valuable to the amateur.
The American National Theatre and Academy (ANTA) will advise
you concerning all aspects of theatre activity. Their New York office
is at 245 West 52nd Street, New York, NY 10019; in Los Angeles, the
office is at 846 North Cahuenga, Los Angeles, CA 90038. General
information on theatre is also available from the American Theatre
Association, 1029 Vermont Avenue, N.W., Washington, DC 20005.

Most major cities support theatrical activity through their county
parks and recreational departments. To find out which professional
plays will be produced in your vicinity and elsewhere, you may contact the Actors' Equity Association office. Information regarding regional theatres can be found by contacting the Theatre Communications Group, at 355 Lexington Avenue, New York, NY 10017.

5. A College Education

Education is of primary importance to an actor. A good education will give you a background in literature, psychology, philosophy, an appreciation of related arts, and a fuller understanding of people. Few of us realize that training of actors in colleges is an innovation of our century; a great deal might be said of its progress, which has not been easily won. When Thomas Wood Stevens led Andrew Carnegie into the newly built Carnegie Tech theatre, he found it wise to describe it to the benefactor as a "lecture hall." Mr. Carnegie never realized he was supporting a drama department. Had the Puritan-minded old Scot observed the "To be, or not to be" carved on the entrance doors he might have realized he was getting the old theatrical, "Nothing is, but what is not."

University drama departments had to solve the problem of how to include practical theatre training, when their charters provided only for a liberal arts education. Each step needed to be carefully planned and cautiously executed. But now college theatres seem to be generally accepted and respected. Many professionals today have degrees from such institutions.

The vastly expanded audience for all the arts has been almost exclusively developed by colleges and universities. And this has come at a most opportune time, when the taste of the Broadway-oriented mass audience has declined to a disturbingly low cultural level. Today our universities are encouraging not only scholars and artists, but also an exclusive and discerning audience. This should portend an upgrading in the cultural values of tomorrow's mass audience. Colleges have hired professional artisans as instructors; for these artists the college has assumed the position of patron once held by the church or the court.

The curriculum offered by most American colleges, universities, and some of the more advanced high schools allows students an invaluable opportunity to learn the art and craft of acting. Violinists may practice alone with their instruments, but actors need other actors and an audience to reach their full potential. Unlike the apprentice system, the university provides a well-ordered and constructively planned series of courses in such important allied skills as dancing, voice production, and fencing, as well as academic studies that encourage mental development.

College drama gets the beginner into roles of importance much sooner than the apprentice method. If this seems somewhat like teaching the baby to swim by throwing it into the lake, it might also be said that the method is quick and decisive. Either the baby swims or drowns immediately.

Of course the college "stars" will one day face the inevitable move into professional ranks, where they must content themselves with parts of much less importance. At such a time they may wonder about the value of their degrees. But the wonder should only be temporary. I have firsthand experience in this, as I entered the pro-

fession holding one of the first degrees ever awarded in drama. As a
novice, the university-trained actor is much more apt than the self-
taught novice to demonstrate the knowledge he has acquired. If his
training has been practical, it will soon be obvious that he can be
entrusted with better parts. In all probability he will also be more
familiar with audiences and audience psychology, a very important
matter.

6. Little Theatre Training

Even avocational acting, while far from ideal, is better than no acting
at all. In little theatres, however, far too much time is apt to be spent
socializing and too little in study and rehearsal. The result is a superficial, imitative, or vanity-oriented performance. Acting experience must have certain standards or it is more destructive than
constructive.

It is important to get before an audience any time in any place,
even if the "theatre" is nothing more than Lope de Vega's "Three
boards, two actors, and a passion." One means of getting before an
audience is by appearing as a guest at local clubs, banquets, civic
groups, and so forth. Select readings that may be delivered standing
at a table without benefit of props or scenery. Prepare these for ten-
or fifteen-minute presentations only, and choose the material ap-
ropos the club, holiday, or particular occasion. You should not expect any reimbursement; you will be repaid in experience. Once established as a solo performer, you can easily use your club contacts
to present short scenes with other actors. By booking an advance
itinerary, your group can have the advantage of getting traveling
expenses on weekends and holidays, and obtaining valuable experience acting before a variety of audiences. Simplicity should be the
watchword in such ventures. Select scenes that are unpretentious;
place your emphasis on careful study of your scenes and characters,
the ensemble work, and communication with your audiences.

7. First Professional Work

Directors, casting offices, or producers prefer to see you act before
they will believe you can handle a part before an audience. It is the
old truism all over again—you can't get a job unless you have experience and you can't get experience unless you have a job. You
won't be hired by making the rounds of casting offices alone. Just as
you learn to act by acting you find work by working. If you work
diligently enough as an amateur, you should be able to get into the
profession.

The best way to obtain employment is to create it yourself. Start
your own group. When you feel prepared, invite an audience. Work
any time, any place and don't be concerned about being paid. Once
you have been paid, you can never act again without remuneration.
You will then be a member of a union. The only exception would be
voluntary appearances for charity or patriotic causes. But member-

ship in a union is no guarantee of getting a job. Our unions do not obtain jobs for members; they protect the actors' interests once they get a job.

There may be times when you will be offered a part in a play you feel is mediocre. If you are a professional and there is nothing better, you will accept. An acting job is not easy to find, and a poor play cannot last forever. But it may lead to getting a part in a good play. Try not to be too critical. Don't assume the job of unhired and unpaid critic. Accept responsibility without question and perform tasks to the best of your ability. Subordinate your personal prejudices. Concentrate that energy on the job at hand. Use your actor's discipline. The world is full of critics, and they are mostly amateurs. That's why excavation companies put peepholes in fences—so that sidewalk foremen can watch workers work.

8. Unions
There are six important unions:

1. *Actors' Equity Association* (AEA, or *Equity*), 226 West 47th Street, New York City. This is the oldest performer's union (formed in 1914), and its realm of interest is the legitimate stage.
2. *Screen Actors Guild* (SAG), 7750 Sunset Blvd., Hollywood, Calif. This is the motion picture union. This includes filmed TV.
3. *American Federation of Television and Radio Artists* (AFTRA), 1551 N. LaBrea, Hollywood, Calif. Live TV and radio.
4. *The American Guild of Musical Artists* (AGMA). Offices in most major cities. Opera, ballet dancers, and concert artists.
5. *The American Guild of Variety Artists* (AGVA). Vaudeville, circus, and nightclub performers.
6. *Screen Extras Guild.* Motion picture extra's union. Together these unions form *The Associated Actors and Artistes of America,* which is chartered by the AFL-CIO.

Keep in touch with Equity or SAG even though you are not yet a member. You'd be surprised at the information all these unions give nonmembers. They might suggest places a young actor can stay on a limited amount of money or inform you about which summer companies are accepting apprentices. In addition to these unions there is *Central Casting,* a nonprofit, nonunion employment agency run by the larger film studios for the benefit of extra players.

All of these unions have similar qualifications. To become a member of SAG, you must either (1) be a paid member in one of the other "four A's" (unions), or (2) have a proffered contract from a producer of a motion picture (but not an extra role). There is an initiation fee plus quarterly dues. Since these are subject to change, it would be best to contact the Screen Actors Guild or Actors' Equity directly. There are nine classifications of dues depending on the annual income of the member.

Actors' Equity Association provides an alternative program for those wishing to gain experience before deciding to become members. A young actor may serve for two seasons as an apprentice in summer stock, provided it is a professional Equity company. At the end of the apprentice period, the actor may become a regular union member.

Most professionals pay dues to two or three unions, as few actors today can depend on any one medium.

Many beginners feel that getting a union card is a big step in their careers. My advice is not to be in a hurry. Many acting opportunities not available to a professional are open to you as an amateur. *Amateur* is a French word, meaning "for love." If you love the theatre, remember that becoming a professional will be like coming home from a honeymoon to marriage. You will be assuming the responsibility of making your love practical, and this will take time.

While you are making a living and "making the rounds" of casting and production offices, your training must not be neglected. Even professionals are constantly rehearsing and acting, when not being paid. Actors' Equity approves of this, provided the audience does not pay. In fact, Equity itself contributes a small production cost to a program set up in New York called Equity Library Theatre. Previously produced plays are cast competitively from among Equity members "in good standing," and these casts rehearse and perform for no wage, as do director, producer, costumer, and stagehands. Such ventures not only keep the actors at their trade, but also serve as "showcases" where they can be seen. Many actors have been cast in commercial stage plays, films, and television because they were seen in Equity productions. Other workshops or "showcase theatres" vary from the greatly publicized New York studios where "young professionals practice their art" to humble stages set up in vacant stores. There are some forty such little groups operating in Hollywood alone. These groups, unlike the theatre that Equity sponsors, are supported by the actors themselves, who pay a fee to cover operating expenses. Sometimes the charge is as little as $15 a month, but the more elaborate New York workshops may cost the actor $100 or more per month. This may all sound very discouraging indeed, but you need to be sure that acting is to be your life's work.

9. Television Commercials

This is the most difficult field of all to get into, even for established professionals, because it is well paid for the time expended. I have seen forty or fifty well-known actors sitting outside an agency office waiting to be called in for an interview for a two- or three-line part in a commercial. Someone named these "cattle calls," and the resemblance is striking.

Many have the erroneous impression that people with no acting experience make commercials and receive fortunes for it. For the most part, people giving endorsements of products on television are professionals who are skillful enough to make you believe they are just ordinary office workers or housewives. Manufacturers are very careful about their public image and would not dare to endanger sales by hiring nonunion actors. There are, however, some fly-by-night agencies that place ads in the classified columns offering to pay for endorsements of a product. Space is hired in an office building, camera and sound are hidden, and as applicants are interviewed, they are recorded and photographed. Those chosen are given a small check and asked to sign a complete release. In other words, there are no residual payments; and it is from residuals that the professional makes his money. Each time a commercial is rescreened, the actors ordinarily receive a small percentage of their original pay. This is the reason actors endure "cattle calls."[7]

10. Making a Living

An established actor can make forty thousand, three thousand, or five hundred dollars a year. It depends entirely on the individual. You might write the Screen Actors Guild for information. In the beginning, and often at odd times during your acting career, the cost of living can be higher than your earning power. So you must think about developing some part-time skill to sustain you. During the thirties, Lloyd Bridges and Russell Conway were part-time package stampers in the New York post office.

11. Agents

There are almost two hundred agents franchised by the Guild in Hollywood, but even the smallest agent is unlikely to take on new clients without seeing them perform. Here is another reason for you to keep working and acting. Some agents will, however, accept a "Broadway name" on reputation alone. Years ago it was customary for agents to have six or eight clients and do very well with them. But that was in the days of the "B" pictures. Today, in spite of the fact that the number of pictures produced in Hollywood has dropped, agents have considerably increased the number of clients they handle. The hope is that by having more clients who work less, the agent can stay in business. This reasoning helps the agent but not the individual actor.

In Hollywood agents are almost a necessity. They are in a much better position to know which studios have films ready for casting. Usually they have been in the business for years and have many acquaintances among producers, writers, directors, and casting agents. In New York, however, casting information is more readily available to the actor. Such publications as *Variety* and *Player's Guide*

---

[7]The smallest initial payment for one commercial is "scale" or minimum salary, as determined by the union.

publish current "legit" news. An actor can consult the bulletin board at the Equity office as to casting and pick up bits of hearsay when making the rounds. Also producers, directors, and casting people are much more available in New York than in Hollywood.

When you are on your rounds in New York or visiting studios in Hollywood, it is wise to carry photographs that you can leave with producers or casting offices.

12. Photographs

These should be eight-by-ten-inch glossy prints. They must be *theatrical portraits* taken by a photographer who understands the particular style. An enlarged snapshot or high school graduation portrait simply will not do. Wait until you get to New York or Hollywood and consult the yellow pages for *theatrical portrait photographers.* SAG, Equity, or your agent may be able to suggest a reliable photographer. Pick four of the best shots and have them made into a composite, then have reproductions made. A composite is usually 8" x 10", divided into four parts, each with a separate photo. Each of the four should be accompanied by descriptions and credits, if possible. Your résumé should be pasted on back of each composite.

13. Résumés

It should be typed double-spaced, and may be mimeographed. Limit information about yourself to one page or less. At the top of the page type your name, address, height, weight, coloring, and other pertinent information. List various phone numbers where you can be reached. Your training and education should be listed next. Broadway, films, and television are headings you might use, if applicable. Information should be simple, direct, and honest. Leave something to talk about at interviews.

When you do get in to see a producer or director, don't put on an act. Don't try to be something you are not. If you are to be interviewed about appearing in a published play, read it beforehand. Dress simply. Don't appear in jeans or any dress that might give the impression you are eccentric. Remember names, shake hands when dismissed, thank the interviewer for considering you, and leave at once. Be neither obsequious nor impudent, but friendly and respectful. Try to leave your prospective boss with the impression that you are intelligent, cooperative, studious, and a worker—in other words, that you would be a valuable and pleasant person to work with. Follow this advice and you will receive only courtesy and consideration.

14. Auditions

Should you be asked to read, it may be in an office or in a dark, empty theatre. In all probability the reading will be "cold"; that is, you will be given only a few minutes to leaf through the play and to concentrate on the lines you are expected to read. Read for *sense*. It is dangerous to try for a characterization or emotion. Generally such readings are to find an actor whose voice and personality match a particular character. Directors or producers are ready to use their imagination.

When we were casting *All the Living,* an actor we were considering haughtily informed us "I never *read—I act*." When he realized I was adamant, he did read for us, but his reading reflected his resentment and petulance—which was exactly the feeling I was hoping to find. He was given the part at once. Later, during rehearsals, he added the "acting" he had mentioned and lost the attitude I had visualized when writing the part.

No one will expect you to give a performance at a reading. It is important that you remain calm and assured and that you show an intelligence and an eagerness at reading. Just try to make sense of the lines and to give a hint of some overall concept of the part.

It is important that you become a good sight reader. You should be able to pick up reading matter you have never seen before and read it aloud with meaning and intelligence. You must not hesitate or stumble over words, and your voice should convey meaning to the listener in a vivid and interesting manner. Make it a point to read aloud to yourself or others at least once every day. Clip out articles from newspapers and magazines that interest you and practice reading these to your family.

As you do, retain eye contact with your listeners. Consider one person as an entire audience and remember you must always hold the interest of your audience. Study facial expressions and if you see evidence of disinterest, do something quickly to regain it. Usually, an audience begins to lose interest when the actor's voice betrays his own disinterest. Believe every word you are reading. Make the words personal to your listeners. Never give up eye contact. Glance down at your paper quickly, photograph a phrase or sentence in your mind, and return to that invaluable eye contact, for you will find it a sensitive barometer of your audience's interest.

Drilling of this kind will also be useful if you have an opportunity to work in radio.[8] The same contact you have developed with listeners can be transferred to work with the microphone. Imagine it as a living person, or as the hearing aid of many living persons. When I first did radio work, I was impressed when I saw more experienced radio actors' attitude toward the mike. They seemed to treat it as another human. They smiled, winked, and frowned at it. Of course they realized that none of these things were making any impression on the device, but it gave them the sense of being in contact with other humans.

---

[8]Radio is far from dead. Many young people have found it receptive to new talent and a stepping-stone to other media.

YOUR FUTURE IN THE THEATRE

The future of the theatre is going to be exciting. All of you have the chance to take part. Perhaps one day you may come to believe that our work together saved you some time and heartbreak.

You are entering a theatre that has greater possibilities than at any previous time in recent American theatre history. In the early 1900s everyone was searching: Eugene O'Neill and Elmer Rice were experimenting with expressionism, George Kelly was writing kitchen drama,[9] and Max Reinhardt was producing his spectacular and thrilling *Miracle.* There seemed no positive direction in America. Great European actors came to the United States: the Moscow Art Players from Russia, Sacha Guitry from France, and Eleanora Duse from Italy.

Then the Depression swept art aside; all that mattered was to exist. Bread lines angered Americans, who determined that these would never happen again. Revolt and anger exploded in the theatre. At last there seemed to be a direction. For the next twenty years playwrights and players preached ideology and propaganda to audiences. Plays included aspects of psychiatry and intellectual dialogues, better read than acted. Theatre was treated as a place to think, rather than a place to feel, to experience, to contact the infinite. We had lost the skill of older theatreworkers to produce the remarkable and the amazing.

To compound the problem, the unions raised prices. At last, audiences realized that those in the theatre were nothing but high-priced bores, and they deserted us. Like every other audience since time began, they wanted excitement in the theatre. They wanted to feel the magic and the illusion of it. They found these things only in the musicals.

But now all over America there are signs of a vast renaissance of legitimate theatre, not localized on Broadway. We are once again finding the skill to act and produce the remarkable and the amazing. Once again we are creating the magic of make-believe. You can be an actor on such a stage.

Hopefully the experience you have gained from this book will help you to realize your goals for personal development. Jack Albertson, whose success came relatively late in life, says, "One has to be resilient to survive professionally but success is the crossroads where preparation and opportunity meet."[10]

MODERN ACTORS: SOME THOUGHTS

Among today's successful actors, there are innumerable examples of the devotion to continuous work that is required in fields as diverse

---

[9]*Kitchen drama* is a theatrical term describing overdone naturalism. It alludes to subject matter and treatment that is exceedingly ordinary.

[10]Janet Rotchstein, "Never Too Late," *Talk* magazine, August 1977.

Richard Chamberlain as Richard II. (Courtesy of Richard Chamberlain.)

as possible. Richard Chamberlain's story seems particularly appropriate in this book, because he has been self-motivating and because he has made a point of broadening his talents, both mentally and physically.

It was only after college graduation, a stint in the army, and several years of serious and energetic study that Chamberlain's first small parts in television began. These finally resulted in a very popular television series, "Dr. Kildare." Although the series lasted for five years, Chamberlain considered it only the beginning of his career.

His humility and courage carried him through three years of work in untried areas, such as legitimate theatre and films. The results were far from outstanding, and he left the United States for England determined to continue his studies with the rigorously demanding repertory theatre there. Through this effort his abilities expanded, so that he was able to play the classics. At last, his Hamlet was triumphantly received.

Chamberlain explains himself as "learning oriented" and highly involved with the "discovery potential" in acting. This description may well be applied to all fine actors for whom a never-ending study of their craft is a way of life.

Lloyd Bridges, in a discussion about his own studies in theatre, traces the beginnings of his career from UCLA drama courses in Shakespeare and Greek drama through variations of the Stanislavski approach, intense work with the Actor's Lab West, and consistent activity in summer theatre repertory. During the interview he was reminded of two historical greats of the theatre, Eleanora Duse and Sarah Bernhardt, who differed extremely in methods and in results. Bernhardt is said to have played *to* an audience while Duse played *with* an audience. Each chose the methods that worked for herself. Bridges's final remark was, "You use what works best for *you*."

Ryan O'Neal has made some pertinent observations. "Legitimate theatre and films," he says, "require two separate techniques. Theatre broadens one's thinking, uses the whole actor, develops confidence and awareness of the physical self. As opposed to films, theatre requires a much larger concept in voice, expression and bodily movement."[11]

O'Neal feels strongly that the actor needs to be aware of his own limitations, so that he can concentrate on the areas in which he needs to work and study. The actor should be able to evaluate the criticisms of others so that what finally emerges has been well sifted and becomes his own special mental and physical expression. In other words, if an actor is too strongly influenced by any one person or point of view, he will deny his own individuality.

Paul Muni was educated in the famed Yiddish Theatre in New

Lloyd Bridges. (Courtesy of Lloyd Bridges.)

[11]Courtesy of Ryan O'Neal. From a personal interview.

York, where he played some three hundred character roles before he was thirty, always resisting leading parts. Muni has said that his own personal style began from a combination of the broad, melodramatic gesture of Theodore Thomashefsky and the more naturalistic approach of Jacob Adler. He was later influenced by the arrival in the United States of the Moscow Art Theatre, as well as Max Reinhardt from Germany. Muni disdained any set theory of acting. He was careful, detailed, and painstaking in his preparation. According to Lee Strasberg, Muni probably spent more time in thorough preparation for a role than any actor in American history. One of Muni's greatest tricks was his ability to capture the attention of an audience simply by means of his rapt attention while listening to a fellow player.[12]

José Ferrer maintains that in order to be as good as you *can* be, you have to go back to Shakespeare, Ibsen, Robert Sherwood, Tennessee Williams, always seeking the widest possible range of experience. Finally, Ferrer has said that you must carve out your own career for yourself.

Ryan O'Neal. (Courtesy of Ryan O'Neal.)

You must keep your mind alert for new trends and fresh attitudes that may appear in the theatre. It is not only possible, but probable, that time will reveal another Brecht, O'Neill, Chekhov, or Pinter. You can only enlarge yourself by remaining curious, neglecting nothing.

Because of the necessity of knowing all phases of theatre, many theatre greats who began in one phase have found themselves successful in another. Good theatre is the result of a large assortment of talents working together. Thus, among the many facets of the theatre, the student actor may very well become the professional director, playwright, choreographer, or scenic designer. In theatre all of these are interdependent, creative processes, and each is totally fulfilling.

Every page in this book has been devoted to explaining just what makes an actor. It has taken thousands of words. A great writer, John Steinbeck, has done it with just a few, in his eulogy to John Emery, a man admired by both Steinbeck and myself as actor and cherished friend. On the opening night of *The Three Sisters* at the Civic Repertory Theatre, John Emery and I walked on stage together for the first time as professionals. We shared a dressing room for the next forty weeks, and during the subsequent years we were in constant contact. Here is what Mr. Steinbeck thought of John Emery, actor:

> *He was an actor, a member of that incorrigible peerage against which, along with gypsies and vagabonds, laws once were made, lest they cause living to be attractive, fear unthinkable, and death dignified, thereby robbing church and state of their taxes on unhappiness.*

[12]Jerome Lawrence, *The Life and Times of Paul Muni* (New York: G. P. Putnam's, 1974).

An actor, a player, not the product of makeup and publicity, but an actor in his blood, six generations back, brother and son of the great and, may we please hope, the permanent fellowship of Burbage, and Garrick, of Booth and Joe Jefferson, of Toto and Emmett Kelly. This was his company, an actor. He played many parts well, whereas most of us play only one—badly.

Sometimes he seemed a child, easily hurt and wryly smiling, but he was wise in friendship and inept in hatred.

He was consistent—professional—responsible—gallant. (A footnote here: Please to remember the time he broke his ankle on stage and played unlimping to his curtain.)

Because of his profession, his life was exposed, down stage, lighted, but none but the stupid, the vain or the vengeful could charge him with ungentleness.

He played larger than life—bravura—and he played small as a mouse. His profession was himself. May all of us hope to come to our curtain as unstained and worthily as he. [13]

FURTHER READING: YOUR FUTURE IN THE THEATRE

Babcock, Dennis, and Boyd, Preston. *Careers in the Theatre*. Minneapolis: Lerner Publications, 1975.

Campbell, Douglas, and Devlin, Diana. *Looking Forward to a Career: The Theatre*. Minneapolis: Dillon Press, 1970.

Cohen, Robert. *Acting Professionally*. 2d ed. Palo Alto, Calif.: Mayfield, 1975. Recommended.

Dalrymple, Jean. *Careers and Opportunities in the Theatre*. New York: E. P. Dutton, 1969.

Engel, Lehmann. *Getting Started in the Theatre*. New York: Macmillan, 1973.

Farber, Donald C. *Actor's Guide*. New York: Drama Book Specialists, 1971.

Horton, Louise. *Careers in Theatre, Music and Dance*. New York: Franklin Watts, 1976.

Hunt, Gordon. *How to Audition: A Casting Director's Guide for Actors*. Chicago: Dramatic Publishing Company, 1977.

Markus, Tom. *The Professional Actor: From Audition to Performance*. New York: Drama Book Specialists, 1978.

Matson, Katinka. *The Working Actor: A Guide to the Profession*. New York: Viking, 1976.

Moore, Dick. *Opportunities in Acting*. New York: Universal, 1963.

Nahas, Rebecca. *Your Acting Career: How to Break into and Survive in the Theatre*. New York: Crown, 1976.

Savan, Bruce. *Your Career in the Theatre*. Garden City, N.Y.: Doubleday, 1961.

Shurtleff, Michael. *Audition: Everything an Actor Needs to Know to Get the Part*. New York: Walker, 1978. Recommended.

[13]Reprinted with permission of John Steinbeck and *Equity Magazine*, January 1965.

ADDITIONAL READING

Besides the works listed at the end of each chapter, the reader will find much of interest in the following:

ACTING

Blunt, Jerry. *The Composite Art of Acting*. New York: Macmillan, 1966.

Burton, Hal, ed. *Great Acting*. New York: Hill & Wang, 1967.

Cole, Toby, and Chinoy, Helen K., eds. *Actors on Acting: The Theories, Techniques, and Practices of the Great Actors of All Times as Told in Their Own Words*. New York: Crown, 1949.

Diderot, Denis. *The Paradox of Acting*. Archer, William. *Masks or Faces?* New York: Hill & Wang, 1957. Two books under one cover.

Funke, Lewis, and Booth, John E. *Actors Talk about Acting: Fourteen Interviews with Stars of the Theatre*. New York: Random House, 1961.

Glenn, Stanley L. *The Complete Actor*. Boston: Allyn and Bacon, 1977.

Lewes, George. *On Actors and the Art of Acting*. New York: Grove Press, 1957.

Matthews, Brander, ed. *Papers on Acting*. New York: Hill & Wang, 1958.

Rockwood, Jerome. *The Craftsmen of Dionysus: An Approach to Acting*. Glenview, Ill.: Scott, Foresman, 1966.

Stanislavski, Constantin. *Creating a Role*. Translated by Elizabeth Reynolds Hapgood. New York: Theatre Arts Books, 1961.

MAKEUP

Buchman, Herman. *Stage Makeup*. New York: Watson-Guptill, 1971. Has excellent sequential photos in color.

Corson, Richard. *Stage Makeup*. 5th ed. New York: Appleton-Century-Crofts, 1975. Long considered the "bible" of complete makeup techniques.

REFERENCE BOOKS

Bowman, Walter P., and Ball, Robert H. *Theatre Language: A Dictionary of Terms in English of the Drama and Stage from Medieval to Modern Times.* New York: Theatre Arts Books, 1961.

Gassner, John, and Quinn, Edward, eds. *The Reader's Encyclopedia of World Drama.* New York: Crowell, 1969.

Hartnoll, Phyllis, ed. *The Oxford Companion to the Theatre.* 3d ed. New York: Oxford University Press, 1967.

Lounsbury, Warren. *Backstage from A to Z.* Seattle: University of Washington Press, 1959.

McGraw-Hill Encyclopedia of World Drama. 4 vols. New York: McGraw-Hill, 1972.

Rae, Kenneth, ed. *An International Dictionary of Technical Theatre Terms.* New York: Theatre Arts Books, 1960.

STAGE COMBAT: ARMED AND UNARMED

American Association for Health, Physical Education and Recreation. *Pamphlet on Fencing.* Washington, D.C.: AAHPER, n.d.

Bernhardt, Frederica, and Edwards, Mrs. Vernon. *How to Fence.* Dubuque, Iowa: Wm. C. Brown, 1961. Paperback.

Gordon, Gilbert. *Stage Fights: A Simple Handbook of Techniques.* New York: Theatre Arts Books, 1973.

Hobbs, William. *Stage Fight: Swords, Firearms, Fisticuffs and Slapstick.* New York: Theatre Arts Books, 1967.

Lidtstone, R. A. *Fencing: A Practical Treatise on Foil, Epée and Sabre.* London: Witherby, 1952.

Palffy-Alpar, Julius. *Sword and Masque.* Philadelphia: F. A. Davis, 1967.

Sports Illustrated, editors of. *Book of Fencing.* New York: J. B. Lippincott, 1962.

Further information on this fascinating, but neglected, aspect of the actor's training can be obtained from The Society of American Fight Directors, 4720 38th N.E., Seattle, WA 98105.

THEATRE HISTORY, GENERAL

(Each of the books listed in this section has an extensive bibliography of works dealing more specifically with particular periods and styles.)

Brockett, Oscar G. *History of the Theatre.* 3rd ed. Boston: Allyn and Bacon, 1977.

Cheney, Sheldon. *The Theatre: Three Thousand Years of Drama, Acting and Stagecraft.* Rev. ed. New York: Longmans, 1972.

Duerr, Edwin. *The Length and Depth of Acting.* New York: Holt, Rinehart & Winston, 1962.

Freedley, George, and Reeves, John A. *A History of the Theatre*. 3d ed. New York: Crown, 1968.

Gassner, John. *Masters of the Drama*. 3d ed. New York: Dover, 1954.

Macgowan, Kenneth, and Melnitz, William. *The Living Stage*. Englewood Cliffs, N.J.: Prentice-Hall, 1955.

Nicoll, Allardyce. *The Development of the Theatre*. 5th ed., rev. London: Harrap, 1966.

Roberts, Vera M. *On Stage: A History of the Theatre*. 2d ed. New York: Harper & Row, 1974.

Stuart, Donald Clive. *The Development of Dramatic Art*. New York: Appleton-Century-Crofts, 1933.

VISUAL AIDS

An excellent and extensive supply of films and filmstrips dealing with theatre history, periods, styles, and acting techniques is available through OLESEN, 1535 Ivar Avenue, Hollywood, CA 90028.

VOICE AND MOVEMENT

(See also the "Further Reading" lists for the chapters on "Discovering Yourself," "Mime," and "The Actor's Voice and Speech.")

Anderson, Virgil. *Training the Speaking Voice*. New York: Oxford University Press, 1961.

Aubert, Charles. *The Art of Pantomime*. New York: Benjamin Blom, 1970.

Blunt, Jerry. *Stage Dialects*. New York: Thomas Y. Crowell, 1967. Includes three dialect tapes.

Brodnitz, F. *Keep Your Voice Healthy*. New York: Harper, 1953. Especially good on care of the voice; written by a medical doctor.

Brook, George Leslie. *English Dialects*. London: British Book Center, 1963.

Chriest, Fred M. *Foreign Accent*. Englewood Cliffs, N.J.: Prentice-Hall, 1964.

Eisenson, Jon. *The Improvement of Voice and Diction*. 2d ed. New York: Macmillan, 1965.

Fairbanks, Grant. *Voice and Articulation Drillbook*. New York: Harper, 1940–61. A standard.

Herman, Lewis, and Lewis, Marguerite. *American Dialects*. New York: Theatre Arts Books, 1947.

———. *Foreign Dialects*. New York: Theatre Arts Books, 1958.

Laban, Rudolf. *The Mastery of Movement*. London: Macdonald and Evans, 1960.

Marash, Jessie Grace. *Mime in Class and Theatre*. London: Harrap, 1950.

Sayre, Gweanda. *Creative Miming.* London: Herbert Jenkins, 1959.

Walker, Katherine Sorley. *Eyes on Mime.* New York: John Day, 1969.

Wise, Claude M. *Applied Phonetics.* Englewood Cliffs, N.J.: Prentice-Hall, 1957. Applies the International Phonetic Alphabet to varieties of American and English speech.

INDEX